The European Higher Ec
Perspectives on a Moving Target

The European Higher Education Area: Perspectives on a Moving Target

Barbara M. Kehm
International Centre for Higher Education Research (INCHER-Kassel), University of Kassel, Germany

Jeroen Huisman
International Centre for Higher Education Management (ICHEM), University of Bath, United Kingdom

Bjørn Stensaker
Norwegian Institute for Studies in Innovation, Research and Education (NIFU STEP), Oslo, and Institute of Educational Research, University of Oslo, Norway

SENSE PUBLISHERS
ROTTERDAM /BOSTON/TAIPEI

A C.I.P. record for this book is available from the Library of Congress.

ISBN 978-90-8790-712-9 (paperback)
ISBN 978-90-8790-713-6 (hardback)
ISBN 978-90-8790-714-3 (e-book)

Published by: Sense Publishers,
P.O. Box 21858, 3001 AW
Rotterdam, The Netherlands
http://www.sensepublishers.com

Printed on acid-free paper

TABLE OF CONTENTS

MINISTER FRANK VANDENBROUCKE

FOREWORD

Re-designing the map of European higher education is a daunting task. Shaping the future European Higher Education Area (EHEA) is an incremental process. Its success depends much on a continuous dialogue with all stakeholders. Until now, the involvement of the community of higher education researchers did not appear clearly. It was a worthwhile initiative to look for their contributions. They have analysed the trends of society and higher education in trying to see and understand the future challenges of and for higher education. The outcomes of the Ghent Conference have demonstrated the value of that exercise. I would like to encourage all higher education researchers to continue their endeavour. They have a task of asking about the values underlying the decision making both at the governmental and the institutional level. They have to address the broad range of questions outlined in the paper 'Higher Education Looking Forward: an agenda for future research'.

We have arrived at the final stages of the Bologna Process, or more precisely: we are about to reach the end of the process as it was originally conceived. The programme of the Bologna Declaration, as signed in 1999, was indeed meant to unroll "within the first decade of the third millennium". The next meeting of European ministers responsible for higher education, in April 2009 in Leuven and Louvain-la-Neuve will hence be the last ministerial conference within the initial time-span of the process. But apart from an elaborate evaluation of the achievements of the Bologna Process, the Ministerial Meeting will also focus on the challenges and objectives for the post-2010 agenda. For we believe that we should take the opportunity to reflect collectively on the needs for the next phase and the objectives that should be realized by 2020.

In preparation of the Leuven Ministerial Meeting, numerous conferences and seminars have been and still are to be organized by various countries and organizations.

BOLOGNA TODAY

In designing the future of the Bologna Process, we first should look at the outcomes and results produced thus far. An independent assessment has been asked for by the European ministers to clarify what has been really achieved and to what extent this has been done. Without anticipating the conclusions of the assessment, one can nevertheless already acknowledge the impressive achievements of the first ten years of the process. The vision that guided the gathering in Bologna in 1999, was to have an integrated higher education area in Europe by 2010, with transparent and readable higher education systems, trustworthy institutions and programmes, and mobile students and professors. That vision was optimistic in the true sense of the word, but also proved to be very mobilizing.

The Bologna Process was also unique in constructing a new method of policy-development. It has set new standards for policy development by its top-down and bottom-up interaction, its active involvement of stakeholders and its ability to generate and mobilize an enormous energy of reform, even if not everyone was always fully aware of certain backgrounds or higher aims. One can truly say that Bologna has led to the mobilization of all relevant social forces in higher education.

When looking into the critical conditions for success of the Bologna Process, besides the ambitious vision and the inclusive nature of the reform process, one should also mention the clarity and relative simplicity of its objectives. The ministers formulated a small number of easily understandable objectives. The Bologna Declaration has set the agenda of reform of European higher education at the right time. Transparency, convergence, and mobility were the strategic objectives European higher education needed in order to unlock its potential, to demonstrate its qualities and thus, and that is of utmost importance, to provide an alternative for an unrestrained global competition.

Indeed, we should probably put more efforts in underlining that Bologna is *not* a big sell-out operation of European higher education, as critics often put up. To the contrary, even, thanks to Bologna, we arm ourselves, all over the continent, with a framework and instruments which allow us to keep the higher education sector within the public domain.

It is true that governments and public authorities all over Europe tend to restrain themselves from deciding on how each and every euro in the university budget should be spent, and where professor so-and-so should be appointed. But that does not mean that they have disappeared from the higher education scene: instead, the focus has shifted towards investing in solid and objective quality assurance systems, developing common qualification levels and descriptors, looking after the social dimension in higher education, and so on. Honestly speaking: as a minister responsible for providing all citizens with equal opportunities for an excellent education, I care much more about these levers and regulatory frameworks, which secure the position of higher education within the domain of public interest, than about the traditional ministerial prerogatives vis-à-vis public institutions, as these prerogatives in themselves do not protect at all against the strikes of the invisible hand of the free market.

To name but one example: Bologna has made us install quality assurance systems – which are, by the way, already demonstrating their positive influence on the (proven!) quality of teaching and research. Don't these quality assurance instruments leave us with much more confidence in our higher education than typical market indicators would ever do, such as market shares or partly earned, partly bought reputations?

BOLOGNA TOMORROW

That is for the past. Together with my colleagues from the other Benelux countries, I had the ambition then to start a new process of collective reflection and debate on what should be the objectives for the next ten years of the Bologna Process. Several seminars and meetings have already taken place all over Europe. There is still a way to go to the Leuven 2009 Ministerial meeting. Yet, a number of provisional statements already can be made on how the strategic objectives for Bologna 2020 should look like.

Before presenting some ideas on the strategic objectives to be set for 2020, I have to make clear that I really believe that we do need a sequel to the Bologna Process. The work is not finished yet. The structural reforms in degree systems, the accompanying regulatory frameworks in quality assurance and credit transfer, the cooperation and mobility realized thus far, they all were established in most countries, but in various modes and at a varying speed. Apart from that, they also seem to be only partial answers to the challenges and needs of today's world. Recognition of qualifications, to name but one example, often still is a problem, in spite of frameworks and instruments, such as quality assurance and accreditation, which have been created or further developed with lots of enthusiasm for the objectives of the Bologna Process. Indeed, while much of the structural reform is already in place, the key challenge now appears to be moving from structure to practice. That is an indispensable move, for popular support for the Bologna reforms – and popular interest in maintaining higher education within the public domain – is to a large extent precisely based on very tangible results and achieve-ments ("why still a procedure for the recognition of my study period abroad?"), rather than on abstractly looking structures.

The general sense of the Bologna Process – transparency, convergence, mobility, quality – is, in other words, still the right one, but it has to be refuelled with new goals and objectives. For we have to be honest about that: the integration of the European higher education area is still rather weak and its global potential not yet realized. A considerable number of countries have joined the process later on, and some of them even quite recently, which challenges these countries, how-ever ambitious they might be, to catch up with the forerunners within a realistic timeframe. But even the forerunners themselves still experience many difficulties in rightly applying the various instruments Bologna has brought about.

STRATEGIC OBJECTIVES FOR BOLOGNA 2020

What then should be the core concepts of the strategic objectives for Bologna 2020, apart from completing the initial agenda, of course? *Transparency* certainly should remain a primary core concept. A lot can be said on increasing complexity and diversity, and most of it is true. We have learnt that heterogeneity and diversity are not the enemies of convergence and integration. As a spontaneous corollary to the convergence realized in the course of the Bologna process, institutions have differentiated themselves. They show ever more variation in mission and ambitions now.

The institutions are right and they should not hesitate continuing along this path. As attractive as it may sound, not least to ambitious policy makers both inside and outside the institutions, the future does not lie in everyone pretending to do the same thing, nor in attempting to assume the many roles society expects higher education to play nowadays. As for me, mission differentiation is a much more promising avenue of future-focused development, contributing to the overall performance of our higher education system as a whole.

But in order to really articulate and value diversity, we should reveal its real nature. Diversity cannot be appreciated if it is kept under the veil of ignorance and ambiguity. The next phase of the process towards transparency therefore should invest much more energy in developing instruments to really address diversity and make it readable and understandable for everyone. Well-designed, multidimensional rankings can be a suitable instrument for that – assuming, and I hope that it can be proven in fact that this is not a killer assumption, that such a type of rankings cannot only be thought of theoretically, but also developed in practice. A realistic assessment of actual learning outcomes will be yet another instrument to make diversity readable and understandable. Regulatory frameworks validating institutional diversity should be developed. For not focusing on making diversity transparent, entails a serious risk: the risk of European higher education being an arena of confusion in which the market is organized as a *bazaar* of undemonstrated reputations. It is not possible to build an attractive European higher education system with a strong collective reputation, if this system is internally not transparent. Thus, transparency of diversity could, however paradoxically it may sound, lead to a new, higher sense of identity and coherence within the European higher education area.

Next to transparency, there is a set of values and ambitions that I would like to summarize in the concept of *social responsibility and responsiveness*. I am strongly convinced that there is no need for differentiation that goes so far as developing a binary divide between a mass higher education system of average quality and an excellent system for the elite. Equality of opportunity for education of excellent quality should be acknowledged as a core value of the European higher education system and a condition for its further success. Despite a successful democratization of higher education in the past, Europe will have to increase its efforts to mobilize its full potential. This implies providing opportunities to *all* talents, especially in those communities where under-participation risks resulting in a real waste of talent. The demographic challenges will force us to mobilize and regularly upgrade all available "brain-power". (Seen from a different angle, one could say that there is no acute need neither to dramatize demographic changes nor to hastily import talent from overseas, given the actual rate of talent still waiting to be discovered and developed on the hand, and the often heavily underexploited potential for life-long learning on the other hand. In many aspects, the higher education sector indeed still has to maximize the impact of learning and research.)

Social responsiveness also requires a new relationship between governments and the public body in general on the one hand and institutions on the other hand. Institutions rightly ask for more autonomy. I do agree that they need more autonomy in order to liberate their potential. But as Isaiah Berlin taught us about the concept of "liberty", we should distinguish two concepts of "autonomy", a negative concept and a positive concept. To be relevant for education policy, "autonomy" should not only be understood in its negative definition, as less government interference. Enhancing autonomy also means: enhancing the capacity to make choices and define strategies, enhancing the capacity to act effectively, and to have impact – in the case of higher education institutions, impact on our society at large. So conceived, autonomy and regulation are not mutually exclusive concepts. I believe in the positive definition of autonomy, in which regulation is seen as a kind of dialogue between responsible actors for the common good. We should look for a new "pact" between higher education institutions, the political authorities and society at large as an alternative both for traditional political regulation and complete political abdication. The challenges ahead for higher education are so crucial for Europe's development in general, that conceptualizing the state-institution relationships in terms of (negative) autonomy and accountability only, may fall short of what actually needs to be done.

Clarity on what governments and social stakeholders expect from higher education institutions should be one of the first goals of such a dialogue. In the context of the knowledge society the public benefits of higher education are ever more increasing, manifold and far-reaching: a better educated and more creative "human capital", up-to-date learning outcomes focusing on generic skills preparing for employability in a changing labour market, new qualifications, new flexible learning arrangements, academic excellence focusing on critical inquiry as well as on knowledge transfer, social and cultural criticism as an invaluable contribution to democracy and critical citizenship.

The paradox of policy-making in higher education is that higher education is becoming so crucial to economic, social, cultural, and even political development, that governments have no alternative but to actively engage in a critical dialogue with institutions and stakeholders, whereas at the very same moment, the institutions themselves claim more autonomy in order to improve their effectiveness. As for the governments, there should be no hesitation in recognizing that the importance of higher education also implies a higher level of funding. I at least have no problem in recognizing the validity of the 2%-norm put forward by the European Commission, and member countries which do not reach this norm, i.e. the large majority, should not hesitate to design an ambitious growth path towards these 2%.

The third concept that should guide us in formulating the strategic objectives for Bologna 2020, is *global attractiveness and global partnership*. The question should not be how Europe guards itself against the tides of globalization or arms itself in the "academic arms race", not even how Europe should organize itself to successfully wage the global war on talent. The question is what Europe can contribute to the global public good: how to unlock not only Europe's but the world's academic potential, how to make ideas circulate around the globe, how to forge partnerships across the continents, how to maintain a global balance between educational needs and educational capacity. That is where the real attractiveness of European higher education really lies. In redefining our ambitions, we should make clear what Europe's contribution should be to answering the global challenges. We should definitely demonstrate the openness of European higher education systems and institutions to the world, rather than establishing a "fortress" against it, despite some feelings of fear and envy against Europe, and despite an overall climate of commercialization or "commodification of knowledge".

CONCLUSION

I took the opportunity to focus on three guiding concepts which could enlighten our road map towards Leuven 2009. These three concepts emerged out of work of the higher education research community. Many more could be added, but let's keep in mind that in moving the Bologna Process further, we should focus our energy upon a relatively small number of strategic objectives. Only by focusing, the Bologna Process will keep on mobilizing energy and interest, not only in Europe itself but also on a global scale.

Frank Vandenbroucke
Vice-Minister-President of the Flemish Government
and Flemish Minister for Work, Education and Training

JEROEN HUISMAN, BJØRN STENSAKER AND BARBARA M. KEHM

BOLOGNA, QUO VADIS?

UNPRECEDENTED CHANGE?

The Bologna process has been characterized as an example of unprecedented change in European higher education. Indeed, who – at the end of the 1980s, a decade before the Bologna Declaration – would have thought that 29 ministers would commit themselves to reach a number of common and far-reaching objectives for higher education in Europe? The sheer quantity of endorsement and commitment as well as the high-stake ambitions are – again from the perspective of the 1980s – astonishing as is its intergovernmental nature. Shortly after the Declaration it transformed into an even more puzzling, multi-stakeholder process, involving various supranational and national agencies.

How different are current developments from two decades ago? At the end of the 1980s, issues like reduction of government spending and the erosion of higher education as a part of the welfare state; increasing attention to new mechanisms of public control over output and performance (the evaluative state); and the withdrawal of the state (Neave, 1988, 1990) were dominating the political agendas. There were no explicit signs that trans-national or supranational issues would soon be on the political agenda. For sure, ERASMUS had been launched by then (1987), but its success was yet to be confirmed and the prominence of (higher) education in supranational policies was still far away. With the Treaty of Maastricht (1992), education received a less ambiguous, but still limited, position in supranational policy-making (De Wit & Verhoeven, 2001). The important 1988 *Magna Charta of European Universities* was indeed a trans-national treaty, but one that dealt primarily with concerns about what the university entails as an institution (Olsen, 2007) and the charter mainly addressed *national* governments, asking them to support the principles set out around institutional autonomy, academic cooperation and the nexus of teaching and research. Even if one would contend that Bologna can be seen as the "logical extension" (Neave, 2001: 186) of various programmes like ERASMUS and COMMETT and experiences of NARICs (National Academic Recognition Information Centres) and ENIC (European Network of Information Centres), the speed of change and the seemingly overwhelming support for the process is surprising.

On the other hand, one should judge the amount of change brought about by the Bologna process with some caution. 'Unprecedented' may aptly denote the change in national regulations in many higher education systems concerning the structure of degree programmes, regarding quality assurance mechanisms, diploma supplements and credit accumulation. However, at the level where it all should happen – the level of individual higher education institutions, there is much more ambiguity in terms of actual change and progress made. Various progress reports indicate that change is visible, but not always fully in line with the expectations (Crosier, Purser, & Smidt, 2007; Huisman, Witte, & File, 2006). From a methodological perspective, Neave and Amaral (2008) adequately point out that "institutional take up" is a rather flexible concept, still far away from execution and institutional embeddedness. Furthermore, other scholarly work points out that the Bologna process was used to achieve particular national reforms (Gornitzka, 2006; Witte, 2006) and there are reasons to extend this perspective to the level of higher education institutions: higher education institutions have translated the expectations of national governments to fit their own strategies. For sure, institutions have to adhere to the national regulations, but beyond that there are many ways in which higher education institutions "take up" elements of the Bologna process.

WHERE DO WE GO FROM HERE?

The above makes it difficult to really pin down the actual amount of change that has taken place in the context of the Bologna process (and the Lisbon process) as well as to disentangle the Bologna process as the prime *explanans* of organizational and systems change from other explanatory factors, such as globalization, changes in national governance arrangements, etc. The *role* of the Bologna process in relation to other explanatory factors could also be disputed. Is the Bologna agenda part of a de-nationalization process, and compatible with other de-nationalization processes such as globalization? Or is it rather a sort of regional response to globalization? Perhaps both interpretations are correct pointing to the complexities of the process as such.

While trying to identify what might come after Bologna, these complexities can be good pointers to a future. First, by the fact that the Bologna process was developed over time, and by new objectives added in a number of ministerial meetings since 1999. Second, by the fact that the Bologna process is closely intertwined with a number of other European initiatives, most noticeable the Lisbon Strategy and the modernization agenda for universities in education, research, and innovation launched by the European Commission. Third, by acknowledging the diversity of instruments and approaches for achieving the objectives stated – ranging from more legalistic approaches exemplified by the recently established register for quality assurance agencies in higher education to the Open Method of Coordination characterized by mutual policy learning and knowledge exchange. These characteristics tell us about a process that has been constantly transforming, open-ended and realized through a number of measures and instruments. Perhaps the greatest challenge for the future is not to identify a number of clear-cut objectives for the next decade, but to design a policy environment that shares some of the same characteristics as the Bologna process in the past. As such, looking back at the achievements is not only an inviting intellectual challenge but also a potential rewarding one for future policy development.

Of course, we already know quite much about the Bologna process. It has been a valuable object of research for scholars in the field of higher education, i.e. those interested in curriculum and organizational change and policy implementation and impact could gather relevant empirical materials to increase our understanding of the phenomena.

Moreover, given the nature of the change process, disciplinary approaches lend themselves perfectly for applications to the Bologna process. Scholars have successfully used political theory and public policy theories, multi-player and multi-level governance approaches, sociological perspectives, (organizational) institutional theory and historical perspectives to analyze elements of the Bologna process. Let us also stress the valuable insights that emerged from analyses from practitioners themselves. As such a body of knowledge emerged – not perfect and certainly not complete – that allowed us to come to terms with process and outcomes of the changes brought about by intergovernmental and supranational dynamics. In this volume, this body of knowledge is built upon to present the state of the art with respect to the most important elements of the Bologna process. And, the reflections on the past will also be used to fuel the debate on the next decade. As such, this book is meant to be a reflective exercise for those involved – in whatever way – in the Bologna process (researchers, teachers, managers, political decision-makers).

While this may sound modest, such reflections are perhaps one of the greatest achievements of the Bologna process in general. Few would disagree in the agenda-setting function of Bologna, but we seldom think about what this means in practice. The agenda-setting functions of Bologna can imply symbolic and strategic use of the process as exemplified when different countries use Bologna to implement reforms with a more domestic agenda. The agenda-setting function of Bologna could also imply expanding our horizons when entering strategic discussions about the future of universities and colleges. Bologna reminds us all that there is another world out there which we can not ignore. At the same time, the agenda-setting function of Bologna can also be a life-line to those that only see anarchy and a more confusing environment to which one needs to adapt. There are indeed many uses of the Bologna process ranging from the concrete and operational to the abstract and conceptual. We have seen Bologna being used to develop, back, refine, identify, and change policy processes in European higher education. Whatever comes after Bologna, we would argue that the process has created a momentum of change that to some extent is self-sustaining in that new networks, actors and groups have been established and closely intertwined. The many meetings, discussions and deliberations taking place under the Bologna umbrella have created a new space for policy-making which indeed is unprecedented in higher education, and making the whole process of policy-making more unpredictable and interesting than ever.

Therefore, we would emphasize that the material is also relevant to those outside of the countries currently subscribing to the process. Not only by including "an outsider's perspective" (see the chapter by Simon Marginson), but we think that the reflections on ten years of Bologna are relevant outside the European area as well (see also Adelman, 2008a, 2008b; Zgaga, 2006).

THE CONTRIBUTIONS TO THIS BOOK

The Flemish Ministry of Education and Training (Department of Higher Education) invited the three editors to produce a volume with chapters discussing topics that are deemed to be most salient in the coming decade (see preface). Based on a tentative list of themes to be covered initially suggested by the Ministry, the editors have solicited contributions from appropriate scholars, experts on the specific topics. The contents (beyond pointing out the general topic of the chapter) were up to the scholars themselves, the editors provided them with a general structure for the presentation of their arguments. Short summaries of the chapters were presented and discussed at the Bologna Seminar *Unlocking Europe's Potential – Contributing to a better World* in Ghent, 19–20 May 2008. The drafts presented in Ghent have later been further refined and extended in collaboration with the editors, and the results can be found in the following chapters.

The contributors to the volume not necessarily agree in their analyses of the Bologna process, but we found – nevertheless – a fair amount of consensus. We summarize the most important topics covered under headings that have been important to the Bologna process in the past, and which we also believe will be at centre stage in our discussions on the future: governance, quality, mobility, and diversity.

Governance

The emergence of a higher education policy arena at the European level is one of the most striking developments in higher education governance in the past decade, but it is certainly not the only one. We have witnessed at the same time (and actually already in the 1980s) national governments stepping back and increasing institutional autonomy, although not in all European countries at the same pace and there are notable exceptions to the trend towards more institutional autonomy. Another governance development is the emergence of the market and network steering as alternative approaches to state steering.

The governance trends as such are recognizable in European higher education, but the picture becomes much fuzzier when we look at what is happening in practice. Some relatively new policy instruments emerge (e.g. contractualization, performance-based funding), but modes of governance interact in particular historical contexts and it becomes unclear what the outcomes are of the new modes of steering. Consequentially, the promise of institutional autonomy may not be at odds with expectations of major stakeholders in higher education. Still, both those in favour of more professional governance and those wanting to maintain more traditional governance arrangements seem to agree that governance is important. Those wanting to see Bologna realizing its potential would emphasize that current reforms in the governance arrangements have not gone far enough. Those pointing to the potential downsides of Bologna would emphasize that change is not taking place due to failing designs and adaptations in the governance area. What everyone agrees upon is also that we do not yet know the full impact of new governance arrangements on higher education in Europe. The paradox emerging is that we may well face another decade of governance reforms in Europe without actually knowing what works and why. Future reformers here will have the double challenge of not only identifying good governance arrangements, but also their applicability in different contexts.

Quality

Trust as a device in professional contexts has been replaced by rational and instrumental forms of control and accountability. Recognition based on estimates of equivalence has, e.g., been replaced by other forms of measurement and assessment and a fair number of new agencies emerged to fulfil new and old accountability roles. This process has also strengthened the call for meta-evaluation and the supranational coordination of assurance mechanisms. Supranational agencies and mechanisms (European Association for Quality Assurance in Higher Education, the European Quality Assurance Register, the ENQA's Standards and Guidelines, European Qualifications Framework, etc.) start to become influential drivers for national and institutional quality assurance practices.

Whereas the latter development is evolving in rather close cooperation with the academic field and academics are still involved in a major way when it comes to quality assessment (peer review), rankings develop in a much more independent way. Rankings can be seen as another mechanism to gain insight into quality, but it would be more accurate to state that currently rankings and league tables are actually measuring prestige. Not only do invalid and unreliable measurements make it impossible for rankings to seriously measure quality, other methodological issues – can we really measure institutional quality? – loom large as well. Whatever our appreciation of rankings is, they are definitely here to stay (Hazelkorn, 2008) and will have a impact on institutional strategies and the higher education landscape in general. Two important – as yet unanswered – questions are: How can we assure and improve quality without ending up with unproductive bureaucracy and how can stakeholders (particularly the next generation of students) be provided with adequate and relevant information on higher education quality? A paradox coming to the fore is perhaps that in the process of creating more trust and transparency while maintaining a high level of efficiency in the sector, we need to re-invent some of the ways quality was secured in the past.

Mobility and Human Resources

The introduction of a tiered structure of study programmes and degrees is not strictly necessary to facilitate temporary intra-European student mobility but will be an advantage for the increase of degree mobility of students from other parts of the world. It remains to be seen how higher education institutions actually deal with recognition (in-depth analysis of student qualifications versus recognition on the basis of trust). The increasing stratification of universities might become a problem for mobility as well. Furthermore, due to many opportunities to go abroad temporary student mobility is experiencing a decline in professional value. This is yet another paradox: the rationale underpinning mobility as part of the Bologna process has been to gain some added value. When everyone is going for the same experience, the added value diminishes. That might make internationalization at home increasingly important. Academic staff mobility is less of success story compared to student mobility and takes place mostly for purposes of research. In this context challenges for career models, employment conditions, and social benefit systems are anticipated.

Some contributions pointed out a number of barriers for increased mobility of students, not least demographic changes and reduced value of temporary mobility for professional careers. Despite the fact that some further increase in intra-European student mobility is foreseen (although it will be increasingly degree mobility rather than temporary mobility), the emphasis is put on increased mobility of students from other parts of the world. For this, no proper preparation is being made as yet. Growing proportions of mobile students from other parts of the world will impact on issues of quality, curricular change to accommodate their needs and expectations, the language in which programmes are delivered, and last but not least on home students and mobile students from Europe. Furthermore, a danger is foreseen that intra-European mobility will tend to concentrate in smaller zones of mutual trust among institutions with similar quality and profiles. For these anticipated development guidelines are needed to deal with potential conflicts and tensions.

Related to mobility is the issue of equity. The social dimension appeared on the Bologna agenda, but it remains to be seen how much progress has been made in realizing some of the objectives. Time may be too short to judge this, given that social inequality has been visible in higher education for centuries and many attempts to balance this have been in vain or have shown only slow progress.

Diversity

Throughout all the contributions the issue of diversity is explicitly (sometimes more implicitly) addressed at various levels and connected to different topics. A number of topics have emerged:
- functional (teaching versus research), geographical, and stratified organisational diversity;
- diversity of the student population and the issue of equity;
- diversity of qualifications and skills (critical academic competencies versus competencies for the knowledge economy) needed by society and economy;
- diversity of markets in which universities will have to compete and to which they will offer their services;
- diversity of stakeholder groups with which universities will have to interact and the interests and needs of which they will have to take into account;
- diversity of funding sources which will have to be developed in order to enable flexible responses to new needs and demands;
- diversity of networks and alliances to be forged and joined by universities;
- diversity/diversification of the academic workforce.

The general concern emerging relates to our final paradox: how to maintain or increase institutional diversity in a European higher education area intended to become increasingly compatible? There are several forces at work that could harm the organizational diversity, but it is difficult to predict how the complexity of interacting drivers will shape the higher education landscape in the coming decade. An undercurrent in some of the writings is that there may be too much diversity. Given the forces pulling and pushing in different directions, there is a risk of diversity gradually heading in the direction of fragmentation. To some extent this has become reality already, e.g. when it comes to the academic profession, but also in terms of the (national, regional, and international) student body. Academics perform a much larger variety of roles in academia and students attending higher education constitute a far from coherent group (background, culture, etc.). Also, at the institutional level, the ongoing competition between higher education institutions may lead to very loosely coupled systems of higher education, although international coherence (networks, consortia) may replace national coherence. It would be too far-fetched to state that academia is falling apart, but it would be worthwhile to keep a close watch on the developments and think about governing mechanisms that would preserve some of the existing coherence and cooperative efforts in higher education.

CONCLUSION

In all, this volume contains a rich set of chapters which seriously – if only for their academic rigour – address the promises and perils of the Bologna process and its preliminary outcomes. A difficult task, given that the process is a target on the move (we are indebted to Neave and Maassen, 2007, pp. 136–137 for this metaphor) and even changing in nature during the process. It is also a difficult task because evidence can be interpreted differently paving the way for new paradoxes and complex interactions between the actors in the field. Consequently we are faced with new questions every time we believe answers to old questions have been found. Still, one lesson learnt from the process is that we (i.e. those involved in policy-making and policy evaluation) should take the evaluation of such large-scale processes more serious than has been done in the past decade. For sure, many insights were gained from evaluation studies but we seem to be still far away from evidence-based policy making in European higher education.

REFERENCES

Adelman, C. (2008a). The Bologna Club: What U.S. Higher Education Can Learn from a Decade of European Reconstruction. Washington, DC: Institute for Higher Education Policy.

Adelman, C. (2008b). *Learning Accountability from Bologna: A Higher Education Policy Primer*. Washington, DC: Institute for Higher Education Policy.

Crosier, D., Purser, L., & Smidt, H. (2007). *Trends V: Universities shaping the European Higher Education Area*. Brussels: EUA.

De Wit, K., & Verhoeven, J. (2001). The higher education policy of the European Union: With or against the member states? In J. Huisman, P. Maassen & G. Neave (Eds.), *Higher education and the Nation State. The international dimension of higher education* (pp. 175–231). Amsterdam etc.: Pergamon.

Gornitzka, A. (2006). What is the use of Bologna in national reform? The case of Norwegian quality reform in higher education. In V. Tomusk (Ed.), *Creating the European Area of Higher Education. Voices from the periphery* (pp. 19–41). Dordrecht: Kluwer.

Hazelkorn, E. (2008). Learning to live with league tables and rankings: The experience of institutional leaders. *Higher Education Policy, 21*(2), 193–215.

Huisman, J., Witte, J., & File, J. M. (2006). *The Extent and Impact of Higher Education Curricular Reform across Europe*. Enschede: CHEPS.

Neave, G. (1988). On the cultivation of quality, efficiency and enterprise: an overview of recent trends in higher education in Western Europe, 1986–1988. *European Journal of Education, 23*(1/2), 7–23.

Neave, G. (1990). On preparing for markets: Trends in higher education in Western Europe 1988–1990. *European Journal of Education, 25*(2), 105–122.

Neave, G. (2001). Anything goes: Or, how the accommodation of Europe's universities to European integration integrates an inspiring number of contradictions. *Tertiary Education and Management, 8*(3), 181–197.

Neave, G., & Amaral, A. (2008). On process, progress and methodology or the unfolding of the Bologna process as it appears to two reasonably benign observers. *Higher Education Quarterly, 62*(1/2), 40–62.

Neave, G., Maassen, P. (2007). The Bologna process: An intergovernmental policy perspective. In P. Maassen and J. P. Olsen (Eds.), *University Dynamics and European Integration* (pp. 135–153). Dordrecht: Springer.

Olsen, J. P. (2007). The institutional dynamics of the European university. In P. Maassen & J. P. Olsen (Eds.), *University Dynamics and European Integration* (pp. 25–53). Dordrecht: Springer.

Witte, J. (2006). *Change of Degrees and Degrees of Change. Comparing Adaptations of European Higher Education Systems in the Context of the Bologna Process*. Enschede: CHEPS.

Zgaga, P. (2006). *Looking Out: The Bologna Process in a Global Setting*. Oslo: Norwegian Ministry of Education and Research.

Part I: Governance

GUY NEAVE

1. INSTITUTIONAL AUTONOMY 2010–2020. A TALE OF ELAN - TWO STEPS BACK TO MAKE ONE VERY LARGE LEAP FORWARD

INTRODUCTION

Autonomy, whether academic or institutional, has been the subject of constant preoccupation for policy-makers, University Presidents and scholars of university affairs for the best part of two decades. What has changed during these twenty years, however, is the way the issue has been posed and debated. *Grosso modo*, the debate can be divided along two lines: first, the defence of the historic construct of academic – or personal, alternatively, positional – autonomy: Second, the gradual modification of that historic model under pressure from reforms throughout the late 1980s and the decade following. Amongst them were closer public control over expenditure, the press for greater institutional accountability, the quest for a more adaptable and flexible relationship between higher education, government and society (Neave and van Vught, 1991) the rise of the Evaluative State (Henkel, 1994; Neave, 2006; Neave, 2008) and the general shift in policy from being driven by social demand to being urged on by "market forces", effectiveness and economy (Dill, Jongbloed, Amaral and Teixiera, 2004).

Before suggesting some issues Institutional Autonomy might pose during the decade 2010 to 2020, a number of *caveats* should be born in mind. The first is the tendency to "over project" – effectively, to underestimate the time need for new developments or practices to embed into institutional routine. An excellent illustration of such over projection in today's agenda of higher education may be seen is the central exercise of implanting a standardized study structure across higher education systems engaged in the Bologna Process (Neave and Amaral, 2008).

The second aspect that merits attention is the process of embedding legislative reform within the individual university and more particularly, whether its importance is real or symbolic. As numerous case studies on both sides of the Atlantic (Pressman and Wildavsky, 1984; Cerych and Sabatier, 1986) into implementing reform in higher education have shown, implementation never follows the tidy path of linear progression that earlier planners counted upon and, as a result, were so often grievously disappointed. Rather, seating policy into the institutional fabric of higher education tends to be reiterative, its thrust blunted by negotiation, interpretation and re negotiation it proceeds (Stensacker, 2004; Weiss, 1977).

B.M. Kehm, J. Huisman and B. Stensaker (eds.), The European Higher Education Area: Perspectives on a Moving Target, 3–22.
© 2009 Sense Publishers. All rights reserved.

THE EVALUATIVE STATE: A FORMATIVE CONCEPT

The experience of higher education in Western Europe these two decades past suggests that institutional autonomy has been under revision far longer than that the legislation which specifically focuses on it today. Prior developments have then to be taken into account.

One of the most important, a "pre conditioner" to institutional autonomy, is the advent of the Evaluative State (Henkel and Little, 1994: Neave, 1998, Kehm, 2007; Clancy, 2007; Henkel, 2007; Neave, 2007). The Evaluative State stands as a transitional stage when many of the issues, later to become key elements in reform at institutional level, are first rehearsed.

The Evaluative State saw Autonomy mutate from a broad-ranging value and a privilege conferred upon universities as a prior condition to their fulfilling their long term task in society[1] (Thorens, 2004) to becoming an operational, multi-faceted, and largely conditional *contract*. The transition from the first definition of autonomy, itself well established in Western Europe's systems of higher education – personal and positional autonomy – to a formally expanded interpretation as institutional autonomy was largely accomplished within the workings of the Evaluative State.

The Evaluative State and its origins

French. The origins of the Evaluative State go back to the mid to late Eighties in France, the Netherlands and Britain, though in each case, the purpose behind these early developments differed considerably. In France, for example, the purpose for establishing the Comité National d'Evaluation in 1986 was less to detect the lack of efficiency amongst individual universities. Rather, it set out on the one hand, to stimulate institutional initiative by using institutional evaluation to disseminate real examples of successful practice, examples to be followed by other universities: on the other, to speed up the pace of change at institutional level. (Neave, 1996)

The French initiative sought to establish a regular feed-back mechanism and to remove one of the major blockages a high degree of legal homogeneity plus the need of formal authorization from central Ministry, imposed on the French university system. (Comité National d'Evaluation, 1989; Staropoli, 1987) In effect, the feedback system *à la française* was designed to strengthen system capacity for change within the existing closed mode of accountability between universities and Ministry by prodding the former into bolder action.

Dutch. This was not, however, the prime concern of the Dutch. In the late Eighties, the Dutch Ministry of Science and Education set out to develop a more radical and far-reaching alternative "steering system" to the classic and detailed "state control" model hitherto dominant. Unlike the French, it did not seek simply to update the procedures of "Legal Homogeneity". Its objectives were broader and more ambitious: How to create a system of coordination which ensured clarity in the strategy at system level, more rapid take-up at the institutional level and, last but very far from least, cut back on the time-consuming procedures of clearance and authorization in short the minutiae of central government control? Initially, this was tackled in terms of applying a "cybernetic" approach to the relationship between government and universities. (van Vught and Maassen, 1988, pp. 64 – 75)

A "self correcting" system held out several advantages: it placed the burden of adjustment on the individual institution whilst opening the possibility for central administration to concentrate on strategic priorities rather than exercising an oversight both close and detailed. Such a concept, later developed under the term "remote steering" (van Vught, 1989) recast the function of central administration, replacing detailed "state oversight" by an arrangement more loosely coupled in which its main task was "facilitatory", that effectively put in place procedures and conditions for rapid and appropriate adjustment at institutional level. (Neave and van Vught, 1991) Unlike the French approach, the Dutch model called for a simultaneous overhaul of central administration, of the capacity to adapt at institutional level as well as a system of feed-back and monitoring, based on academic performance and output indicators entrusted to the Dutch Universities' Association. (Jenniksens, 1997)

Both the French and Dutch reforms shared the belief that central to providing the higher education system with an inbuilt capacity to adapt rapidly to change required a greater margin of initiative at the institutional level, by updating management and revising the structures of governance. This agenda, however, was not presented as extending institutional autonomy, though such revisions to internal management and governance may certainly be seen in this light.

British. The situation was very different, however in the United Kingdom. Paradoxically, the British university system had long been identified – and very certainly so in the minds of its denizens – by certain unique operational features which, ironically possessed a degree of kinship with the vision entertained by the Dutch, though not by the French. The British university system was largely self-regulating, driven by the initiatives of individual universities and progressed in what is best described as an organic manner. By contrast to both French and Dutch universities, their British fellows were not legislatively driven. British universities possessed an extremely high degree of institutional autonomy, legally guaranteed by each university's founding Charter and upheld by a very particular relationship between central government and individual university which reflected the classic interpretation of the "proper" relationship between government and university, which owed much to 19th century English Liberalism. (Rothblatt, 1998) and very particularly in university affairs: State intervention was best reduced to a minimum.

Under this agreement, appointment to positions of leadership, (Neave, 1991) academic recruitment, promotion, the granting of tenure, the holding of – and sometimes, the canvassing for – endowment capital, the selection of individual students, the determination of curricular content and the methods used to evaluate student performance as indeed the award of degrees from Bachelor through to Doctorate, were very real instances of the institution's self-governance and the substantial nature of its autonomy. Other differences followed: not least the view that Institutional Autonomy was the prior condition that guaranteed Academic Autonomy. To the British academic, without the first, the second is precarious at best. This is a very different way of interpreting the ties between Academic Autonomy and Institutional Autonomy. By contrast, the Humboldtian Concordat looked to the State[2] to uphold academic or positional autonomy. The Jacobin university in France looked to the State to sustain the same principle by preventing the incursion of occult or particular interests into the affairs of academe. The British, however, in not untypical eccentricity, looked to Institutional Autonomy laid down in the terms of the individual University Charter, to protect the University and Learning from the State itself. (Neave, 2008).

Institutional Autonomy was the central and basic principal permeating British Universities. It set them aside from their European counterparts. Indeed, until the late 1980s system-wide legislation – the basis of the principle of Legal Homogeneity (Neave & van Vught, 1994) – was unknown. The legal basis of each university, its structure, patterns of governance and administrative procedures were enshrined in an individual Parliamentary Act, which constituted the individual University's Charter, specifically tailored to the purpose and mission the founding fathers laid upon a particular university. This founding legislation laid down the individual university's responsibilities, structure, inner workings, regulations and procedures. Powers of oversight and verification that in Europe formed part of the University's responsibility to the collectivity, in Britain were vested in the individual university and exercised in keeping with the terms of the Founding Charter – or its modification.

The Evaluative State: national variations on a strategic theme

French. The rise of the Evaluative State carried with it subtle variations in national priorities. In France, the introduction of the principle of "Contractualization" – that is, negotiation between individual university and central Ministry over the objectives to be attained for the coming five years (Chevaillier check) in no way compromised the status of the university as a public service, still less its commitment to meeting social demand. (Neave, 2004a) If the press for more efficient resource usage, improvement in quality and competition were present, the latter applied to a very different sphere. Rather than pitting one university against another for resources, the French version of the Evaluative State was grounded in rhetoric of competition abroad and national cooperation and solidarity at home. (Neave, 2004b)

Dutch. By contrast, the Dutch operationalization of the driving principles of modernization, marketization and institutional efficiency, enthusiastically applied on the home front were very definitely seen as an "exportable" model, both within Europe and farther afield.

British. In Britain, the emergence the Evaluative State impelled higher education from being grounded in a species of organic development towards a "regulated" system, with a growing emphasis on active government steering, exerted through specially created "agencies of public purpose" (Henkel, 2007) intermediary bodies which effectively reversed the pattern, long sustained by the University Grants Committee.[3]

Through the new stratum of oversight and verification, the will of government was injected into the university world. System-wide re-engineering resulted in system-wide legislation in the shape of the Education Reform Act of 1988, the 1992 Higher Education Act and the Higher Education Act 2004. The 1998 Act was an unprecedented example of the first Framework Act (Loi d'orientation, Rahmengesetz) ever to be applied to British higher education. The second created a unified system by granting university status to Polytechnics, outlined a national system for funding higher education. It laid down a corporate model of institutional governance, standardized in role, size and composition across all institutions raised to university level. (Williams, 2004) The third ushered in a further round of national standardization together and differential tuition fees. It set system wide conditions that determined the amount individual universities could charge their students. (DFES, 2003)

Three Remarkable Truths

British strategy yielded three remarkable truths. First, that whilst government certainly possessed the means to refine institutional autonomy, previously, it chose not to exercise them. By acting, it demonstrated, that the distinction between institutional autonomy as an inalienable right and academic freedom as a theoretically revocable privilege could, in practice be rendered rather less distinct than once believed.

Second, that the very feature around which other systems were building their strategy of modernization through institutional self-adjustment and self-correction – that fundamental concept of "organic development" which historically lay at the heart of the British university system – was not sufficiently adaptable – or to be more nuanced, was not *sufficiently* adaptable *within the time frame* envisaged by the British authorities. (Brown, forthcoming)

Third, in the absence of a "market" mechanism in higher education, central government found itself having to act as an Ersatz, hopefully temporary. With government acting as a 'pseudo market' ushered an unprecedented degree of juridification into British higher education. Whilst in no way comparable to the Legal Homogeneity that historically "steered" higher education in Western Europe, juridification was evident and very certainly so in a system that had long evolved without it. As one long-term student of British higher education observed: "… government in the UK employs the rhetoric of the market in connection with higher education, but since government controls the price universities can place on their services and the amount and variety of services they can sell, universities operate not in a market but in something like a command economy." (Trow, 1996, p. 310)

And their Consequences

There is a further perspective, which draws a contrast more stark still between the rise of the Evaluatory State in Britain and on mainland Europe. It involves "dual lines of accountability" in Western Europe, sometimes described as a "bi-cephalous model of administrative control" (Lane, 1982).

Prior to the Evaluative State, this bi-cephalous arrangement was the key underpinning to Legal Homogeneity, linking university and ministry (Lane, 1982; de Boer. 2003, pp. 253 – 255). It rested on a *descending administrative* hierarchy emanating from ministry to university, terminating in the person of the Secretary General in French universities, the *Regiringscommissaris* in their Flemish counterparts, with the *Kanzler* in Germany and the Administrative Director in Sweden, civil servant administrators who exercised legal oversight within individual universities on behalf of the ministry. An *ascending academic* hierarchy ran in parallel, culminating in the person of the *Président d'Université,* or the Rector as the first amongst equals in the academic estate.

By extending the bounds of institutional self-management, the Evaluative State formally weakened the descending administrative hierarchy, whilst strengthening the administrative responsibility laid upon the head of the ascending academic hierarchy. Not untypical was the Dutch Law for Modernizing University Governance of March 1997 (*Modernisering Universitaire Bestuursorganisatie*). (de Boer, 2003) It strengthened institutional self-management, opened up new ties with local interests and concentrated executive authority, hitherto dispersed across Senate and Board of Curators, into a three member Executive Board. For the first time in their history, Dutch universities were run by a monocephalic administrative structure. (de Boer, 2003, p. 256)

In mainland Europe, the Evaluative State shortened and concentrated the *descending* administrative hierarchy at institutional level. By contrast, the British authorities *brought a dual hierarchy into being,* at the very moment it was being phased out in mainland Europe. The British edition of the descending administrative hierarchy, which took shape during the early to mid Nineties, was more redoubtable than its earlier European counterparts: it was constructed around agencies of public purpose wielding oversight for regular assessment, evaluation and verification of institutional achievement. The descending hierarchy *à la britannique* was powerful precisely because it formed an evaluatory mechanism linking institutional funding to institutional performance.

The Significance of Evaluatory Homogeneity

The presence of a technically sophisticated and deeply penetrative system for evaluating performance and quality, which is the heart of the Evaluative State, redefined the procedures involved in Accountability. By focusing on the *individual* university rather than on whole sectors or on institutional types, which were the operational focus of *Legal* Homogeneity. (Teichler, 2007) Instead the principal of Homogeneity changed its location. The new version was bought to bear and operationalized *a posteriori,* thereby modifying control over higher education previously exercised *a priori.* (Neave, 1998)

The Evaluative State, by counterbalancing *Legal* Homogeneity, did so via *Evaluative* Homogeneity, set standardized criteria for minimum levels of performance and quality, applied to the individual University. (Neave, forthcoming) Nor did it subscribe to the basic assumptions of Legal Homogeneity. It did not assume institutional capacity to meet change to be similar across different types of institution.

Evaluative Homogeneity

The Evaluative State fulfils two principal functions. It is a powerful instrument for the organizational integration of higher education through operationalizing and applying standardized procedures and uniform rules in the area of quality assessment and accreditation. (Blieklie, 2007, p. 397) When the twin principals of transparency and public accountability are added into Evaluatory Homogeneity, the Evaluative State becomes central to society's understanding how its higher education system and within the system, how individual universities, perform. As its name implies, the Evaluative State brings together a basic instrumentality, which systematically, in standardized format and regularly updated, makes information on higher education publicly available. Such information on institutional output, performance and achievement shapes society's readiness to fund individual establishments, influences the choice students make between different institutions and courses. It provides a feed-back for leadership to determine institutional strategy and priorities by allowing leadership to compare output and performance with other institutions of a similar condition or to identify those whose achievements are worth emulating.

Thus, the Evaluative State acts as the central construct in the relationship between higher education and the legislator and the priorities the latter wishes to be reflected in higher learning. By the same token, it also represents the termination with extreme prejudice of what was presented earlier as the historic "Concordat" between higher education and society in Western Europe. For whilst the earlier Concordat was grounded in the State's acting as protector of the University, so the Evaluative State re-defines the role of the State primarily as the protector of society's interests – economic, social and developmental – vis a vis the University. To make no finer point, having resigned its historic role as the "Guardian of Learning" the (Evaluative) State now acts as "Overseer of the Market for higher education". (Neave, 2008b)

Evaluative Homogeneity: Its Potential

Yet, in the transition from *Legal* Homogeneity to *Evaluative* Homogeneity as the prime driver in coordinating higher education it is not surprising that interpretations as to its viability, potential and the exact ways it may shape higher education, are by no means clear-cut. On the one hand stands the argument that Evaluative Homogeneity is a counterweight to institutional diversity and overlap, in programmatic provision, modes of study – on site or distant ~ and in means of diffusion. (Huisman and Kaiser, 2001) By operating through standardized criteria, dimensions and procedures, focused on higher education's output, coherence and order are maintained at the very moment when the national community fragments, when regional interests assume greater importance in shaping institutional priorities and when institutional identity, under press from both markets and competition has increasingly become the thing of institutional self –advertisement rather than being the long accumulation of repute built up over the years.

Viewed thus, Evaluative Homogeneity modernizes *but does not alter* the basic characteristic of higher education. It remains a regulated system. Indeed, one of the perverse effects of policies of "de-regulation" has been to bring regulation to new and surreal heights of conformity and constraint. (Daxner, 2006, pp. 231–240; Amaral and Magalães, 2008) Evaluative homogeneity and its operational instrumentality ensure a central and additional objective – that market forces now have their place as the prime policy driver. Fragmentation of the national community in no way diminishes regulation. On the contrary, when both evaluation and funding are "repatriated" to the regional level, regulation is better aligned with regional concerns by a physically more immediate control over institutional performance and achievement.

Evaluative Homogeneity brings clarity at a time when institutional diversity is all the more evident precisely because the historic administrative framework of higher education, if not dissolving, at very least, is subject to increasing overlap. (Huisman and Kaiser, 2001)

Stratification, Differentiation and Evaluative Homogeneity

Institutional stratification and differentiation are not exclusively the work of evaluative homogeneity. Though sometimes taken for granted in such decentralized systems as the United Kingdom and the United States, these system characteristics have always existed *de facto* in Western European systems, even if strenuously denied *de jure*.

Legal Homogeneity did not take either differentiation or stratification into account save in terms of broad sectors whose component establishments were nevertheless held to be on a footing of legal equality. The status of individual universities was thus defined by their inclusion in a particular legally and administratively defined sector. Standing and identity were then collectively defined by "institutional types". Belgium, for instance, provides a particularly nice example. Higher education, like Caesar's Gaul, is divided into three segments – university, long course higher education outside the university, (*Hoger Onderwijs buiten universiteit HOBU*) short course higher education outside the university. (Verhoeven & Devos, 2002)

The mutation of Legal Homogeneity into Evaluative Homogeneity dissolves both stratification and differentiation as the means of distinguishing *different types* of establishment on the basis of their collective standing in a given sector. It *individualizes* institutional status. In contrast to Legal Homogeneity for which legal stratification and differentiation served as devices for assigning *permanent* status and identity to Universities, Evaluative Homogeneity employs stratification and differentiation as *provisional* and dynamic driving forces. Irrespective of whether they bring reward or penalty in their train, these two characteristics perform a central and strategic function in system coordination as opposed to acting, as they did under Legal Homogeneity, as a *descriptive registration.* Thus, institutional status is explicitly linked with, and made dependent upon, institutional services and performance. In turn, the same criteria determine the standing, repute and recognized excellence the individual University commands– or lacks!

The Evaluative State and Institutional Autonomy.

The setting up of macro steering systems – analysed in terms of increased efficiency, performance, output on the one hand, and on the other as a search by governments for a focused and reiterative mechanism rapidly to transplant national strategy into institutional execution – is clearly central to the change which is redefining academic autonomy from being personal or positional and re-constructing it in terms of institutional autonomy.

Some scholars have argued that institutional autonomy and personal autonomy are the heads and tails of the same coin. (Bleiklie and Kogan, 2007, p. 477) Historically, this holds good only in the Anglo Saxon systems of higher education. The equivalent construct in Western Europe extolled *positional* autonomy. It never conceded universities were *autonomous* institutions. (Hirsch and Weber, 2001, pp. 52–67) Regardless whether one agrees with the term "institutional autonomy" to describe offloading responsibility from central national administration to the institution, or placing additional conditions and responsibilities upon the individual university, both certainly require a very different pattern of internal institutional power (for an English perspective on this see Smith, Adams and Mount, 2007).

Positional autonomy is a very ancient pattern of governance, which endured many centuries namely, internal governance shared amongst senior scholars in the Academic Guild (de Groof, Neave and Svec, 1998) This today is translated as "collegiality." This construct contrasts with the rising notion, visible in the Netherlands and UK, though by no means limited to those systems, of institutional decision-making vested in a strong institutional Executive, backed by a team of professional managers. (Whitchurch, 2006) It derives rather from corporate management and business practice in the belief that managerialism may be associated with academic success though there is remarkably little evidence to support this conviction. (Smith, Adams and Mount, 2007, p. 8) The shift of institutional governance away from "academic community" and "collegiality" to "managerial professionalism" (Rhoades, 2005) reflects that change in higher learning's purpose and culture from the contemplative and spiritual to the applied, the productive and the expeditive.

Institutional autonomy may be justified on much the same grounds as its earlier *positional* counterpart. It ensures conditions necessary and conducive to sustained, creative and original thought which, maintained at a consistently high level and over time, begets excellence. Its contemporary construction, however, has to do with the management of the university as a public institution, more particularly with creating optimum effective administrative structures that permit institutional leadership to develop and carry out those strategic decisions that enable the institution to discharge the responsibilities and tasks which external interests and stakeholders have laid upon the university and to do so with speed and within cost. To meet the culture of production, power and authority, rather than being collegial and thus dispersed, are concentrated around institutional leadership and delegated in the form of an administrative chain of command.. (Bolden, Petrov and Gosling, 2008) In other words, the principles of good husbandry and accountability to major stakeholders – of which the government is one –assume organizational form. Institutional autonomy becomes both an operational task and the individualization of a once shared and collective responsibility.

What is an Autonomous Institution?

The range of responsibilities placed on individual institutions begs the question: "what are the essential functions a university must control if it is to exercise Institutional Autonomy as a genuine rather than as a symbolic condition?"

In 1994, the German sociologist Rudolph Stichweh identified a number of key functions necessary if Institutional Autonomy was to have substance. Amongst them, Stichweh believed, was the University's right and competence
– To decide independently the areas, which would engage its commitment.
– To endorse specific value systems and to define capital, career systems and incentives.
– Independently to decide on the basic institutional principles and forms of institutional governance.
– To control the criteria of access both for students and for academic staff.
– To define its strategic tasks and to set institutional goals.
– To determine both the formal and informal links to be developed with other sectors of society.
– And the obligation to assume full responsibility for the decisions taken and to be fully accountable for them. (Stichweh, 1994 cited in Nybom, 2007)

As a theoretical typology *of Institutional* Autonomy that appeared during the 1990's, Stichweh built on the same basic propositions as *positional* autonomy. Internal self-governance of academia by academia is enlarged from, and extended beyond, the fundamental freedoms of teaching and learning to embrace and include all activities undertaken within the purlieu of the individual university. Strategic planning, setting institutional goals, the ties between university and external community are, under such a schematic, internally determined by the Academic Estate, with the Administrative Estate serving in an executive capacity.

Institutional Autonomy as Stichweh presented it, is driven by an internal dynamic, grounded in the principle of academic self-government, tempered by the obligation to be accountable to government and society. Under this construct, Institutional Autonomy is driven by the disciplinary and epistemic evolution within the university. It is an interpretation remarkably close to its British counterpart,[4] particularly in selection of students and staff nomination and appointment which, in the German context of the day, were highly heretical.

Institutional Autonomy Reshaped

Stichweh's theses allow us to identify and thereby to contrast, the features of Institutional Autonomy as they emerged first within the rise of the Evaluative State and second, when set against the changes in distribution of power and authority within the institution itself. Indeed, the overall thrust of recent legislation stands at the antipodes of Stichweh's vision. Whereas Stichweh regarded Accountability as flowing from the nature of internal academic self-government, its contemporary edition puts accountability at the centre of the university's obligation. The repositioning of accountability and the obligation *to submit* to assessment of performance, achievement, financial efficiency and good husbandry is a natural concomitant of Institutional Autonomy in the Knowledge Economy. Nevertheless, it reverses the relationship between university and external society, by replacing distance by proximity and involvement. The task of the new Institutional Autonomy is to permit the university to set up those procedures, administrative structures and qualified administrative personnel to enable it to deal with external society reaching in.

The upshot, as Kogan and Bleiklie pointed out in a recent review of organization and governance in universities of Western Europe, is the creation of powerful managerial infrastructures, running in parallel, where not supplanting, academic structures built around Deans, Heads of Departments and the Professorate, once the personification and apotheosis of *positional autonomy*. (Kogan and Bleiklie, 2007, p. 479) It is unclear, for the moment, whether Institutional Autonomy in its new guise is a constraint upon, or is relatively neutral vis a vis academic autonomy in its positional definition. Swedish evidence suggests that its impact is relatively marginal: more important, *both* institutional and academic autonomy appear increasingly to be dependent on external actors. (Bladh, 2007, pp. 243 – 249)

Dependency and Conditionality

Dependency alone does not differentiate the contemporary edition of Institutional Autonomy from its positional predecessor. It may equally well be argued that the latter was just as dependent on the government's upholding the Humboldtian Concordat as it was on the state budget. Nor is dependency any the less when transferred from Prince to Merchant, from public revenues to private contracts, eked out by payment for commissions and services.

More important than dependency, is conditionality. Conditionality implies instability, though this is rarely recognized. Just as the boundaries of Institutional Autonomy are subject to continual negotiation in keeping with the expeditive ethic which requires higher education keep abreast of continual and largely unpredictable change through permanent negotiation between government, the market and academic institutions, (Henkel, 2007, pp. 87–99) so too are the conditions that determine whether the individual institution is able – quite literally – to afford even the remnants of *positional* autonomy within it. Both are subject to the same constraints. Henkel's proposition that neither Institutional nor Academic Autonomy today are fixed in stone and for all time, cannot be gainsaid, either for the United Kingdom or, for those systems of higher education currently committed to re-constructing the Knowledge Society's equivalent of Institutional Autonomy. But to see Academic Autonomy in terms of boundaries contested between the state, the market and academic institutions merely confirms – though in an alternative vocabulary – the basic unpredictability to which academic autonomy is now hostage. For if academic autonomy is not entirely out of the control of academia, by the same reasoning, neither is it wholly within the powers of academia. And this is tantamount to admitting its oscillating and unpredictable quality.

This view is partly shared by Kogan and Bleiklie. The Academic Estate with its collegial "style" of decision-making has, they argue, become integrated into the Administrative Estate less as decision-makers than as the executors of institutional policy. Collegiality gives place to top-down line management. Collegiality's end transfers the basis of legitimacy from the Academic to the Administrative Estate. (Kogan and Bleiklie, 2007, p. 479) Thus, inverting the relationship between the Academic and the Administrative Estates is one of the more significant developments in Institutional Autonomy's mutation from a broad ranging value and organizational ethic to becoming a form of intellectual shorthand for the strengthening of managerial hierarchy as the prime vehicle to ensure demonstrated efficiency and expedition under the new rubric of that term.

Leadership

Though Britain has a long way still to go before individuals can make a life-time career as 'professional' President – a practice well established in the United States (Kerr & Gade, 1986) – significant developments are to be noted. In particular, the balance between managerial acumen and a proven track record for institutional development may be a pointer both to the weakening of academia's power to organize their institution and to placing it in the hands of "manager professionals' rather than scholar/managers. (Rhoades, 1998) The gradual extension of the descending administrative hierarchy within the institution – the advent of the "professional Dean" as manager rather than as academic, the assimilation of "Pro Vice Chancellors" as senior managers rather than senior academics ((Smith, Adams and Mount, 2007, p. 8) point to the transfer of authority within formally autonomous institutions from the community of scholars to the world of managers. And thus to redefining the bounds of positional autonomy. (Whitchurch, 2006 p. 9)

Strengthening of leadership is far from being British exclusivity. On the contrary, it stands well to the fore in France, where recent legislation in the shape or the Law of August 10th 2007 – the so called "Pécresse Law" named after the Minister of Higher Education and Research, Valérie Pécresse – concentrates power in the hands of the University President. (Montlaur-Creux, 2007) whilst simultaneously diluting that of academic staff. (Berger, 2007) A broadly similar trend is equally evident in Norway (Stensaker, 2006) Portugal. (Amaral, 2008) and the Netherlands. In the latter instance, the 1996 Law on University Governance, revised the basic duality in mentioned earlier and at institutional level reinforced the descending administrative hierarchy. The Governing Board is smaller. The President is re-cast as the direct and explicit representative of external interests. Still formally elected from amongst the senior Professorate, the Dutch Rector's executive powers over institutional management are reinforced. However, the Rector reports to the President. The President represents civil society. He replaces the classic descending chain of oversight that bound Ministry to University. The President serves in a strategic role as intermediary between civil society and university, whereas he Rector is responsible for the execution of the strategy determined in the Governing Board and serves as intermediary between Board and the constituent interests *within* the University. (De Boer, 2003)

The Danish University Act of 2003 stands as a further variation on the general theme of reforming governance. The managerial aspect, which is a central characteristic in the present day version of Institutional Autonomy, is clear. Executive Management is vested in a Board, not greatly dissimilar to the American Board of Trustees. Whilst the Dutch version has outside interests speaking through the person of the President, membership of the Danish University Board has an external majority of members of whom the Chairman is one.

Looking Ahead: A Very Dark Glass

As we turn to issues that are likely to follow from re-engineering Institutional Autonomy, it is as well to recall three indisputable verities. They bear directly on aspects likely to cause concern over the decade before us.

The first is that the reforming impulse in its entirety, which has lasted over twenty years, was ushered in by a severe economic crisis, by structural changes in the economy, by major restrictions in the higher education budget and, as this analysis has argued, by major additions to the instrumentality of system steering through evaluating institutional performance, efficiency and achievement.

The second lies in aligning higher education's purpose and mission with the canons of one particular School of Economic Thought, – or its derivatives in higher education – variously qualified as Neo- Liberalism or Ultra-Liberalism.

The third truth is that Institutional Autonomy, reinterpreted in the light of the demands of the Knowledge Economy, sets the specific purpose upon the University to expedite its response to the specific demands of external interests for knowledge, useful and relevant to their purposes. The instrumentalization of Institutional Autonomy reflects the unavoidable fact that today the market is deemed to be the prime driving force of higher education. It also reflects the dependency of the university on the state of the economy to which it is deemed to be a partner with a varying geometry of indispensability, and depending on the particular faculty involved. Like Animal Farm, some faculties are more indispensable from industry's standpoint than others.

Identifying key issues is complicated further by the crisis, which so far few have had the courage publicly to admit, though it is generally agreed that the economies of Europe show disquieting signs of creaking under the combined strain of a second oil shock and of grossly imprudent behaviour by another of Neo Liberalism's "axial" institutions, namely Banking. If the universities from the mid 80's through to early 90's were weighed in the balance and found wanting by the canons of Neo Liberalism, the viability and sustainability of the reforms enacted in the meantime cannot but be subject to similar heart-searching and reassessment, as will be the assumptions of Neo Liberalism itself – one of the many fallouts from the present querulousness in the economies of Europe.

Other Consequences of Marketization.

It is a basic axiom of Neo Liberalism that just as in a buoyant economy the privatisation of profit is an excellent thing, so in a morose economy, the socialization of loss – that is, the responsibility of the ordinary citizen to bail the imprudent out – is no less imperative. If some governments have admitted the necessity for bailing out Banks in the interests of the short term, can they deny the *bien fondé* of the same argument when applied to universities, which under the action of those same governments have become increasingly focused on the short term, whilst nevertheless retaining a commitment that extends over the long?

Precisely because higher education is today more closely coupled to the market than ever before, so it is more vulnerable than ever before and more speedily so, to the market's vagaries and fortunes. Seen from this perspective, it is precisely the re-definition of Institutional Autonomy to serve as instrument for an expeditive managerialism, that bids fair to drive the impact of external down-turn rapidly into the Groves of Academe. No less worrisome is the possibility that precisely those universities that have gone out of their way to diversify to the utmost their reliance on contracts with industry, business, information technology – the cream of the Entrepreneurial Universities – that will suffer most. If business lays off its own employees, management and cadres, will it continue to back university research or buy university services to the same degree as before? Will the pendulum of policy fashion swing in the opposite direction with the possibility that regulations put in place to extract more initiative and responsiveness from higher education, are uncoupled and dissociated from the Neo Liberal ethic? How far will the growing regulation of certain key areas such as research, see the role of governments and the European Union acting as quasi-permanent "pseudo markets"?

Economic crisis has prompted reforms more radical and more sustained than economic prosperity ever did. One has only to compare the 1960s with the 1980s and 1990's in Western Europe to see how far this axiom is born out. One has to admit that the fortune-teller's crystal ball is more than usually clouded when turned to the coming decade. The futurologist's glass becomes darker still, when we bear in mind that reforms in performance assessment, governance, leadership – initiatives that took root during the 1990s – could not have been deduced, even less predicted – on the basis of cost-cutting exercises undertaken the previous decade.

Abiding Issues

There are, most certainly abiding issues that arise from re-defining Institutional Autonomy as the central construct in higher education. First, how far, and to what type of establishments, is it to be applied? Another way of posing this question is: How far is the transition of Institutional Autonomy as a pervasive and universal value to an operational *modus administrandi,* nearing completion? There are two sides to this; first, Autonomy whether institutional or positional, serves to identify and to confer status on institutions. It also serves to differentiate them. Thus, short cycle higher education, whether in the form of French *Instituts Universitaires de Technologie,* German *Fachhochschulen* or Polytechnics – whether British or Portuguese – tended, by and large, to come under closer and more direct oversight from Ministry or Local Education Authorities. (Pratt and Burgess, 1976: Amaral and Carvalho, 2008) Differences in the range and scope of Institutional Autonomy between university and non-university sectors has given rise to much ill-will, not to mention being the root cause of "academic drift". (Kyvik, 2007) and "policy drift" (Neave, 1979) Various remedies have been applied.

In the United Kingdom, integrating and nationalizing Polytechnics as new universities, in Portugal under pressure from the Polytechic interest, the removal of pedagogic autonomy from the universities under the terms of Law 26/2000 and of Law 1/2003. (Amaral and Carvalho, 2008) are timely reminders of the tensions that differential distribution of Institutional Autonomy causes.

As yet, the issue of Institutional Autonomy as a new management construct applies mainly to the university sector. This policy tends to disregard that over the past twenty years, the universe of learning has undergone two changes in definition, from university to higher education and, more recently, from higher to tertiary education. (OECD, 1998) The expanding universe of post school provision begs the question exactly where the lines are to be drawn – and how justified – between post school establishments where Institutional Autonomy applies and those where it does not.

This is a matter of the utmost nicety. It is clearly an issue falling fairly and squarely under the responsibility of national authorities. How far, where and to what degree are the boundaries of Institutional Autonomy to be set? On what criteria they are to be delimited? This issue is present in all systems where non-university, short cycle higher education exists cheek by jowl with "research universities". On geographical criteria alone, it is a matter with a "European" dimension, even though the power to act is most assuredly a Member State concern.

Other scenarios also follow from re-defining Institutional Autonomy. There is an "inclusive and maximalist" definition. Likewise, there is an "exclusivist and minimalist" edition. The latter appears to be emerging in various forms in Germany, France, Sweden and the UK within the setting of identifying and preserving, excellence – in essence, a policy of *triage*. Yet, the search for excellence and the evident and well-advertised advantages that recognition brings, raise two other questions. Are the excellent to be accorded separate status? Is the purpose of such public benediction to set aside a few "super" or "European" universities – say, 200 or so out of the 4,100 in Europe *sensu lato*? What will be the consequences for the type of Autonomy, whether Institutional or positional, accorded to the excellent? Will there be any substantive differences between that enjoyed by the Elect and that granted to the commoners? Thus, the well-worn issue of whether variations in the degree of institutional autonomy are a privilege – temporary, ephemeral and revocable – or whether the institutional autonomy granted to the majority is an institutional right, returns in full force.

Such scenarios are very far from being a pipe-dream as certain Scandinavian governments contemplate quite amazing reductions to their university base. This option unearths another interesting possibility, namely the return to a "Guardian Relationship" for just some of Europe's leading establishments whose recognized excellence is so outstanding that to let them sink without trace would compromise the very visibility Europe reckons it ought to have in the vast world.

The Guardian Relationship Resurrected?

Resurrecting a highly-focused and selective "Guardian Relationship," built around a few highly-performing establishments, may not be wholly within the canons of Neo Liberalism. It may, paradoxically, be the way of sustaining Europe's viability in a global economy. If it were, such an arrangement would cast a further and no less interesting light on the relationship between government, university and society. For, regardless of whether the recognition of excellence is a passing or a permanent thing in the advantages it secures, it is a very clear example of further stratification. The new Guardian Relationship may anticipate a system profile akin to the current configuration in Brazil, where the elite universities are public sector and the mass sector, private. (Schwartzman, 1998) An alternative to this vision could well see the emergence in Europe's higher education systems of a "temporarily protected" sector, consisting of highly-performing research universities at the apex and at the base a "market-driven" mass sector . The latter, whilst not private, would nevertheless compete ferociously for public funding and for whatever largesse it could garner from private sector sources.

What such an arrangement would entail for Institutional and positional Autonomy is not difficult to see. If the purpose of Institutional Autonomy is to allow the individual higher education establishment to determine its best strategy for demonstrating performance and achievement, from this it follows that positional autonomy is the reward for excellence demonstrated rather than a right that attaches unconditionally to the individual academic by the nature of his or her employ. What this suggests is that indeed, positional autonomy where it is recognized at all, will be dependent on, and conditioned by, the success Institutional Autonomy may reap. In turn, this situation suggest that positional autonomy will become a matter of privilege and circumstances, both conditional upon institutional success, not as a professional right. (7492words)

NOTES

[1] All too little attention has been paid to the often very specific connotations and *sous entendus* that accompany this term when transposed from one nation-state system of higher education to another. In part, this arises from the very nature of Autonomy as the central "taken for granted" in any one system of higher education. Matters are complicated yet further by the belief, largely unspoken, even – or perhaps, above all – amongst the denizens of academia itself, that because the same term is often shared across different systems, it carries with it the same operational outcomes. Or has been the result of similar experience. This, however, is very rarely the case. Take for instance, the French rendition of university autonomy – *les libertés universitaires*. There is a world of difference as any philosopher is aware, between Freedom in the singular and Liberties in the plural, the first being a permanent and inalienable condition, the second as a theoretically revocable privilege. (Thorens, 2004; Neave, 2008) The systematic exploration of the different connotations that attach to this term across different systems is very far from being a sterile exercise in socio-linguistics. It merits further and sustained attention.

[2] Humboldt saw the Monarch as the best guarantor and through him the apparatus of state. However, the elevation of the Prussian monarch as Protector of Universities was realized only in 1848. (Nybom, 2004)

[3] The furious multiplication of such bodies on the British higher education landscape from 1992 onward was unprecedented. In addition to the four Higher Education Funding Councils for England, Scotland, Wales and Northern Ireland, went the Quality Assurance Agency, the Adult Learning Inspectorate, the Teacher Training Agency, the Higher Education Staff Development Agency, the Institute of Learning and Teaching in Higher Education, not to mention the further division of the main Research Councils which alone constituted seven separate bodies. To this, discussion in 2003 –2004, proposed Learning and Skills Councils and Sector Skills Councils dispersed at regional level. (For a more elaborate treatment of this curious phenomenon see Guy Neave, (2005) "The supermarketed university: reform, vision and ambiguity in British Higher Education", *Perspectives* vol.9, No.1 January, pp. 17 – 22.

[4] This point is developed above.

REFERENCES

Amaral, Alberto (2008) "The reform of Higher Education in Portugal". In Amaral, A. (org.) *Políticas do Ensino Superior: Quatro temas em debate* Lisboa, Conselho Nacional de Educação, pp. 17–37

Amaral, Alberto and Antonio Magalhães. (2007) "Market Competition, Public Good and Institutional Governance," *Higher Education Education, Management and Policy*, 19.1: 63–76.

Bladh, Agneta (2007*)* " Institutional Autonomy with increasing dependency on outside actors", *Higher Education Policy*, vol. 20, No.4, pp. 243–259.

Berger, Anne E, (2007) "La Loi Pécressse et le modèle américain," *Liberation*, December 20th 2007, http://www.liberation.fr/rebonds/299182.FR.php

Bleiklie, Ivar (2007) "Systematic integration and macro steering", *Higher Education Policy*, vol. 20, No.4, pp. 291–413.

Bleiklie, Ivar and Kogan, Maurice (2007) "Organization and governance of universities", *Higher Education Policy*, vol. 20, No.4, pp. 477–494.

Bolden, Richard Petrov, Gregory and Gosling, Jonathon (2008) *Developing collective leadership in higher education: Final Report*, London, Leadership Foundation for Higher Education.

Brulin. Goran (2006) "The Third Task of Universities or How to get Universities to serve their Communities" in Peter Reason, and Hilary Bradbury (eds) *Handbook on Action Research: Participative Inquiry and Practice*, London, Sage.

Cerych, L & Sabatier, P (1986) *Great Expectations: implementing reform in Europe's higher education*, Stoke-on-Trent (England) Trentham Books

Clancy, Patrick (2007) "Resisting the Evaluative State: Irish academics win the Battle but loose the War" in Juergen Enders and Frans van Vught (eds) *Towards a Cartography of Higher Education Policy Change*, Enschede, CHEPS, pp.111–118.

Comité National d'Evaluation (1989) *Priorités pour l'Université* , Paris, La Documentation française.

Daxner, Michael (2006) "Challenges to academic conduct and their implications for university development", *Higher Education in Europe*, vol. 31, No.3, pp. 231–240.

de Groof , Jan Neave, Guy & Svec, Juraj (1998) *Governance and Democracy in Higher Education, vol. 2*. in the Council of Europe series *Legislating for higher education in Europe*, Dordrecht, Kluwer. 392 pp.

de Boer, Harry (2003) *Institutionele Verandering en professionele autonomie: een empirische en erklarende studie naar de doorwerking van het Wet 'Modernisering Universitaire Bestuursorganisatie (MUB)* Enschede, CHOBS.

Dill, David Jongbloed, Ben Amaral, Alberto & Teixeira, Pedro [Eds] (2004) *Markets in Higher Education: rhetoric or reality?* Dordrecht, Kluwer Academic Publishers.

European Commission (2007) "Towards the European Higher Education Area: responding to challenges in a globalized world", *Conference of European Higher Education Ministers; Contribution of the European Commission,* Bruxelles (xerox)

Eustace, Roland (1998) "The United Kingdom" in Husén, Torsten Postlethwaite, T. Neville, Clark, Burton R. and Neave, Guy (Eds) *The Complete Encyclopedia of Education* CD ROM Oxford, Elsevier Science.

Henkel, Mary (2007) "Can academic autonomy survive in the Knowledge Society? A perspective from Britain", *Higher Education Research and Development*, vol.26, No.1, March, pp. 87–99.

Henkel, Mary and Little, Brenda (1999) *Changing Relationships between Higher Education and the State* London, Jessica Kingsley.

Hirsch, Werner Z. & Weber, Luc E. [Eds] (2001) *Governance in Higher Education: the University in a State of Flux*, London/Paris/ Geneva, Economica, pp.52–67.

Huisman, Jeroen Maassen, Peter and Neave, Guy. (2001) *Higher Education and the Nation State,* Oxford, 2001, Elsevier-Pergamon for IAU 267 pp.

Jenniskens, Ineke (1997) *Governmental steering and curriculum innovations : a comparative study of the relation between governmental steering instruments and innovations in higher education curricula.* Utrecht, De Tijdstroom

Kehm, Barbara (2007) "The Evaluative State and Higher Education Policy in Germany", in Juergen Enders and Frans van Vught (eds) *Towards a Cartography of Higher Education Policy Change*, Enschede, CHEPS, pp. 139–148.

Kerr, Clark & Gade, Marion L. (1986) *The Many Lives of Academic Presidents: Time, place, character,* Washington DC, Association of Governing Boards of Universities and Colleges.

Lane, Jan-Erik (1982) "Das Hochschulwesen in Skandanavien in einer vergleichenden Uebersicht" in L. Hueber (Ed) *Europeaeischen Encyclopedie Erziehungswissenschaft*, Hamburg, Klett-Kotta Verlag.

Leslie, L. L. & Slaughter, S. A. (1997). "The development and current status market mechanisms in U.S. postsecondary education." *Higher Education Policy*, vol. 10. No.2 pp. 239–252.

Brown, Roger (forthcoming), "Effectiveness or economy? Policy drivers in UK higher education, 1985-2005". In: Jeroen Huisman (ed.), International perspectives on the governance of higher education: Alternative frameworks for coordination. London/ New York, Taylor and Francis.

Marton, Susan (2007) "University Autonomy under Threat? – a case study from Sweden," http://www.flackattack.org/faw/index.php?title=University_Autonomy_under_Threat%3F

Montlaur-Creux, Carine (2007) "Loi n°2007-1199 du 10 août 2007 relative aux libertés et responsabilités des universités » Pau, November 2007, Université de Pau et des Pays de l'Adour, Direction des Affaires juridiques (power point presentation)

Musselin, Christine (2004) "Commentary on 'The Bologna Process and the Evaluative State: a viticultural parable,' " in Kogan, M. (ed) *Management and Evaluation in Higher Education, UNESCO Forum Occasional Paper series, Paper No.*7 Paris, 2004, UNESCO, pp.35–38.

Neave, Guy (1979) "Academic drift: some views from Europe", *Studies in Higher Education,* vol. 6, No. 2, Autumn 1979.

Neave, Guy (1991) "On the procedures of Elevation: or, how the mantle of Elijah falls upon the shoulders of Elisha", *Organisation und Management von Universitäten: Verhaltnis von Staat und Universität, Plenum* 1/1991 [Vienna] pp. 44–49

Neave, Guy (1996) "The Evaluation of the higher education system in France," in Robert Cowen [Ed] *World Yearbook of Education 1966 The Evaluation of Systems of Higher Education,* London, Kogan Page, pp. 66–81-

Neave Guy (2004a) "The Bologna Process and the Evaluative State: a viticultural parable" in Kogan, M. (ed) *Management and Evaluation in Higher Education, UNESCO Forum Occasional Paper series, Paper No.7* Paris, 2004, UNESCO, pp.11–34.

Neave, Guy (2004b) "The Temple and its Guardians: an excursion into the Rhetoric of Evaluating Higher Education", *Journal of Finance and Management in Colleges and Universities* (Tokyo) vol.1, No.1, pp 212–227.

Neave, Guy (2006) "The Evaluative State and Bologna: Old Wine in New Bottles or simply the Ancient Practice of 'Coupage'? *Higher Education Forum,* vol.3, March 2006, Hiroshima (Japan), Hiroshima University Research Institute for Higher Education, pp. 27–46.

Neave, Guy (2008) "From Guardian to Overseer; Trends in Institutional Autonomy, Governance and Leadership" in Alberto Amaral (ed) *Reforma do Ensino Superior: Quatro temas em Debate,* Lisboa, 2008, Conselho Nacional de Educacão.

Neave, Guy (forthcoming) "The Evaluative State as Policy in Transition: an anatomical study," in Robert Cowen & Andreas Kazamias (eds) *International Handbook of Comparative Education,* Dordrecht, 2009, Springer Verlag.

Nybom, Thorsten (2008) "University Autonomy and academic freedom: political rhetoric or institutional reality?" *Keynote presentation to the Conference 'Transition to Mass Higher Education Systems: international comparisons and perspectives',* Haifa, [Israel]The Technion Israel Institute of Technology, December 4th – 6th 2008 14 pp

OECD (1998). *Redefining Tertiary Education,* Paris: OECD.

Portugal (1988) Assembly of the Republic *Law 108/88 September 24th University Autonomy,* Lisboa, Centro de Informações sobre a Reconhecimento Académico de Diplomas.

Pressman, J L.; Wildavsky, A B. (1984*) Implementation: How great expectations in Washington are dashed in Oakland: or, why it's amazing that federal programs work at all, this being a saga of the Economic Development Administration as told by two sympathetic observers who seek to build morals on a foundation of ruined hopes,* 3rd edition. Berkeley: University of California Press.

Purser, L & Crosier, D (2007) "Trends V: Key Messages*", 4th Convention of European Higher Education Institutions,* Lisbon, March 2007 (power point presentation).

Rhoades, Gary (1998) *Managed Professionals: unionized faculty and restructuring academic labour,* Albany NY, SUNY Press.

Rhoades, Gary (2005) "Capitalism, academic style and shared governance" *Academe* vol. 91, No.3.

Rothblatt, Sheldon (1998) *The Modern University and its Discontents; the Fate of Newman's Legacies in Britain and America*, Cambridge University Press.

Smith, David, Adams, Jonathon and Mount, David, (2007) *UK Universities and Executive Officers: the changing role of Pro Vice Chancellors: Final Report*, London, Leadership Foundation for Higher Education.

Staropoli, André (1987) "The Comité National d'Evaluation: Preliminary Results of a French Experiment" *European Journal of Education*, Vol. 22, No. 2, pp. 123–131.

Stensaker, Bjorn (2004) *The Transformation of Organisational Identities. Interpretations of policies concerning the quality of teaching and learning in Norwegian higher education.* Enschede, CHEPS

Stichweh, Rudolf (1994) *Wissenschaft, Universitaet, Professionen*, Frankfurt/Main, Suhrkamp.

Teichler, Ulrich (2007) *Higher Education Systems; conceptual frameworks, comparative perspectives, empirical findings*, Rottedam, Sense Publishers.

Thorens, Justin (2006) "Liberties, Freedom and Autonomy: A Few Reflections on Academia's Estate", *Higher Education Policy* vol. 19, No.1, pp. 87–110.

Tjeldvoll, Arild (1998) *A Service University in Scandinavia*? Oslo University, Institute for Educational Research.

Trow, Martin (1975) "The public and private lives of Higher Education", *Daedalus*, No. 104 November pp. 113–127.

Trow, Martin (1996) "Trust, Markets and Accountability in Higher Education: a comparable perspective", *Higher Education Policy*, vol. 9, No.3, p. 310.

Ullman, Walter (1961) *Principles of Government and Politics in the Middle Ages*, New York, Barnes & Noble.

van Vught, Frans and Maassen, Peter (1988) "An intriguing Janus head: The Two Faces of the New Governmental Strategy for Higher Education in the Netherlands" *European Journal of Education*, Vol. 23, Nos. 1/2 (1988), pp. 65–76.

Weiss, Carole (1977) "Bridging Research and Policy. Research for policy's sake: the Enlightenment Function of Social Research," *Policy Analysis*, vol. 3, No.4, pp. 531–545.

Whitchurch, Celia (2006) *Professional Managers in UK higher education: preparing for complex futures Interim Report*, London, Leadership Foundation for Higher Education.

Williams, Gareth (2004) "The Higher Education market in the UK" in David Dill, Ben Jongbloed, Alberto Amaral & Pedro Teixeira [Eds] *Markets in Higher Education: rhetoric or reality?* Dordrecht, Kluwer Academic Publishers, pp. 241–270. (8951).

JUSSI VÄLIMAA

2. THE RELEVANCE OF HIGHER EDUCATION TO KNOWLEDGE SOCIETY AND KNOWLEDGE-DRIVEN ECONOMY: EDUCATION, RESEARCH AND INNOVATION

INTRODUCTION[1]

Universities are an indigenous product of Western Europe, where the organization and the idea of university was first developed during the eleventh and twelfth centuries on a 'utilitarian soil'. According to Cobban (1988, 10), 'Europe's earliest universities were institutional responses to the need to harness the expanding intellectual forces of the eleventh and twelfth centuries to the ecclesiastical, governmental and professional requirements of society.' The originality of the European university – compared to other forms of higher learning in the world – was based on the social innovation of its organization. The universities were privileged corporate associations of masters and students with their statutes, seals, administrative machinery and degree procedures (see Cobban 1988, 1).[2] However, the development of a guild of masters or students into an organization using the name 'university' was contributed to by the four principles of university, which have become deeply embedded in the European universities. According to Cobban (1988, 11–14), those are "*1) the belief in the dignity of man, who, even in his fallen state, was capable of impressive mental and spiritual growth, 2) the belief in an ordered universe which was open to rational understanding, 3) the belief in the prospect of man's mastery of his environment through his intellect and his mounting knowledge and experience, and 4) culture in which questioning and analytical approach to both classical and contemporary material was encouraged.*" One of the objectives of this paper is to reflect on how higher education institutions continue to respect their 'utilitarian soil' and whether the founding principles still are the cornerstones in and of European universities.

Even though the aim of this paper is not to run through the history of higher education, it should be noted that the second critical period in the development of European universities took place during the Europe of Napoleonic wars in the beginning of the nineteenth century. As a solution to the crisis of universities, this era saw the establishment of the University of Berlin (in 1810), which helped to create the globally influential Humboldtian idea of university. The unity of teaching and research combined with academic and institutional freedoms laid the basis for the crucial social roles universities played in the processes of modernization during the nineteenth and twentieth centuries. Universities and other higher

B.M. Kehm, J. Huisman and B. Stensaker (eds.), The European Higher Education Area:
Perspectives on a Moving Target, 23–41.

education institutions have not only promoted, but they have also greatly benefited from the processes of modernization, which supported the current knowledge explosion and occupational specialization and strengthened the nation state as a central unit of and in modernization processes. Higher education institutions took the advantage from the ally with the nation state, able to provide more and new resources for universities. In return, universities provided the nation states with new cultural identities and skilful labour for both public service and industrial production, as Wittrock (1993) has sharply stated looking at the modernization from the perspective of higher education.

One reason for beginning this chapter with a glimpse at the history of European universities is the fact that we are now witnessing another period of potential transformation of universities, which may challenge the founding principles of universities. The globalization, massification and mission overload of higher education are all concepts that describe the changing and increasing societal demands of and for higher education. The growing importance of knowledge, research, innovation and evolving perspectives on expertise are changing the social role of universities in the globalized world. One of the most popular concepts used for approaching these changes is 'knowledge society' together with a number of other conceptualizations (Knowledge Economy, Information Society, Learning Society), which aim at illuminating the nature of societal change. These conceptualizations both challenge higher education to change and force it to test – once again – the foundational principles of European universities. The main research question of this paper is: What is the relevance of higher education for Europe in the (new) era of knowledge society and knowledge-driven economy?

I will begin this chapter by analysing 'knowledge society' and its related concepts 'knowledge economy,' 'learning society' and 'information society.' This analysis will be followed by a discussion on the relationship between higher education and society through the topics of private and public goods and 'world-class universities' (also cf. contributions of de Boer and Texeira in this volume). I will also focus on the main *Zeitdiagnose,* namely, mode 1 and 2 and the 'triple helix', and on academic capitalism and entrepreneurial universities as more empirical approaches to recent changes. In Section 4, the focus of the article is on 'knowledge society' as a political goal in national, regional and global contexts. Section 5 changes the perspective and analyses the changes in higher education challenged by ICT, knowledge production, the training of professionals and the development of civic societies. Section 6 sums up the themes of the paper.

ON THE KNOWLEDGE SOCIETY AS A SOCIAL PHENOMENON AND AS AN INTELLECTUAL DEVICE

Michael Peters (2007, 17) states, "concepts have histories. They also have homes." 'Knowledge society' has been developed by sociologists, 'knowledge economy' by economists and 'learning society' by educators. These concepts – or their developers – do not, however, normally really communicate with each other in the academic world. Their communication – or confrontation – takes place in the realm of public policy, where conceptualisations rather than academic theories operate like *performative ideologies* (Peters 2007). This insight is fruitful, especially for higher education research, which is often utilized – or debated – in public policy making processes. This study aims, therefore, at identifying and analysing the origins of the central concepts surrounding 'knowledge society.' The argument is that we need critical analyses of concepts as intellectual devices and their uses in different public policy arenas in order to ascertain the relationship between the changes taking place in higher education institutions, higher education policies and societies.

'Knowledge Society' is often used as a slogan in a number of political contexts. In Japan, for example, it supports the ideas of lifelong learning and the need to train the labour force that is both technically skilful and has good communication, leadership and team working skills. In the European Union, in comparison, 'knowledge society' is related to the employment issues and the global competition with other R&D superpowers, whereas in many European nation states it is connected with national innovation policies (like in Finland). Therefore, the concept of knowledge society has created a discourse which is based on intellectual assumptions about the social dynamics of modern societies. In a knowledge society discourse, everything related to knowledge and knowledge production can be included and interconnected, regardless of whether it concerns individuals, organisations or entire societies. The knowledge society discourse also describes the current situation in which the knowledge society is both the objective of policies and debates, and an agent promoting policies and debates concerning its potentials.

A Short History of Knowledge Society as an Intellectual Device

The given title of this paper contains two crucial concepts: 'knowledge society' and 'knowledge-driven economy.' Intellectually, the latter belongs to the tradition of the knowledge economy, which will be discussed below. The term 'knowledge society' requires more attention because it is a social theory explaining social change.

According to Bell (1973), postindustrial society can be characterized as a knowledge society in a double sense: the sources of innovation are increasingly derivative from research and development, and the weight of the society is increasingly in the field of knowledge. The same ideas have been advanced by Castells when analysing key differences between previous modes of development with the societal dynamics of the digital world. According to Castells (1996, 17), "in the new, informational mode of development the source of productivity lies in the technology of knowledge generation, information processing, and symbol communication."[3]

As a concept, 'knowledge society' has its own history.[4] The use of the term 'knowledge society' began to expand with the studies of researchers such as Robin Mansell and Stehr (1994) in the 1990s (UNESCO 2005). While Mansell et al. (1998) focused mainly on information and communication technology (ICT) as a driving force of a knowledge society or 'an information society, the aim of Stehr was to create social theories based on the notion of knowledge society. This was because theory that focused primarily on the relationships between labour and property (capital) no longer provided the intellectual insight necessary for describing, understanding and explaining modern societies. Stehr does not argue that labour and capital dynamics disappeared. He also points out that previous social structures are not eliminated with this extension or enlargement. However, his assertion is that societal relationships cannot be explained without integrating the primacy of dynamics related to knowledge. In creating his theory of modernization, Stehr suggests that modernization is not as deterministic as Marxism would suggest; rather, 'modernization essentially involves multiple and necessarily unilinear processes of 'extension' and 'enlargement' (Stehr 1994, 29–32). The sociological question is, 'Does the nature of knowledge production change societies, cultures and economics?' The mere popularity of the term 'knowledge society' itself functions as evidence of modern societies understood as knowledge-based societies.

Knowledge and the uses of knowledge are, however, nothing new for mankind that understands itself through languages, which are symbolic systems for cultivating and transferring knowledge. In fact, the capacity to gather, analyse and use knowledge has been a crucial element throughout the history of mankind (McNeill and McNeill 2006). What makes the idea of knowledge society exceptional is the quantity of knowledge (and information) produced daily and the use of ICT in data-intensive processes. It may well be that the modernization processes within the knowledge society are processes of extension rather than social transformation that defines a fundamentally new era of human existence.

In short, as an intellectual device, the knowledge society aims at describing a new situation in which knowledge, information and knowledge production are the defining features of the relationships within and among societies, organisations, industrial production and human lives. Furthermore, the social theory of knowledge society aims at explaining the fundamental role knowledge plays in economics, culture and the politics of modern societies. In addition to being a social theory, the knowledge society is a concept that has been used widely in different domains of societies including economics, politics, popular media and culture – and academic research.

Associated Concepts: Learning Society, Information Society and Knowledge Economy

Alongside 'knowledge society,' a number of related concepts reference potential relationships between knowledge and change in society. The most important of these are 'learning society,' 'information society' and 'knowledge economy.' The discussion on learning societies and lifelong education for all coincide with the expansion of the knowledge society (UNESCO 2005). Originally, the concept of learning society referred to a new kind of society in which the old distinctions between formal and nonformal education were no longer valid (Hutchins 1968; Husén 1974). In this new context, lifelong learning becomes indispensable because there is a need to change workplaces and professions and to update knowledge during one's career. The crucial new skill in a learning society is the ability to 'learn how to learn'. Furthermore, learning is no longer the privilege of an elite or one age cohort; rather, these notions cover the entire communities and individual life spans (UNESCO 2005).

The discourse about the information society began in the 1960s. However, according to a number of writers, this concept provides a rather limited and technically oriented description of the challenges in a modern society, because the information society focuses on the 'production, processing, and transmission of a very large amount of data about all sorts of matters – individual and national, social and commercial, economic and military' (Schiller 1981, 25; Stehr 1994, 12). The main sociological critique against this economic perspective emphasizes the fact that knowledge always has a social function, which is rooted in the production, distribution and reproduction of knowledge. These issues are political and not technical because the quality of information and knowledge is related to social structures and the use of power in society.

Economic theories emphasizing the importance of knowledge in societies have their own history. According to Peters (2007), the tradition of 'Knowledge Economy' began with the work of Hayek (1937) who emphasized the importance of knowledge for economic growth. In his critique against socialism and state planning, he asserted that the best way of organizing modern society was market logic. The central element in his vision of liberal democracy envisioned science and markets as self-organizing systems. The price system communicates information, because "prices can act to co-ordinate the separate actions of different people in the same way as subjective values help the individual to co-ordinate the parts of his plan" (Hayek 1945). According to Peters (2007), the second wave of (what is now known as) neoliberal thinking paid attention to the formalization of economics, developing information theory and the economics of information, whereas "concurrent third waves might include Machlup's (1962) groundbreaking work on the production and distribution of knowledge in the US economy and Becker's (1964) human capital theory,[5] although these research traditions proceed from different assumptions and use different methodologies."

The reason for introducing these schools of thought is drawing attention to the fact that Knowledge Society as a sociological concept and Knowledge Economy as an economical concept often confront each other in the field of higher education policy making. This communication is not, however, based on the rules of academic argumentation, but on the political usefulness of their ideas.

KNOWLEDGE SOCIETY AND HIGHER EDUCATION

The idea of social change based on extension and enlargement is familiar to higher education researchers, too. Martin Trow's (1974) assumption, according to which the social role of higher education changes with the expansion of student body, has been accepted as an insightful conceptualisation of mass higher education. A similar trend has been noted by Burton Clark (1983), who maintains that the main source of social dynamics in higher education is the expansion of knowledge, which leads to new research fields, creating a demand for new chairs and professorships to be established for the emerging fields of research and disciplines. It also creates the need to establish new training programmes and new higher education institutions. To put it briefly, the logic of expansion in research-based knowledge, the number of students, staff and higher education institution creates a situation, where this expansion changes the social dynamics of higher education institutions and national systems of higher education. This expansion has taken and is taking place simultaneously with the development of knowledge societies. Stehr's interpretations indicate that the emergence of the knowledge societies and the expansion of higher education have a causal relationship. This is because knowledge production in and of itself supports growth in industrial production and creates new business activities.

Knowledge as a Private and a Public Good

The debate on private and public goods in higher education is a relevant example of a knowledge society discourse on the public policy intersection of the knowledge society and knowledge economy. Marginson (2006, 50) discusses the nature of knowledge when he criticises the problems of traditional liberal distinctions (see Samuelsson 1954) between the private and the public (goods) in higher education: "For example, language and discourse and knowledge as 'know-how', as distinct from knowledge expressed in particular artefacts such as texts, are about as close to natural public goods as we can get. The mathematical theorem retains its value no matter how many people use it. Nor are its benefits confined to individuals for long: knowledge can only ever be a temporary private good". Marginson's assertion that questions the ownership of knowledge needs to be taken seriously in global knowledge societies, where intellectual property rights are one of the issues at stake. Furthermore, the commodification of knowledge is crucial not only in research but also in teaching (see Naidoo and Jamieson (2005)).

There are two interrelated issues here. The first concerns the ownership of innovations. In a number of countries, the problem has been addressed through the legislation that regulates the intellectual property rights of academics and universities. The first such act was the 1980 Bayh–Dole Act in the United States, which gave ownership of intellectual property, arising from federally funded research, to universities (Slaughter and Rhoades 2004). The second issue is related to student tuition fees. The question of 'who benefits' from higher education is often translated into the question 'who should pay' for education. When these questions are combined with budget reductions in higher education, they easily tend to produce debates on the problems of public higher education institutions, as has been the case especially in the Anglo-American cultural sphere (Naidoo and Jamieson 2005). Whether this is a crucial European topic is not perhaps an essential question, but is now becoming problematic in the continental European higher education discourse. An example of this argumentation, fuelled by neo-liberal reasoning, would be the demands for 'world class universities' and the increasing use of league tables in national higher education debates (Dill 2006).

The political objective to establish 'world-class' universities is a global goal, despite the problems of defining a 'world class' university (see Altbach 2007). According to one of the definitions, "world-class should mean an established record and sustainable ability of creating new knowledge and sound evidence of contribution to economic prosperity, enhancement of competitiveness, and an effective role in the empowerment of students and citizens." (Sadlak and Cai 2007, 21.) From the perspective of European medieval universities, this list of responsibilities looks like an updated version of their principles. It has a strong belief in the education of man, a good belief in the possibility of rational reasoning and a firm belief in the mastery of environment. When saying this I would like to contextualize it historically. Namely, the 'real innovation' of world-class university discourse is the introduction of status hierarchies to national systems of higher education. Sadlak and Cai (2007, 20) say, 'it needs to be pointed out that a higher education institution aspiring to be a "world-class university" will find this goal expensive. Therefore, it is legitimate to pose the question: how many such elite institutions do a given country or region not only need but can also support (and support only through public funding)?'

The Transformation of Universities and Research: Zeitdiagnose vs. Empirical Analyses

The discourses of knowledge society are supported by two main perspectives concerning the transformation of science and the university (see Tuunainen 2005). The first asserts that a radical metamorphosis is taking place in the relationship between knowledge production and university as an institution. Gibbons et al. (1994), Nowotny et al. (2001) and Etzkowitz et al. (2000) propose that governments have promoted national prosperity by supporting new lucrative technologies together with the universities which become 'engines' of their regions. Gibbons et al. (1994) argue that a new form of knowledge production, "mode 2," is replacing the traditional one, "mode 1". Mode 1 knowledge has been produced within autonomous disciplinary contexts, governed mainly by academic interests of a specific community, whereas mode 2 knowledge is produced within the context of its application. Mode 2 knowledge is transdisciplinary research, characterized by heterogeneity, and it is more socially accountable and reflexive than mode 1 knowledge. In addition, the proponents of the concept argue that universities are losing the monopoly of knowledge production because knowledge can be acquired in a variety of organizations and institutions.

The other variant of the metamorphosis thesis is the "triple helix" thesis, which states that universities can play a crucial role in innovation in the increasingly knowledge-based societies. Etzkowitz and Leydesdorff (2000) assert that the previously isolated institutional social spheres of university, government and industry have become increasingly intertwined. This has brought academic, economic and wider networks of social actors together in new constellations comprising triple helix knowledge dynamics. Based on systems theory, Etzkowitz et al. (2000) assert that four processes describe the major changes in the production, exchange and use of knowledge in the triple helix model. These are the internal transformation in each of the helices (academia, state and industry) followed by the influence of one institutional sphere on another. The third process is the creation of a new combination of trilateral linkages, networks, and organizations among the three helices, while the fourth describes the effect of these inter-institutional networks both on their originating spheres and society, as a whole.

Mode 2 knowledge production has been perhaps one of the most influential conceptualisations of the change of higher education in modern societies. However, the main limitation of this characterization of knowledge production dynamics involves being "one-eyed and reductionist," focusing on a "relatively small – albeit significant and dramatically changing – domain of the diverse landscape of science in society" (Elzinga 2002). It has also been argued that the dichotomy between Mode 1 and 2 presents two discrete ideal types that probably never existed in the real world. In addition, Weingart (1997), Peters (2007) and Häyrinen-Alestalo (1999), among others, have both pointed out the ideological connection between this discourse and political neo-liberalism.

The same type of critique has been levelled at the concept of "triple helix of university–industry–government relations" (Etzkowitz and Leydesdorff 1997). In this vision the university is a hybrid organization incorporating economic developments together with scientific research and education. The problem with this assumption is, however, the leap of abstraction that infers that twenty-first century universities are 'entrepreneurial universities,' and it is an irresistible, unavoidable development (Etzkowitz 2002 in Tuunainen 2005, 278–279).

While these types of ideas offer a basis for analysis, they are neither social theory, nor can they be universally established by empirical research. What these various notions have in common is that they all are attempts to characterize the defining features of the era we now live in. Noro (2000) characterises this "third type of sociological theory" as the sociologically driven need to seek answers to existential questions such as 'who are we?' and 'what is the nature of our epoch?' According to Tuunainen, these *Zeitdiagnose* 'usually combine familiar materials in a novel way, are normative in nature and pursue a topical insight.' They can be used as conceptual devices and points of departure for policy making (see Tuunainen 2005, 283), as was illustrated by the use of Mode 2 knowledge in South African policy making context (see Kraak 2000). Owing to the nature of *Zeitdiagnose*, these abstractions imply that not only higher education has changed, but society is also changing.

A second, more moderate view of the changing nature of knowledge production and universities holds that academic capitalism is challenging the traditional values found in higher education institutions, where an attempt is underway to substitute old practices with neoliberal values and management practices. Universities become a fertile ground for entrepreneurial universities and academics (Slaughter and Leslie 1997; Slaughter and Rhoades 2004; Marginson and Considine 2000). According to an empirical study by Marginson and Considine (2000), it is indeed evident that there is a general pattern of modelling universities along the lines of enterprises. This new form of 'enterprise university' may be described as follows: "it has a strategically centralised leadership highly responsive to the external setting, the wide use of corporate and business forms, the 'emptying out' of academic governance and the weakening of disciplinary identity" (Marginson 2006). However, Marginson and Considine do not proclaim that mode 2 or triple helix dynamics constitute global trends, because knowledge production plays out differently in distinct types of universities. Older, established universities with strong academic and disciplinary cultures possess more field-specific power (Bourdieu 1988) and are able to resist, even generate change, while other types of higher education institutions are more vulnerable to neoliberal management ideas (Marginson and Considine 2000, in Tuunainen 2004).

On the basis of his empirical findings, Tuunainen (2005, 292) argues that the "commercialization of the academic research through spin-off companies turned out to be in conflict with the other university activities, most apparently, with publicly funded research and university teaching." Furthermore, it has been noted that universities increasingly emphasize the importance of scientific quality under the pressure of market-orientation and commodification of research outcomes (Alestalo-Häyrinen and Peltola 2006). These findings suggest that there is a "need for seeing scientific work and universities as complex and, occasionally, contradictory entities whose developmental trajectories are shaped by multiple historical, political and cultural characteristics" (Tuunainen 2005, 293).

One of the main aims of theorists, who chronicle the transformation of higher education, is to highlight the changing social role of higher education and how this change is connected to changes in knowledge production in universities. Furthermore, the aim is to argue that empirical analysis of this topic challenges the picture painted by *Zeitdiagnose*. Situations in universities are complex and conflicted and routinely elude many theoretical abstractions.

THE KNOWLEDGE SOCIETY AS A POLITICAL GOAL

In order to highlight some of the political perspectives and expectations related to the knowledge society discourse, I will pay attention to three political levels: national, regional (EU) and global.

Nation States

At the level of nation states the knowledge society can be seen to have taken on distinct forms. Castells and Himanen (2002) assert the following three alternative routes to the knowledge society: 1) Silicon Valley – a market driven, open society (USA), 2) Singapore – an authoritarian model of the knowledge society and 3) The Finnish model – which describes an open, welfare-state-based knowledge society. This typology highlights the variety of possible ways of defining, approaching and using knowledge society as a political goal. A fruitful suggestion made by Castells and Himanen is their assumption that the social structure of the informational age is based on networks (Castells 1996). According to Castells (1996, 470–471), "networks are open structures, able to expand without limits, integrating new nodes as long as they are able to communicate with the network, namely as long as they share the same communication codes (for example, values or performance goals). A network-based social system is a highly dynamic, open system, susceptible to innovation without threatening its balance."

Networking as the Social Organisation of Knowledge Society

When applying network analysis to the Finnish model, Castells and Himanen (2002) further develop the argument that a knowledge society is organised in and through networks. They assert that networks illuminate the way power is organised in general in Finland. The nation state plays a significant role through various social actors, which bring researchers and business companies together to focus resources on problems deemed to be of economically strategic importance. These are either development agencies that support cooperation between business and research,[6] or public organisations that promote cooperation between the world of business and academe.[7] Politically significant is the fact that the National Technology Council, chaired by the prime minister, defines national strategies for technology and innovation. It is in this context where the role of higher education policy becomes important. In Finland, universities are seen and defined as part of the national innovation system, which aims at increasing the capacities of Finnish enterprises and the nation state in general with regard to the international market (Miettinen 2002).

The Regional Dimension: "The Most Competitive and Dynamic Knowledge-based Economy in the World"

In addition to European nation states, the knowledge society discourse has opened up an imaginary social space in the European Union itself. This argument is emphasized on the European Commission's knowledge society homepage, which begins with the central objective of the Lisbon strategy: "to become the most competitive and dynamic knowledge-based economy in the world, capable of sustainable economic growth with more and better jobs and greater social cohesion."[8]

This citation, in and of itself, indicates the importance of the topic for the European Union. In order to reach this objective "Europe's education and training systems need to adapt both to the demands of the knowledge society and to the need for an improved level and quality of employment." The European Commission is confident of the potential this type of society offers for its citizens. According to the cited webpage, the knowledge society means: "new employment possibilities, more fulfilling jobs, new tools for education and training, easier access to public services, increased inclusion of disadvantaged people or regions."

These EU web pages indicate both the objectives and the Commission's definitions and understandings of the knowledge society. European employment strategy is highlighted in these documents, the main emphasis being on how policy on the knowledge-based economy can promote employment in Europe. Quite naturally, education and training are prominent. It is more interesting to note that innovation and research – as topics – are more hidden in the documents.

However, the promotion of knowledge-based economy is a crucial objective in creating the European Research Area (see Key 2005). The fact that Europe produces most research in the world is defined as a problem in this knowledge economy discourse, which assumes that technological progress, innovation and human capital are the sources of economic growth. Research production is defined as a problem, because Europe fails to exploit its scientific base (Key 2005, 13). The report also defines the main building blocks of a 'knowledge system' crucial for promoting knowledge economy, noting that "in this system, science, technology/ innovation and industry are central, but not sufficient to ensure economic growth, competitiveness and job creation. The education and training system, human resources and the labour market, and the financial system all have a substantial impact on the performance of 'Science–Technology–Industry'." The report also emphasizes state intervention because it plays a horizontal role promoting cooperation between crucial institutions. (Key 2005, 20.)

Social Responsibilities of Higher Education in Global Information Societies

The UNESCO World Conference on higher education emphasised the many meanings that relevance of higher education means for the development of global information societies.[9] The impressive list of social responsibilities expected from higher education clearly indicates that world communities have high expectations regarding higher education. It also indicates that the social role of higher education in the global information society is seen crucial for the development of societies. Furthermore, the list of expectations highlights the central roles universities play as producers of knowledge and educated experts in knowledge societies (UNESCO 2005, 97).

HIGHER EDUCATION AND THE NEEDS OF THE KNOWLEDGE SOCIETY

Having described various types of knowledge society discourses and contexts, I change the focus to key topics which highlight society from the perspective of higher education. The key challenges are presented by ICT, knowledge production, training of professionals and development of civic society.

Information and Communication Technology

One of the challenges for the internal development of higher education institutions is created by the implementation of the rapidly changing information technologies. Higher education institutions are not only producing and supporting technological innovations, but are at the same time intensive users and subject to the limitations of ICT. The ICT revolution already has significant impacts on students' learning processes (e.g., through the availability of virtual learning environments and new sources of information), challenging both students and teachers to reassess their conceptions about learning and instruction (Hasenbegovic et al. 2006). Therefore, the challenges related to the use of ICT are not only technical, but are also related to pedagogical thinking and organisational structures (Laurillard 2002). New technologies require new professionals, not only to maintain and upgrade ICT support, but also to work in teaching development units and centres, which address the pedagogical (re)training of professors (Rhoades 1998). ICT is restructuring the institutional fabric of higher education and is influencing the academic work carried out by university teachers, as much as it is changing the nature of support functions accomplished by staff administrative personnel.

Knowledge Production and Innovations

This theme has been approached above from the perspective of knowledge society in the discussion on the changing role of universities in the knowledge production. Looking from the perspective of higher education institutions, we can define two main challenges. The first one is how to mitigate the increasing pervasiveness of academic capitalism and strengthen the traditional tasks of the university. When saying this, I would like to emphasize (following Slaughter and Rhoades 2004; Ylijoki 2003; Marginson 2006) that academic capitalism is not something any person or group 'does to us' as much as 'it' is something 'we do to ourselves.' However, there are significant disciplinary differences in the academic world with regard to their relationship with society (see Becher and Trowler 2001; Slaughter and Rhoades 2004). Higher education institutions should be able to take into account the cultural differences inside academia (see Välimaa and Ylijoki 2008). Secondly, the topic of knowledge production is related to knowledge transfer from higher education to society (which includes, naturally, business enterprises). According to Teichler (2004), the major modes of knowledge transfer include 1) knowledge media (books, films, letters, e-mail messages, etc.), 2) physical mobility of scholars and students, 3) collaborative research and joint teaching/learning project and 4) trans-national education. Metaphorically, the knowledge transfer from universities to society and to knowledge-driven economy resembles more a drizzly rain of ideas than an innovation thunderstorm (see Lester and Sotarauta 2007). It would be quite narrow-minded to understand the knowledge production of universities mainly as innovations. Furthermore, when speaking about innovations, one should also make the distinction between *technical innovations* and *social innovations.* Technical innovations refer to different kinds of new ways of improving production or creating new products, whereas social innovations refer to new ways of organizing social behaviour, whether it takes place in the existing organizations or in new emerging social forms. Higher education institutions can have a role in both of these innovation processes through collaborative research and development projects, and through the physical mobility of students from higher education institutions to enterprises and public sector jobs.

Higher Education and Working Life

The notion of the learning society reveals many aspects of the knowledge society. They both emphasize the centrality of knowledge production and lifelong learning of the labour force. The imperative of this ethos can be summed up by the phrase 'learning how to learn.' Furthermore, *human capital theory* seems to explain much of the empirical data gathered on the European labour market (Machin 2005) because improving the educational level and the qualifications of the labour force has a positive impact on GDP, even though it is difficult to measure the exact impacts of educational investments.

The human capital aspect is also seen essential in the European Union, where knowledge society discourses strongly emphasize employment-related topics and themes. However, in higher education institutions, discourses on the knowledge society challenge universities to develop and to adopt new collaborative teaching practices in the training of professionals. It has been noted that the development of expertise often takes place both in formal training (in higher education institutions) and in workplaces. This cooperation between the world of work and academia challenges higher education institutions to develop both their traditional structures and their pedagogical practices (see Tynjälä, Välimaa and Sarja 2003).

There is extensive literature on the relationship between higher education and work (see Teichler 1998). However, Rhoades and Slaughter (2006, 19–25) have elaborated five assumptions concerning the relationship between higher education and working life that can not be supported by empirical research. According to them, it is quite problematic to assume that work equals private sector employment because it does not reflect the empirical realities of employment in many parts of the United States and in other countries. It has also been assumed that work equals employment in large companies. Even though this equation maps very nicely onto the pattern of academic capitalism and the new economy, it does not reflect the realities of employment in the private sector in the United States. Thirdly, it is assumed that education for work equals fitting in and assimilating to existing workplaces, even though "working life is changing dramatically, and it is a worthwhile question whether the sole function of higher education is to adapt to those changes." According to the fourth assumption, preparing for work equals developing new job skills. "Yet, it reflects a particular theoretical perspective about education and employment that has been empirically called into question". Finally, it is assumed that work equals paid employment, even though this assumption "overlooks the realities of demographic patterns and public policy challenges in most countries" (Rhoades and Slaughter 2006, 24–25).

Higher Education Institutions in Civic Society

What are the main roles of higher education in a civic society? As noted in the Dearing report (1997) and the UNESCO World Conference (UNESCO 2005), many of the social responsibilities of higher education emphasise that the cultivation of civic virtues shapes a democratic and civilized society. In addition, higher education institutions are expected to contribute to the culture and cultural development of societies. This implies that higher education institutions are expected to initiate and maintain a critical discussion within societies.

DISCUSSION: THE CHALLENGES FOR HIGHER EDUCATION IN GLOBALIZED KNOWLEDGE SOCIETIES

The knowledge society discourse is understood differently in various social arenas of societies. In the context of employment and the world of work, it supports the ideas of lifelong learning and the need to update the skills of the labour force in a learning society. For individuals, it focuses on the need to keep up with the continuously expanding ocean of knowledge in information societies. As for higher education institutions, the knowledge society discourse is translated into a need to serve knowledge-driven economy because of the need to be more efficient in innovation production. In higher education policies the trend is to create world-class universities as a response to the challenges posed by globalized knowledge societies.

In all different knowledge society debates, higher education institutions are expected to be more efficient actors in the knowledge-driven economy. This political objective is rooted in the underlying common sense assumption that higher education institutions should produce more information and facts (through research) to promote innovations. However, it may be argued that the real challenge for higher education institutions is not only to produce new facts, but to increase our understanding. One of the challenges universities face in a knowledge society is to develop theoretical thinking which reduces the complexity caused by the exploding flows of information. This is not to say that universities should have nothing to do with the innovation production. The argument is that universities are really useful and active members of knowledge societies, if they develop theoretical understanding on the changing world because there are no other societal institutions which have the luxury of reflecting on the world from nonutilitarian perspectives. In this regard, critical thinking and theorising is the most useful activity in globalized knowledge societies.

Having said that, it should be added that it is more fruitful to understand universities as a part of knowledge systems, rather than as lonely heroes solving the problems of globalized knowledge societies. It is, therefore, crucial to pay attention to the interactions between higher education institutions and the other parts of knowledge systems because higher education institutions are related to their societies and cultures through education, service and research. It should also be remembered that popular *Zeitdiagnose* are rooted in certain ideological ways of thinking (see Peters 2007). The problem with *Zeitdiagnose* is not necessarily their normative tone, but the fact that they give all too monolithic and simplistic description of higher education institutions. According to a number of empirical studies and an array of theoretical perspectives, universities are complex organizations because they have many historical layers and many disciplines, all of which have a distinct relationship to the society.

Homo Economicus and the Future of Higher Education

The future challenges for European higher education are greatly influenced by the grand narrative of neoliberal thinking. This narrative is encapsulated in the notion of *homo economicus,* which is an ideal type of human behaviour based on universalist assumptions of individuality, rationality and self-interest of human beings (Peters 2007, 167). Therefore, in higher education policy discourses, it is no more fashionable to speak about students or academics. Instead, we are supposed to use a new language in which students are 'customers' or 'clients' and academics are 'providers'. This turn is not merely linguistic. It aims to change the way of thinking about higher education by changing the relation between teaching and learning into a contract between the buyer and the seller. The crucial question is how does this way of reasoning change the basic functions of universities?

Let us, then, reflect on how the ideal of *homo economicus* challenges the foundational principles of European universities to see what kind of future perspectives neoliberal reasoning opens for European higher education. The most radical changes are taking place with the first principle, *the belief in the dignity of man,* in other words, the belief in education and the growth of human beings through education. According to this, ideal type 'customer students' are not interested in mental growth but getting 'value for money'. The remaining three founding principles are maybe less radically influenced by *homo economicus* because the rationality of man is not questioned, but it is only seen from an economical perspective. The belief in the man's mastery of his environment through his intellect is, however, defined differently by *homo economicus* because higher education institutions are expected to be innovative members of societies. Simultaneously, the context of higher education institutions is becoming more fragmented because of the increasing variety of different social expectations. The fourth principle of universities, *questioning and analytical approach,* is not threatened in open societies because *homo economicus* represents itself an academic ideal, which may be challenged by other academic ideals.

What are the consequences of *homo economicus* policies for the relevance of higher education in a knowledge economy? From the perspective of education, the answer seems to be evident. In the global competition for students, the reputation of higher education institutions will be the currency. This easily means the strengthening of status hierarchies between universities because a *homo economicus* student will choose the 'world class higher education institution' that gives the best value for money – no matter how impossible it is to define 'a world-class university' (Altbach 2007).[10] In the national systems of higher education, this creates pressures to make status hierarchies steeper between higher education institutions in all European national systems of higher education.

As for research, the implications seem to be evident. The trend of decreasing public funding and the increase in externally funded research seem to continue, which makes the competition harder and promotes academic capitalism in higher education institutions. The fact that research funding needs to be earned has made the management of universities "like running a small business" (Henkel 2007, 42). This leaves less time for fundamental research, because of the fact that the borderline between fundamental and applied research is blurring. The challenge for universities lies in how to sustain their integrity in the changing contexts (Henkel 2007). As for the production of innovations, the public support of institutional activities is essential because creative work is always done in the basic units and commercial activities often conflict with fundamental research (see Tuunainen 2005).

These future scenarios that borrow their social dynamics mainly from the US system of higher education are, however, not the only possible vision for the future. The future of the European higher education is essentially a political question. As the success of the Bologna Process has shown, new change strategies can be developed for the purpose of enhancing European higher education. The combination of political negotiations and pragmatic will to develop European higher education in the format of a process is a remarkable political achievement. Therefore, alternative ways for the future development may be discovered in the traditions of European universities, in which the combination of teaching and research and service to society with collegial responsibilities to academia have been indispensable for the development of the universities as academic and national institutions. Politically, creating the 'European way' to meet the future challenges of higher education could be the future goal of the Bologna process.

NOTES

[1]   This paper is partly based on the article 'Knowledge Society Discourse and Higher Education' by Välimaa and Hoffman, in *Higher Education* (forthcoming).

[2]   The term *universitas* was commonly applied to several types of corporate bodies such as craft guilds or municipal councils. When applied to universities, *universitas* for long referred to the guild of masters or of students or of masters and students combined, not to the university as a complete entity (Cobban 1988).

[3]   According to Bell (1973, 212), knowledge is "a set of organized statements of facts or ideas, presenting a reasoned judgement or an experimental result, which is transmitted to others through some communication medium in some systematic form".

[4]   See Stehr (1994) for a comprehensive discussion on the origins of the concept 'Knowledge Society'.

[5]   According to Marginson (1993), human capital theory is based on two hypotheses: "First, education and training increase individual cognitive capacity and therefore augment productivity. Second, increased productivity leads to increased individual earnings, and these increased earnings are a measure of the value of human capital."

[6]   TEKES The Finnish Funding Agency for Technology and Innovation (see: http://www.tekes.fi/eng/tekes/)

[7]   SITRA is the Finnish National Fund for Research and Development under the supervision of the Finnish Parliament (see:http://www.sitra.fi/en/)

[8]   For more details see: http://ec.europa.eu/employment_social/knowledge_society/index_en.htm).

[9]   According to UNESCO World Conference the relevance of higher education means: 1) being politically responsive, 2) being responsive to the world of work, 3) being responsive to other levels of the education system, 4) being responsive to culture and cultures, 5) being responsive to all, 6) being responsive everywhere and all the time, 7) being responsive to students and teachers. As a conclusion the declaration says: "In these circumstances, higher education can truly help to underwrite the generalized spread of knowledge within industrialized societies and in developing countries." (UNESCO 2005, 97)

[10]   There are no universal criteria for defining a world class university, which makes it rational to assume that good institutional reputation develops historically and is related to the social reproduction of elites of their societies (see Bourdieu 1988).

REFERENCES

Alestalo-Häyrinen, M. & Peltola, U. (2006) The Problem of a Market-oriented University. *Higher Education*, 52: 251–281.

Altbach, P. The Costs and Benefits of World-Class Universities, in J. Sadlak & L. N. Cai (eds.) *The World-Class University and Ranking: Aiming Beyond Status.* Bucharest: UNESCO-CEPES. Cluj-Napoca: Presa Universitara Clujeana, 363–370.

Becher & Trowler, P.R. (2001). *Academic Tribes and Territories. Intellectual Enquiry and the Cultures of Disciplines.* Second Edition. Buckingham: SRHE & Open University Press.

Becker, G.S. (1964, 1993) *Human Capital: A Theoretical and Empirical Analysis with Special Reference to Education.* Chicago: Chicago University Press.

Bell, D. (1973), The Coming of Post-industrial Society: A Venture in Social Forecasting. New York: Basic Books.

Bourdieu, P. (1988). *Homo Academicus.* Cambridge, Polity 1988.

Castells, M. (1996). *The Information Age: Economy, Society and Culture.* Volume I: The Rise of the Network Society. Oxford: Blackwell.

Castells, M. & Himanen, P. (2002) *The Information Society and the Welfare State: the Finnish Model.* Oxford: Oxford University Press.

Cobban, A. (1988). *The Medieval English Universities: Oxford and Cambridge to c. 1500.* Berkeley and Los Angeles: University of California Press.

Clark, B. R. (1983) *The Higher Education System.* Berkeley: University of California.

Dearing Report (1997) Higher Education in the Learning Society, Norwich: HMSO.

Dill, D. (2006) Convergence and Diversity: The Role and Influence of University Rankings. *CHER 19th Annual Conference "Systems Convergence and Institutional Diversity?".* Kassel, September 7–9, 2006.

Elzinga, A. (2002) New Production of Reductionism in Models Relating to Research Policy. Paper to the Nobel Symposium, Science and Industry in the 20th Century, Stockholm 21-23, November at the Royal Swedish Academy of Sciences.

Etzkowitz, H. & Leydesdorff, L. (1997). (eds.) *Universities and the Global Knowledge Economy: a Triple Helix of University-industry-government Relations.* London: Pinter.

Etzkowitz, H. Webster, A. Gebhardt, C. Cantisano Terra, B.R. (2000). The Future of the University and the University of the Future: Evolution of Ivory Tower to Entrepreneurial Paradigm. *Research Policy,* 29 (2), 313–330.

Etzkowitz, H, Leydesdorff, L. (2000). The Dynamics of Innovation: from National Systems and "Mode 2" to a Triple Helix of University-industry-government Relations. *Research Policy,* 29 (2), 109–123.

Etzkowitz, H. (2002) The Norms of Entrepreneurial Science: Cognitive Effects of the New University-industry Linkages', *Research Policy* 27 (8), 823–833.

Gibbons, M., Limogenes, C., Nowotny, H., Schwartzman, S., Scot, P. and Trow, M. (1994) *The New Production of Knowledge: The Dynamics of Science and Research in Contemporary Societies.* London: Sage.

Hasenbegovic, J., Gruber, H. Rehrl, M. & Bauer, J. (2006) The Two-Fold Role of Epistemological Beliefs in Higher Education: A Review of Research About Innovations in Universities. In P. Tynjälä, J. Välimaa & G. Boulton-Lewis (eds.) *Higher Education and Working Life – Collaborations, Confrontations and Challenges.* Amsterdam: Elsevier, 163-176.

Hayek, F. (1937) Economics and Knowledge. *Economica* IV, 33-54. In Http://www.virtualschool.edu/mon./Economics/HayekEconomicsAndKnowledge.html .

Hayek, F. (1945) The Use of Knowledge in Society. *American Economic Review,* No.4, September, 519-30. In Http://www.virtualschool.edu/mon./Economics/HayekEconomicsAndKnowledge.html

Häyrinen-Alestalo, M. (1999) The University Under Pressure of Innovation Policy – Reflecting on European and Finnish Experiences, *Science Studies* 12(1), 44-69.

Henkel, M. (2007) Academic Boundaries: Are They Still Needed? *Higher Education Forum* 4. Research Institute for Higher Education. Hiroshima University, 33–46.

Husen, T. (1974) *The Learning Society*. London: Methuen.

Hutchins, R. (1968) *The Learning Society*. London: Penguin.

Kraak, A. (2000) Changing Modes: New Knowledge Production and its Implications for Higher Education in South Africa. Pretoria: Human Sciences research Council.

Key Figures 2005. Towards a European Research Area. Science, Technology and Innovation. European Commission.

Laurillard, D. (2002) Rethinking Teaching for the Knowledge Society. *EDUCAUSE Review*, 37 (1), 16-25.

Lester, R. & Sotarauta, M. (eds.) 2007. Innovation, Universities and the Competitiveness of Regions. Technology Review, 214/2007. Tekes. Helsinki. (AND *Universities, Industrial Innovation, and Regional Economic Development: A Report of the Local Innovation Systems -project*. Industrial Performance Center, Massachusetts Institute of Technology. Cambridge: USA)

Machin, S. (2005) Education and the Labour Market. Talk for *Seminar on the Economics of Education*. Helsinki, September 21.

Machlup, F. (1962) The Production and Distribution of Knowledge in the United States. Princeton: Princeton University Press.

Mansell, R. & When, U. (1998*) Knowledge Societies: Information Technology for Sustainable Development*. New York: UN Commission on Science and Technology for Development. Oxford University Press.

Marginson, S. (1993) *Education and Public Policy in Australia*. Cambridge: Cambridge University Press.

Marginson, S. (2006) Putting 'Public' Back into the Public Universities. In *Thesis Eleven*, No. 84: 44–59. London, Thousand Oaks: SAGE Publications

Marginson, S. & Considine, M. (2000*) The Enterprise University*. Cambridge: Cambridge University Press.

McNeill, J.R.. & McNeill, W.H. (2006) *Verkottunut ihmiskunta. Yleiskatsaus maailmanhistoriaan*. Translated by Natasha Vilokkinen. The Human Web. A Bird's-Eye View of World History. Tampere: Vastapaino

Miettinen, R. (2002) National Innovation Systems: Scientific Concept or Political Rhetoric. Helsinki: Edita.

Naidoo & Jamieson (2005) Knowledge in the Marketplace: The Global Commodification of Teaching and Learning in Higher Education. In P. Ninnes & M. Hellstén: *Internationalizing Higher Education. Critical Explorations of Pedagogy and Policy*. Dordrecht: Springer, 37–52.

Noro, A. (2000) Aikalaisdiagnoosi sosiologisen teorian kolmantena lajityyppinä, *Sosiologia* 37(4), 321–329.

Nowotny, H., Scott, P. & Gibbons, M. (2001). *Re-thinking Science. Knowledge and the Public in an Age of Uncertainty*. Cambridge: Polity Press.

Peters, M.A. (2007) *Knowledge Economy, Development and the Future of Higher Education*. Educational Futures, Rethinking Theory and Practice. Vol 10. Sense Publishers: Rotterdam/Taipei.

Rhoades, G. (1998) Managed Professionals. Unionized Faculty and Restructuring Academic Labor. Albany: State University of New York Press.

Rhoades, G. & Slaughter, S. (2006) Mode 3, Academic Capitalism and the New Economy: Making Higher Education Work for Whom? In P. Tynjälä, J. Välimaa & G. Boulton-Lewis (eds.) *Higher Education and Working Life – Collaborations, Confrontations and Challenges*. Amsterdam: Elsevier, 9–33.

Sadlak, J. & Liu Nian Cai (2007) Introduction into the Topic: Expectations and Realities of World-Class University Status and Ranking Practices, in J Sadlak & Liu Nian Cai (eds.) *The World-Class University and Ranking: Aiming Beyond Status*. Bucharest: UNESCO-CEPES. Cluj-Napoca: Presa Universitara Clujeana, 17–24.

Samuelsson, P. (1954) The Pure Theory of Public Expenditure, *Review of Economics and Statistics* 36(4): 387–9.

Slaughter, S. & Leslie, L.L. (1997). *Academic Capitalism -Politics, Policies and the Entrepreneurial University.* Baltimore & London: Johns Hopkins University Press.

Slaughter, S. & Rhoades, G. (2004) *Academic Capitalism and the New Economy. Markets, State and Higher Education.* Baltimore & London: Johns Hopkins University Press.

Stehr, N. (1994) *Knowledge Societies.* London. Sage.

Teichler, U. (1998) *Higher Education and the World of Work: Changing Conditions and Challenges.* paper for the UNESCO World Conference in Higher Education, Paris.

Teichler, U. (2004) The Changing Debate on Internationalisation of Higher Education, *Higher Education,* vol 48 (1), 5–26.

Trow, M. (1974) Problems in the Transition from Elite to Mass Higher Education. Policies for Higher Education. Conference on Future Structures of Post-Secondary Education. Paris

Tuunainen, J. (2005) Hybrid Practices? Contribution to the Debate on the Mutation of Science and University' in *Higher Education* 50: 275–298.

Tynjälä, P. Välimaa, J. & Sarja, A. (2003) 'Pedagogical Perspectives on the Relationship between Higher Education and Working Life', *Higher Education* 46, 147–166.

UNESCO 2005. *Toward Knowledge Societies.* Unesco World Report. http//www.unesco.org/publications.

Välimaa, J. & Ylijoki, O.H. (2008) (eds.) *Cultural Perspectives to Higher Education.* Springer.

Weingart, P. (1997) 'From Finalization' to "Mode 2": Old Wine in New Bottles?' *Social Sciences Information* 36(4), 591–613.

Wittrock, B. (1993). The Modern University: The Three Transformations, in S. Rothblatt, & B. Wittrock (eds.) *The European and American University since 1800.* Cambridge: Cambridge University Press, 303–362.

Ylijoki, O.-YH. (2003). Entangled in Academic Capitalism? A Case-study on Changing Ideals and Practices of University Research. *Higher Education* 45: 307–335.

PEDRO TEIXEIRA

3. ECONOMIC IMPERIALISM AND THE IVORY TOWER: SOME REFLECTIONS UPON THE FUNDING OF HIGHER EDUCATION IN THE EHEA (2010-2020)

INTRODUCTION[1]

Although economists' interest for higher education is somehow recent, it has become a decisive force in shaping the social and political views about it. One of the aspects on which economics' influence has been most prominent is funding matters. With the continuous expansion of higher education during recent decades, many European countries have now to deal with mass systems and the subsequent financial challenges it poses. Moreover, this expansion of higher education systems has been taking place in a context of reassessment of the role of governments in many social activities. These trends have fostered important developments and experiments in the funding of higher education, which are likely to remain relevant, and even more so, in the coming years.

The main purpose of this chapter is to discuss some possible scenarios in the funding of higher education in the EHEA for the coming decade. This will be done through the identification of some major current trends in European higher education funding. Following the first section describing the growing influence of economic rationality on higher education thinking, the second section concerns some basic reasons why higher education is a relevant topic for economists and why it is likely that it will continue to be so in the coming years. The third section discusses the current situation of higher education funding in Europe and its main trends, concerns and policy challenges. Finally, the fourth section presents some major issues that are likely to influence decisively the funding scenario of higher education in Europe during the coming decade.

SETTING THE SCENE – ECONOMICS, MARKETS AND HIGHER EDUCATION

Nowadays, we are so much used to the influence of economics on higher education that we tend to overlook the fact that this is the result of recent decades of growing interest to apply economic tools to the analysis of higher education matters. The initial impulse promoting this shift came from the exploration of individual and social motivations when allocating resources to higher education.

B.M. Kehm, J. Huisman and B. Stensaker (eds.), The European Higher Education Area: Perspectives on a Moving Target, 43–60.

Higher Education as an Economic Subject

The idea that higher education can provide benefits, even economic ones, is certainly an old one. Until the mid-twentieth, century most economists paid little attention to the economic analysis of higher education, though in the postwar this has changed quite significantly (Teixeira, 2005). This change was prompted by several developments that converged to give increasing prominence to the economic effects of education. One of those changes relates to the analysis of the distribution of income and the belief that education could be one among the major explanatory factors of these differences, thus, a major instrument to promote social mobility. The second important change was the postwar revival of growth debates that, alongside the expansion of educational systems in most Western countries, led to an increasing emphasis on the qualification of the labour forces as a key factor in explaining differentiated growth performances. Last, and certainly not least, there was the neoclassical ascendancy in economics in general and labour in particular that played down the importance of the labour market and paved the way for the systematic application of neoclassical economics to this area of research. In this context, a group of economists, including T. W. Schultz, Gary Becker and Jacob Mincer, devoted increasing attention to the economic role of education, based on the idea of human capital. This would not only shape the views not only of many economists about education but also of other social scientists and policy-makers.

These developments launched a process of reformulation of the economic perspective about educational matters. The latter received significant attention due to its economic and social prominence. By stressing the economic motivations of individuals and governments for the expansion of education, economists opened the door for reconceptualizing the role of educational institutions themselves. By regarding educational decisions as being largely motivated by economic factors and calculus, economics has contributed decisively to educational institutions being considered (also) as economic institutions.

The interest of economist in higher education is founded in its relevance as an economic subject. Higher education is relevant because it uses resources that society could allocate to other activities and that therefore have an opportunity cost. Moreover, the activities developed by higher education institutions produce effects that are relevant from an economic point of view. Finally, the decisions taken in the realm of higher education are also influenced by economic motivations and calculus.

Higher education is a relevant economic subject because it also faces the basic questions that economics attempts to deal with. Economics is about finding answers for the complex equation of human needs and material possibilities. Whereas the latter is regarded as limited, at any moment in time the former is assumed by economics as being unlimited. Thus, although the material possibilities may be expanded, their level will always be beyond the level of satisfaction of all human needs. Thus, economics tries to deal with the basic problem of scarcity of resources and the choices regarding the allocation of resources in order to maximize any chosen measure of welfare. Economists have been trying therefore to provide answers to the following: to what activities should be allocated resources, how much should be awarded to which activity, how to develop each activity and whom should benefit from the results of that labour.

Higher education is not different in that respect from any other economic activity. In every system and in every institution, one is faced with those basic questions. What activities should be developed in each higher education institution? How many resources should be allocated to the different missions that each institution chooses to fulfil? How to organize those activities (be it teaching, research or the so-called third mission)? And whom should be the primary beneficiaries of the products that each higher education system and institution delivers? These are basic questions that one constantly faces, either at the system level or at the institutional one, to which economists attempt to contribute with their expertise. Moreover, by regarding educational institutions increasingly as a kind of economic unit, economists quickly moved to encompassing the educational system into the basic economic framework of the market system.

Markets and Higher Education

Mainstream economics tends to regard markets as effective mechanisms of social choice that, through rational utility-maximizing behaviour of individuals, will allocate resources to activities in a way that no one could be better-off without making anyone else worse-off (the so-called Pareto optimality conditions). However, economists are also aware that markets do not always produce the optimal outcome from a society's point of view; that is the case with market failures. The development of public economics has led to greater attention to the issue of market failures, the main types being those of public goods, the existence of externalities, information problems and natural monopoly.

The issue of public good is normally a source of controversy in the way economists discuss higher education. Many individuals argue that the application of market forces to higher education is inappropriate because higher education is a public good. The common usage of the term 'public' would refer to the provision of higher education, which has historically been dominated by public powers in most of Europe. However, when economists talk about public goods they refer to the nature of the good. The conditions for higher education to be considered a public good would be the existence of nonrivalry and nonexclusion of consumption (Barr, 2004), the former meaning that the quantity consumed by one individual would not reduce the amount available for the remaining ones and the latter, that there are no effective mechanisms to prevent individuals from enjoying good. Goods that satisfy this condition will be unattractive for private providers, since these cannot earn a profit on their production, and therefore their production needs to be both publicly financed and publicly supplied.

The goods and services provided by higher education do not seem to meet those criteria. In fact, there are plenty of examples of situations around the world where all the main outputs of higher education are produced through markets. The issue therefore is not so much whether markets will finance and produce higher education for those who wish to purchase it, but to what extent the amount and types of goods and services thus produced will be efficient for society. Since higher education provides relevant social benefits, it is in the interest of society to contribute to higher education in order to maximise social welfare. Hence, most economists prefer calling higher education a merit good rather than a public good. By this they mean that governments should promote private consumption of this type of good because of its individual and social benefits, but need not be concerned with its public provision.

The other types of market failures discussed by economists are also relevant to higher education (Johnes, 1993). The issue of externalities is certainly a very important one since it refers to a situation in which individual decision-making, which is assumed to be rational and self-interested, does not take into account the fact that investments in higher education will affect others in a positive way. Thus, individuals may spend on higher education less than what it would be socially desirable.[2] A second type of market failure refers to information problems. In a situation where the level of information is poor, individuals may not choose the best alternative available.[3] Finally, there is the case of natural monopolies, which refers to a situation when the economic conditions of a certain sector prevent the development of a great number of providers, thus limiting the positive role that competition is supposed to have. Although it is not very likely that natural monopolies exist in the case of higher education, market power may be concentrated in a selected number of providers giving them the potential to distort the way the system operates. These market failures have provided the economic rationale for government intervention (Wolf, 1993).

However, economists also consider it is problematic to think that government intervention is the answer to all these problems. Rather, they consider that some degree of market regulation may have a positive effect in the way higher education operates. This view has had a decisive influence upon governments' willingness to strengthen market mechanisms (see Teixeira et al., 2004), which has been visible through three main vectors: the promotion of competition in the system, the enhancement of privatisation – either by the development of private higher education or by stimulating some forms of 'privatisation' of public institutions, and finally the promotion of growing institutional autonomy to enhance their responsiveness to the external environment. The introduction of these three vectors has led to what has been called the development of so-called quasi-market mechanisms, in which decisions on demand and supply are coordinated using mechanisms in which only some aspects of markets are introduced, often gradually (Jongbloed, 2006).

The growing influence of economic rationality and the strengthening of market forces in higher education is a controversial matter (Teixeira et al., 2004). Several authors have voiced concerns over these developments, maintaining that they have contributed to organisational fragmentation, increased administrative bureaucracy or even to a crisis of identity in HEIs (see Amaral et al., 2002). Others have counterargued that there have been significant achievements in terms of cost reductions. However, it should be noted that market mechanisms have by far been more prominent in political rhetoric than in actual policy changes. The difference presently is the existence of a more intensive scrutiny of governments' role in higher education and a stronger willingness to discuss possible alternatives to government regulatory powers.

The growing interest of economists in higher education has had a significant influence on shaping the political and social discourses about that sector. It has become a truism to speak about the economic relevance of higher education and expressions such as 'human capital' and 'investment in education' have become part of the public jargon. The economics' analytical apparatus of markets has also pervaded the policy debate about higher education and made it a present reality in many higher education systems, even if mostly at a rhetorical level. This increasing influence of economic analysis on higher education policy has become particularly relevant in the choices concerning higher education funding, to which we turn our attention.

BRAVE NEW WORLD? - THE ASCENDANT OF EFFICIENCY AND THE FUNDING OF HE[4]

Despite the fact that many of the essential ingredients of markets are not in place for higher education, market-type coordination mechanisms are becoming increasingly popular in higher education policy making (Teixeira et al., 2004). Their emergence in particular can be observed in the area of funding, whose promarket policies have been the subject of debate and policy experimentation in several countries. In this section, we analyse the main current trends in higher education funding and the ways economic rationality is playing a significant role in those trends.

Dealing with Limitations in Public Funding

Arguably, the dominant issue in recent years in higher education funding in Europe as much as elsewhere has been that of financial constraints (see Williams, 1991 and Kaiser et al., 1992). The so-called crisis of the welfare state has challenged the sustainability of the traditional financial reliance of higher education on public funding. Governments in almost every Western country have tried to contain the growth of public expenditure, an objective that is significantly difficult due to the expanding inertia of many components of public expenditure (Barr, 2004). The pressures for expanding resources being allocated to areas such as healthcare and social security have forced many governments to rethink their financial engagement in other areas. Education in general has become one of the potential areas for cost containment. This context has certainly been enhanced by the growing political visibility of the so-called grey vote. Thus, the likelihood that higher education could see expanded its level of public resources is rather small, and many higher education institutions have been preparing themselves for a context of declining or at least stagnant public support.[5]

Part of the explanation for those financial difficulties has to do with the fact that even when the overall level of funding has increased it did not keep up with the growth in enrolments, and the demand for higher education has continually expanded during the last decades. European universities have been under significant strain to accommodate not only an ever-growing population, but also to extend access to parts of the population traditionally under-represented. This increase in rates of participation has in most cases largely outpaced demographic declines of young adult populations experienced in recent decades in most European countries. The data available point out to the existence of some rigidity in the level of funding per institution; thus, those institutions and those systems where the expansion was absent or less significant did better than those where there was a rapid expansion of enrolments. In the latter case, the expansion of funding had more difficulty in keeping up with levels of enrolment.

The financial challenges created by this massive expansion of European higher education systems became more problematic due to the increasing trends on the cost side. There has been some discussion about this trend. It could argue that this is due to inefficiency, and it would not be difficult to find some casual examples of that in the way most institutions operate. However, it seems awkward that the level of inefficiency would increase precisely at a time when most higher education institutions have been under significant pressure to be more efficient in the way they operate. Other potential explanations to these steeping costs lie in the use of more costly resources and in increasing quality. The emphasis on research universities as a role model has definitely contributed to enhance this trend, as suggested by the fact that the increase in cost has been clearly more visible in research universities (Clotfelter, 1996). Although it is certainly difficult to measure quality with rigour, the use of more expensive factors is easier to be traced. In fact, there are signs that in many European institutions additional investments have been poured into the enhancement of research capability and especially of the qualification of their academic and nonacademic staff. This has inevitably increased the labour costs of higher education, which in many institutions represent three quarters or more of the total running costs. Other factors such as rising costs with libraries, IT and other equipment have added to this trend.

One of the main factors usually presented to explain this rise in costs has to do with the nature of higher education as a labour-intensive activity. This is what has been christened in the sixties by Baumol and Bowen as cost-disease (see Getz and Siegfried, 1991). This refers to the rising relative unit cost phenomenon in labour-intensive activities that have more difficulty in increasing their levels of productivity due to the limitations in replacing labour by capital and technology. Higher education institutions seem unable to benefit on a large scale from the kind of productivity enhancements typically associated with the goods-producing sectors of the industrialised economies, in which firms can replace labour with capital or outsource production to countries with lower labour costs (Johnstone, 2006). Institutions in these sectors will find hard to contain costs because their workers expect their salaries to follow the increase in the living costs that is being pushed by those sectors experiencing greater productivity increases (Geiger, 2004).

This financial context has led to greater concerns with the level of external and internal efficiency of the system.[6] As regards the latter, like in many other public services, in recent years, it became a rather common statement that higher education institutions should be more efficient in their use of taxpayers' resources (Cave et al., 1990). The increase of the so-called accountability procedures had important consequences for the working of higher education institutions. The claim for more accountable institutions of higher education suggests that European societies have become less confident in the internal working of those institutions, based on the belief that institutions do not spend available resources in an efficient way. Moreover, most current policy discussions assume that higher education institutions do not spend resources as efficiently as possible or as society wanted. The efficiency concerns were not restricted to the internal operation of higher education institutions, but they also extended to their articulation with the external environment. Thus, many governments, namely European ones, have been devising policies to strengthen the external efficiency of the higher education system, i.e., to improve the ability of higher education to fulfil the needs of the national economy and of the entire society. This required the promotion of more responsive higher education institutions.

These rising concerns about efficiency have had a clear impact on the relationship between higher education institutions and their main financial provider, which has tried to transmit to the institutions the claims for proefficient behaviour. This has been visible in changes in the sources and mechanisms of funding of higher education in Europe.

Rationalizing the Sources of Funding

One of the most hotly debated topics in Europe about the efficiency of higher education funding has to do with the main sources of financial support to institutions. The traditional reliance of higher education funding systems on government support has been under increasing scrutiny from the ascending economic rationality in higher education discourses. According to mainstream economics, the rationale for public funding of higher education should be based on the externalities produced by higher education, i.e., effects that are not adequately handled by the market mechanism (see for instance Barr, 2004 and Johnes, 1993). This is in line with the view that higher education should not be properly considered as a public good, according to the economic definition, but as a merit one.

The analysis of higher education demand has been significantly influenced by the human capital perspective about education (Becker, 1994). According to this view, both society and the individual should asses to what extent it is economically attractive to allocate resources to higher education through a cost-benefit analysis. Most economists tend to consider that in the case of higher education the larger portion of the benefits tend to have a private nature, namely, higher lifetime earnings and greater employability (the duration and length of unemployment has been shown to be persistently lower for higher education graduates than for workers with lower levels of education) (see Card, 1999). Higher education graduates also benefit from several other benefits associated with a degree such as higher social status and access to jobs of greater social prestige and desirability (even if not always of higher income).

This type of cost-benefit analyses has been instrumental to the recent debates about changing the sources of funding in higher education and the introduction of cost-sharing in higher education (Teixeira et al., 2006). Cost-sharing is mostly associated as the introduction of tuition fees to cover part of the costs of instruction (Johnstone, 2006). The introduction of fees has been regarded by most economists as a positive factor since economics tends to consider that there is a greater efficiency when there is a charge (price) that reflects at least in part the costs incurred in the provision of higher education (Barr and Crawford, 2005). Tuition fees are expected to play an important role in rationing supply across consumers and providing price signals to consumers, which are expected to be more careful about their educational decisions. Tuition fees are expected to stimulate students both to work harder and to be more perceptive and demanding as a higher educational consumer.

Economists tend to consider that policies of low-cost or free tuition are negative not only on efficiency grounds, but also on equity ones. The public subsidies tend to benefit disproportionately offsprings of the wealthy social groups, because these are over-represented in higher education and therefore reap a big portion of the private benefits, while all taxpayers bear the cost. Wealthier groups have not only more income but also greater cultural capital, and they tend to be more familiar with the kind of methods of work and with the aspirations that lead to academic success. Thus, we may face a situation of redistribution from low-income groups to wealthier ones. Although some have expressed concern about the potential negative effects of the potential demand of introducing tuition fees, the evidence available suggests that in the European context the effects on participation rates are small.

One of the major arguments towards the introduction of tuition fees in Europe has been a pure necessity. The expansion of higher education has been taking place in times of increasing pressure for greater parsimony in the use of public funds and the diversification of higher education's financial basis where possible. The increasing competition for public funds has shown that higher education may face difficulties against other social needs such as healthcare and social security, and future societal trends (such as ageing populations) will weaken further higher education's bargaining capacity. Although public funding is likely to remain the major source of income for European public HEIs, the current situation has forced many countries to rethink the way higher education costs are funded and to discuss the potential diversification of sources of funding.

There are not many available studies with comparable data on the composition of funding of higher education institutions. Recent evidence indicates that the role of government has slightly diminished in its share of overall institutional funding. However, this decline has often been partly offset by the increase in contract funding. In any case, in most European countries governments continue to represent by far the largest source of funding to public higher education institutions. As regards the other sources, they still represent a small portion of funding and in several cases have not shown signs of becoming significant. This is particularly the case with tuition fees, arguably the most debated alternative source of funding in European higher education policy. There is significant diversity in Europe regarding the existence and the level of tuition fees, though they seem to be significant only for (most) English higher education institutions. However, in some cases the increasing financial participation of families and students has made an expansion of the system financially more viable and certainly eased the financial difficulties of several institutions.

Economic Incentives and Mechanisms of Funding

The growing necessity of funds and the need to find more efficient modes of dealing with expanding higher education systems have become prominent items on the agenda of policy makers and administrators. This difficult balance between growing needs and scarce resources has led many governments to test different approaches to manage the higher education system, often through the introduction of some market mechanisms.

Presently, the funding of higher education in many European countries takes place by means of allocating grants to higher education providers. These funds are often determined through funding formulas that reflect certain criteria that may be adjusted according to the government priorities to the higher education system. This process was clearly associated with the strengthening in many countries of institutional autonomy, thus giving higher education institutions greater freedom to administer the resources allocated to them by public authorities.

However, the criteria to determine the amount of funding, allocated to each institution, present some signs of change. In recent decades, there has been a prevalence of funding higher education based on input measures rather than output ones. However, governments seem increasingly concerned with the results of higher education institutions. This has led to two important changes. One has been the introduction of output criteria in the calculation of funding. The other has been the growing popularity of instruments such as performance-based funding and contract funding. Altogether, these trends have contributed to increase the complexity of funding mechanisms, and nowadays it may be less clear what the priorities of governments are when funding higher education institutions.

The emphasis on performance-based funding is surrounded by some great expectations about the behaviour of higher education institutions, not unlike the ones being promoted on managerial modes (Herbst, 2006). It is expected that those changes will promote greater efficiency of the institutions and foster competition between them. However, the adoption of performance-based mechanisms of funding in a period of significant financial parsimony means that those systems will tend to have relevant distributive effects that will favour the more effective institutions vis-à-vis the poorer performers. Moreover, if performance-based funding becomes an instrument to disguise some budgetary cuts in which good performers will receive less money but not less than poor performers (Orr et al., 2008), it means that poorer performers will suffer even more.

The change towards performance funding also signals a different type of relationship between governments and institutions. The level of fetail of some of these experiments can create some fuzziness about the actual degree of autonomy of many institutions, because these may feel constrained to behave in a certain way, especially when those performance-based mechanisms are complemented by the introduction of targeted mechanisms (see Orr et al., 2008). Formula funding was often introduced alongside the development of institutional autonomy; but the trend towards performance-based funding may suggest that governments rely less on higher education institutions' capacity to respond to societal needs and feel the need to steer them through the definition of a set of criteria and exogenously defined institutional priorities. This may also create some tensions with the degree of equity in the system and the way governments relate to each institution.

In several countries, governments have started funding institutions on the basis of contracts and business-like output targets, notably focusing on completion rates and the average length students take to complete degrees. This indicates that governments position themselves increasingly as contractors buying services from autonomous (external) institutions, rather than looking at public institutions as part of the public macrostructure. This growing relevance of contract funding points out to other important trends such as some concentration of this type of funding in some institutions, in which case this has become a very important source of funding (see Lepori et al., 2007).

There is a growing willingness to give a more prominent role to consumer demand in the way higher education is funded. This orientation towards the presumptive customers is aimed at reducing inefficiency since students can influence how higher education institutions serve them and increase the responsiveness of education providers to them. One of the most debated instruments for introducing this orientation towards the demand of higher education would be through a voucher system, which has been presented as an instrument to enable students to make their own choices regarding the institution, the programme and the mode of study. In recent years there has been significant debate about the possible experimentation with vouchers in higher education, namely, in a few European countries (The Netherlands, Finland and the UK) and outside Europe (Australia, New Zealand and the USA) (see Jongbloed and Koelman, 2000 and Kaiser et al., 2002). However, the significant political resistances that this type of mechanisms seems to raise have prevented thus far any significant experience.

The defence of this type of changes in funding mechanisms is based on the assumption of rational choices by students. However, the choice of a particular programme or institution is a complex decision for the student that needs to be carefully assessed, especially because it is a costly decision and not reversible. Many observers question not only the degree of the rationality of student choices but also their ability to deal altogether with such complex choices at an early age. Others argue that the problem is due to the fact that student will tend to value certain aspects, i.e., the consumption aspects of higher education, that should not have a prominent role in these career choices. Finally, some have argued that the difficulty of those choices has to do with the specificity of higher education as a peculiar type of good and less with the rationality of the students.

There was a clear degree of controversy associated with some recent changes in mechanisms of funding. A significant resistance to these changes is provided by HEIs, because they expect this produces grater instability in the amount of public resources they receive. Moreover, some of these changes have introduced significant tensions between institutions. Others have also argued that the stimulus towards greater responsiveness to students' needs could make some institutions develop a bias towards short-term strategies. This emphasis on a business-like approach could be damaging to some academic values (Bok, 2003). Possibly, the main issue is that those changes would possibly have consequences in the geometry of the whole system. Although there is a reasonable amount of evidence that students are able to make on average rational choices, it does not necessarily mean they will not choose what governments and institutions want them to choose. It is not clear whether policy-makers and HEIs are prepared to accept that.

Rethinking Student Support Mechanisms

The changes in funding have had implications for mechanisms of student support, which in the case of Europe have normally been regarded as very generous when compared to other areas of the world. European student support mechanisms have also seen a growing concern for efficiency and for cost-benefit analysis in higher education policy debates.

The changes in funding have created new challenges to mechanisms of support to students and stimulated some major trends. The trends towards the introduction of and the increase in tuition fees in many European countries have enhanced the risk that some students may be prevented from getting higher education or would drop out during their studies due to the financial pressure. Another relevant change in recent years refers to the criteria through which students should be supported and to the mechanisms through which public support should be awarded. In the former aspect, one sees a growing willingness to give more relevance to issues of merit and less to need. In the mechanisms of support, there has been a growing popularity of loan schemes that reduced the prior hegemony of grants as the main mechanism of support.

Many economists have been championing the promotion of loan schemes as an essential part of student support mechanisms, because of their potential contribution to promote greater efficiency (see Barr, 2004). First, most economists argue that loans are preferable to grants because the latter tend to distort the demand's behaviour by making higher education too cheap and to promote some excessive demand for higher education. Second, most economists assume that individuals are highly sensitive to financial incentives. Thus, if they know that they will have to repay later a portion of their costs, they will tend to be more careful about the choices they make regarding higher education. Finally, the advocates of loan schemes have also tried to make their case on equity grounds. By making loans widely available, governments were helping overcome the limitations associated with investments in human capital since this is different from other types of investments, where borrowers cannot provide any collateral that could cover default risk. The existence of a public support mechanism that would cover that risk would overcome that market imperfection and make more viable for students to maximize their intertemporal allocation decisions. Furthermore, some authors have argued that the introduction of loan schemes reduces the level of regressiveness that has traditionally characterised public higher education funding.

The recent popularity of loans is due to several reasons. On the one hand, it is far more bearable financially for governments facing expanding enrolments and financial austerity. On the other hand, the loans would be consistent with the human capital view that, although stresses the need to overcome the current financial constraints of students, also emphasises that in the long-term students are the main beneficiaries of a higher education degree. Thus, the purpose of the support mechanism should be financing students in the present, but asking them in the future to use some of the additional income to repay the support provided in the form of a loan.

The growing popularity of loans as an apparently ideal mechanism of support has faced some controversy about students' debt-aversion. This potential problem has been pointed out to be more significant in students from less favourable social backgrounds that may be less willing to incur debts (see Callender, 2006). There is also growing concern in many countries about the effects of increasing levels of student debt on participation in higher education.

These concerns have been one of the main arguments to the introduction of income contingent loans. In this type of loans, repayments are done as a share of the graduate's income, until the total amount of debt is repaid. In this case, the length of the repayment period is not fixed as it depends very much on how successful is the graduate's transition to the labour market. Since its initial Australian experience, this type of loans have become an increasingly popular instrument in student support schemes and most observers concur that in that case there were no detrimental effects on access (see Chapman, 2006 and Barr and Crawford, 2005).

Despite the relevance of financial issues, these are not the only obstacle for students to enrol in higher education. Even in cases where generous financial arrangements exist, students from different socioeconomic backgrounds may differ in their choices (Aamodt, 2006). Many potential students, especially from poorer backgrounds show insufficient knowledge about mechanisms of financial support that could help them to cope with the costs of higher education. Thus, if governments are interested in improving the equality of educational opportunity in higher education, they should address those issues, especially by promoting more information about opportunities available for students to fund their higher education studies. This would also have a clear positive effect in the efficiency of student demand.

SOME REFLECTIONS ABOUT FUTURE TRENDS IN HIGHER EDUCATION'S FUNDING

These current trends in the funding of higher education have fostered important developments which will have significant implications for the development of higher education in the coming years. For example, the current trends highlight potential tensions between the increasing influence of economic rationales in the funding of higher education and the possibilities for change within the political framework. We will now turn our attention to these potentially conflicting dimensions in the European context.

Expanding Financial Needs

Higher education is expected to persist as an important priority in policy terms, especially due to its increasing economic valuation. In recent years governments have increasingly regarded the advanced qualification of human resources as a key factor in promoting national economic competitiveness. The recent economic discourse based on models of endogenous growth has but strengthen this view that the accumulation of human capital can improve the economic prospects of a certain community. This will therefore call for further expansion of the quantity and quality of higher education available in each European country and in Europe as a whole.

The expansion of higher education is also likely to continue to be significantly pushed by individual behaviour. A higher education degree is likely to remain on average a very attractive personal investment, as shown by persistently high private rates of returns observable in many countries. Moreover, the evidence from labour market studies suggests that higher education graduates persistently enjoy advantages of employability regarding workers with less education. Thus, in times of increasing flexibility and change in the labour market, a higher education degree will continue to be a major instrument to get access to the noblest part of the labour market. The social demand for higher education is therefore expected to remain very strong, especially in those countries whose rates of enrolment are still clearly below OECD averages.

These expectations regarding the persistent of strong demand poses financial challenges for further expansion of higher education supply. One the one hand, there is a major question on how to continue funding the system, especially when the likelihood for expansion to be based in the public system is still strong. On the other hand, there is the question on how to guarantee that the solutions regarding funding this increasing cost will not be detrimental in terms of access and affordability. The issue of how to fund this continued expansion of costlier higher education is certainly not trivial, especially considering the limitations that many governments face to expand (or even maintain) the public contribution to higher education.

Strengthening Market Forces

One of the most likely responses to those financial challenges will be through strengthening market mechanisms in European higher education, namely by increasing the privateness of the system. However, this is likely to be a complex and controversial issue in many European countries. Despite the increasing willingness of Western governments to adopt market-like mechanisms, the existence of private institutions remained minimal in most of these systems. In fact, privatization of the systems occurred mostly by increasing the private-like aspects of the dominant public system, through stimulating competition in terms of students and funds, rather than through promoting or even allowing the emergence of a significant subsector of private higher education (with the exception of Eastern Europe and Portugal).

The private sector in higher education may become a significant issue in many European countries in the coming years. The relevance of private higher education may be strengthened due to not only the financial constraints but also a response to some of the shortcomings of past massification. In those countries where the patterns of enrolment are still growing rapidly, the expansion of the private sector will tend to focus on the absorption of unfulfilled demand. However, in the more common post-massification cases, private institutions may position themselves as a high-quality/high-cost alternative to the mass/low-cost public higher education. This more specialized approach may refer to issues such as the type of programmes offered or the methods of teaching. There are already some examples of Western European countries where the private sector has been developing this kind of strategy.

The other dimension of increasing privateness of European higher education systems has to do with the reinforcement of the market orientation of public higher education institutions. One of the expected consequences of this private orientation of European public institutions has to do with the sources of income. The pressure to find sources of funding other than governmental ones will not recede. On the contrary, most institutions will be under greater pressure to diversify their funding sources. In this respect one cannot help but thinking that the introduction and the increase of tuition fees will be even more on the agenda, especially in those countries where until now the degree of public controversy has prevented its introduction or its increase from becoming a symbolic value.

This market orientation in funding is also expected to contribute to more changes in the mechanisms of funding. One can expect that the concerns over the external and internal efficiency of higher education institutions will provide additional pressures for greater responsiveness and institutional competition. Thus, instruments to strengthen the demand-oriented mechanisms of funding, such as vouchers, are likely to be very much on the policy agenda during the coming decade. The current trends also suggest that governments will tend to strengthen the use of performance-based funding, namely as an instrument to promote a closer steering of the system through the definition of specific priorities by targeting funding to certain objectives. The coming years will certainly bring more relevance to contract funding and to competition for additional funds, not only in research but also in teaching. Overall, one could say that governments will tend to regard themselves increasingly as contractors of higher educational services of autonomous institutions, which in many cases happen to be publicly owned, rather than as a provider of public higher education.

Regulatory Challenges

The combination of the aforementioned trends of growing concern over the economic outputs of higher education and a stronger market orientation of funding may contribute to the emergence of greater differentiation and segmentation of funding within the EHEA. Although many European governments are clearly concerned with the relevance of the contribution of higher education and research to national competitiveness, they have also given signs that they would prefer to concentrate some resources in some institutions in order to improve the effectiveness of those resources. The trend towards contract funding and performance-based funding will erode even further the traditional approach, present in many European countries, of governments treating all public institutions on equal terms. These developments suggest that the cohesion of many higher education systems will be under significant strain in the coming years.

The stability of European higher education systems will also be under pressure on another front. European systems have tended to promote diversity as an important value and the way institutions are funded may have a significant impact in that respect. Several of the trends discussed above point out to the increasing competition between institutions and to the growing rewards for those that appear to be more effective in responding to prescribed policy objectives. Although not all institutions enjoy similar conditions, they may be tempted to mimic strategies that appear to be financially successful. Mechanisms of funding can become a strong force towards institutional isomorphism, if institutions realize that they reward certain types of institutional behaviour. Thus, the expected increasing diversity in funding mechanisms may not necessarily foster diversity among higher education institutions.

As for student support mechanisms, one of the most important issues, especially with regard to the consolidation of the EHEA, will be that of portability. Currently, most European countries seem to take a rather cautious approach, namely on direct mechanisms of support (Vossensteyn, 2004). With the expected increasing integration of higher education systems and greater mobility of students, it will be interesting to see if governments will take a more liberal stance and privilege the funding of the students regardless of the nationality of institutions in which they enrol, or rather, if the financial restrictions will prevail on a more reductionist approach. On the other hand, since the current trends suggest that loans, especially of income contingent ones, will become a more frequent mechanism of support, especially vis-à-vis grants, it will be interesting to see if and how these mechanisms will also internalise that growing European dimension.

Although the trends point out to the strengthening of market forces and to the reduction in some of government regulation, the picture may be more complex. The increasing dimension and complexity of the system would recommend that governments retreat from centrally trying to steer the system and also from financial mechanisms. In a system as large and diverse as most European higher education systems, a reasonable degree of competition is recommended. However, the human capital theory seems to have convinced most policy-makers only on the surface or mostly on that part that recommended that human capital activities could have a powerful growth effect. When confronted with big changes in the funding of higher education, governments have difficulty in giving away power they once controlled, often with the argument that students will not be able to make adequate choices.

Accordingly, the strengthening of market forces does not mean that governments should retreat from any kind of regulation. On the contrary, like in any other market, some kind of regulation is needed and higher education is no exception to that (Teixeira et al., 2004). The more governments strengthen the role of markets in higher education, the more they need to give attention to issues such as the quantity and quality of the information available in the system, the consequences of enhanced institutional competition and the level of equity (either at the individual or at the institutional level).

Between the Scylla of Inefficiency and the Charybdis of Controversy

Altogether, the trends described in this chapter indicate that economic analysis has made significant inroads in the way policy-makers discuss and organize mechanisms of funding, and this is likely to endure in the coming decade. The financial pressures felt by many governments and institutions to use resources in a more efficient and economic seems to become a permanent feature of higher education systems. These will only be able to deal effectively with the financial challenges posed by an expanding and more costly higher education system if policy-makers and institutions are able to be ingenious about sources of revenue and the incentives embedded in funding mechanisms.

However, many of the changes suggested by an economic approach to the funding of higher education are far from uncontroversial. In many cases, the degree of political feasibility may be rather limited due to the controversy and resistances arising from changes in funding mechanisms. This is especially the case with the introduction of major symbolic changes such as tuition fees, loans or vouchers. The political sensitiveness of some of these changes require that, in order to be effective, great care should be taken in preparing them. This highlights the complexity of the various steps concerning the design of those policy changes and their political and technical implementation (Barr and Crawford, 2005). Although many policy-makers often prefer limited debate and swift changes to minimize the risk of protest, the relevance of the issues concerning the funding of higher education require a significant degree of public debate and, if possible, of public consensus upon the need and the rationales underlying those changes.

If higher education funding may greatly benefit from the contribution of economic analysis, one could also say that it is certainly too important to be left only to economists. The economic and social relevance of higher education require broad and persistent political support that can only be achieved if economists and policy-makers are willing to engage the European public opinion in an often difficult but necessary debate.

NOTES

[1]   Despite being the sole responsible for the views expressed in this text, I would like to express my intellectual gratitude to many colleagues whose views have shaped mine on this subject, and in particular to Alberto Amaral, Ben Jongbloed, David Dill and Bruce Johnstone.

[2]   Some of the main externalities associated with more education refer to health benefits, benign behaviour is aspects such as crime, impact on other worker's productivity, and greater political and social cohesiveness. Although it is not obvious to qualify empirically, several economists have been trying in recent years to document the size of those social benefits provided by higher education (see McMahon, 1999).

[3] This may lead to myopic behaviour of students that under-invest in higher education because they can not assess properly the future benefits of a higher education degree. One also faces important information-related problems in the higher education sector when it comes to assessing the outcome (including the quality) of the efforts of academics and students (see Dill and Soo, 2004).

[4] The following discussion will not analyse issues related to the funding of research. Although this is a very relevant topic for the funding of many European HEIs, it would require an individual chapter in order to receive an adequate treatment.

[5] The observed recent trends in funding in many European countries show nevertheless a less clear picture. Whereas in some countries there are signs of stagnant funding, especially in those that have traditionally generously funded their higher education systems, in others the signs of austerity are less visible. A recent study shows several examples of European countries where the level of funding per institution seems to have grown in real terms in recent years (cf. Lepori et al., 2007). According to some observers this could be because the cuts took place mostly in the 1980s and early 1990s and current evolution did not help institutions to recover.

[6] Economic theory usually distinguishes two main types of efficiency: allocative and technical. One institution of higher education is allocative efficient when its educational outcomes (e.g. graduates, publications, services to the community) correspond to society's educational demands, at a marginal level. One institution of higher education is technically efficient when it achieves the maximum level of outputs (e.g., graduates, publications, services to the community) attainable given the level of inputs available (e.g. financial and human resources).

REFERENCES

Aamodt, Per-Olaf (2006) "Access to Higher Education within a welfare state system: developments and dilemmas" in Teixeira et al (2006)

Amaral, A. and Jones, A.G. and Karseth, B. (eds.), 2002, "Governing Higher Education: National Perspectives on Institutional Governance", Amsterdam, Kluwer

Barr, N. (2004), Economics of the welfare state, (4th edition) Oxford: Oxford University Press.

Barr, N and Ian Crawford (2005) Financing Higher Education – Answers from the UK, Routledge

Becker, Gary (1993) Human Capital; Chicago University Press

Bok, Derek (2003) Universities in the Marketplace; Princeton: Princeton University Press

Callender, Claire (2006) Access to Higher Education in Britain: the impact of tuition fees and financial assistance, in Teixeira et al (2006)

Card, David (1999) "The Causal Effect of Education on Earnings", in Orley Ashenfelter and David Card (ed.) Handbook of Labor Economics, Vol. 3, Amsterdam: Elsevier

Cave, M.; M. Kogan and R. Smith (1990) - Output and Performance Measures in Government: The State of the Art, Jessica Kingsley, London

Chapman, Bruce (2006) Income related student loans: concepts, international reforms and administrative challenges, in Teixeira et al (2006)

Clotfelter, Charles (1996) Buying the Best - Cost Escalation in Higher Education, Princeton U Press; Princeton

David D. Dill and Maarja Soo (2004) "Transparency and Quality in Higher Education Markets, in Teixeira et al (2004)

Geiger, Roger (2004) Knowledge and Money; Stanford UP

Getz, Malcolm and John Siegfried (1991) "Costs and Productivity in American Colleges and Universities", in Clotfelter, Charles; Ehrenberg, Ronald; Getz, Malcolm and John Siegfried, Economic Challenges in Higher Education; Chicago: Chicago University Press and NBER

Herbst, Michael (2006) Performance Based Funding; Springer: Dordrecht

Jongbloed, Ben (2006) Strengthening Consumer Choice in Higher Education, in Teixeira et al (2006)

Jongbloed, B. and J. Koelman. Vouchers for Higher Education? A Survey of the Literature. Enschede: CHEPS, 2000.

Johnes, G. The Economics of Education. London: MacMillan Press, 1993.

Johnstone, Bruce (2006) "Cost-Sharing and the Cost-Effectiveness of Grants and Loan Subsidies to Higher Education", in Teixeira et al (2006)

Kaiser, Frans; Hans Vossensteyn and Jos Koelman (2002) Public Funding of Higher Education – A Comparative study of funding mechanisms in ten countries; CHEPS

Kaiser, Frans; Raymond Florax; Jos Koelman and Frans van Vught (1992) - Public Expenditure on Higher Education - A Comparative Study in the Member States of the European Community, Jessica Kingsley Publishers, London

McMahon, Walter (1999) Education and Development – Measuring the Social Benefits; Oxford: Oxford University Press

Orr, Dominic; Michael Jaeger; Astrid Schwarzenberger (2008) "Performance-based funding as an instrument of competition in german higher education"; in Alberto Amaral (ed.) Higher Education Policy Reform in Portugal – 4 Themes of Debate; Portuguese National Education Council; Lisbon; pp 177–208

Teixeira, Pedro (2005) 'The Human Capital Revolution in Economic Thought', History of Economic Ideas, XIII, 2, pp. 129–148

Teixeira, Pedro; Johnstone, D. Bruce; Rosa, Maria João and J. J. Vossensteyn; (2006) A Fairer Deal? Cost-sharing and accessibility in Western Higher Education; Springer-Kluwer, Dordrecht

Teixeira, P.; Dill, D.; Amaral, A. and Ben Jongbloed (Eds.) (2004) Markets in Higher Education, Kluwer, Amsterdam

Vossensteyn, J.J. (2004) Portability of Student Financial Support. An Inventory in 23 European Countries. Main Report. CHEPS, Enschede

Williams, Gareth. Changing Patterns of Finance in Higher Education. Milton Keynes: Open University Press, 1991.

Wolf, C. Markets or Governments: Choosing Between Imperfect Alternatives. Cambridge, MA: MIT Press, 1993.

HARRY DE BOER, JÜRGEN ENDERS AND BEN JONGBLOED

4. MARKET GOVERNANCE IN HIGHER EDUCATION

Higher education governance has changed significantly across Europe over the last two decades. In almost all countries we have witnessed governance reforms, although with different pace, depth, impact and timing (Center for Higher Education Policy Studies, 2007; Kehm and Lanzendorf, 2006). Generally speaking, we witness various forms of governance blending, in which elements of hierarchy (traditional governance), market (self governance) and networks (network governance) are present (van Kersbergen and van Waarden, 2004). The coordination of service delivery takes increasingly place through interconnected policy levels, ranging from the local to the global level, with a substantial number of actors who in networks of interdependent relationships influence processes of agenda setting, policy development, policy determination, policy implementation and evaluation (de Boer, 2006). Moreover, teaching, research and innovation systems are increasingly becoming intertwined, emerging into several dynamic and complex networks without a single dominating decision-making entity. We face 'multi-actor, multi-level, multi-subject governance'. Because of this 'multi-dimensionality', governance seems to be a Gordian knot of actors, rule structures and policy levels that can hardly be disentangled properly.

In this paper we want to mark the contours of a particular governance concept that qualifies under the heading of 'new governance'. It concerns the idea of 'market governance', which "refers to the use of the market mechanism of supply and demand in governance processes. In this governance mode, government interventions are focused on the shaping of a level playing field, which facilitates self-regulation (…)" (Fenger and Bekkers, 2007). Moreover, we will discuss some implications of introducing this governance concept to higher education at the European level. Point of departure in our reasoning is the overall tendency in Europe over the last the decades to modernise public sectors in which governments (intend to) steer from a distance and institutions of higher education become more autonomous in order to be competitive (Center for Higher Education Policy Studies, 2007; Eurydice, 2000). In many countries, bringing in competition in public sectors has been regarded as a welcome supplement to traditional state regulation. In the eyes of many observers of the public domain, centralized steering through directives has become obsolete and the basic assumptions of the effectiveness of government intervention have been questioned. In Osborne and Gaebler's words: "The kind of governments that developed during the industrial era, with their sluggish, centralized bureaucracies, their preoccupations with rules and regulations, and their hierarchical chains of command, no longer work very well. (…) Hierarchical, centralized bureaucracies (…) simply do not function well in the

B.M. Kehm, J. Huisman and B. Stensaker (eds.), The European Higher Education Area: Perspectives on a Moving Target, 61–78.

rapidly-changing, information-rich, knowledge-intensive society and economy of the 1990s" (Osborne and Gaebler, 1992: 11-12). Since the 1980s and 1990s changes have taken place and present-day relationships between state and service providers are increasingly characterized by marketisation with autonomous institutions, competitive environments and liberalized rule-systems (e.g. Teixeira, et al., 2004). We assume that in the foreseeable future it is likely that 'market governance' will remain an appealing concept to key decision makers in higher education. In this respect, market governance is to our opinion more than a fashion and therefore this way of coordinating the provision of public services deserves our sincere attention.

We will argue in the first part of this contribution that the shifts in governance have frequently been initiated by or are the result of state-imposed reforms. The new modes of governance are placing states in a dilemma. Bearing responsibility for the performances of the public sector at the system level on the one hand, and stepping back on the other hand, creates a schizophrenic blend of being 'absent and present' at the same time (Raad voor Maatschappelijke Ontwikkeling, 2002: 31). How can the state effectively step back and simultaneously act decisively to live up to the expectations? Does the concept of market governance offer an answer to this problem? In exploring the concept of market governance, we address the basic conditions for higher education markets and the responsibilities of states in this concept. And is this concept of market governance applicable to the European higher education area (EHEA)?

Our contribution is structured as follows. First, we address 'governance', the changes in governance and the resulting dilemmas for the state. Then we characterize the nature of higher education services and ask ourselves to what extent such services can be traded on markets. In the second part of the contribution we focus on market governance (the conditions to create markets in higher education, followed by a discussion on the potential roles of states in market-based higher education systems). In the final section the implications of regulated markets in higher education at the European level are discussed.

We like to stress that in this contribution we explore the meaning of market governance in higher education because we foresee that most likely market-based steering will be one of the guiding concepts. To what extent we should welcome this way of system steering is a different question; one that will not be answered in this contribution.

CHANGES IN GOVERNANCE

'Governance' has attracted a lot of attention over the last two decades, both from practitioners and researchers and both in private and public sectors. Nevertheless a univocal definition of governance does not exist. Etymologically governance refers to 'piloting', 'rule-making' or 'steering' (Kjaer, 2004: 3). Generally governance refers to the rule structures and means of achieving direction, control and co-ordination of wholly or partially autonomous individuals, organisations or sectors on behalf of interests to which they jointly contribute (Lynn, et al., 2000: 2). In much of the literature it has become a shorthand term for a particular set of changes, signifying a shift in the way in which the state seeks to steer society (Newman, 2001).

In principle, the increased attention for governance relates to government failures[1] (e.g. Pierre and Peters, 2000). More specifically, we see five general reasons, also applicable to higher education, why governance is in the centre of interest.[2] To some extent these reasons are interrelated and have reinforced each other. A first reason to rethink system governance concerns the economic recessions and the resulting problems of public expenditures in continuously growing higher education systems ('massification'). Particularly in the 1980s, the underlying rationale to reassess system governance was budget-driven and aiming to make first and for all savings. Affordability and cost awareness were key issues in the search for new governing mechanisms. A second reason relates to the changing context for higher education. Europeanization, internationalization and globalization pose new governance questions for at least two reasons. 'Games without frontiers' bring up new issues that need to be dealt with and reveal bottlenecks in existing rule structures. Student mobility, for instance, raises questions about degree structures and recognition or about portability of student loans. Moreover, new influential actors have entered the scene of higher education (e.g. the European Union, the World Bank, the World Trade Association or the Organisation for Economic Co-operation and Development), leaving their imprints on the systems' coordination. As a third reason, we mention the disappointing achievements of (national) governments. There has been a disillusion with and distrust of statism. In many cases states could not live up to the expectations with respect to resolving societal problems. This is not only due to the limited effectiveness of traditional government intervention, but also to towering high expectations from society. Learning from those experiences many governments developed a more modest attitude towards coordinating the higher education system. A fourth reason to rethink governance concerns the ideological shift towards the market, emphasizing new value systems and mechanisms. Universities have been exposed to marketisation and encouraged to 'sell' their services at various markets. Third party funding, tuition fees, vouchers and competition for research grants are examples of this incline towards the market. Finally, we mention the rise of new public management as a new organisational approach for the public sector that has stimulated the rethinking of governance. According to this approach universities should be managed in a more business-like way (Pollitt, 1993: Reed, 2002). Within the universities rationalization of authority distributions and decision-making structures took off. Generally, we can observe a strengthening of the (top) executives ('strong leadership') and a decline of the (formal) powers of deliberative bodies.

Obviously, each country, given its historical roots, has developed its own wave of reforms to adjust its higher education system to modern times. In the mid-1990s, the OECD concluded, for example, that "Certainly countries differ at the level of individual reforms. They place different emphasis on different aspects and implement reforms at varying speeds. The rate of take-up of reforms shows considerable variation among countries: not all countries are reforming the areas described. There are several important divergences in reform objectives. Some countries, for example, have set a reduction in the size of the public sector as a specific objective, while others put more stress on improving its performance and strengthening its role" (Organisation for Economic Co-operation and Development, 1995: 25). However, some general tendencies, varying in terms of fine tuning due to specific situations can be observed. Lane (2000: 6) argues that "some countries have tried one or two of these kinds of reforms whereas other countries have embraced all of them: decentralization, privatization, incorporation, deregulation and reregulation, the introduction of executive agencies, internal markets or the use of purchaser-provider split, as well as tendering/bidding schemes". While the reform movements vary in depth, scope, and success by country, they are remarkably similar in their rhetoric, the goals they pursue and the technologies they utilize (Kaboolian, 1998; Pollitt, 2001). In fact, many public sector reforms have become "part of the new consensus" (Eliassen, 2008). In many countries right wing governments introduced the marketisation and modernization agenda, but their views were soon largely accepted by the political left.[3] Without downplaying the differences, the 'third way' in the UK and 'similar consensual' views in continental Europe did neither reverse the trend of trying to reduce the scope of the state nor stop the development of moving from public administration to new public management (Eliassen, 2008). Political parties compromised about the direction of the public sector: more autonomous service providers, more marketisation, new funding arrangements (performance- or output-based) and the advent of new 'accountability' schemes (e.g. Sociaal-Economische Raad, 2003).

THE STATE'S DILEMMA

From the angle of the state, the developments described so far concern shifts in governance in the form of 'moving up', 'moving down' and 'moving out' (e.g. Pierre and Peters, 2000). A number of authorities and responsibilities have moved from the nation-state to the European level. The EHEA is one example of this tendency. At the same time, some powers are transferred from the state to the higher education organisations, i.e. 'moving down'. Compared to the past, universities are increasingly developing towards corporate actors with an empowered and professionalised leadership and management (e.g. de Boer, et al., 2007). This change to establish semi-autonomous agencies responsible for operational management is referred to as 'agencification' (Kjaer, 2004). It is a key element of the NPM-agenda and a clean break with the past because it separates strategic goal setting for the sector and policy execution. The third shift is 'moving out': the transfer of 'public' tasks to private organisations and the privatisation of public agencies. Contracting out is another 'moving out' option. In this case the state is the purchaser of services, which are delivered by the private sector. Examples of contracting out are catering in or cleaning of universities, keeping salary records or executing student loan schemes. These three 'moves' indicate that state powers have slimmed down, since many activities are carried out 'elsewhere'.

The intention to limit the state's role and to make the public sector work better are two general reform goals (e.g. Pollitt and Bouckaert, 2004). The first goal refers to the minimalist or liberal state, meaning rolling back the frontiers of the state. Addressing issues such as 'what is the public interest', 'what are the core objectives of the state', and 'how much can a state effectively handle', have led to the state's withdrawal from a number of tasks and to focus on its redefined core businesses. State strategies to 'minimise its role' concern the privatization or contracting out of services and the introduction of markets (liberalization) (Eliassen, 2008). Following Pollit and Bouckaert (2004), we witness the state's minimise and marketise strategy to change the coordination of the public sector. In higher education, both marketisation and privatisation have attracted attention. The second goal – improving service delivery – aims at multiple goals such as gaining in efficiency, effectiveness, savings, and quality. It implies a public sector re-organisation, often sold as 'modernisation'. One of the most popular ways to achieve these goals is by devolving authorities and empowering the organisations that deliver the services. Across Europe many higher education reforms are aiming to enhance the university autonomy and to stimulate universities to become 'public entrepreneurs' with clear and distinguishing profiles (Center for Higher Education Policy Studies, 2007). Universities are more and more empowered to become 'modern service providers' that carefully 'listen' to customer needs.

Apart from questioning to what extent state strategies of minimising and marketising have been successful, it is important to stress that stepping back not automatically implies a less powerful state. It is quite conceivable "that what we are witnessing a reconfiguration of, rather than a decline in, state power (…)" (Newman, 2001: 19). The number of rules set by the state is in most countries still impressive; "the minimal state remained both large and hyperactive" (Rhodes, 1997: 89). And Hirst (2000) argues, that rather than being hollowed out, the state has become merged with other public and private actors to exercise control and is still a significant player. We would argue that in the case of higher education, by setting strategic directions the state's impact on the ultimate outcomes of the sector remain big, may be even bigger than in the past (Goedegebuure, et al., 1993). The more interesting question is "not how much government, but rather what can government do and how can it do that best?" (Jongbloed, 2003: 131).

THE STATE, THE MARKET AND THE NATURE OF THE GOODS AND SERVICES

In debates on the performance crises of the public sector, market coordination was for a while primarily seen as an alternative to state coordination: the state versus the market. Nowadays we speak of the state *and* the market. Markets are to a large extent created and regulated by the state. Establishing institutions for markets requires complex regulations (e.g. Eliassen, 2008). In fact, institutionally markets might be even more complex than the state providing public services. Markets are valued because theoretically they offer the best way – the most efficient – of allocating goods and services. Markets, having suppliers trying to maximize their profits and consumers trying to maximize their utilities, reach optimal outcomes under a set of conditions such as perfect competition or absence of information asymmetries. However, in real life perfect markets do not exist and for that reason legitimize state regulation. In fact, there are several reasons why states regulate the provision of services or why they take responsibility for safeguarding the public interest (realizing socially desirable outcomes).

The two main categories for state intervention are: market failures, resulting in not producing enough services or providing services for an unfair price, and political preferences. The first well-known market imperfection is related to the nature of the services. A pure public good prevents potential providers to produce the socially desired outputs. In economics, a public good is defined by 'non-rivalness' and 'non-exclusiveness'. The consumption of a good by a person does not reduce the amount of the good available for others and no person can effectively be excluded from using the good. Only if these two conditions are met we speak of a public good. On the contrast, if persons can be excluded from consumption and the good cannot be used again after consumption by someone else, we speak of a private good. There are also mixed forms. Club goods mean that persons can be excluded from consumption, but if it is consumed it does not reduce the consumption by others. An example of a club good is cable television. Common (pool) goods refer to non-excludable goods with rivalry: a lake is there for every one but once I catch a fish you can't catch it anymore. What kind of good is higher education?

Enders and Jongbloed (2007: 12) start by arguing that the central product of universities, knowledge, is a public good. If a person 'consumes' scientific knowledge it does not prevent others for consuming it too. In principle, persons can also be hardly excluded from consuming knowledge. Therefore, "in theory, we may thus conclude that the central product of higher education and research has characteristics of a pure public good" (Enders and Jongbloed, 2007: 12). However, they continue, in practice things look differently. Access to scientific knowledge is limited because much of this knowledge is only accessible for particular scientific communities with their own 'language' and journals. Knowledge in the form of research outcomes is not always immediately made public, which means that persons are excluded, at least for a period in time, to consume that knowledge (patents are a good example of scientific knowledge that is temporarily not a public good). Third party funded research is another example of knowledge as a product that can be traded.

Education, another university product, is in principle a private good (e.g. Onderwijsraad, 2001). Persons can be excluded from it (e.g. entry selection) and there is rivalry (e.g. attention by a teacher given to one student goes at the expense of attention for another). If one relaxes the rivalry criterion, education can be regarded as a club good; after being selected ('not being excluded') a student 'joins the club' (his participation goes not at the expense of somebody else). It means that in principle education is a marketable commodity, as we widely observe in the real world of higher education. If we consider education as a private good, state intervention on the basis of this potential market imperfection is not justified.

A second market imperfection is the existence of externalities. In the case of externalities not all the benefits or costs are included in the calculations upon which production decisions are based, leading to undersupply or oversupply from a social perspective. Externalities have positive or negative effects for third parties that are not (fully) included in the product's price. Higher education supposedly has positive effects, e.g. on the nation's economic welfare as well as on 'good citizenship'. If this assumption is correct, state support to increase higher education consumption is legitimate.

A third market failure relates to the existence of increasing returns of scale and declining marginal costs which may create market concentrations such as monopolies. If this is the case, competition resulting in optimal quality-price ratios will not occur ('single price setting'). Governments may respond by issuing directives (e.g. antitrust regulations) to prevent the emergence of monopolies. In higher education the emergence of (regional) monopolies is conceivable. In many countries scale enlargement – mergers, strategic alliances, creating critical mass and (closed) networks – has taken place, frequently imposed or encouraged by legislatures. This may (regionally) lead to power concentrations that potentially block new competitors and obstruct fair competition. On the other hand, one can correctly argue that through scale enlargement these merged organisations can function more efficiently and, consequently, increase their competitiveness. Encouraging the establishment of critical mass (reduction of the number of competitors) and preventing power concentrations (maintaining or increasing the number of competitors) is a delicate policy dilemma. The point we want to stress here is that state intervention in higher education is legitimized when it intends to prevent concentration of market powers, which indeed may occur in higher education. In such a case, the state acts as a watchdog, overseeing and protecting fair competition.

Finally, market imperfections may result from a lack of transparency. Consumers and producers need to be well informed on prices and quality of products in order to optimize their decisions. Governments may intervene to enhance transparency.

Apart from market failures, governments may intervene because of wider social goals. This is the second main category for state intervention, i.e. for political reasons. Examples are access to services, security of supply, ensuring minimum standards, setting safety standards, protecting the interests of future generations or of 'endangered species'. It concerns political decisions and it may well be that even in the case of pure private goods governments decide to interfere. Examples of interventions in higher education based on political grounds are the promotion and protection of broad access. Seeing higher education as a merit good states develop policies for 'free' access, even if higher education is seen as a private good. Accreditation as a condition for public funding can be regarded as a procedure to ensure minimum quality standards. Higher education has also its 'endangered species'; due to a mismatch between supply and demand, vulnerable subjects in teaching and research may not survive the harsh realities of the market. If such subjects are considered to be of importance from a social or economic point of view, state intervention seems legitimate (see, for example, Higher Education Funding Council for England, 2005).

Thus, there can be various reasons for state involvement in higher education: "In some cases public provision of a good or service is preferred because public policy is seen as more efficient than private provision through the market. In other cases the resort to public provision is the result of market failure, as in the case of monopolies and the potential for exploitative behaviours. In a further set of cases goods are seen as part of the public realm because this is the only place where an equitable outcome can be guaranteed" (Considine, 2005: 36).[4]

We take the point of view that higher education is a collective good or a public interest. There is a commitment from the state to a publicly defined interest, having the characteristics of a private good that is bound by state regulations for reasons of externalities (social benefits) and wider social values such as access. It implies that the state bears responsibility for this collective good. Arguably, access to higher education, efficient use of public funds, and quality of education are cornerstones of a state's responsibility towards higher education ('a good and efficiently produced service available for all'). If higher education is regarded this way, the next question is how can the state best fulfil its responsibility? In principle, there are five options.

First, the state can decide to provide the services itself: state-owned universities offering teaching programmes prescribed by the state. Second, private organisations are brought in to deliver the services ('contracting out') and the state purchases the collective good from private providers or provides subsidies for the services. Third, autonomous public organisations offer teaching programmes and the state subsidises or purchases the services from autonomous public agencies. Fourth, there is the combination of the second and third option: the state creates a market space within which both private and public organisations are offering their services and bidding for the customer's favour. Irrespective of the legal status of the providers, the state bears its responsibility by subsidizing services (e.g. programmes or the number of (successful) users of the service). Finally, instead of supporting the supply-side, the state can decide to (financially) support the users of the services (demand-side driven support). Students instead of universities receive a state subsidy to consume the programmes of their liking.

Apart from the first option, the higher education market seems to play a role. In the remainder of the paper, we will zoom in on this higher education market space. We will ask ourselves what it means to have or create a real higher education market.[5] What are the kinds of conditions for an open higher education system with minimal state regulation, i.e. a system that does not distinguish between public and private providers?

CONDITIONS FOR AN OPEN SYSTEM OF HIGHER EDUCATION

An open system of higher education means that every provider of higher education programmes can qualify for public funding. In practice it means that private organisations – e.g. private universities and/or other private companies – will have equal opportunities to compete with (public) providers for public funds. The underlying rationale for an open system of higher education is that as the number of providers grows, competition increases and that more competition leads to more efficiency, higher quality, more innovation, more differentiation, and more choice for consumers. In other words, more competitors make the system of delivering a collective good perform better. Obviously this 'market' rationale can be questioned: does competition increase when there are more providers, and does more competition indeed lead to more innovation, more choice or higher quality?

As we explained in the previous section, also in a system where every provider develops its own programmes, the state has system responsibility, since higher education is regarded as a collective good. As a purchaser or financial donor the state applies its standards for the services it wishes to pay for (see also the next section on the state's role). In an open system for higher education, two aspects concerning these standards are important. First, both the number and 'weight' of the standards should be kept to a minimum in order to invite as many providers as possible; otherwise it can not be seen as an open system. Second, if a provider meets these standards it receives public money for delivering its services, irrespective whether it concerns a regional, national, international, public or private provider.

There are also potential downsides of an open system of higher education. First, some teaching programmes may disappear because they are not economically viable (e.g. due to a lack of demand), which leads to a decrease of variety, destruction of capital and may have consequences for research programmes (if a teaching-research nexus exists). The disappearance of economically vulnerable subjects – the wild orchids – is problematic if it concerns goods that are desirable from a social perspective ('cultural value') or from an economic perspective ('strategic value') (e.g. Higher Education Funding Council for England, 2005). If vulnerable subjects do not disappear, the market does not what it is supposed to do ('survival of the fittest'). Second, having more providers also implies a fragmentation of budgets (Sociaal-Economische Raad, 2003: 135). Third, having more providers could lead to bigger aggregated claims on public budgets. Without increasing the levels of public budgets, the average costs will drop. Fourth, phenomena of 'cherry picking' or 'cream skinning' can pop up and may result in an unbalanced supply of programmes. These phenomena refer to organisational strategies that (only) focus on profitable programmes. Only highly profitable services will be offered; risky consumers will be avoided – e.g. offering business administration programmes, or selecting only the best students. Some providers offer a broad range of programmes using profitable programmes to cross-subsidise less profitable ones. When there are many providers using cherry picking strategies this cross-subsidy strategy is jeopardized since too much pressure is put on them. Particularly, the danger of losing the 'orchids' and cherry picking strategies can reduce the system's overall diversity (see also the final section of this contribution). Most of the possible downsides of an open system can be prevented by state intervention, for example, through regulations or financial incentives. This however in turn limits the openness of the system. It is a trade-off between the perceived benefits of the openness of the system and state regulation to avoid the potential downsides. In order to establish an open system of higher education and to further competition, providers of educational programmes must have free entry and exit to higher education markets. Currently many higher education systems are to a large extent closed because conditions to qualify for public funding are very tough. In fact, in practice the number of publicly funded higher education institutions expands only when the state considers this wise (e.g. for reasons of regional development). In most countries, it is difficult, if not impossible, for new providers to qualify for public funding.

In principle, in an open higher education system the conditions for getting public funding are the same for every provider. This refers to having a level playing field. It implies, for instance, that entry rules are the same for every provider. If a provider's educational programme meets the quality standards set, they receive public funding. By the same token, both public and private providers can lose their accreditation. There is however a second interpretation of creating a level playing field, which refers to providers having the same expectations on profits. In this case, the rules are not the same for everyone, but are consciously made different. For example to give new providers a fair chance to become a real competitor they are temporarily advantaged, i.e. the advantages of vested interests are taken away. Such entry rules might increase the number of providers. A level playing field means that *ultimately* the rules and conditions are the same for everyone. The assumption is that low entry barriers lead to more providers and, consequently, to more competition. However, even if low entry barriers do not (immediately) result in an increasing number of providers, they may cause market-type behaviours of the (few) current providers on the market. The threat of potential competition may provoke attitudes of increased cost awareness, better value for money, or more quality awareness. This is the central thesis of contestable markets, assuming that opening up a market puts pressure on current providers because new providers *can* easily enter the market (Baumol, 1982). The threat of potential competition increases further if not only the barriers of entry but also the barriers of exit are low. The latter may cause problems of 'take the money and run' strategies, which could seriously undermine the stability of the system.

Apart from low entry and exit barriers for providers there are more conditions to be met to have fair competition on the supply-side as well as on the demand-side. In discussing the possibilities and desirability of markets in education, the Educational Council of the Netherlands mentions eight conditions with respect to perfect markets: four on the supply-side and four on the demand-side. On the supply-side providers must:

– have free access to the market space (already discussed),
– have freedom to develop their own products (e.g. length of programme, content of programme),
– have freedom on the use of 'means of production' (e.g. the selection of students and staff as well as financial discretion),
– be free to set the price and the quality of their product (e.g. tuition fees).

With respect to all these conditions a level playing field is needed. For providers these conditions mean that they are enabled to act as entrepreneurs or corporations. Nothing new for private providers but for public institutions it implies significant changes (both structurally and culturally). Public entrepreneurialism, requiring 'full' substantial autonomy, contributes to more responsiveness to societal needs, more client-orientation, more innovativeness and risk-taking and to developing more tailor-made services. Entrepreneurs control their own organisational borders. For the moment many states strictly control the borders of their higher education organisations. As we have argued elsewhere, if universities are supposed to be autonomous they should set their own boundaries (de Boer, et al., 2007). This means that not the state but the universities – just as the private providers – should define the content and length of teaching programmes, select the students, employ university staff and set labour conditions. In addition, they should set the price for their services. Other financial discretions required to act as 'market actors' are lump-sum funding schemes as well as the possibility for these entrepreneurs to make profits or at least the possibility to build up monetary reserves. Strictly speaking, in an open system public institutions can not only lose their accreditation (as a condition for public funding), but can go bankrupt too. Anyway, if the market conditions on the supply-side are met, then public and private as well as national and international providers are able to compete on the kind, the quality and the price of their services. In fact, all providers become 'private' organisations that are publicly subsidised. The latter is being justified by the fact that higher education is regarded as a collective good.

Jongbloed (2003: 128) applied these four market-type conditions to the Dutch situation (in 2002-2003) and argues that Dutch universities have considerable autonomy when it comes to product development and the use of resources. At the same time, entry barriers for educational service providers are high and fee levels (for European students) are set by the state.[6] In this respect, one might say that the Dutch are halfway towards an open system (as regards the supply-side conditions).

Conditions on the demand-side are that consumers must be free to choose the products and providers of their liking. Adequate information on price and quality is required to make just choices. It means that students have the opportunity to be well-informed about 'all' programmes' strengths, weaknesses, and costs, so that they can opt for the programme that satisfies their needs best. Of course students are bounded in their rationality; they can not process all the pros and cons of all programmes offered. They point is that real markets should be transparent, in the sense that if a student wants information on a particular programme, this information should be easy accessible and reliable. Based on this information the student decides where to study what (free choice of provider and programme). For the moment, the general opinion is that the transparency of higher education markets leaves much to be desired, although several initiatives have been taken to improve transparency and to better inform students. Moreover, the student must cover the costs of his/her education. In private higher education this is usually the case; in public higher education however students rarely bear the full costs.

If the conditions on the demand-side are violated, state intervention is legitimised. It may issue regulations to protect the customer, for instance, to make it mandatory for providers to periodically make public the outcomes of quality assessments in a particular format. Or to mention another measure, the state decides to directly fund the student (instead of the university) in such a way that the student can actually cover the costs of received education.

It is clear that while many higher education systems are moving into the direction of markets, the eight conditions for perfect markets are not met in any single higher education system. Market failures and the nature of the products all conspire to make the free market an unlikely contender in higher education: "Visible hands are the order of the day, and the question is what these hands should look like" (Meek, 2000: 23). In answering our main question – how can the state effectively step back and simultaneously act decisively to fulfil its responsibilities – we will now turn to the roles of the state in a market-based higher education system.

THE ROLE OF THE STATE IN A MARKET-BASED SYSTEM OF HIGHER EDUCATION

There are various roles of the state to protect the public interest in market-based systems of higher education (see also Plug, et al., 2003). Our sense of higher education's public interest refers to 'a high quality, efficiently produced service available for all'. In the concept of market governance the state is engaged in the allocation of (equal) positions in the market space (the process of inclusion and exclusion of providers) and in defining the boundaries of this space. Additionally, state action can "be focused on the definition of playing rules that the actors in the arena should comply with in the negotiation processes they undertake in order to achieve collective action" (Fenger and Bekkers, 2007: 23). The state is however not directly involved in defining the specific outcomes of the collective behaviour within the level playing field. The sector's outcomes are the product of self-regulation among the actors involved (Fenger and Bekkers, 2007). In this context we believe the state has the following parts to play:

- Market or competition engineer: it has to define the institutions for the higher education market;
- Sponsor: if higher education is considered as a collective good then the state must financially sponsor the delivery of services (subsidise the providers or the customers);
- System-wide agenda setter: the state is responsible for translating public interests into a strategic agenda, i.e. the state as policy maker. At the system level it must operationalize the public interest. What are, for instance, the minimum quality standards for a programme? What are strategically important or economically vulnerable subjects requiring 'protection' from the market?
- Supervisor and controller: the state assesses the performances of the higher education system in relation to its strategic agenda. This requires accountability and monitoring schemes.
- Upholder of justice: the state oversees if the game is played according to the rules of fair competition (this role could also be carried out by a separate, general or sector-specific agency);
- Commissioner: if the provision of collective goods and services will be left to 'market organisations', then the state must develop tendering and contracting systems. This implies that the public interest in higher education will be translated into concrete assignments and contractual conditions.

In other words, the state must define the public interest of higher education, promote and protect these interests, define fair rules for competition and minimum standards for the services and the delivery, and conclude and oversee contracts. This enumeration of state roles clearly shows that markets without government involvement are fiction. Second, sometimes the various roles are incompatible or at least full of tension. Making choices (on policies and rules) on the one hand and supervising them on the other hand may be tricky. Third, the state does not take up these roles in 'isolation'. The strategic agenda, for instance, is the outcome of a political process that ideally involves consultations with stakeholders in society.

Stakeholders might also participate in defining the (minimum levels of) quality of teaching programmes.

THE EUROPEAN HIGHER EDUCATION AREA AND THE MARKET GOVERNANCE CONCEPT

Higher education is a collective good which inevitably means state intervention. This intervention is, for instance, related to the setting of minimum standards for quality, access and efficient use of public resources. Moreover, the state can set standards for internal governance such as staff and student representation in strategic decision-making and standards for public accountability (see, for instance, the principles of good governance).[7]

Such a mixed model of market and state combines top-down and bottom-up steering. At the bottom consumer and provider sovereignty determine system outcomes (self-regulation via demand and supply). These system outcomes will be evaluated by the state. This means that the state has to inform itself about system performances in one way or another. Apart from assessing system performances (monitoring role), the state must also define system goals (translating the public interest), create the rules of the game (market engineer), commission contracts and financially sponsor higher education. In other words, market governance assumes some degree of coordinated action for which the state seems to qualify best. What does this mean for the EHEA? How can the different roles of the state be organized at the European level?

In principle there are two options. First, the nation-states transfer their authorities to the European Union. The European legislature is authorized to make binding decisions in higher education. Over the last decades, however, higher education has been one of the policy areas considered to be a 'national affair'. We expect that the principle of subsidiarity will continue to dominate the European higher education landscape, at least in the midterm. The nation-states seem not to be willing to give up on their powers to steer 'their' higher education. This means that the European Union will not fulfil this role of coordinator in the EHEA.

The second option for coordinated action in the EHEA is intergovernmental decision-making. In this case the 'capitals of Europe' bargain and negotiate about the issues that come forth out the state roles mentioned in the previous section. The political decisions can be executed by agencies at the European level. The nation-states collectively have to fill in their role as market engineers and, to give some examples, deal with the following issues. What are the standards with respect to the quality of educational programmes? In terms of access policies, should they develop a European student loan scheme to give equal opportunities to students all over Europe? They may consider taking measures to prevent regional monopolies and to take care for regional spreading (guarantees for geographical access). They should think about vulnerable subjects in order to avoid the disappearance of certain subjects in particular regions. And what will be the standards to qualify for public funding? Should there be only conditions related to the quality of the programmes, or also to access and to organizing principles of the providers (e.g. to have student and staff representation in organisational decision-making). One of the key questions concerns the definition of the public interest of higher education at the European level and the translation into a strategic agenda. Of course big budgetary decisions need to be taken. The design of a level playing field also immediately touches upon a highly sensitive issue: equal rules for all, or different rules to give the less advantaged systems a fair chance to prepare for competition?

It is unlikely that these issues will be solved at short notice. At present states have different attitudes towards their higher education. They have different perceptions and preferences about the state roles they should perform in a market-based governance concept. To overcome such differences requires sophisticated political competences as well as a willingness to create a real market-based EHEA. This may be hard but not impossible. The Bologna process is showing that inter-governmental action can be successful, in the sense that voluntary agreements on complex issues have been made and (partly) implemented. Of course this inter-governmental process also lays bare many obstacles to implement such comprehensive agreements and shows how difficult and laborious such processes are. The year 2020 may be too soon to expect 'political miracles' in higher education.

FINAL REMARKS

We want to conclude with three issues not mentioned earlier in this paper. It concerns the issues of information asymmetry, democratic deficit and diversity. First, a system where states are setting the strategic goals of the EHEA and private and autonomous public organisations are implementing the policies bears the risk that these states will increasingly be poorly informed about the performances at the shop-floor level. Distance created by separating policy formation and policy execution is likely to increase the information asymmetry. Being ill-informed is problematic as it complicates the state's responsibility of safeguarding the public interest. Performance monitoring systems can be put in place, but will inevitably lead to costs. Incomplete information is always a problem; it leads both to government and market failures (de Boer, 2002), but by separating policy formation and implementation the increased distance between policy maker and service provider worsens the situation. This is all the more problematic when the states need such information to formulate the next set of strategic goals. It means that a lack of information hinders both policy making and supervision. This underscores once more the importance of developing effective monitoring and accountability schemes: do they really provide the information needed and do the accompanying costs outweigh the (assumed) efficiency gains of a market-based system? The information asymmetry problem is likely to be even a bigger problem in European higher education than in national higher education systems.

Another issue concerns the potential democratic deficit. Separating system goal setting and service provision puts pressure on the traditional mode of accountability in representative democracies. To what extent can a minister be held responsible for poor service delivery provided by private or highly autonomous public organisations? In markets, outcomes are the result of interactions among demand and supply without direct government involvement. Can we blame the minister for poor outcomes then? What are the options for citizens to protest against poor services? If the market of higher education is working perfectly, the answer is that customers can be voting with their feet: they change providers if they don't like the services offered. And if they don't like the system as such they vote for a different government. However, markets are not perfect and voting with one's feet may not be effective. And, particularly at the European level the impact of a single vote to change the higher education system is close to zero. Alternatives might be to further elaborate upon the idea of 'horizontal accountability' and the idea of 'associative democracies'. In both cases stakeholders (or customers) will be more actively engaged in the (supervision of) provision of goods. As regards horizontal accountability stakeholders have a right to be informed about the performances of the service provider. Associative democracies refer to functional and/or territorial representation of interest groups in university decision-making, a kind of 'empowering' industry and citizens at the organisational level. This kind of representation might take away the problem that "institutions that are granted more autonomy and capabilities lack the representative channels to ensure electoral input and accountability" (Pierre and Peters, 2000: 116). At present in many higher education systems we see the emergence of new institutional governing bodies, or changes in the composition of existing ones, aiming to include external and/or internal stakeholders into university's strategic decision making. In practice, the development of effective horizontal accountability systems and functional representation appears to be difficult.

Finally, we conclude this contribution with a short word on higher education markets and diversity, although this highly complex relationship would require (and deserve) a lengthy debate (e.g. Codling and Meek, 2006: Fairweather, 2000: Meek, 2000). Codling and Meek (2006) argue, for instance, that diversity rests on the interplay of five factors: the environment, policy intervention, funding, competition and co-operation, and ranking. The assumption embraced by many policy makers advocating market mechanisms in higher education, that competition in higher education will lead to more diversity is too simplistic and false at many instances (although empirical evidence is thin). Ignoring the complex interplay of the various factors for the moment, and focussing on completion only, there are two possible responses to increased market competition: "institutions can diversify in an attempt to capture a specific market niche, or they can imitate the activities of their successful competitors" (Meek, 2000: 36). The response of innovative behaviour to occupy niches versus copying the performance of the more successful seems to depend on the 'economic environment'. Taking into account Geiger's (1996) notion of 'hard times encourage diversity' on the one hand, and the processes of isomorphism on the other hand, Codling and Meek (2006: 15-16) express two propositions:

- during periods of high student demand and resource flow in higher education markets, the potential for institutional convergence increases; in this situation the institutions have the resources to mimic successful performers;
- during periods of low students demand and resource flow in higher education markets, the potential for diversity increases; in this situation institutions are faced with survival and forced to innovate and to seek new markets in order to survive.

Following this line of argument, the extent to which an open market for higher education in Europe leads to homogeneity or diversity depends on Europe's higher education economic environment. If there will be a situation of economic prosperity, more competition is likely to result in convergence rather than in diversity. According to Meek (2000) this has been the Australian case over the last two decades. Finally, we would add that in an open system of higher education vulnerable subjects are likely to disappear, which basically means a reduction of diversity at the system's level. Taking these arguments together Meek's conclusion (2000: 37) that diversity – serving the diverse needs of society – rests on a policy decision and cannot be left solely to the market to resolve, makes sense. But, in turn, such state intervention could easily undermine the concept of an open system for higher education. Further research on 'markets and diversity in higher education' is required.

NOTES

[1] Here we mean government failures in a broad sense. There exists also a body of political-economy literature using government failure in a more narrow sense. They argue that governments are subject to failures as much as markets do and therefore government intervention does not lead to an efficient allocation of services. See, for instance, (LeGrand, 1991: Wolf, 1979).

[2] In slightly different words, Fenger and Bekkers (2007:17-19) mention five crises of the welfare state that have contributed to the emergence of the governance paradigm: the financial, regulatory, rationality, implementation and complexity crisis. Limited budgets in situations of increasing demands, the jungle of detailed rules, incomplete knowledge of causal as well as means-end relations, the involvement of multiple agencies during the implementation and the continuing functional differentiation and fragmentation with highly specialized, autonomous yet interdependent subsystems have contributed to rethink traditional governance structures (Fenger and Bekkers 2007).

[3] As mentioned above, there are variations among countries. Green-Pedersen (2002) argues that NPM reforms have been implemented to a different extent because political parties adopted different strategies. Party politics explain some of the variety, but some general tendencies are noticeable (Green-Pedersen, 2002).

[4] Considine (2005: 36) gives the following provisional list when it comes to policy interventions: indivisibility, administrative ease, common pool resources, cultural goods and equity goods. Most of these imperatives have been addressed in this section.

[5] We realise that universities are engaged in various types of markets each having their own institutions (student, research and academic labour markets). Our focus is on 'student markets'.

[6] Universities decide on the level of tuition fees for non-European students, with a maximum set by the state.

[7] The European Commission mentions five principles of good governance: openness, participation, accountability, effectiveness and coherence (Commission of the European Communities, 2001).

REFERENCES

Baumol, William J. "Contestable Markets: An Uprising in the Theory of Industry Structure." *The American Economic Review* 72, no. 1 (1982): 1–15.

Center for Higher Education Policy Studies. "The Extent and Impact of Higher Education Governance Reform across Europe. Final Report to the Directorate-General for Education and Culture of the European Commission." Enschede: CHEPS, 2007.

Codling, Andrew, and V. Lynn Meek. "Twelve Propositions on Diversity in Higher Education." *Higher Education Managment and Policy* 18, no. 3 (2006): 1–24.

Commission of the European Communities. "European Governance. A White Paper." Brussels: COM (2001) 428, 2001.

Considine, Mark. *Making Public Policy.* Cambridge: Polity Press, 2005.

de Boer, Harry. "Trust, the Essence of Governance?" In *Governing Higher Education: National Perspectives on Institutional Governance,* edited by Alberto Amaral, Glen A. Jones and Berit Karseth, 43-61. Dordrecht: Kluwer Academic Publishers, 2002.

de Boer, Harry F. "Governance in Het Hoger Onderwijs." In *Vernieuwing in Het Hoger Onderwijs. Onderwijskundig Handboek,* edited by Hans van Hout, Geert ten Dam, Marcel Mirande, Cees Terlouw and Jos Willems, 327-40. Assen: Van Gorcum, 2006.

de Boer, Harry F., Jürgen Enders, and Liudvika Leisyte. "Public Sector Reform in Dutch Higher Education: The Organizational Transformation of the University." *Public Administration* 85, no. 1 (2007): 27–46.

Eliassen, Kjell A. "Introduction: Liberalising and Modernising Public Services." In *Understanding Public Management: Privatisation, Liberalization and Modernization of Public Services,* edited by Kjell A. Eliassen and Nick Sitter: Sage, 2008.

Enders, Jürgen, and Ben Jongbloed. "The Public, the Private and the Good in Higher Education and Research: An Introduction." In *Public-Private Dynamics in Higher Education. Expectations, Developments and Outcomes,* edited by Jürgen Enders and Ben Jongbloed. Bielefeld: transcript Verlag, 2007.

Eurydice. "Two Decades of Reform in Higher Education in Europe: 1980 Onwards." Brussels: Eurydice, 2000.

Fairweather, James S. "Diversification or Homogenization: How Markets and Governments Combine to Shape American Higher Education." *Higher Education Policy* 13 (2000): 79–98.

Fenger, Menno, and Victor Bekkers. "The Governance Concept in Public Administration." In *Governance and the Democratic Deficit,* edited by Victor Bekkers, Geske Dijkstra, Arthur Edwards and Menno Fenger, 13-34. Aldershot: Ashgate Publishing Limited, 2007.

Geiger, R.L. "Diversification in Us Higher Education: Historical Patterns and Current Trends." In *The Mockers and the Mocked: Comparative Perspectives on Differentiation, Convergence and Diversity in Higher Education,* edited by V.L. Meek, L. Goedegebuure, O. Kivinen and R. Rinne, 188-203. Oxford: Pergamon, 1996.

Goedegebuure, L., F. Kaiser, P. Maassen, L. Meek, F. van Vught, and E. de Weert. "International Perspectives on Trends and Issues in Higher Education Policy." In *Higher Education Policy. An International Perspective,* edited by Leo Goedegebuure, Frans Kaiser, Peter Maassen, Lynn Meek, Frans van Vught and Egbert de Weert. Oxford: IAU & Pergamon Press, 1993.

Green-Pedersen, Christoffer. "New Public Management Reforms of the Danish and Swedish Welfare State: The Role of Different Social Democratic Responses." *Governance* 15, no. 2 (2002).

Higher Education Funding Council for England. "Strategically Important and Vulnerable Subjects. Final Report of the Advisory Group." HEFCE, 2005.

Hirst, Paul. "Democracy and Governance." In *Debating Governance,* edited by J. Pierre. Oxford: University Press, 2000.

Jongbloed, Ben. "Marketisation in Higher Education, Clark's Triangle and the Essential Ingredients of Markets." *Higher Education Quarterly* 57, no. 2 (2003): 110-35.

Kaboolian, L. "The New Public Management: Challenging the Boundaries of the Management Vs. Administration Debate." *Public Administration Review* 58, no. 3 (1998): 189–93.

Kehm, Barbara M., and Ute Lanzendorf, eds. *Reforming University Governance. Changing Conditions for Research in Four European Countries.* Bonn: Lemmens, 2006.

Kjaer, Anne Mette. *Governance.* Cambridge: Polity press, 2004.

Lane, Jan-Erik. *New Public Management.* London and New York: Routledge, 2000.

LeGrand, Julian. "The Theory of Government Failure." *British Journal of Political Science* 21, no. 3 (1991): 423–42.

Lynn, Laurence E., Carolyn J. Heinrich, and Carolyn J. Hill. "Studying Governance and Public Management: Why? How?" In *Governance and Performance: New Perspectives*, edited by Carolyn J. Heinrich and Lawrence E. Lynn, 1-34. Washington DC: Georgetown University Press, 2000.

Meek, V. Lynn. "Diversity and Marketisation of Higher Education: Incompatible Concepts?" *Higher Education Policy* 13 (2000): 23–39.

Newman, Janet. *Modernising Governance. New Labour, Policy and Society.* London: Sage publications, 2001.

Onderwijsraad. "De Markt Meester?" Den Haag: Onderwijsraad, 2001.

Organisation for Economic Co-operation and Development. "Governance in Transition: Public Management Reforms in Oecd Countries." Paris: OECD, 1995.

Osborne, David, and Ted Gaebler. *Reinventing Government: How the Entrepreneurial Spirit Is Transforming the Public Sector.* Reading, Mass.: Addison-Wesley Pub. Co., 1992.

Pierre, Jon, and B. Guy Peters. *Governance, Politics and the State.* Edited by B. Guy Peters, Jon Pierre and Gerry Stoker, *Political Analysis.* Houndmills Basingstoke: Macmillan press, 2000.

Plug, Peter, Mark van Twist, and Ludy Geut. *Sturing Van Marktwerking. De Bestuurlijke Gevolgen Van Liberalisering En Privatisering.* Assen: Koninklijke Van Gorcum, 2003.

Pollitt, Christopher. "Clarifying Convergence: Striking Similarities and Durable Differences in Public Management Reform." *Public Management Review* 3, no. 4 (2001): 471–92.

———. *Managerialism and the Public Services. Cuts or Cultural Change in the 1990s? (Second Edition).* Oxford: Blackwell Publishers, 1993.

Pollitt, Christopher, and Geert Bouckaert. *Public Management Reform. A Comparative Analysis (2nd Edition).* Oxford: University Press, 2004.

Raad voor Maatschappelijke Ontwikkeling. "Bevrijdende Kaders. Sturen Op Veratnwoordelijkheid." Den Haag: RMO, 2002.

Reed, Michael I. "New Managerialism, Professional Power and Organisational Governance in Uk Universities: A Review and Assessment." In *Governing Higher Education: National Perspectives on Institutional Governance*, edited by Alberto Amaral, Glen A. Jones and Berit Karseth, 163-86. Dortrecht: Kluwer Academic Publishers, 2002.

Rhodes, R.A.W. *Understanding Governance. Policy Networks, Governance, Reflexivity and Accountability.* Buckingham: Open University Press, 1997.

Sociaal-Economische Raad. "Kennis Maken. Kennis Delen. Naar Een Innovatiestrategie Voor Het Hoger Onderwijs." Den Haag: SER, 2003.

Teixeira, Pedro, Ben Jongbloed, David Dill, and Alberto Amaral. *Markets in Higher Education. Rhetoric or Reality?* Vol. 6, *Higher Education Dynamics.* Dordrecht: Springer, 2004.

van Kersbergen, Kees, and Frans van Waarden. "'Governance' as a Bridge between Disciplines: Cross-Disciplinary Inspiration Regarding Shifts in Governance and Problems of Governability, Accountability and Legitimacy." *European Journal of Political Research* 43 (2004): 143–71.

Wolf, Charles. "A Theory of Nonmarket Failures: Framework for Implementation Analysis." *Journal of Law and Economics* 22, no. 1 (1979): 107–39.

JAN DE GROOF

5. EUROPEAN HIGHER EDUCATION IN SEARCH OF A NEW LEGAL ORDER

INTRODUCTION

The 'Legal Order' Is Challenged

1. - Major changes have taken place in higher education in the Wider Europe over the past decade. Most large-scale changes were initiated through the legislator, the government, the international community, the socio-economic environment and donors. The reform of the universities has been a laborious process, but not spurred on by the universities themselves. Usually the political government, as defender of the interests of society, had to take the decisive initiative to bring the passivity of the universities to an end.

The changing size and shape of higher education became a constant characteristic of the institutional landscape. Globalisation implies also the changing nature of higher education providers. The growth in *private* and/or *transnational* education institutions, commercial or not for profit, offering *contact* or *contract* (distance) education, has been quite dramatic during the last 15 years. The sector was dominated during decades or even centuries by universities, often with *public status*. It became a 'market'. But competition with the new providers led also to an innovation of curriculum, flexibilisation of the academic organisation and shaped the core business of the universities.

Creating and expanding market conditions for the provision of public education within the nation and the growth of private and transnational education and tuition-based institutions contributed to a market economy and the opening up of national borders. But some states were being forced to invoke moratoria and regulatory arrangements to circumscribe non-governmental education. New providers provoked a decline in enrolments of 'classic' universities. But in all countries government subsidization and legislative priority given to the latter will be questioned, referring to *fair and equal treatment of all accredited institutions and/or programmes, to free trade and to competition law.* Due to the new public/private relationship in the higher education sphere, governmental regulations restricting access to private and/or international providers will also being questioned.

2. - It is interesting to note that the way in which higher education has diversified in Europe has varied widely from one country to another[1]. Although there is no need of an 'Europe-wide model'[2] and there always will be more systems of higher education than countries in Europe, these tendencies need *common and coherent*

B.M. Kehm, J. Huisman and B. Stensaker (eds.), The European Higher Education Area:
Perspectives on a Moving Target, 79–104.
© *2009 Sense Publishers. All rights reserved.*

legal approaches, contributing to the (already existing voluntary) convergence and internationalisation within the EU and EHEA. National legal systems are fully separate (in terms of public law) from one another, and are interconnected by means of another type of legal system, public international law, which is based on the equal sovereignty of its original subjects, i.e. the States. A new legal mechanism of *public or private law* seems to be a condition for efficient transnational education and research[3].

Furthermore it has been predicted that the market-oriented approach or the *'market culture'* of the university would clash with the Humboldtian education ideal and its accompanying *'basic assumptions and beliefs'*. In the higher education legislation of all Member States a balance should be found in the triple mission of the university and the university colleges as well as through their associative institutional networks. The new generation of education legislation has to be screened on the 'European characteristics' of the university. The law should clarify, specify and tighten the core functions and values of the university, with broader attention for tasks geared towards society and the market.

Higher education has been brought under the influence of the EC by the European Court of Justice (ECJ). The argument was at first that higher education was preparing for the labour market. For this reason, it was considered to fall under the four freedoms of the internal market. The Court has now also chosen *the citizen* as the starting point. By taking the European citizen as the new basis of the jurisprudence, the Court has implicitly begun thinking in terms of a European system of Higher Education. This can force the member states to make agreements about the central financing of one European Higher Education system.

The next paragraphs also focus on tendencies that will question and challenge legal frameworks dealing with higher education.

Changing Patterns of Legislation: the 'Juridification' of Higher Education

3. - The 'juridification' and 'judicialisation'[4] of the higher education system has pejorative overtones involving excessive recourse to legal procedure to resolve issues previously settled by negotiation or informal agreement or by the tertiary education institutions themselves. Here, however, juridification is to be understood as that part of the broader process of 'incorporation' which brought the higher education institutions into the formal ambit of either administrative or constitutional law as the main instrument for regulating the boundaries of systems of governance whilst also giving formal legal recognition to powers and areas of responsibility previously defined internally by practice, tradition and custom within and by, the academic guild.

The rule of law implied codifying the ties between government and university so that due process or its violation could be ascertained. But, it also had the task of defining the boundaries within which autonomy could be exercised as well as defining the nature of that autonomy. The boundary between the 'public' and the 'private' lives of the university[5] were drawn in keeping with the Humboldtian principle of the freedom to learn and to teach.

A philosophy of 'steering at a distance' was introduced: a move towards a *result*-oriented, rather than *rule*-oriented responsibility for the institutions involved. Government's role changes[6]. From the role of sole provider and detailed regulator with the responsible minister as the important actor, it has redefined its role to that of supervisor of a level playing field.

4. - The changing role of the government, the trend towards deregulation, a certain diversification of institutes, the gearing of national politics to the international context are the factors of change which affect higher education. The university has to deliver new answers on 'if', 'what', 'when' and 'how' education and research will be organized.

On all legal dimensions of university life autonomy was questioned. "Education is more closely audited, assessed and centrally controlled than at any time in history. This has formed an important part of the centralisation of power over the direction of education policy and the management of the system to meet various political and economic goals. The relationship between law and politics in the context of education reform is important to an understanding of the way that the politicisation of education during the past 30 years has shaped its legal framework and the structure of control and regulation within the system."[7]

From the 1990s, the concept of autonomy was fiercely juxtaposed with the requirement for accountability. A range of external policies created new demands on universities which were regarded as leading to an erosion of autonomy. The transnational cooperation within the higher education landscape directly provoked changes in the institutional behaviour. In a short period of time, government had intervened quite directly in higher education institutions both to guarantee quality management and also to require compliance with a new regime of academic and funding regulations. This raised charges against government on the basis of infringing on institutional autonomy[8].

In conclusion, it does not seem to be contradictory to state that the increasing delegation of powers to the institution level is accompanied by an increasing power and number of norms of the central authority. States should guide the university sector through a framework of general rules, policy objectives, funding mechanisms and incentives for education, research and innovation. In return for being freed from over-regulation and micro-management, universities should accept full institutional accountability to society at large for their results.[9]

"L'erreur sur le caractère dynamique du droit vient de la succession rapide des lois"[10] – *On the Law on Higher Education*

5. - Education policy-makers also identified *deregulation* as an overall objective. Policies cope with the apparent contradiction between drafting framework law enabling institutions to implement autonomy and the differentiated systems of accountability. In all European countries there were criticisms of the role of the ministry and complaints about the unsupportive mix between too much and too hurried prescriptive legislation.

Complaints were also frequently voiced about either premature or unnecessary administrative overregulation which interfered with institutional autonomy. The expanding governmental and legal instrumentarium contradicts whatsoever with the finding that the dependence of the public-funded system of higher education institutions on government grants has continued to reduce with the development of a more market-oriented approach and with the changes in the tuition fee structure, even for undergraduate degree courses.

In modern higher education, few major decisions are made without considering the legal consequences, and though the core functions of higher education – instruction and scholarship – are remarkably free from external legal influences, no one would plausibly deny the increase of legalization on campus[11].

The *Law on Higher Education* is dealing with practically all aspects of the university, with governance and management and the budget, with higher education as businesses, with property and estate issues and dispute management, and – chiefly – with staff and students. In the last decade, there has been growth in the key areas with respect to the impact of the law upon the campus, including the application of the principles of consumer law to the student–university contract; the issue of the degree of affirmative action/positive discrimination over admissions, not only with reference to race/ethnicity; but also increasingly concerning socio-economic background; the exercise of expert academic judgement in terms of probing whether the university really has delivered the academic content that the prospectus has promised; a greater emphasis on alternative and preventive dispute resolution in handling disputes with students and employees.[12]

The higher education world tended to think of itself as removed from and perhaps above the world of law and lawyers. "Higher education (...) was often viewed as a unique enterprise that could regulate itself through reliance on tradition and consensual agreement. It operated best by operating autonomously (...). An outsider would, almost by definition, be ignorant of the special arrangements and sensitivities underpinning this environment. And lawyers and judges as a group, at least in the early days, were clearly outsiders."[13]

But 'justice and efficiency go hand in hand'[14], so long at least as the law does not impose excessive refinements. The national legislative reform of higher education should make use of the comparative set of legal indicators[15].

THE INTERNATIONAL LEGAL SETTING

Severe Paradoxes on the Level of National-Supranational Competence

6. - "The new legal order" started in the last decade.

As art. I.3 *GATS Treaty* excludes "services supplied in the exercise of governmental authority", if not supplied "on a commercial basis" nor "in competition with other service suppliers", the applicability of the Treaty to some education sectors remains questioned. The last years witnessed explosive growth in international trends in services, particularly at the tertiary level among a great diversity of public and private players.

The *Treaty of European Union* (1992) included education as one of the policies of the Community in order to help it "meet its severely amended and extended objectives". Art. 3(9) stipulates that the EU shall deliver a "contribution to education and training of quality" and the Treaty introduces consequently art. 149 and 150 (ex art. 128 and 129).

As a result of the expansive interpretation by the ECJ of the concept '*Professional Training*', positively mentioned in the EC Treaty, '*education*' is part of the Community arena, as a consequence of the application of the non-discrimination principle of Member State subjects regarding access to education and of the principle of free movement. In a sense, articles 149 and 150 are the reflection of the series of European programmes that had been developed by the *Community* before the *Union* expressly included education, professional training and culture as a community objective – albeit within the framework of an application of the subsidiarity principle[16].

The Union's sphere of action increased evermore, although it was the result of a voluntary system, of incentive measures and competition. While the original distrust that originally accompanied the creation of art. 1 of the second European Convention on Human Rights (ECHR) Protocol started to wane[17], there grew a sense that the European dimension had a positive influence on the national education system.

The *Bologna* process is also a paradox. On the one hand, it is part of the community momentum; in that sense Bologna belongs to the community actions and programmes. But on the other hand it goes beyond the treaty stipulations. The intergovernmental nature of the Bologna process has prevented a careful assessment of the detailed *criteria and procedures of the subsidiarity principle* – as described in the Treaty – including the monitoring by national parliaments and the principle's influence on the central, regional and local level[18].

The aforementioned articles 149 and 150 have thus become largely obsolete, certainly as far as higher education is concerned, also as a result of how the facts have changed, even though the Member States are refusing to admit to this in so many words. They refer to the lack of resistance when applying tools such as *benchmarking*, *good practices* and *open coordination*, even though they are the ones who determine the relevancy of the legal (European) interpretation. 'Fewer' European norms and procedures can therefore lead to 'more Europe'. '*Harmonisation*' is an explicit objective, but only if it falls outside of the standard procedures.

7. - The focus within Europe on *diversity* referring to the national educational system and as a consequence of the Member States' *exclusive* competence – unlike in the field of 'research', which has become an area of *shared* competence – and the variety of language and culture, are continuously repeated as being the guiding principles, also in the field of quality assurance. However, the Commission is now granted a more important role than simply carrying out administrative duties and financing symposia. The Commission is expected to monitor the process and the European Council has integrated the Bologna process in its benchmarks and recommendations. In line with art. 149 EC Treaty, the Economic and Social Committee is also given a role.

The fact that the Member States and parties have no legal obligation under the Bologna process and therefore tend towards harmonisation, forces legal experts not only to take a more modest view, but also to design innovative techniques. The update of the "European Constitution"[19] and the Treaty of Lisbon amending the Treaty on European Union and the Treaty establishing the European Community missed however the chance to present the Member States involved with this opportunity. But the support of the Council of Europe, together with the implementation of art. 149, par. 3 EC Treaty, offers an opportunity for opening up to other countries.

Democratic deficit in the decision-making process regarding the fundamental choices that are made regarding the future of higher education in Europe seems also a paradox. There are grounds for criticism, but reference must be made to the decision-making process in each of the Member States and the direct involvement of the institutions in the draft legislation. For the initial lack of debate, the universities and colleges are also partially to blame. However, unlike the *benchmarking* exercise and the *Lisbon* strategy, we notice that the academic community has taken ownership of the restructuring of higher education. We are immediately reminded that the autonomy and accountability of institutes of higher learning are still of *constitutional tradition* in several Member States[20].

Educational users can only stake their claims if solid strategies and processes are included in the legislation. The question of legal status of policies therefore appears to be a decisive argument in favour of measuring the democratic deficit. Legislation should be analysed from this perspective without hampering the European momentum

The Relative Autonomy of National Education Law

8. - The 'complementary role of the Union' in educational matters continues to be stressed in the European Parliament[21], whether a further mutual sharing of responsibilities between the Union and the Member States depends on the specific measures in accordance with the relevant community educational programme. As yet there is no detailed common European *policy* but on the other hand the *loyalty requirement* in respect of Europe will constantly question the national administration.

Even though the right to education "*is calling by its very nature for regulation by the State, regulation which may vary in time and place according to the needs and resources of the community and of individuals*", according to the ECHR[22], the conformity of national law to EU and ECHR[23] will have to be carefully checked in future. Here the interpretation will be considered of the basic rights as 'general principles of Community Law', where these rights arise from Art. 6 (ex art. F) of the *Maastricht Treaty*[24] arising from the 'common constitutional traditions of the Member States', albeit within the (educational) competence of the Union[25].

In view of the 'complexity of (national) educational law' and despite the fact that the sphere of activity of the European Union with respect to education was regarded with suspicion, there was a growing realization that no Member State (party to the respective Conventions) could allow itself to (continue) to be isolated. The Community educational space demands a 'common national educational policy' and must be supported by the same principles of law, leading to coherent regulation.

It can be argued that European practice correctly must lead to 'harmonisation', used in its correct legal definition and meaning 'coordination' – but not 'unification'. '*Harmonisation*' refers to the integration process that does *not* lead to the creation of uniform law, but rather to the creation of common frameworks or rules, establishing a common goal, which leaves room for divergent specification. '*Unification*' aims at the establishment of common uniform (EC)rules replacing national ones.

EU Law should be amended in this sense. The higher education policies show that we are living now in the *post art. 149-150 era.*

The Inevitable Enforceability of the International Norm

9. - Common objectives and standards do not prevent education from continuing to be embedded in national traditions and based on specific cultural, social and confessional values, as well as on a diversity of social and economic policies. "It is fair to say that no other sector of law and administration reflects the traditions and culture of a people as much as does its provision for education."[26]

Both European educational policy and basic rights relating to education, however, raise a continuous series of questions about the discretionary space that the Member States dispose of. National regulation should be more (emphatically) justified in respect of its European and human rights dimensions. It may be expected that when settling educational disputes, the national courts will invoke international legal standards more than in the past. There is no reason to believe that the impact of ECHR in the constitutional sphere will continue to have a minor influence on education[27].

The ECHR becomes visible as a result of the observance of legal principles in educational matters, including the problems of hierarchy in connection with basic rights in the event of internal conflicts between rights and freedoms. The criteria for 'justifiable unequal treatment' and application of the *non-discrimination principle*, for example, as determined by the ECHR, serve as model for internal jurisprudence. Comparative law is invoked in the approach to *third party action* (occasionally with the applicability of basic rights in private relationships).

The systematic penetration of international conventions and declarations into the domestic legal system is inevitable. Every validly signed treaty forms an integral part of the internal legal system. And, in principle, the direct effect of a treaty leads to enhanced legal protection. It may be expected that the citizen will more than ever invoke interpretations of internal legal standards that conform to the convention and where applicable to (one of the degrees of) its direct effect. (Constitutional) Courts have derived a *standstill obligation* from Art. 13 of the 'International Pact of Economic, Social and Cultural Rights' (IPESCR) in connection with the desire to promote access to higher education.

The opinion that the consistent recognition of the *ius cogens* of the international legal standard in educational matters, as set out in Art. 13 IPESCR[28] should be avoided, appears to be outdated. This also counts for higher education. Conventions cannot be ignored by national lawmakers. Some provisions are apparently *self-executing*; provisions of conventions require states party to the convention in all cases to adopt suitable measures via a regulatory intervention.

On European Legal Methodology in Higher Education: 'Nova et Vetera'?

10. - Higher education legislation and policy became surprisingly the privileged domain of different classic and/or recent European law principles. Their accumulation makes soft law rather 'hard'.

a) The Principle of Trust

Regardless of which procedures are used with respect to national and European legislation relating to diplomas, i.e. 'recognition', 'equivalence' or the procedure of 'harmonisation', all these various mechanisms in fact refer to the principle of 'mutual *trust*' – which, for that matter, remains an essential community principle. Regardless of the quality assurance techniques that are provided by national legislation, the international (quality) standards are converging into general frameworks, for both accreditation of programmes and of institutions. The *meta-evaluation* or *meta-accreditation* or recognition of accreditation agencies examines the credibility of the national systems. Sooner than expected, internationalising is becoming a guideline in the reform of national legislation. Full transparency will become a new interpretation for the free movement of students, teachers and researchers, based on proven mutual trust.

b) Community Loyalty

Article 10 EC demands from the Member States that they take all "appropriate measures, whether general or particular, to ensure fulfillment of the obligations arising out of this Treaty or resulting from action taken by the institutions of the Community", and that they at the same time shall "abstain from any measure which could jeopardize the attainment of the objectives of this Treaty". This negatively and positively formulated prescription fulfils the obligation towards cooperation in good faith that is the responsibility of the Member States in their relation with the Community and in their mutual relationships[29]. This principle obliges the Member States e.g. to assess whether the diploma of the EC national is the equivalent of the domestic diploma[30].

c) Convergence leads to Mobility

'Convergence' – i.e. focusing on a shared frame of reference is becoming a reality for European higher education and not just because of the Union's '*supporting, coordinating or supplementary actions*' and the '*Declarations*' or '*Agreements*' in this field. The integration of the labour market and professional training and lifelong learning systems are also a contributing factor. The hope is that increased workers' mobility, and, as a result, an increasing mobility of parents, will have a 'mobilising' effect. Another form of convergence relates to the institutions. The associations between universities and colleges, e.g. in Flanders, play a decisive role in the so-called 'academisation' of trainings (i.e. making non-university programmes consequently 'academic' in nature).

d) Harmonisation

The prohibition of harmonisation is valid only insofar as the action of the Community is based exclusively on articles 149 and 150 EC Treaty, not in the case where the community action rests on different provisions. The obligation to take into account the "community *acquis*" implies that harmonisation measures based on other treaty provisions remain possible. This paper argues that harmonisation does not mean '*unification*'.

e) The Subsidiarity Principle

The principle is being formulated as follows: "In areas which do not fall within its exclusive competence, the Community shall take action, in accordance with the principle of subsidiarity, only if and in so far as the objectives of the proposed action cannot be sufficiently achieved by the Member States and can therefore, by reason of the scale or effects of the proposed action, be better achieved by the Community" (art. 3B ECT). In reality, the spill-over effect of the considerable Community influence meant a centralisation of competences. As the Community Institutions (and specifically the European Commission) were granted a facilitating role in the *Bologna process*, albeit reluctantly, the distinction between the *Bologna* process and the general competences granted to the Community under article 149 of the EC Treaty is fading. It is possible that, as a result of both mechanisms, legally speaking there is an 'open coordination', but that it does not appear anymore from the *de facto* situation. It should not be concluded that this is inevitably in conflict with the subsidiarity principle and with the exclusion of harmonisation, as mentioned in article 149 of the EC Treaty. In our opinion, the convergence between the *Bologna* process and the competences granted to the Community under the EC Treaty leads to a (legal) balancing exercise on the tight-rope[31].

f) Soft Law?

The Bologna process is considered as the perfect example of soft law. The use of the term 'soft' could be questioned. '*Mobility*' and '*recognition*' – two major EU-principles in education law – are used as the dominant techniques shaping the Wider Europe, – the Founding Fathers of the original EC Treaty could just dream of. The process can be interpreted as of a *para*-law rank, with a *quasi*-binding effect. The Bologna process already appears to belong to the *acquis communautaire* and if there is no strict need for EU legislation, there are other ways to enforce soft law. 'No legally binding force' does not equal 'no legal effect at all'. The technique debates the traditional (*top down* and *supranational*) EU-method and explores to what extent new forms of European governance (*intergovernmental* and *non-governmental*) can be promoted. It seems an alternative to the formal adaptation of the EC Treaty, aimed at more effectiveness of transparent community action. It contributes to the enlargement of the Union. New members may accede, simply by agreement of existing members. But no procedure is foreseen for ejecting members who do not succeed in their (voluntary engaged) commitment.

g) The Open Method of Coordination?

The Lisbon strategy introduces a philosophy of governance that is new for *education* policy. As before, the Union used this method for the Member States' social policy, specifically concerning employment policy and retirement issues. The method contains anyway an important drawback, as policy-measures depend on the goodwill of national governments and a common education area remains largely hypothetical or even haphazard when a party chooses to opt out. The 'Europe moving at different speeds' is becoming more of a reality and also a Europe of mobile students and scientist, of 'citizens' if you will.

THE APPLICATION OF EUROPEAN LAW IN HIGHER EDUCATION (EU)

The Application of Competition Law?

1) In General

11. - *"Are schools commercial undertakings?"* In the sense of European or national competition law, education institutions that provide a service that complies with *compulsory* education are not treated as a commercial undertaking, even though they are engaged in competition and advertising, and to an extent follow a business logic. Case law of the ECJ shows that what is used as a criterion is the fact that schools are given little room to manage their income, content, educational performance, administration and organisation of services. They have no 'own interest'.

But government cannot simply provide every possible public service, even if it wanted to, neither can it meet all *higher* education needs. The requirement of diversification is fulfilled by external pluralism. There is no reason to assume that the application of competition law to education will remain taboo.

Is a liberalisation of education conceivable, just like in other sectors where, until recently, the State enjoyed a monopoly (like the public transport system, electricity)? Higher education institutions, as competing service providers whereby the performance required is laid down by contract? The question may even be asked whether a progressive liberalisation could perhaps not contribute to the general well-being by better satisfying the need for diversification of the educational offering, obviously with quality control. This is more meaningful, perhaps, than a collection of restrictions that may or may not be necessary for the goal envisaged, namely compulsory education.

There is no natural legal incompatibility between compulsory and non-compulsory education and liberalisation of education. After all, every legal system may contain stipulations that provide for a corrective system of solidarity with less affluent families.

12. - At the time the Treaty establishing the EC was adopted, policy fields which were supposed to be in the public interest, like public health, social security, culture, youth policy and education were supposed to belong completely to the jurisdiction of the Member States. They were not supposed to be affected by the provisions of the Treaty, such as the provisions concerning the internal market and European Competition law.

The anxiety in the Member States for too much influence of the internal market led to several articles in the *Treaty of Maastricht* and *Amsterdam*, meant to safeguard these policy fields against harmonisation on the legal basis for regulating the internal market. Even though the Member States still have some room for regulatory measures in these fields, it became clear that European competition law applies and imposes its limits.

Since the abovementioned fields not just belong to the jurisdiction of the Member State but are also supposed to be government influenced if not regulated, the question arises whether the same applies to education. Of the policy fields mentioned above, the ECJ always acknowledged the jurisdiction of the Member States. In the field of education, the Court went one step further by actually naming it as a typical government activity.[32]

If European law (competition law) is applicable, it takes precedence over every statutory exception the member attempts to make.

2) Positive European Norms on the Provisions of Competition Law

13. - The EC Treaty, just like many of its national competition counterparts, basically prohibits undertakings *to form a cartel* (art. 81 ECT) and concerns abuse of a *dominant position* (art. 82 ECT).[33]

Many undertakings achieve a dominant position by actually providing for a service which belongs to the public interest. For these specific undertakings article 86 EC provides an exception in the sense that competition law is only applicable to these undertakings as long as it does not hinder the exercising of the service in the public interest. The service in the public interest itself is, therefore, exempt from the application of competition law.

What has all this to do with educational institutions? The concept of enterprise in community law is a broad one.[34] An enterprise is defined as every entity which occupies itself with an economic activity. Economic activities are those activities from which profit might be derived. It does not matter whether the entity actually makes a profit, which legal status it has or whether it is an enterprise in the strict sense of the word. This means that parts of the government may be characterised as enterprise in the sense of the EC Treaty, in case they occupy themselves with a economic activity.[35] Only in specific cases the entities concerned are not covered by the provisions concerning competition. According to the Court, an entity which operates in a statutory system of social security under strict supervision of the state, without discretionary freedoms and is not allowed to make a profit, will not be regarded as an enterprise.[36]

With such a broad concept of undertaking, it is not exactly predictable that educational institutions which compete will be exempt from the application of these provisions.[37]

For Member States it is prohibited to give state-aid. According to article 87 EC Member States are not allowed to provide undertakings with financial support, unless the Treaty itself allows the support, or the Commission declares the support conforming to the EC Treaty.

Secondly the articles 3g, 10, and 81 and 82 EC do not allow the Member States to legalise, support or strengthen behaviour of undertakings, which in itself would violate the articles 81 or 82 of the Treaty. The prohibition derived from the combination of these three provisions means that the Member State is not allowed, for example, to sanction in a statutory provision entrepreneurial behaviour which in itself would be a cartel or an abuse of dominant position. Such laws violate the Treaty and are eligible to be challenged in court.[38] Only measures limiting competition taken by the Member State without any involvement of the undertakings concerned will survive this prohibition.[39]

3) Applicability of Competition Law to Higher Education Institutions

14. - The acceptance of education as belonging to the public interest allowed Member States to regard educational institutions to be free of the influence of competition law. If competition between educational institutions only concerns competition for students, because higher numbers of students will result in more government funding, the provisions regarding competition in the Treaty most probably will not apply. In that case the competition between the institutions is only used as a means to allocate government funds.

This may be different, however, once educational institutions are entering competition with commercial educational institutions operating on the market. Once government-funded educational institutions start selling courses or 'modules' at market prices to students or other interested parties, they are actually a commercial activity. Consequently there would be no reason not to apply competition law to them. Obviously, in between these two extremes is a large grey area. To decide whether competition law is applicable must be done on a *case by case* basis.

In many European countries educational entities provide for education on a commercial basis. Obviously these entities must be regarded as undertakings within the scope of the EC Treaty. Sometimes the Member State even acknowledges the diplomas these institutions may provide as equal to the diplomas provided for by state-funded or otherwise acknowledged national educational institutions. In that case such a commercial institution may eventually be seen as an enterprise providing for a activity in the public interest and be protected by the exception of article 86 EC.

If government-funded educational institutions enter the market of commercial education, it is only fair to apply competition law to their activities. Otherwise these institutions might have enormous advantages over the commercial entities. Without applicability of competition law, government-funded institutions have the opportunity to cross-subsidise their commercial activities with government funds by allocating lecturers and professors who are paid with government money to their commercial courses. Moreover, without applicability such institutions would be able to combine forces in an educational cartel offering a much more extensive list of courses which basically might drive commercial institutions off the market. Under article 81 EC such competition-limiting behaviour is prohibited.

If a government-funded university wants e.g. to start a commercial business school which competes on a regular basis with other commercial business schools, it may find itself to be an undertaking in the sense of community law, but could be characterised as an undertaking with an activity in the public interest in the sense of article 86 EC This means that competition law will only apply to the activity of public interest (the regular educational courses) as far as it does not hinder the exercising of this task. Under community law the entity as a whole will be seen as such an undertaking.[40] Contrary to national law, there is no splitting off of the commercial activity from the government activity.

Any subsidies to the entity must be regarded as state-aid. State-aid is, as we have seen, prohibited under article 87 EC and has to be notified to the European Commission. This also applies to funds provided to an undertaking in the sense of article 86 EC, supplied to finance the service of public interest. Such aid is usually declared in conformity with the EC Treaty, if the funds do not exceed the amount of money needed for the exercising of the service of public interest[41]. This means that the extent of the service itself is not determined exclusively by the Member State anymore[42].

The article 86 EC-status ensures that universities mostly will be able to cooperate with regard to their regular activities and also maintain their networks throughout Europe. But e.g. for the business schools, cooperational activities may be suspect and not always in conformity with community law.

15. - What applies to educational courses also applies to research. If universities allow research institutes to compete extensively with commercial research bodies, the universities may become undertakings in the process.

It is arguable that universities, on which the duty of doing research in the public interest is imposed, may subsidise their fundamental (government-funded) research with the income earned by doing commercial research. As long as the commercial research only forms a small part of the sum of activities of the university as a whole (including education), which still is the case[43], the doctrine of broadening the activity of public interest may have as its consequence that universities are not characterised as an undertaking.

But the ECJ allowed the Member States to broaden the scope of the exclusively assigned public services in the sense that these may encompass certain commercially attractive activities, when this is considered necessary to maintain a healthy entrepreneurial balance. So if these commercial activities aim to compensate for the disadvantages the execution of a service of public interest brings with it, the scope of the public service may be extended.[44]

Non-Discrimination Principle

16. - Central element of the internal market in general and the free movement of persons in particular, is the principle of *non-discrimination.*

The jurisdiction pertains in particular to discrimination during admission of students to a vocational education program in a Member State of which they do not possess citizenship. Such students have the right to admission under the same conditions as those that apply to national applicants. Recent case law declares that holders of secondary diplomas awarded in other Member States can gain access to higher and university education under the same conditions as holders of secondary education diplomas awarded in the Member State.[45]

Implementing article 39 of the Treaty, a higher education institution is not entitled to refuse a position to an EU national applicant on ground only of nationality. There is an exception for employees in the public service but the ECJ has not allowed the institutions to rely on that provision to avoid the rules where no issue of public security arises.[46]

The question on discrimination on the basis of nationality or as legitimate test of eligibility for employment will still be at the agenda for national legislators and the higher education institutions themselves.

Higher Education and the Free Movement of Persons and Services

17. *Can university education be qualified as a service in the sense of article 50 EC?* The ECJ has excluded from the definition of services within the meaning of article 50 EC courses offered by certain establishments forming part of a system of public education and financed, entirely or mainly, by public funds.[47] By establishing and maintaining such a system of public education, financed as a general rule by the public budget and not by pupils or their parents, the State did not intend to involve itself in remunerated activities, but was carrying out its task in the social, cultural and educational fields towards its population.[48]

However, the Court has held that courses given by educational establishments essentially financed by private funds, notably by students and their parents, constitute 'services' within the meaning of article 50 EC, since the aim of those establishments is to offer a service for remuneration.[49] It should be noted here that it is not necessary for private financing to be provided principally by the pupils or their parents. According to consistent case law, Article 50 EC does not require that the service be paid for by those for whom it is performed.[50]

In a recent case, the Court however has held that a teaching activity carried out by a taxpayer of one Member State for a legal person established under public law, in the present case a university, situated in another Member State comes within the scope of Article 49 EC, even if it is carried out on a secondary basis and in a quasi-honorary capacity.[51] This implies that the State has to keep on carrying the largest part of the costs of education in order to maintain education outside the regime of services of the EC.

But one has to keep in mind that the amount of tuition fees for education financing recently has grown and that universities are now behaving more competitive and market-directed.[52] A complicating factor is the fact that the EC is a member of the WTO on behalf of the Member States concerning the common policy. In 1995 the EC has taken on behalf of the member states the obligation to open the market for private-financed basic, extended and higher education and vocational training.[53] According to the recent Lisbon Convention of December 17th 2007, no unanimity is needed any more before starting the WTO negotiations.

18. - The free movement of persons, one of the key elements of the internal market of the EC, consists of two groups: the free movement of workers (Art. 39 ff EC) and the freedom of establishment (Art. 43 ff EC). In surprisingly expanding ways these touch upon education law: European legislation and case law in this field have definitely moved into education issues stipulating that both the free movement of workers and the freedom of establishment can be achieved by means of diploma recognition[54]. Close links exist between freedom of movement for workers, employment and vocational training, particularly where the latter aims at putting workers in a position to take up offers of employment from other regions of the Community; such links make it necessary that the problems arising in this connection should no longer be studied in isolation but viewed as inter-dependent.[55]

Articles 39 and 43 of the European Treaty are relevant to the *rights of entry and residence* within the Member States of academics and students who are European Economic Area (EEA) nationals and the families of EEA nationals whatever their nationality. The legal European framework Directives and Regulations provides for free movement for workers, the self-employed, providers and recipients of services, students, and members of the families of any of these categories. EEA students have the right to enter and remain in order to pursue their studies. Both employees and students can be accompanied or joined by their families. The position is governed by the Immigration (EEA) Order[56] which provides that an EEA national shall be admitted on production of either a valid national identity card or passport issued by an EEA state.

Directive 93/96 used to rule the position of *students*. Students could potentially be qualified as a worker; it did not matter that the employment might be part-time or that the pay might be at a level which attracts family credit, so long as the employment was 'effective and genuine'. If the student could not fall within the definition of a worker, self-employed person, or provider or recipient of services, then to obtain a residence permit as a qualified person the student would need to be studying full-time on a vocational course, be covered by comprehensive sickness insurance, and declare ability to self-support without recourse to public funds.

From the *Directive 2004/38* on amending directive 93/96 all union citizens have the right of residence on the territory of another Member State for a period of longer than three months if they are students. They should be enrolled at a private or public establishment, accredited or financed by the host Member State on the basis of its legislation or administrative practice, for the principal purpose of following a course of study, including vocational training. The financial independence of directive 93/96 remains.[57]

A striking fact is that students were not the aim of the internal market, but workers were.[58] But all non-economically active persons gained additional rights through secondary European legislation: relatives of workers, retired persons, and students in their role of future workers.[59] In this way, several measures were taken which affected education while not being aimed at doing so. In the meantime, the role of the European Union concerning education was laid down in the EC Treaty in Art. 149 EC Treaty through the Treaty of Maastricht[60] as being subsidiary and supporting. This development occurred side by side with the development concerning the free movement of students as a form of free movement of persons.

In the *Bernini*[61] case, the Court decided and confirmed that the student grant awarded by a Member State to the children of workers forms a *social benefit* for a migrant worker in the sense of Article 7, paragraph 2, of Regulation 1612/68, when the worker continues to provide for the support of his child. Under such circumstances, the student can call upon Article 7, paragraph 2, to obtain a student grant under the same conditions as those which apply to children of national workers, and in particular *without that a further condition as to his residence* can be set.

19. - *Study grants*, however, is a policy area which has a strong link with a national financial system, like health insurance. This is the main reason why there is no EU legislation concerning harmonization of study grants of any kind.

The Court held in *Lair and Brown* (paragraphs 15 and 18 respectively) still that "at the present stage of development of Community law assistance given to students for maintenance and for training falls in principle outside the scope of the EEC Treaty for the purposes of Article 7 thereof [later Article 6 of the EC Treaty, now, after amendment, Art. 12 EC]". In those judgments, the Court considered that such assistance was, on the one hand, a matter of education policy, which was not as such included in the spheres entrusted to the Community institutions, and, on the other, a matter of social policy, which fell within the competence of the Member States so far as it was not covered by specific provisions of the EC Treaty.[62]

Thus, in addition to the supporting measures to the free movement of students, the free movement of persons has had a direct impact on study financing.

In the *Meeusen case*,[63] for instance, the Court of Justice ruled that the fact that the mother of a Belgian student worked for a few hours a week in another Member State, the Netherlands, led to a right for the daughter to student financial support in the Netherlands. This was constructed through a reference to the free movement of persons: because the mother had always paid taxes in the Netherlands, she had obtained a right to social benefits, including student financial support for her children. There was no residency requirement for the daughter attached to this right to student financial support.

Several Member States have announced that they are re-considering the limitations to residency requirements for study grants as stated above, an important principle of the EC education policy is comprised in the theme of the liberalisation of the internal market. Thus, the particular competences are grafted onto the so-called four liberties, namely the free movement of goods, persons (workers and establishment), services, and capital. As mentioned above, this path has been challenged by the Court in favour of the emphasis on the *citizen.*

In education matters, it is especially the free movement of persons which is important. More particularly, the migrating worker or self-employed person has the right to follow educational courses under the same conditions as a national subject. *Recent case law* ruled that art. 17 and 18 EC precludes a condition in accordance with which, in order to obtain an education or training grant for studies in a Member State other than of which the students applying for such assistance are nationals, those studies must be a continuation of education or training pursued for at least one year in the Member State of origin of those students.[64]

The mobility of third-country national students was regulated in a special directive[65] and agreement has been reached in the Council on another directive aiming at the liberalisation of the mobility of researchers[66]. Both directives are supposed to contribute to the Lisbon targets by attracting high quality researchers and students to the European research and educational space.

20. - According to article 43 EC, restrictions on the freedom of establishment must be lifted. Following article 44 sub 1 EC, the Council, acting in accordance with the procedure referred to in Article 251 and after consulting the Economic and Social Committee, shall act by means of directives.

What the freedom of establishment means for education law has become apparent in a series of cases concerning diploma recognition for lawyers.

Lawyers form a special category in the case law of the Court of Justice because legal studies are by nature bound to a Member State; a lawyer knows his own national system, hardly ever a different national legal system. This has made it difficult to create a system of diploma recognition for lawyers. In the *Vlassopoulou case,*[67] a Greek lawyer with many years of work experience in Germany, wished to start her own office in Germany. She was refused by the German bar because she did not have a German law degree. The Court of Justice decided that this was discrimination on the basis of nationality and that Ms Vlassopoulou had to be given the opportunity to prove that she possessed adequate knowledge of German law.

Many Member States have created such a possibility for foreign lawyers by having special tests. However, Ms *Morgenbesser* was not allowed to take such a test in Italy.[68] She had a French law degree, and had immediately started working at an Italian law firm. She did not take the French bar exam but had finished her legal education at the university. The Court of Justice ruled that such a view by

Italy was not allowed either because it blocked Ms Morgenbesser's rights as an EU citizen.

Recent case law shows that art. 18 EC which lays down generally the right for every citizen of the Union to move and reside freely within the territory of the Member States, finds specific expression in the provisions guaranteeing the freedom to provide services. Art. 18 EC precludes legislation which allows taxpayers to claim as special expenses conferring a right to a reduction in income tax the payment of school fees to certain private schools established in national territory, but generally excludes that possibility in relation to school fees paid to a private school established in another Member State.[69]

After working with the sectoral system and the three general systems for a number of years, a first step towards consolidation has been taken by the Directive 2001/19/EC and a second, larger step, has been taken with the adoption and implementation of Directive 2005/36/EC on the recognition of professional qualifications which had to be implemented by the Member States until October 2007. This directive replaced fifteen existing directives in the field of recognition of professional qualifications[70].

The recognition of professional qualifications and diploma recognition in the European Union is another expression of the freedom of establishment in education law.

In recent communications[71], the Commission already considered the compatibility and transparency of the educational systems insofar as qualifications have to be recognised. None of recent policy papers, communications and Council conclusions address clearly the inter-linkage between professional recognition and academic recognition as well as the consequences for professional mobility and labour migration based on the existing treaty provisions, secondary legislation as well as case law of the Court of Justice.

Developments related to the mobility principle and the internal market concept seem not to have reciprocal influence on actions taken by the Community institutions in the field of education. Case law of the Court of Justice nevertheless will be of direct influence on the development of a European Area of Higher Education[72].

Another sphere of strong reciprocal influence with the Bologna process will be the Council of Europe/UNESCO Conventions covering academic recognition in Europe.

On 11 April 1997 the *Lisbon Convention* was adopted and entered into force on 1 February 1999 as the main instrument for the recognition of diplomas in Europe. Most Member States of the European Union have ratified this Convention during the last five years. The general principle is that foreign diplomas must be recognised unless there are substantial differences. This applies for applications of recognition concerning the entrance into higher education, study periods and final degrees. The charge of proof of these substantial differences lies with the evaluation body.

It is considered to be a key instrument for the Bologna Process aiming to establish a European Higher Education Area by 2010, the main goals of which include improving mobility of students, staff and graduates, facilitating the recognition of qualifications and increasing the transparency of higher education systems in Europe.

European Union Citizenship

21. - In the Treaty of Maastricht, a "European citizenship" was established[73]; still a vague concept but refined by the ECJ expanding the discrimination ban to receivers and *potential* receivers of services and thus to all EU (economically non-active) citizens[74].

The Maastricht Treaty however did not go that far. Article 18 EC determines that "every citizen of the Union shall have the right to move and reside freely within the territory of the Member States, subject to the limitations and conditions laid down in this Treaty and by the measures adopted to give it effect"[75], but the proportionality principle must be respected[76].

The implementation of the education sector within the concept of European Union Citizenship should be seen as a privileged opportunity for Member States.

LEGISLATION AS A TOOL FOR GOVERNMENT CONTROL IN HIGHER EDUCATION?

22. - The 'juridification' and *judicialisation* of higher education should not necessarily be seen in a negative light. After all, the articulation of the legal norm not only defines rights, freedoms and responsibilities, but it also serves a more dynamic higher education policy. The traditionally conservative reflexes of the academic corps and institutions often compel political decision-makers to think proactively. To an extent, *regulation* is indicative of an '*enterprising government*' that will not be held back by the, to some extent slowly evolving, viewpoints within the academic corps.

Yet the exponential growth in legal rules and, in consequence of the statutory powers of the institutional authorities, the equally noticeable proliferation in self-regulation compromises the democratic *involvement*, the *manageability*, as well as the *implementability* and *controllability* of regulation at *macro*, *meso* and *micro* level.

We are, it would appear, confronted not so much with a 'talking' or 'negotiating State'[77] as with a '*codifying and modifying State*'. The evidence from the past decade would also seem to confirm that education legislation is amongst the least accessible regulatory frameworks in the country's housekeeping.

There are strong indications that regulations governing universities will continue to evolve towards an imbalance between an initially detached lawmaker and government on the one hand and the so-called autonomy of the universities on the other. Under the explicit banner of deregulation and administrative autonomy, competency in a wide range of areas has been left to the institutional authorities. It was apparently the legislator's intention for the institutional authorities henceforth to be able to regulate at their own discretion in core decision areas. Solemn statements regarding the relatedness of institutional autonomy and greater restraint in government regulation are reaffirmed on a regular basis. To restrict government control to the main outlines fits into the evolution from '*government*' to '(*good*) *governance*' which is manifesting itself across Europe. It is linked with the notion of delegation to the most functional level and the simplification of regulation (regulatory management). 'Good governance' also aims to replace one-sided, imperative government prescriptions with clear agreements, and it is based on reciprocity, voluntarism and flexibility.

Increasingly, however, the question arises whether the legislator has since committed to continuing to couple *responsibilization* of the institutions with the intention of broadening the autonomy of the universities. Or has the pendulum perhaps swung the other way and have the contours of the autonomous space that is to be safeguarded consequently shrunk? Certainly at a moment when the uniformity/convergence in regulation seems almost complete for all universities – irrespective of the legal status of the organising authority, the notion of *normative autonomy*[78] assumes an even greater urgency.

Hence, the question is whether the "*amended regulation that is to be re-amended*" will jeopardise adherence to the principles of care and transparency in governance, as well as the continuity and quality of internal policy-making. Democratic decision-making presupposes the accessibility and *implementability* of regulations for all users of and sections within the universities. This principle should always be a concern for the regulator[79] and draft legislation should invariably be tested against it. With every new legislative initiative, one must therefore consider whether it might not increase rather than reduce the regulatory and administrative obligations of the institutions.

If new regulation will demonstrably worsen the *planning burden* – or, if you will, the degree of 'bureaucratisation'[80] – then the regulator must question its necessity and efficacy, in accordance with the principles of good legislation.

But there is more. When looking at ways of reducing the legislative *corpus*, invariably questions arise with regard to the regulatory role of government in higher education, as well as the future profile of the administrative authority and its toolset. Apparently, then, regulation encompasses aspects of both the *state supervision* and the *state control model*[81]. The questions arise which competencies the State should never shed and how the regulator should translate this into practical terms.[82] The accelerated developments in education and the consequences of internationalisation for institutions of higher education require an up-to-date answer.

23. - Overregulation and discontinuity in the legislative technique in relation to higher education has been rife in some countries. There was more at stake than merely a '*re-regulation operation*'. Such a legislative process does not (necessarily) correspond with the rules of good lawmaking, and in particular the principles of *efficiency*, *necessity*, and *transparency* of regulation. To this, one may quite justifiably add the requirements of *clarity*, *coherence* and *implementability*; indeed, quite an illustration of the adage '*patere legem quam ipse fecisti*' for new regulations.

There are other criteria of quality legislation that need to be respected in modern regulatory technique, including those of *efficiency* and *effectiveness*. The classic authors on legislative technique always used to emphasise the primacy of 'accuracy, correctness and accessibility', followed closely by the principles of legal security and trust, which conflicts with the practice of frequently changing the legal norm. Although any 'simplification of the legal rule' should concern quality rather than quantity, restricting the extension of a legal norm may contribute directly to its 'implementability' or 'sustainability', as well its (internal and external) controllability.

It seems as relevant as ever to recall that the approval of a decree as such does not 'steer society': "The choice for law as a tool is not rarely based on overstrained expectations of what laws and the authorities can achieve. The political ambitions are great; the possibilities for government to induce behavioural change are however quite limited."[83]

Are universities and other institutions of higher education not moving from a regime where "anything goes if sufficiently motivated" to a situation where "nothing goes unless permitted by law"? It would seem to make sense to consider a *screening* of prevailing regulation from the perspective of its capacity to increase the autonomy of the institutional administrations – albeit within the confines of a correct interpretation of the legality principle. This is also the basic premise of a new movement in favour of the deregulation process that is proposed in relation to educational legislation[84]: deregulation proposals should be tested for the extent to which they enhance autonomy and keep intact the core business of government[85].

At the same time, the Dutch Educational Council, in one of its studies, insists on research into the 'policy utilisation and effect' of (de)regulation: *"There have, in recent years, been few targeted studies into the effects of deregulation, and those that do exist often do not consider such effects on the basis of the criteria of quality, accessibility, efficacy, freedom of choice and social cohesion"*. Specifically in relation to higher education, the Educational Council observes 'contrary developments' between 'self-direction towards strategic behaviour' and 'adherence to agreements at the level of the entire sector'.[86]

The question has arisen of whether 'the primacy of the legislator' in educational affairs is intact if the regulator relinquishes so much normative competency to other bodies. To what extent does the government's resignation of power give rise to a *democratic deficit*? This question has previously surfaced in relation to the original and now broadly interpreted competencies of the Dutch–Flemish accreditation organisation or NVAO[87]. Its array of competencies apparently stretches beyond the *Visitation Protocols* – an aspect of self-regulation on the part of the Flemish Interuniversity Council (VLIR) and the Association of Universities in the Netherlands (VNSU).

In a democratic state, the legislative power does not necessarily have a regulatory monopoly. However, delegated regulation should in any case adhere not only to the constitutional legality principle, but also to prevailing legal requirements, including those of democratic decision-making[88] and enhanced public control. Would it therefore not be desirable to scrutinise whether the *evaluation/assessment/ accreditation/registration/recognition/licence/planning and other* mechanisms that have been laid down by law are actually in keeping with such fundamental democratic principles?

To conclude: the *legality principle*, as the cornerstone of legal equality and security, requires that government action should rest on a statutory basis. Other stakeholders in the field may also be expected to adhere to this principle.

24. - A sustainable law only regulates where necessary to safeguard public interests. The review of higher education legislation may take a three-track approach: a *legal–technical* simplification, i.e. "simple, clear and fewer laws"; an alleviation of the *administrative* burden; and/or the development of a methodology for prior assessment of the likely effects of legislation, i.e. a system of *"regulatory impact analysis"*.

The foundation of a proper regulatory framework for higher education comprises, among other things, the outlining of principles of good legislation, a set of assessment tools and methods, and the processing of the various levels of lawmaking: *inventorying, consolidation, coordination,* and *codification.* The greatest potential for simplification lies in the actual codification.

As far as 'university regulation' is concerned, *codification* would also appear to be the priority; 'codification', that is, in the sense of a coherent and systematic re-organisation or review of general and abstract rules[89], with a view to resolving the prevailing unfamiliarity of the law. Codification must, in this instance, encompass the possibility of *modification*, including through deregulation and the 'responsibilisation' of institutional authorities: changes in legislation and regulation are necessary in order to allow for a better through-flow, demand orientation and greater diversity.

It would appear that the call for a more transparent regulation of administrative relationships on the basis of the broadest possible concept of autonomy and flexibility for institutions in the organisation of the educational process is also relevant to other areas. An experimental space for certain elements merits a legal foundation. The regulator, too, ought to permit himself some flexibility. New control tools might be considered and the *'contractualisation'*[90] of (the organisation and provision of) university education and research policy has various precedents. The 'new Legal Order' led to the introduction of instruments of private law and contract-like institutions/students, institutions/staff, institutions/State, intra institutional relations and management contracts. Universities must be adequately equipped to function competitively in the transitional space between market and government. The economic dimension of higher education requires structural adjustments[91].

'Deregulation' does not stand in the way of 'government control'. It does however require choices in relation to the limitations that government may set for itself and the obligations which it may impose on the institutions. After all, one of the most forceful arguments in current legislative doctrine is that *evaluation of legislation* as a tool for enhancing the quality of the law can no longer be ignored. It is a fundamental characteristic of democracy that it entails the possibility of self-correction, through an openness to debate, the revocability of decisions and the precarious nature of the positions of power.

This applies all the more strongly during the phases of coordination, codification and modification. Even more relevant than Montesquieu's claim that "one should not touch the law but with trembling hands" is the adage that any first rule of law must be written with huge circumspection. In higher education, it appears, 'legality' often overtakes 'reality'.

NOTES

[1] E.g. SCOTT P., Back to the Future? The Evolution of Higher Education Systems, in KEHM, B.M. (Ed.), *Looking Back to Look Forward. Analyses of Higher Education after the Turn of the Millennium*, Kassel: INCHER, 2007 p. 24–25.

[2] SCOTT P., Unified and Binary Systems of Higher Education in Europe, in BURGEN A. (ed.), *Goals and Purposes of Higher Education in the 21st Century, Higher Education Policy Series 32*, London, 1996, p. 49.

[3] *The European Grouping of Territorial Cooperation-EGTC*, European Union, Committee of the Regions, 2007, p. 18. DE GROOF J., HENDRIKS Fr., Accreditatie in het hoger onderwijs in Vlaanderen en Nederland, *Tijdschrift voor Onderwijsrecht en Onderwijsbeleid*, 2005–2006, nr. 4–5, p. 247–356.

[4] Namely, the involvement of the judiciary in higher education issues.

[5] TROW M., The 'public' and 'private' lives of academia, *Daedalus*, 1978, vol. 2, pp. 113–127.

[6] MOUWEN C.A.M., VAN BIJSTERVELD S.C., *De Hybride Universiteit: Het Onverenigbare verenigd? De Integratie van taak en Markt in de Universiteit van de Toekomst*, The Hague: Elsevier, 2000; See also PROSSER T., Regulation, Markets and Legitimacy, in JOWELL J. and OLIVER D., (eds.), *The Changing Constitution*, 4th Edition, Oxford: O.U.P., 2000, p. 229–257.

[7] HARRIS N., *Education, Law and Diversity*, Oxford: Hart Publishing, 2007, p. 31–32.

[8] See DE GROOF J., JANSEN J., *The 21st Century Dean. A Manual for Effective Management and Authentic Leadership*, Pretoria University Press, 2003.

[9] Activities of the European Union Summaries of Legislation, Education and training: general framework, lifelong learning, Modernising Universities.

[10] RIPERT G., *Les forces créatrices du droit*, Paris, 1955, p. 133.

[11] Comp. with. "We know surprisingly little about the law's effect upon higher education, but virtually no one in the enterprise is untouched by statutes, regulations, case law, or institutional rules promulgated to implement legal regimes.", OLIVAS M., The Legal Environment. The Implementation of Legal Changes on Campus, in ALTBACH P., BERDAHL R. and GUMPORT P. (eds.), *American Higher Education in the Twenty-First Century. Social, Political, and Economic Challenges*, 2nd Edition, Baltimore: John Hopkins University Press, 2005, p. 226.

[12] See e.g. our *De Universitaire Regelgeving – Coördinatie en Annotatie*, Nijmegen: Legal Wolf Publishers, 2005, 1170 p and *De Hogeschoolregelgeving – Coördinatie en Annotatie*, Nijmegen, 2007, 1019 p. with forthcoming supplements (2008) !; FARRINGTON, D.J. and PALFREYMAN, D., *The law of higher education*, Oxford University Press, 2006.

[13] First chapter ('Overview of Postsecondary Education Law'), in KAPLIN W.A. and LEE B.A., *The Law of Higher Education*, 1995, p. 1–75.

[14] WADE H.W.R., FORESYTH C.F., *Administrative Law*, 9th ed., 2004.

[15] DE GROOF, J. and LAUWERS, G., 'Improving the Regulatory Environment for the Implementation if the Right to Education', in *Onderwijs en onderwijsrecht in een pluriforme samenleving, opstellen aangeboden aan prof. mr. dr. D. Mentink*, Boom Juridische Uitgevers, 2008, 39–55.

[16] LENAERTS K., Subsidiarity and Community Competence in the Field of Education, in DE GROOF J. (Ed.), *Subsidiarity and Education. Aspects of comparative Educational Law*, Leuven, 1994, p. 117–144; DE WITTE B., Equivalentie van studieperiodes en erkenning van diploma's, *Tijdschrift voor Onderwijsrecht en Onderwijsbeleid*, 1992–1993, nr.5–6, p. 290.

[17] Cf. DE GROOF J. and LAUWERS G., *No Person Shall be Denied the Right to Education*, Nijmegen, Wolf Legal Publishers, 2004.

[18] cf. art. 9, 3 Part III Draft Treaty establishing a Constitution for Europe.

[19] *PbEG* 2007, C 306.

[20] Cfr. GLENN Ch., DE GROOF J., *Balancing Freedom, Autonomy and Accountability in Education*, Nijmegen: Wolf Legal Publishers, 2005, 3 vol.; DE GROOF J., *La Révision Constitutionnelle de 1988 et l'Enseignement. La Paix Scolaire et son Application*, Bruxelles, Cepess, 1989.

[21] See e.g. the '*Lamassoure report*', in the *Committee on Constitutional Affairs* (*European Parliament*), preparing the European Union's *Charter of Fundamental Rights*, signed as a political declaration (December 2000) in preparation of the *Convention*.

[22] In its first judgement on the principle dated 23 July 1968, Series A no 32.

[23] See also BERKA W., 'Human Rights: A Challenge to Educational Law: A Survey within the Systems of the European Convention on Human Rights', in DE GROOF J., MALHERBE R. (eds.), *Human Rights in South African Education*, 1997, p 199 et seq; MENTINK D. and GOUDAPPEL F., The Education Provision in the Charter of Fundamental Rights of the European Union: a Bleak Perspective, in *European Journal for Education Law and Policy*, vol. 4, nr. 2, 2000, p. 145–148; BERKA W., The Right to Education in the Charter of Fundamental Rights in the European Union, in *European Journal for Education Law and Policy*, vol. 5, nr. 1, 2001.

[24] Dated 7 February 1992 'concerning the European Union'.

[25] Compare with USA: LENAERTS K., 'Fundamental Rights in the European Union', *European Law Rev.*, 2000, 575.

[26] GLENN Ch., DE GROOF J., *op.cit.*, vol. I, p. 56.

[27] See the special issue of the *Tijdschrift voor Onderwijsrecht en Onderwijsbeleid* , 1993–1994, no 5–6. On Higher Education, see also 2005-2006, nr. 4–5 and 2007-2008, nr. 1–2.

[28] And not alone Art. 13, sections 1 and 3.

[29] KAPTYEN P. and VERLOREN VAN THEMAAT, *op.cit.* p. 97 and LENAERTS K., *op.cit.*, p. 514–522.

[30] See the judgment in *UNECTEF v Heylens* [1987] ECR 4097, paragraph 13; *Kraus* (1993) ECR I-1663.

[31] See also section 8.

[32] Case 147/86, *Commission vs Greece* (*Frontisteria's*), 1988 ECR 1637.

[33] An enterprise has a dominant position as soon as it is able to behave independently from it consumers ad its suppliers.

[34] Case C-41/90, *Höfner*, 1991 ECR I-1979.

[35] In case C-309/99, *Wouters vs Algemene Raad van de Nederlandse Orde van Advocaten*, 19 February 2002, 2002 ECR nyr a public body regulated in the Dutch Constitution was characterised as a association of entrepreneurs and its decisions are therefore covered by the article 81, 82 and 86 EC.

[36] Joined cases C-159 en C-160/91, (*Poucet en Pistre*), 1993 ECR I-637; case C-218/00, *INAIL*, 22 January 2002, 2002 ECR nyr.

[37] STEYGER E., Competition and Education, in DE GROOF J., LAUWERS G. and DONDELINGER G., *Globalisation and Competition in Education*, Nijmegen: Wolf Legal Publishers, 2003, p. 275–280.

[38] Case 267/86, *Van Eycke*, 1988, ECR 4769; case C-153/93, *Delta Schiffahrts- und Speditionsgesellschaft*, 1995 ECR I-2517; case C-96/94, *Centro Servizi Spediporto*, 1995, ECR I-2883; case C-35/96 *Commissie vs Italie*, 1999 ECR. I–135.

[39] Case C-2/91, *Meng*, 1993, ECR. I-5751; case C-185/91, *Reiff*, ECR 1993 ECR. I-5801; case C-245/91, *Ohra*, 1993 ECR I-5851.

[40] Case C-309/99, *Wouters vs Algemene Raad van de Nederlandse Orde van Advocaten*, 19 February 2002, 2002 ECR nyr.

[41] Case T-106/95, *FFSA*, 1997 ECR II-229: Case C-332/98, *CELF*, 2000 ECR I-04833; this case law is still developing, see C-53/00, *Ferring*, 2001, ECR I-9067 and the Conclusion of A-G Jacobs, 30 April 2002 in case C-126/01, *Ministre de l'économie, des finances et de l'industrie v GEMO SA*, pending.

[42] STEYGER E., *ibidem*.

[43] LAMBERT R. BUTLER N., *The Future of European Universities*, Centre for European Reform, London, 2006.

[44] Case C-320/91, *Corbeau*, 1993 ECR I-02533.

[45] *Commission of the European Communities/Republic of Finland v. Republic of Austria*, C-147/03, 7 July 2005.

[46] *Allue and Coonan v University of Venice*, Case C-33/88 [1989] ECR 1591; *Scholz v University of Cagliari*, Case C-419/92 [1994] ECR 1505.

[47] See to that effect *Humbel and Edel*, paragraphs 17 and 18 and *Wirth*, paragraphs 15 to 16.

[48] *Schwarz v. Finanzamt Bergisch Gladbach*, C-76/05, 11 September 2007.

[49] *Wirth*, paragraph 17.

[50] See, for example, Case 352/85 *Bond van Adverteerders and Others*, 1988, ECR 2085, par. 16; Joined cases C-51/96 and C-191/97 *Deliège*, 2000, ECR I-2549, par. 56; *Smits and Peerbooms*, par. 57; and *Sklandia and Ramstedt*, par. 24 in *Schwarz v. Finanzamt Bergisch Gladbach*, C-76/05, 11 September 2007.

[51] *Jundt v. Finanzamt Offenburg*, C-281/06, 18 December 2007, par.39.

[52] DAVIES G., "Welfare as a service", (2002) 29 (1) *Legal Issues of Economic Integration*, 27, 29.

[53] See http://tsdb.wto.org/wto/WTOHomepublic.htm.

[54] DE GROOF J., Overview of European Education Law, I and II, in *2000* and *2001 Yearbook of Education Law*, New York, 2001, 2002.

[55] 1968R1612-EN-30.04.2006 – 002.001-2 "Regulation (EEC) No 1612/68 of the Council of 15 October 1968 on freedom of movement for workers within the Community."

[56] Immigration (European Economic Area) Order 1994, SI 1994/1895, as amended by SI 1997/2981; also numerous Regulations of which the latest are the Immigration (European Economic Area) Regulations 2006, SI 2006/1003.

[57] Table of correspondence between directive 2004/38/EC and current EC legislation on free movement and residence of union citizens within the EU, p. 9.

[58] See Art. 39 EC for the basis of the free movement of workers.

[59] Council Directive 93/36/EEC of 29 October 1993 on the right of residence for students.

[60] 1992.

[61] Judgment of the Court of 26 February 1992, Case C-3/90, *Bernini* [1992] ECR p. I-1071.

[62] Bidar case, already mentioned.

[63] *Meeuwsen*, case C-337/97, 8 June 1999.

[64] *Rhiannon Morgan v. Bezirksregierung Köln / Iris Bucher v. Landrat des Kreises Düren*, C-11/06 and C-12/06, 23 October 2007.

[65] OJ 2004 L For the original proposal, see COM (2002) 548.

[66] Council docs. 14473/04, 18 November 2004 (agreed text of Directive) and 10388/04, 11 June 2004 (agreed text of Recommendation). For the original proposals, see COM (2004) 178.

[67] Judgment of the Court of 7 May 1991, Case C-340/89, *Vlassopoulou* [1991] ECR p. I-2357.

[68] Judgment of the Court of 13 November 2003, Case C-313/01, *Morgenbesser* [2003] ECR p. I-13467.

[69] *Schwarz v. Finanzamt Bergisch Gladbach*, C-76/05, 11 September 2007.

[70] The mechanism of recognition established by Directives 89/48/EEC and 92/51/EEC remains unchanged.

[71] "The role of universities in the Europe of knowledge", COM (2003) 58 final.

[72] "Great potential is found in the Vlassopoulou, Morgenbesser and Hocsman rulings and their application in future procedures before national authorities and courts. If the Bologna process will lead to an increasing mobility of students, shopping from one educational system to the other will become a normal professional qualification process" : SCHNEIDER, H. and CLAESSENS, S., "The recognition of Diploma's and the Free Movement of professionals in the European Union: Fifty years of Experiences" (working paper, 2008). See also SCHNEIDER, H., *Die Anerkennung von Diplomen in der Europäischen Gemeinschaft*, Antwerp, MAKLU, 1995.

[73] Now in Art. 17 EC.

[74] *Cowan*, Case 186/87 (1989) ECR-195, par. 17.

[75] See also Judgment of the Court of 17 September 2002, Case C-413/99, *Baumbast and R* [2002] ECR p. I-7091.

[76] *Valentina Neri v European School of Economics*, Case C-153/02, (2003) ECR I-13555.

[77] VAN HEFFEN O., MAASSEN P., VERHOEVEN J., et al., *Overheid, Hoger Onderwijs en Economie. Ontwikkelingen in Nederland en Vlaanderen*, Cheps, Utrecht, 1999, p. 163.

[78] Cfr. DE GROOF J., NEAVE G., SVEC J., *Democracy and Governance in Higher Education*, Kluwer Law International, The Hague, Council of Europe, 1998.

[79] See the studies by the Schoordijk Institute of the University of Tilburg – Centre for Legislative Studies, and, among others, GEELHOED L.A., Deregulering, Herregulering en Zelfregulering, in

EIJLANDER Ph., GILHUIS P.C., PETERS J.A.F., *Overheid en Zelfregulering,* Zwolle, 1993, p. 33 ff.; ZOONTJENS P., Naar een Wet Algemene Bepalingen Onderwijs?, in EIJLANDER Ph., et al., *Wetgeven en de Maat van de Tijd,* Zwolle, 1994, p. 191 ff.; EIJLANDER Ph., *De Wet Stellen,* Zwolle, 1993.

[80] See the finely nuanced considerations by the Audit Commission for Quality Care in Academic Education in Flanders, *Aandacht voor Kwaliteit in de Vlaamse Universiteiten,* Brussels, 1998, p. 47.

[81] See for example MAASEN P.A.M., *Governmental Steering and the Academic Culture,* Cheps, 1996, p. 69 ff.; DE GROOF J., NEAVE G., SVEC J., *ibidem.* Compare also with the reflections of VAN HEFFEN O., VERHOEVEN J., DE WIT K., Higher Education Policies and Institutional Response in Flanders, in JONGBLOED B., MAASSEN P., NEAVE G., *From the Eye of the Storm. Higher Education's Changing Institutions,* Cheps, Dordrecht, 1999, p. 291

[82] Which evolutions are unfolding with regard to the basic concepts, as formulated by KELLS H.R., *Self-regulation in Higher Education,* London, 1992, p. 57 ff.

[83] DE GROOF J., Onderwijs en regelgeving. Enkele notities, *Tijdschrift voor Onderwijsrecht en Onderwijsbeleid,* 1996–1997, no. 4, pp. 201–208.

[84] In confirmation of the observation that outlining the core objectives in legislation does not necessarily increase the autonomy of the educational institutions, see GLENN Ch., DE GROOF J., *Balancing Freedom, Autonomy and Accountability in Education 3 volumes,* Wolf Legal Publishers, 2004.

[85] EIJLANDER Ph., RIETVELD J.J.W.M., ZOONTJENS P., *Modernisering Onderwijsregelgeving. Eindrapport,* Schoordijk Institute, Centre for Legislative Studies, October 2001. The report concludes, among other things, that the time would appear to be ripe for deleting obstructive and superfluous rules, and for replacing detailed but sometimes ineffective regulations with more general principles. (*ibid,* p. 3).

[86] MASLOWSKI R., HUISMAN J., Deregulering en Autonomievergroting in Relatie tot Onderwijsvernieuwing en Onderwijsopbrengsten, in *Onderwijs in thema's,* Nederlandse Onderwijsraad, 2005, pp. 79–80.

[87] Cfr. DE GROOF J., HENDRIKS Fr., *art. cit.*

[88] In decision-making, all the relevant spheres of interest should be treated equally; the formal legislator retains the ultimate competency.

[89] The previously mentioned report by the Schoordijk Instituut (UTilburg) '*Modernisering onderwijsregelgeving*' (2001) argued in favour of the introduction of 'general principles of educational quality'(*ABOs*) to replace the existing, excessively detailed regulation. These principles had already been mentioned in *Onderwijskwaliteitsbrief 2000,* where they were however defined as 'general principles of good education (ABBOs).

[90] Comp. KWIKKERS P., Governance through checks and balances: an approach to drafting regulations for higher education and research, *European Journal for Education Law and Policy,* 1997, nr. 1–2, p. 57–80; DE GROOF J., *Flexibilisering mits Contractualisering ?* V.L.O.R., Brussels, 2008.

[91] Cf. VAN DAMME D., Higher Education in the Age of Globalisation: the Need for a new Regulatory Framework for Recognition, Quality Assurance and Accreditation, in DE GROOF J., LAUWERS Gr., DONDELINGER G., *op.cit.*

Part II: Quality

MAREK KWIEK

6. THE CHANGING ATTRACTIVENESS OF EUROPEAN HIGHER EDUCATION: CURRENT DEVELOPMENTS, FUTURE CHALLENGES, AND MAJOR POLICY ISSUES

INTRODUCTION: THE GROWING COMPLEXITY OF THE ACADEMIC ENTERPRISE

The strength (and attractiveness) of higher education in Europe is a research topic which seems to be most usefully discussed with reference to other dimensions of higher education These include high-quality teaching; cutting-edge research; the future of the combination of the two academic missions in increasingly differentiated systems; adequate and more diversified (both public and private) funding under pervasive fiscal pressures in most European economies; more differentiated institutions and consequently a substantially more stratified academic profession. It is difficult to define either the strength or the attractiveness of European higher education as both are relative and elusive terms: to be strong and to be attractive means different things in different contexts (local, national, European), at different (micro-, meso-, and macro-) levels and for different constituencies (or stakeholders). On top of that, we are discussing multiple future social and economic developments and their possible, relatively uncoordinated, if not chaotic, impacts on higher education systems. The paper will focus on the different – and often conflicting – senses of the attractiveness of European systems and institutions to students, academics, the labor market, and the economy. Universities need to be attractive to increasingly differentiated student populations (and to cater for their increasingly different needs) but they also need to be attractive workplaces and provide attractive career opportunities for academics. In the face of ongoing restructuring of the public sector in general in many parts of Europe (see e.g. Gilbert 2004, Taylor-Gooby 2004, Iversen 2005, Kwiek 2007a, Kwiek 2007b), universities also need to keep the respect for traditional academic values, and in the face of the competition with other parts of the world, they still need to be open to such values in their teaching and research. Their attractive curricula need to match transformations in the labor market and in the economy in general. Finally, to be attractive, European higher education needs to be distinctive from higher education in other parts of the globe (Zgaga 2007: ix). Both public and private institutions are under multi-faceted pressures to change today, with various intensities in various parts of Europe. These institutions include governmental agencies, institutions of the corporate world, institutions of civil society, and the

B.M. Kehm, J. Huisman and B. Stensaker (eds.), The European Higher Education Area:
Perspectives on a Moving Target, 107–124.

core institutions of the public sector. In general terms, we are experiencing the shattering of a stable world governed by modern institutional traditions, and in this context universities are increasingly expected to adapt to the changing social and economic realities (see Scott 1999, EC 2003b, OECD 2007a). In a European context, in light of a sustainable future of higher education systems, the following ideas are highly relevant: the introduction or increase of tuition fees and student loans (cost-sharing as an access, equity, social stratification, mobility, and status issue, see Johnstone 2006); academic entrepreneurship and "academic capitalism" as ways to diversify institutions' funding basis (see Shattock 2005, Shattock and Temple 2006, Clark 1998, Williams 2003, Kwiek 2008b); the ongoing reformulations of the European welfare state and the European social model (privatization of some public services, especially in new EU member countries, see Deem 2007, Kwiek 2007a); and finally the revised EU social agenda and new supranational visions of higher education (see EC 2005a on the "Social Agenda" or a report on "The Future of Social Policy", and numerous recent World Bank and OECD publications on tertiary education). Educational strategies for 2010–2020 will need to take into account the complex nature of the academic enterprise today and the powerful role of traditions of the modern European university which may be acting both as inhibitors to changes and as their activators.

MORE MARKET MECHANISMS AND NEW INCOME-GENERATING PATTERNS

Which developments with direct impact on the attractiveness of European higher education systems can be expected? Firstly, with the growing relevance of the market perspective and increasing financial austerity for all public services (accompanied by growing competition in public expenditures), strengthened by globalization and internationalization processes, European higher education institutions in 2010–2020 are expected to be responding to changing financial settings basically by revenue-side solutions: seeking new sources of income, largely non-state, non-core, and non-traditional to most systems. They may include various forms of academic entrepreneurialism in research (consulting, contracts with the industry, research-based short-term courses, etc.) and various forms and levels of cost-sharing in teaching (tuition fees), depending on the academic traditions in which the systems are embedded (and the relative scale of underfunding). Attractive institutions and systems will be prepared to use these revenue-side solutions, apart from using some painful cost-side solutions (well-known especially in transition countries).

Attractive European higher education systems will be able to find a fair balance between the impacts of general trends of globalization and internationalization and the impacts of regional (European and national) responses to make sure that academia still retains at least major characteristics of postwar higher education systems and retains its traditional attractiveness as a workplace and an opportunity for a professional academic career (so far, as Enders and De Weert confirm in their comparative study of the academic profession in Europe, European systems in general offer "low financial rewards" and "uncertain future prospects for university employment", Enders and De Weert 2004: 22). Globalization brings about direct competition between business and non-business models of organizations, and in the case of public institutions the competition between more traditional collegial types of university management and governance and new business types of management and governance, known so far in Europe mostly from private higher education institutions, can be expected (Kwiek 2008a, 2008b). In the times of the imminent reformulation of current welfare state systems in most parts of Europe (as Pierson stressed, "while reform agendas vary quite substantially across regime types, all of them place a priority on cost containment. This shared emphasis reflects the onset of permanent austerity ... the control of public expenditure is a central, if not dominant consideration", Pierson 2001: 456), attractive institutions and systems in 2020 will be able to balance the negative financial impact of the gradual restructuring of the most generous types of welfare state regimes in Europe on public funding for higher education. Higher education in general, as opposed to healthcare and pensions sectors, and top research-intensive universities in particular, are perceived by European societies as being able to generate their own additional income through e.g. entrepreneurship or cost-sharing (where fees are legally possible). Ironically, the more successful public entrepreneurial universities are today, the bigger the chances are this becoming an unavoidable expectation in the future. Along with the efforts to introduce market mechanisms in pension systems (multi-pillar schemes instead of pay-as-you-go ones) and healthcare systems (privatized systems based on additional, private, individual insurance policies), especially but not exclusively in European transition economies, the most far-reaching consequences of this marketization/privatization trend can be expected for public funding for higher education and research. As William Zumeta stressed recently, "unlike most of the other state budget components, higher education has other substantial sources of funds that policy-makers feel can be tapped if institutions need to cope with deep budget cuts" (Zumeta 2005: 85).

Another expected development is the promotion across Europe – as a mostly new and reasonable policy solution to the current problem of underfunding of European universities – of a more substantial inflow of both private research funds from the business sector and of more private teaching funds from student fees. The EC is becoming much more positive towards student fees (it stressed recently that "it has been shown that free higher education does not by itself suffice to guarantee equal access and maximum enrolments" and invited member states to consider whether "their current funding model ... effectively guarantees fair access for all qualified students to the maximum of their capacities", EC 2005c: 8, 10). Trends in European demographics – whose social consequences from a larger comparative perspective are shown periodically by such popular datasets as *Pensions at a Glance* (OECD 2007b) or *Health at a Glance* (OECD 2007c) – will be affecting directly the functioning of the welfare state in general, but only indirectly, through the growing pressures on all public expenditures in general will it be affecting universities. Strong higher education institutions will be able to steer the changes in funding patterns for higher education in their countries rather than to merely drift with them. The impact of public sector reforms on the attractiveness of academia to new generations of academics is another expected development and it seems especially negative in Anglo-Saxon countries and in transition countries (see Deem

2006: 292 and Deem and Brehony 2005, see also a report on the UK academic staff by Oliver Fulton in Enders 2000 or Kwiek 2003 on Poland). The overall policy call of the EC that Europe needs to "respond to new social realities" – caused by globalization and demographics – through "a new approach to the social agenda with implication for both national and European levels" (EC 2007a: 4) may have indirect impacts, translated into different national contexts, on public higher education as well.

The possible redefinition of higher education from a public (and collective) good to a private (and individual) good is a tendency which may further undermine the idea of heavy public subsidization of higher education (see Calhoun 2006, Marginson 2006). In a stakeholder society, the fundamental relationship between higher education institutions and their stakeholders is always "conditional" – which introduces an element of "inherent instability", Neave 2002: 22). The economic rationale for higher education is changing: as Philip Altbach stresses, "the private good argument largely dominates the current debate" and it results from a combination of economics, ideology, and philosophy (Altbach 2007: xx). The possible gradual redefinition of higher education as a private good is parallel to two other processes visible in Europe: the reconsideration of the role of tuition fees as a smaller scale process (e.g. in transition countries) and, more generally, the reconsideration of funding of public services in general as a way to tackle the financial austerity of European welfare state regimes, as a large-scale process.

There is a clear paradox: higher education is seen as more important than ever before in terms of the competitiveness between nations, but although the importance of "knowledge" in our societies is greater than ever, at the same time, along with the pressures to reform current welfare state systems, the capacity of national governments to finance higher education and R&D is considerably weaker than in previous decades. Knowledge is increasingly produced by other sectors than higher education, and increasingly funded by the business sector, though – see the role of private R&D in OECD economies (OECD 2006: 67–73, OECD 2007a: 30–40, and Eurostat 2007). In the OECD area, R&D performed by the business sector has increased steadily over the past two decades and in 2005, R&D performed by the business sector reached 68% of total R&D. The tension between the general attitude of governments and populations (education perceived as perhaps the primary asset of the individual) on the one hand and the inability or unwillingness of the very same governments to increase current levels of public funding for higher education and research in public universities – is stronger than ever before. As the EC put it recently elegantly but firmly, "to attract more funding, universities first need to convince stakeholders – governments, companies, households – that existing resources are efficiently used and fresh ones would produce added value for them. Higher funding cannot be justified without profound change: providing for such change is the main justification and prime purpose for fresh investment", EC 2005c: 8). Consequently, incentives for transformations in functioning of higher education may come through new funding arrangements (referred to by the EC as new "contracts" between universities and societies).

In the last half century, despite an immense growth in enrollments, public higher education in Europe remained relatively stable from a qualitative point of view and its fundamental structure remained unchanged. But, as Malcolm Skilbeck put it, things got substantially changed: "the University is no longer a quiet place to teach and do scholarly work at a measured pace and contemplate the universe as in centuries past. It is a big, complex, demanding, competitive business requiring large-scale ongoing investment" (Skilbeck, quoted in OECD 2004: 3). The forces of change worldwide are similar (see Johnstone 2008) and they are pushing higher education systems into more market-oriented and more competitive arenas (and towards more state regulation combined with less state funding) – which is another expected development. For centuries, "the market" had no major influence on higher education: the majority of modern universities in Europe were created by the state and were subsidized by the state (see Rüegg 2004, de Ridder-Symoens, 1994). Over the last 200 years, most students in Europe attended public institutions and most faculty members worked in public institutions (within all major models of the university in Europe which served as "templates" for other parts of the world, be it the Napoleonic, the Humboldtian, or the British models). Today market forces in higher education are on the rise worldwide: while the form and pace of this transformation are different across the world, this change is of a global nature and is expected to have an impact on higher education systems in Europe. Market forces formulate the behavior of the new providers and, more importantly, increasingly reformulate the missions of existing traditional public higher education institutions. It is still unclear how the competition between public and private institutions in various parts of Europe (especially in CEE, though) will influence the core mission of public higher education generally.

NEW STAKEHOLDERS AND THE CHANGING TEACHING/RESEARCH NEXUS: TOWARDS STUDENT-CENTERED UNIVERSITIES?

Within the European Higher Education Area in 2010–2020, the role of new (and previously significantly less important) stakeholders will be growing, both in discussions at national levels and at the level of the European Commission. Universities under conditions of massification will be increasingly expected to be meeting not only the changing needs of the state but also changing needs of students, employers, labor market and the industry, as well as regions (see Arbo and Benneworth 2006, Goddard 2000, OECD 2005) in which they are located. The expected developments in 2010–2020 may fundamentally alter relationships between stakeholders, with the decreasing role of the state (especially in funding), the increasing role of students and the labor market for the more teaching-oriented sector, and the increasing role of the industry and the regions for the more research-oriented sector.

On a more general plane, massification of higher education is tied with the growing significance of those new stakeholders (as Guy Neave put it regarding the developments in Continental Europe, "the rediscovery of 'stakeholders' as a dimension in higher education policy is intimately tied with the rise of the mass university", Neave 2002: 17). At the same time, in order to flourish, which means to be both attractive and competitive, universities also need to continue to meet (either traditional or redefined) needs of academics. Increasingly differentiated student needs – resulting from differentiated student populations in massified systems – already lead to largely differentiated systems of institutions (and, in a parallel manner, a largely differentiated academic profession). The expected differentiation-related (or stratification-related) developments may fundamentally alter the academic profession in general, increase its heterogeneity, and have a strong impact on the traditional relationships between teaching and research at European universities.

The traditional Humboldtian model of the university was combining research and teaching, and was basically faculty-centered (see Fallon 1980, Röhrs 1995, Readings 1996, Kwiek 2006a: 81–138, 2006b). An Anglo-Saxon model deriving from, among others, Cardinal Newman, was largely teaching-oriented and student-centered (see Pelikan 1992, Rothblatt 1997, Rüegg 2004). These two competing 19th century ideas on what universities should be doing continue well into the 21st century. The questions of how to combine teaching and research as university missions, in which types of institutions they should be combined, and based on which funding streams for which (non-)priority research areas (e.g. public/private) will become crucial in 2010–2020. Are strong and attractive universities in 2020 going to be closer to the American (Anglo-Saxon) university model which has traditionally been much more student-oriented than continental university models in Europe? Most probably, the answer is in the positive. For the time being, most non-elite institutions in Europe are already teaching-oriented while universities are still able to combine teaching and research. Formulations about the need for systemic changes regarding teaching at universities figure prominently in the 2007 London Communiqué (which assumes "a move towards student-centered higher education and away from teacher driven provision", 2007: 2). Transformations of European higher education until 2020 may look like a paradigm shift to traditional universities, both those embedded in the German Humboldtian tradition and those embedded in French Napoleonic tradition, and perhaps especially to institutions in new EU member countries in Central Europe which are still mostly elitist, conservative, and faculty-oriented. University missions are already being strongly redefined, and their redefinition, for instance, along the lines suggested above, may require a fundamental reconstruction of roles of educational institutions (as well as a reconstruction of tasks of academics). The main characteristics of current European systems may be strongly redefined. Implications of Bologna at both European, national, institutional, and individual (academics') levels seem still not fully realized. The conclusions Bruce Johnstone and Pamela Marcucci reach in this context confirm the general trend discussed here:

"The public and governments alike tend to think of universities and colleges as places for *instruction*. The important *research* missions of those institutions that are properly labeled universities may thus drop to an even lower priority or become otherwise distorted by the rising student-faculty ratios and the need to spend more time teaching or searching for entrepreneurial revenue or both ... . Research may fall to only a few universities, or fall mainly to the universities and research institutes in the advanced countries ... or may fall mainly to business and private investment" (Johnstone and Marcucci 2007: 3).

The social, political, cultural, and economic world is changing, and so are changing student populations and educational institutions. Higher education is subject to powerful influences from all sides and all – new and old alike – stakeholders: the state, the students, the faculty, employers, and industry, and on top of that, it is becoming a very costly business (as Burton Clark put it, "more income is always needed: universities are expensive and good universities are very expensive", Clark 1998: 26). The expected development is that stakeholders may increasingly have different needs from those they traditionally had, and their voice is already increasingly taken into account (as in the case of students who are living in the highly competitive, postnational, and postmodern world and who, in general, are expecting a more vocational orientation in their education, as opposed to e.g. the orientation towards traditional *Bildung*, or the cultivation of the life of the mind, see Kwiek 2006a: 139–228, Neave 2000, Readings 1996, Delanty 2001). Institutions are expected to transform themselves to maintain public trust (and use public subsidies). As Neave described it, the passage to the "Stakeholder Society" involves a redefinition of the "community in terms of those interests to which the university should be answerable" (Neave 2002: 12). Also the role of the market in higher education (or of government-regulated "quasi-markets", see Teixeira et al. 2004) cannot be ignored as the market is reshaping our lives as humans, citizens, and finally as students/faculty (on the failure of Bologna in conceptualizing the role of the market in European – especially Central European – higher education, see Kwiek 2004). Never before has the institution of the university for so long been under the pressures of so many different stakeholders; never before has it been perceived by so many, all over the world, as a failure in meeting the needs of the students and the labor market (the literature on the supply/demand mismatch is substantial, see Brown 2004, Perryman et al. 2003). Therefore the question is which directions higher education systems will be taking while adapting to new social and economic realities, in which the role of the market is growing and the education received by graduates is increasingly linked to their professional and economic future.

Following transformations of all public sector institutions, universities in Europe – traditionally publicly-funded and traditionally specializing in both teaching and research – are under powerful pressures to review their missions in view of permanently coping with austerity in all public sector institutions (see Pierson, 2001) and to compete for financial resources with other public services heavily reliant on the public purse. The consequences for the teaching/research agenda are far-reaching. As Rosemary Deem alarmingly put it recently, "scarce public funding may be also a crucial factor in the unfolding saga about the future role and purposes of universities in respect of teaching and research. Teaching-only universities *per se* (as opposed to higher education institutions in general) do exist in both public- and privately-funded forms in many countries, but at the present time this is not the norm in most of Europe. However, this may not continue to be the case in the future" (Deem 2006: 285). The trend of disconnecting teaching and research in higher education has already started: as Vincent-Lancrin (2006: 12) summarizes his analyses of OECD datasets, "academic research might just become concentrated in a relatively small share of the system while the largest number of institutions will carry out little research, if any" (which is challenging the traditional Humboldtian principle of the unity of research and teaching, *die Einheit von Forschung und Lehre*, see the German idea of the university in Kwiek 2006a: 81–138 and 2006b).

European higher education systems will be attractive if, amidst the changes, there is still enough space for traditional universities following the above multiple missions: teaching, research, and service to society. The supranational trend (revealing itself in EC, OECD, and World Bank publications) to institutionally engage in the substantial reformulation of their missions is strong, both globally and in European transition countries (e.g. the idea of research to be done only by "flagship" universities in Poland, suggested by the new government in 2008). The European Commission at the moment seems convinced that teaching and research are mutually dependent and reinforce each other. There are signs of hesitations, though, and one of the differences between the Bologna process goals and the Lisbon strategy goals could be that the former is interested in reforming all higher education institutions while the latter is interested in reforming universities which are research-intensive and which can contribute directly (rather than indirectly via the increased qualifications of the European labor force) to European economy's competitiveness via innovations, patents, and technology transfer (see e.g. EC 2004 on "Science and Technology, the Key to Europe's Future").

The distinctiveness (and attractiveness) of European higher education has traditionally been in its ability to combine the two core missions. The Humboldtian tradition in this respect has been surprisingly strong across Europe – but not in other regions, especially not in Latin America, India, China and, generally, in the developing countries which have been expanding their higher education systems rapidly in the last decades and which have been largely teaching-oriented, with research carried out in selected elite institutions only. The tendency of locating research outside of universities, which additionally influences the research/teaching separation, has been particularly strong in Europe and in Anglo-Saxon countries in the last two decades. Both public and private funding for research increasingly goes to the business research and development sector. New products and innovative technologies are most closely related to business research and development. Consequently, the possibility of teaching/research separation at universities (and not only at higher education institutions in general) – as a development threatening the traditional attractiveness of the academic profession to new generations of scholars – is also reinforced by new flows of public and private research funds. The EC's idea of the goal of "3% of GDP" to be spent on research and development does not assume that increased research funds will go from public sources to public universities; instead, increasingly, private business research funds will go to private research institutions.

EUROPEAN HIGHER EDUCATION IN COMPETITION WITH OTHER REGIONS

By 2020, the role of competition in higher education will grow substantially, and in several dimensions. The world, including the graduate labor market, is becoming extremely competitive. Academic institutions will most probably focus more on the competitive advantages of their graduates as a substantial part of their missions (and will be ranked accordingly, especially nationally, apart from the research-based global rankings). Strong European higher education will be based on competition (see Huisman and Van der Wende 2004): excellence in research is driven primarily by competition – between individuals, institutions, and countries. As a recent EC report on "frontier research" put it, "the desire to be first to make a major new discovery or a significant advance in theoretical understanding drives researchers to devote themselves single-mindedly and for long hours. Researchers compete with one another all the time – for funds, for new equipment, for the best technicians, to get their publications accepted in the leading journals, and for prizes ... and other recognition-based measures of esteem" (EC 2005b: 35). Competition and cooperation come together, and Europe is currently very strong in both respects.

As a whole, the EU lags behind both the USA and Japan in tertiary attainment and in competitiveness ranking. Relatively few young people in the EU enroll in higher education (which brings an EC analysis to a conclusion that "higher education in Europe is still not an attractive option for a significant part of pupils having completed upper secondary education", EC 2005b: 11). Also too many enrolled students leave universities in Europe without their degrees – the survival rate in Europe is comparable to that in the USA (66%) but lower than in OECD (70%), in Korea (79%) or in Japan (94%). The active population of the EU has lower levels of higher education attainment than its main competitors – it is 23% for the EU, while twice as much (43%) for Canada, 38% for the USA and 36% for Japan (EC 2005b: 11–13). The Bologna-supported introduction of the BA level of graduation would probably attract more students into higher education, though. The strength of EU systems of education is that they produce a considerably higher number of new PhDs – however they have fewer researchers active in the labor market than the USA. Strong European higher education needs to be able to attract best talents from other parts of the world, be they students, scholars, and researchers. Currently, compared with other world regions, spending on higher education in Europe (EU-25) is relatively low. Total investment in higher education in the EU is about 1.1% of GDP, at similar levels as Japan but below Australia (1.5%), and significantly below Canada (2.5%), the USA (2.7%) and Korea (2.7%). As the EC put it in financial terms, "to close the spending gap on the USA the EU would have to spend an additional 150 billion Euro per year" (EC 2005d: 21). The EU thus needs to improve access to higher education, to increase higher education attainment levels, and to increase total (public and private) investment in higher education. To reach the levels of enrolment in higher education of young people (aged 18–24 years) in the US, European institutions would have to increase enrolment by 50% (i.e. from 25% to 38%). Thus European systems in 2010–2020 are expected to experiment widely with tuition fees, and accompanying loan programs (on fees and loans from an equitable access perspective, see especially Johnstone and Marcucci 2007, Johnstone 2006, Salmi 2006, Salmi and Hauptmann 2006, on CEE countries, see Kwiek 2008a, 2008c).

MEETING CONFLICTING DEMANDS AS A CHALLENGE TO THE ACADEMIC PROFESSION

Massified educational systems (and corresponding an increasingly massified academic profession) unavoidably lead towards various new forms of differentiation, diversification, and stratification. The need for differentiation in quality is stressed by the EC when it states that "mobilising all Europe's brain power and applying it in the economy and society will require much more diversity than hitherto with respect to target groups, teaching modes, entry and exit points, the mix of disciplines and competencies in curricula, etc" (EC 2005c: 5). Universities in most European countries seem still quite faculty-centered and their responsiveness to student and labor market needs is low (as the OECD notes, most current reforms "aim to improve the responsiveness of universities and government research institutions to social and economic needs", OECD 2006: 11). But students are increasingly being reconceptualized as "clients" or "customers" of higher education institutions (which is consistent with New Public Management and which is especially evident in the private sector booming in CEE countries). Public institutions in Europe are still in most cases either "Humboldtian" or "pre-Humboldtian"; and only in a few cases called "post-Humboldtian" (see Schimank and Winnes, 2000 for an interesting taxonomy) such as e.g. the UK, Sweden, Norway, or the Netherlands, universities are less faculty-centered and there is no universal link between teaching and research (see Deem 2006: 291). The broadening of the debate of universities with employers, students, parents, and other stakeholders about graduates employability (in order to "enhance trust and confidence in the quality and relevance of institutional engagement", *Trends V*: 11) can be expected in 2010–2020. The EUA report suggests that employability has grown in importance as a driver of change – in 2007, 67% of institutions considered the concern for employability as "very important" (as opposed to 56% in 2003) (*Trends V*: 35). And employability (despite its inherent vagueness as a concept) is expected to be a key notion in rethinking the attractiveness of European institutions.

European universities will be attractive if they are able to meet the above (and sometimes conflicting) differentiated needs. These needs sometimes seem to run counter to the traditional twentieth-century social expectations from the academic profession in continental Europe, though. Consequently, attractive European higher education systems will have to find a fair balance between expected trans-formations so that the academic profession is not deprived of its voice. Close relationships with the industry, the responsiveness to the labor market and meeting students' needs have not been traditionally associated with the core values of the academic profession in continental Europe, perhaps despite verbal declarations of the academic community and despite universities' mission statements (see large international comparative studies by Boyer et al. 1994, Altbach 2002, Enders 2004). It is unclear to what extent these core values will need to be renegotiated, or are already under renegotiation, in massified higher education systems.

Universities in 2020 will be strong and attractive to the academic profession only if the changes will be fair and balanced. Overburdened, overworked, (relatively) underpaid and frustrated academics will not be able to make European universities in general strong and attractive. And they will not be useful in the realization of the "more growth/more jobs" Lisbon strategy of making Europe a "knowledge-based economy" (and society). Unfortunately, current trends, both globally and Europe-wide, show the diminishing attractiveness of the academic career, academic workplace and academic remuneration and, consequently, may indicate growing future problems in the retention of best talents in academia in 2010–2020. Attractive higher education systems should be able to offer academics competitive career opportunities. One of the possible options in times of financial austerity (reported for OECD economies in relation to universities already in the 1990s by Gareth Williams, OECD, 1990) might be further differentiation of the sector by 2020, with subsequent targeted research funding and further concentration of research (with the eligibility of selected top institutions only) and possibly flexible salary brackets, depending on national classifications or rankings of higher education institutions, with increased opportunities of academic mobility between them. This is basically the overall philosophy of the Lisbon strategy with reference to universities. For this goal, it would be especially useful if there were various rankings and different – for different quality levels – European accreditation agencies. The widening of the gap in economic status of academics and other professionals needs to be stopped, at least in top national institutions, to avoid further "graying" of the academic profession in 2010–2020 and to make universities a career option for the best talents. It would consequently stop what Alberto Amaral recently called "the gradual proletarisation of the academic professions – an erosion of their relative class and status advantages" (Amaral 2007: 8).

Differentiated student populations in Europe require also increasingly differentiated institutions, and (possibly, consequently) different types of academics. This may mean the decline of the high social prestige of higher education graduates (counted today in millions) and of the high social prestige of most academics (counted today in hundreds of thousands in major European economies). The universalization of higher education is already having profound impact on the social stratification of academics, especially in those countries where the expansion in enrolments was especially significant ("the conditions of academic work have deteriorated everywhere", Altbach 2002: 3).

ACADEMIC VALUES, CHANGING RESPONSIBILITIES AND THE FRAGILITY OF THE STATUS QUO (AN EU CONTEXT)

People, traditions, and values matter in higher education. The Bologna Follow-Up Group strategy stresses, "innovations and renewal can, however, only be successful if they build on an awareness of traditions and values" and the process as a whole should "build on Europe's heritage, values and achievements" (BFUG 2007: 2). The apparently powerful role of values in European higher education systems needs to be maintained as these distinct core values have so far proved a successful "European dimension". Challenges to both academic values and the organization of academic work in Europe have probably never been so powerful in the last half a century than today. And in 2010–2020, they are bound to intensify. A new general context for universities may be the one in which the social trust in public institutions can no longer be guaranteed, which is a substantial change of social mood prevailing in postwar Europe, with relatively lavish public funding guaranteed and high social prestige of public universities and of the academic profession taken for granted. The questions to consider would be how to achieve in the European higher education area common academic values – such as critical inquiry, disinterested science, intellectual freedom, a commitment to objective knowledge etc – which are universal values (Scott 2003: 296). Traditional academic values, closely associated with the public service responsibilities of universities and science, Scott argues, "have to come to terms with a new moral context in which the superiority of the public over the private can no longer be taken for granted" (Scott 2003: 299). This new "moral context" has been widely supported by emergent EU social policies, especially social policies advocated in CEE countries, experimenting widely with various forms of privatization of social services (Ferge 2001, Kwiek 2008c). European institutions need to continue its reliance on traditional academic values (especially academic freedom and institutional autonomy) to be strong and attractive.

Higher education in the EU context has been put in a post-national (and distinctly European) perspective in which interests of the EU as a whole and interests of particular EU member states (nation-states) do not have to be the same. The reason for the renewed EU interest in higher education is clearly stated by the Commission: while responsibilities for universities lie essentially at national (or regional) level, the most important challenges are "European, and even international or global" (EC 2003b: 9). The divergence between the organization of universities at the national level and the emergence of challenges which go beyond national frontiers has grown, and will continue to do so in 2010–2020. Thus a shift of balance is necessary, the arguments of the EC go, and the Lisbon agenda in general, combined with the emergence of the European Research Area in particular, provide new grounds for policy work at the European level (see Keeling 2006, Kwiek 2004, 2006b).

The construction of a distinctive European educational policy space – and the introduction of the requisite European educational and research policies – has become part and parcel of EU "revitalization" within the wide cultural, political, and economic Europeanization project (see Lawn 2003). The response to major challenges facing Europe (losing its heritage and identity, losing out economically, giving up on the aspiration of developing its own vision of a desirable future for humanity, giving up the European Social Model etc.) should be, according to a recent influential *Frontier Research: The European Challenge* report published by the EC, through education, knowledge, and innovation:

> "The most appropriate response to these challenges is to increase the capacity of Europe to create, absorb, diffuse and exploit scientific and technical knowledge, and that, to this end, education, research and innovation should be placed much higher on the European policy agenda" (EC 2005b: 17).

European higher education systems are expected to be in dialogue with its stakeholders with respect to ongoing and future curricular reform – especially with respect to its vocational role, but also in its generalist ones. Both OECD and the EU have been supporting very strongly the idea of universities meeting the changing needs of students, employers, the labor market, the industry, and the region. The traditional type of continental university seems currently largely unable, and unwilling, to meet these needs, unless undergoing a radical transformation. In the European Commission's view, universities today face an imperative need to "adapt and adjust" to a series of profound changes Europe has been undergoing (EC 2003b: 6). They must rise to a number of challenges and they can only release their potential by undergoing "the radical changes needed to make the European system a genuine world reference" (EC 2003b: 11). They have to increase and diversify their income in the face of underfunding. The European Commission is suggesting "targeted increases" in public investment in higher education in certain key areas only, and a bigger contribution from the private sector – reminding generally that, to quote the title, "The Success of the Lisbon Strategy Hinges on Urgent Reforms" (EC 2003a: 7). EU and national research and development programs should complement each other and EU-wide priority research facilities will have to be identified – in those cases where resources need to exceed the capacity of individual member states (EC 2007b: 14). The EC views (some form of) restructuring of higher education as necessary, and a much wider idea of European integration applied to the higher education sector (integration via "spill-over", where integration in some economic areas leads to functional pressures to integrate in related areas, in this case in education, as in neo-functionalism in integration theories, see Barkholt 2005: 23), expressed in the ideals of a common European higher education area and common European research area, seems useful. The university's goal is the creation of an area for research where scientific resources are used "to create jobs and increase Europe's competitiveness" (EC 2001: 1). This implies a new discourse on the purpose of higher education in Europe, distant from a traditional one in which the role of external stakeholders other than the state (and other than academics) was limited. The change in discourses and concepts used for the discussion of the future of public universities is a reflection of much wider socio-economic processes which seem to affect the whole public sector in Western economies. In view of the above, the status quo – or the current social and economic *modi operandi* of universities in Western societies – is very fragile: the multi-faceted impacts, trends, and challenges are far-reaching, long-term, and structural in nature.

CONCLUSIONS AND SUMMARY OF POLICY ISSUES

The major policy issues related to the future strength (and attractiveness) of European higher education systems include the following: (i) how to combine the attractiveness of European universities to different stakeholders whose interests in, and expectations from, increasingly differentiated higher education get substantially changed in new social and economic realities; (ii) how to meet the needs of students, the labor market and the economy without fundamentally transforming traditional values and modes of operation common to best European universities today; (iii) how to combine the (necessary) restructuring of higher education systems towards meeting new needs epitomized in "more growth/more jobs" Lisbon strategy with the traditional values associated with academic teaching and research; (iv) how to attract the best talent to academia amidst the deteriorating job satisfaction and changing working conditions of the academic profession; (v) how to view the traditional unity of academic teaching and research in universities in the context of the prioritization of research areas and the concentration of research funding, and more targeted and more competitive research funding expected and in which types of institutions the traditional combination of teaching and research is still fundable; (vi) what is the wider impact of changing public and political views (increasingly regarding the university as private good) on the future of cost-sharing (student fees) and academic entrepreneurship in research funding; (vii) how governments can cope with growing differentiation of both student populations, institutions and their educational offers, and finally of the academic profession itself; (viii) to what extent higher education policies in Europe are becoming part and parcel of much wider social (political, ideological, and philosophical) welfare state policies and public sector policies, and how the uniqueness of the university sector *vis-à-vis* other public services could still be maintained in the future; (ix) to what extent the impact of globalization and demographics on policy thinking about other public services (healthcare, pensions) will change policy thinking about higher education, especially in terms of funding and governance structures; and (x) how can the "European dimension" be saved as part of the attractiveness of European higher education to other regions of the world in the context of market-related changes to universities worldwide which are global in nature, similar in kind, and not specific to Europe?

The most general, structural policy issues with regard to public universities (as presented in the EC, OECD, and World Bank documents of the last decade, especially regarding funding) do not seem substantially different from structural policy issues discussed with reference to other segments of the public sector. The major difference – namely, the widely acknowledged fact that universities have much wider options to diversify their income – may lead to viewing universities as even more financially self-reliant than before, and potentially being much more open to new funding patterns. The policy challenge at national levels is to what extent particular countries are willing and able to accept global thinking about the future of public sector institutions in general (and of public universities in particular), and to what extent responses to this new way of thinking can vary between the countries. Surprisingly, the worldwide reform agenda for universities in the 1990s, as observed by Bruce Johnstone, was remarkably consistent: there were "very similar patterns in countries with dissimilar political–economic systems and higher educational traditions, and at extremely dissimilar stages of industrial and technological development" (Johnstone 1998: 1). Historically, and based especially on the US experience, we know that budget cuts in higher education in harsh times have always been disproportionately higher than in other public services, and that, from a longer perspective, "a constant element of the history of the universities, and certainly in the Middle Ages and early modern times, is the lack of financial resources. ... there is no doubt that many institutions were hardly able to function decently, and always lived, as it were, below the breadline" (de

Ridder-Symoens, 1996, pp. 183–184). New policy contexts in which state-subsidized public universities will operate are in the making; therefore being conclusive in a world that is changing faster than ever before, and in which the role of contingent events grows, is difficult – constructing future scenarios for higher education is a very risky business.

REFERENCES

Altbach, Philip G. (2007). "Introduction" to P.G. Altbach and Patti McGill Peterson (eds.). *Higher Education in the New Century*. Boston: CIHE.

Altbach, Philip G. (2002). *The Decline of the Guru: The Academic Profession in Developing and Middle-Income Countries*. Boston: CIHE.

Amaral, Alberto (2007). "Higher Education and Quality Assessment. The Many Rationales for Quality". In: *Embedding Quality Culture in Higher Education*. Ed. by Lucien Bollaert et al. Brussels: EUA.

Arbo, Peter and Paul Benneworth (2006). *Understanding the Regional Contribution of Higher Education Institutions*. Paris: OECD/IMHE.

Barkholt, Kasper (2005). "The Bologna Process and Integration Theory: Convergence and Autonomy". *Higher Education in Europe*. Vol. 30. No. 1. April 2005.

BFUG (2007). *European Higher Education in a Global Setting. A Strategy for the External Dimension of the Bologna Process*. Bologna Follow-Up Group Report.

Boyer, Ernest L, and Philip G. Altbach, Mary Jean Whitelaw (1994). *The Academic Profession. An International Perspective*. Ewing: the Carnegie Foundation.

Brown, Philip (2004). *The Changing Graduate Labour Market: A Review of the Evidence. Technical Report*. Cardiff: Cardiff University.

Calhoun, Craig (2006). "The University and the Public Good". *Thesis Eleven*. No. 84. February 2006.

Clark, Burton (1998). *Creating Entrepreneurial Universities. Organizational Pathways of Transformation*. New York: Pergamon Press.

Delanty, G. (2001). *Challenging Knowledge. The University in the Knowledge Society*. Buckingham: SRHE and Open University Press.

Deem, Rosemary (2007). "Introduction: Producing and Reproducing the University". In: Debbie Epstein et al (eds.). *World Yearbook of Education 2008: Geographies of Knowledge, Geometries of Power*. New York: Routledge.

Deem, Rosemary (2006). "Conceptions of Contemporary European Universities: to Do Research or Not to Do Research?". *European Journal of Education*. Vol. 41. No. 2.

Deem, Rosemary, and Kevin J. Brehony (2005). "Management as Ideology: the Case of 'New Managerialism' in Higher Education". *Oxford Review of Education*. Vol. 31. No. 2 June 2005.

EC (2007a). "The European Interest: Succeeding in the Age of Globalisation". Brussels. COM(2007) 581 final.

EC (2007b). "Strategic Report on the Renewed Lisbon Strategy for Growth and Jobs". Brussels. COM(2007) 803 final.

EC (2005a). "Communication from the Commission on the Social Agenda". Brussels. COM(2005)33 final.

EC (2005b). *Frontier Research: the European Challenge*. Brussels. European Commission.

EC (2005c). "Mobilising the Brainpower of Europe: Enabling Universities to Make Their Full Contribution to the Lisbon Strategy". Brussels. COM(2005) 152 final.

EC (2005d). "European Higher Education in a Worldwide perspective". Commission Staff Working Paper. Brussels. SEC(2005) 518.

EC (2004). "Science and Technology, the Key to Europe's Future – Guidelines for Future European Union Policy to Support Research". Brussels. COM(2004) 353 final.

EC (2003a). "'Education & Training 2010'. The Success of the Lisbon Strategy Hinges on Urgent Reforms". Brussels. COM(2003) 685 final.

EC (2003b). "The Role of the Universities in the Europe of Knowledge". Brussels. COM(2003) 58 final.

EC (2001). "Report from the Commission. Concrete Future Objectives of Education Systems". Brussels. COM(2001) 0058 final.

Enders, Jürgen, ed. (2000). *Employment and Working Conditions of Academic Staff in Europe*. Frankfurt: GEW.

Enders, Jürgen and Egbert de Weert (2004). *The International Attractiveness of the Academic Workplace in Europe*. Frankfurt: GEW.

EUROSTAT (2007). *Science, Technology and Innovation in Europe*. Brussels: European Commission.

Fallon, D. (1980). *The German University*. Boulder: Colorado Associated University Press.

Ferge, Zsuzsa (2001). "European Integration and the Reform of Social Security in the Accession Countries". *The European Journal of Social Quality*. Vol. 3. Issue 1&2.

Fulton, Oliver (2000). "Academic Staff in the United Kingdom". In: Jürgen Enders (ed.), *Employment and Working Conditions of Academic Staff in Europe*. Frankfurt a/Main: GEW.

Gilbert, Neil (2004). *Transformation of the Welfare State. The Silent Surrender of Public Responsibility*. Oxford: Oxford UP.

Goddard, John (2000). "The Response of HEIs to Regional Needs". Newcastle upon Tyne.

Huisman, Jeroen, and Marijk van der Wende, eds. (2004). *On Cooperation and Competition. National and European Policies for the Internationalisation of Higher Education*. Bonn: Lemmens.

Iversen, Torben (2005). *Capitalism, Democracy, and Welfare*. Cambridge: CUP.

Johnstone, D. Bruce and Pamela N. Marcucci (2007). *Worldwide Trends in Higher Education Finance: Cost-Sharing, Student Loans, and the Support of Academic Research*. Prepared for the UNESCO Forum on Higher Education. Available from: www.gse.buffalo.edu/org/IntHigherEdFinance.html

Johnstone, D. Bruce (1998). "The Financing and Management of Higher Education: A Sttaus Report on Worldwide Reforms". Report to the UNESCO World Conference on Higher Education, Paris, October 5–9, 1998.

Johnstone, D. Bruce (2006). *Financing Higher Education. Cost-Sharing in International Perspective*. Boston: CIHE.

Keeling, Ruth (2006). "The Bologna Process and the Lisbon Research Agenda: the European Commission's Expanding Role in Higher Education Discourse". *European Journal of Education*. Vol. 41. No. 2.

Kwiek, Marek (2008a), "On Accessibility and Equity, Market Forces and Entrepreneurship: Developments in Higher Education in Central and Eastern Europe". *Higher Education Management and Policy*. Vol. 20, issue 1 (March).

Kwiek, Marek (2008b), "Academic Entrepreneurship and Private Higher Education in Europe (in a Comparative Perspective)". In: Michael Shattock (ed.). *Entrepreneurialism in Universities and the Knowledge Economy: Diversification and Organizational Change in European Higher Education*. Maidenhead: Open University Press.

Kwiek, Marek (2008c). "The Many Faces of Privatization in Higher Education in Poland. Its Impact on Equity and Access". In: Jane Knight (ed.). *Financing Higher Education: Access and Equity*. Sense Publishers: Rotterdam.

Kwiek, Marek (2007a). "The University and the Welfare State in Transition. Changing Public Services in a Wider Context". In: Debbie Epstein et al (eds.). *World Yearbook of Education 2008: Geographies of Knowledge, Geometries of Power*. New York: Routledge.

Kwiek, Marek (2007b). "The Future of the Welfare State and Democracy: the Effects of Globalization from a European Perspective". In: Ewa Czerwinska-Schupp (ed.). *Globalisation and Ethical Norms*. Frankfurt – New York: Peter Lang. 2007.

Kwiek, Marek (2006a), *The University and the State. A Study into Global Transformations*. Frankfurt a/Main and New York: Peter Lang.

Kwiek, Marek (2006b). "The Classical German Idea of the University Revisited, or on the Nationalization of the Modern Institution". Poznan: Center for Public Policy Research Papers Series. Vol. 1. Available from www.cpp.amu.edu.pl.

Kwiek, Marek (2004). "The Emergent European Educational Policies Under Scrutiny. The Bologna Process From a Central European Perspective". *European Educational Research Journal*. Vol. 3. No. 4. December.

Kwiek, Marek (2003). "Academe in Transition: Transformations in the Polish Academic Profession". *Higher Education*. Vol. 45. No. 4. June 2003.

Lawn, Martin (2003). The 'Usefulness' of Learning: the Struggle over Governance, Meaning and the European Education Space. *Discourse: Studies in the Cultural Politics of Education*. Vol. 24. No. 3.

London Communiqué (2007). "Towards the European Higher Education Area: Responding to Challenges in a Globalised World". London. May 18, 2007.

Marginson, Simon (2006). "Putting 'Public' Back into the Public University". *Thesis Eleven*. No. 84.. February 2006.

Neave, Guy (2002). "On Stakeholders, Cheshire Cats and Seers: Changing Visions of the University". In: *The CHEPS Inaugural Lectures 2002.*. Enschede: CHEPS.

Neave, Guy (2000). "Universities' Responsibility to Society: An Historical Exploration of an Enduring Issue". In: Neave, Guy, ed., *The Universities' Responsibilities to Societies. International Perspectives*. Amsterdam: Pergamon Press. OECD (2007a). *OECD Science, Technology and Industry Scoreboard 2007*. OECD: Author.

OECD (2007b). *Pensions at a Glance. Public Policies Across OECD Countries*. OECD: Author.

OECD (2007c). *Health at a Glance 2007. OECD Indicators*. OECD: Author.

OECD (2006). *OECD Science, Technology and Industry Outlook*. OECD: Author.

OECD (2005). *Supporting the Contribution of Higher Education Institutions to Regional Development. The OECD Programme on Institutional Management in Higher Education*.

OECD (2004). *On the Edge: Securing a Sustainable Future for Higher Education*. OECD. Author.

OECD (1990). *Financing Higher Education. Current Patterns* [written by Gareth Williams]. Paris: Author.

Pelikan, Jaroslav (1992). *The Idea of the University. A Reexamination*. New Haven: Yale University Press.

Perryman S. and E. Pollard, J. Hillage, L. Barber (2003). *Choices and Transitions. A Study of the Graduate Labour Market in the South West*. A HERDA-SW report.

Pierson, Paul (2001). "Living with Permanent Austerity: Welfare State Restructuring in Affluent Democracies". In: Pierson, ed., *The New Politics of the Welfare State*. Oxford: Oxford UP.

Readings, Bill (1996). *The University in Ruins*. Boston: Harvard University Press.

Ridder-Symoens, Hilde de, ed. (1996). *A History of the University in Europe. Vol. II. Universities in Early Modern Europe (1500–1800)*. Cambridge: CUP.

Rothblatt, Sheldon (1997). *The Modern University and Its Discontents. The Fate of Newman's Legacies in Britain and America*. Cambridge: CUP.

Röhrs, Hermann (1995). *The Classical German Concept of the University and Its Influence on Higher Education in the United States*. Frankfurt am Main: Peter Lang.

Rüegg, Walter, ed. (2004). *A History of the University in Europe. Vol. III. Universities in the Nineteenth and Early Twentieth Centuries (1800–1945)*. Cambridge: CUP.

Salmi, Jamil (2006), "Student Loans in an International Perspective: The World Bank Experience", available from http://www1.worldbank.org/education/lifelong_learning/ publications/student_loans.pdf.

Salmi, Jamil and Arthur Hauptman (2006), "Innovations in Tertiary Education Financing: A Comparative Evaluation of Allocation Mechanisms". Dijon, June 2006.

Shattock, Michael (2005), "European Universities for Entrepreneurship", *Higher Education Management and Policy*. Vol. 17. No. 3.

Shattock, Michael, and Paul Temple (2006). "Entrepreneurialism and the Knowledge Society: some conclusions from cross national studies", a paper presented at the EAIR Forum, Rome.

Schimank, Uwe and Markus Winnes (2000). "Beyond Humboldt? The Relationship Between Teaching and Research in European University Systems". *Science and Public Policy*. Vol. 27.

Scott, Peter (2003). "Challenges to Academic Values and the Organization of Academic Work in a Time of Globalization". *Higher Education in Europe*. Vol. XXVIII. No.3.

Scott, Peter (1999). „Globalization and the University". *CRE-Action* 115.

Taylor-Gooby, Peter, ed. (2004). *New Risks, New Welfare. The Transformation of the European Welfare State*. Oxford: Oxford UP.

Teixeira, Pedro, and D. Bruce Johnstone, Maria J. Rosa, Hans Vossensteyn, eds (2006). *Cost-Sharing and Accessibility in Higher Education: A Fairer Deal?*. Dordrecht: Springer.

Teixeira, Pedro, and Ben Jongbloed, David Dill, Alberto Amaral, eds. (2004). *Markets in Higher Education. Rhetoric or Reality?* Dordrecht: Kluwer.

Trends V (2007). *Universities Shaping the European Higher Education Area*. Brussels. European University Association.

Vincent-Lancrin, Stéphan (2006). "What Is Changing in Academic Research? Trends and Future Scenarios". *European Journal of Education*. Vol. 41. No. 2. June 2006.

Williams, Gareth, ed. (2003), *The Enterprising University: Reform, Excellence and Equity*. Buckingham: SRHE and Open University Press.

Zgaga, Pavel (2007). *Looking Out: The Bologna Process in a Global Setting*. Oslo: Norwegian Ministry of Education and Research.

Zumeta, William (2005). "State Higher Education Financing. Demand Imperatives Meet Structural, Cyclical, and Political Constraints". In: Edward P. St. Johns and Michael D. Parsons, *Public Funding of Higher Education. Changing Contexts and New Rationales*. Baltimore: Johns Hopkins UP.

BJØRN STENSAKER AND ÅSE GORNITZKA

7. THE INGREDIENTS OF TRUST IN EUROPEAN HIGHER EDUCATION

INTRODUCTION

In a world increasingly characterised by interpersonal and interorganisational relations across national borders, trust is a key issue. It is plausible to assume that trust between people and institutions is more easily developed and invested within the nation state than across nation states. Hence, processes of globalisation, internationalisation and Europeanisation also entail shifts in trust in higher education at several levels and a challenge as to how actors can manage to move from a state of distrust to a trusting relationship. Trust is a core issue within national systems of higher education – between higher education institutions and society (students, parents, employers) and in the governance relationship between government and universities and colleges, and also within higher education institutions and the academic community. The autonomy granted to institutions and academics is founded on the idea that they are "entrusted" to act according to professional and academic standards and with institutional integrity. The more they are trusted the less there is need for imposing strict control regimes. This kind of trust relationship is embedded in a notion of a higher education system that also is based on a fairly stable and ordered relationship between higher education institutions, society and government. Many of the elements that uphold such an order are absent in an international relationship between two or more actors. While social and economic interactions in most states are well regulated often by law, such regulations are not as well developed and consequential internationally. Most states have also built up several organisations and institutions with a specific purpose to build trust in society and its subsectors. Actors share a history, and maybe even an identity, and have tacit knowledge of the way a higher education system works. Internationally, far fewer organisational and institutional arrangements exist focusing on such issues. Finally, size matters for the overview and transparency of a higher education system, and when interaction in higher education involves an expanding number of actors, it involves interaction "among strangers" and actors who have comparatively less knowledge about each other. In general, one can assume that trust is more difficult to obtain in larger higher education systems or between higher education systems.

Although trust is a general issue when discussing Europeanisation, internationalisation and globalisation, it has specific relevance to the Bologna Process and the aim of building a European Higher Education Area (EHEA). Seemingly, the EHEA scores low with respect to the key trust-building characteristics

B.M. Kehm, J. Huisman and B. Stensaker (eds.), The European Higher Education Area:
Perspectives on a Moving Target, 125–139.

mentioned above. The Bologna declaration lacks the backup of enforceable international laws and regulations specifying how relationships within the EHEA should be structured. There is a historical lack of established organisational and institutional arrangements within the EHEA that focus on building trust. There is a considerable knowledge and information gap between states, institutions and individuals as the number of countries participating in the Bologna process, especially signatory countries, has increased to 46 and with the prospect of further expansion.

The paradox concerning this situation is that despite the seeming lack of trust-building characteristics related to the Bologna Process, it is still, at least politically, regarded as a success and, according to a recent survey, there is much support for the aims of the process among teaching professionals in European higher education institutions (Eurobarometer 2007). Also according to a survey among the national unions organising academics in Europe, there is a high level of trust in the Bologna Process potential both for making interaction across national systems easier and for increasing a sense of belonging to common higher education community in Europe (Gornitzka and Langfeldt 2005). However, the implementation of the Bologna Process advances at different speeds in different countries and accomplishments in some areas are not in line with the political optimism (Neave & Maassen 2007: 138) is an indication that building trust between the political and societal level and the 'shop floor' of higher education perhaps is one of the greatest challenges for the future. As part of the expansion of and growing competition within the sector stemming from deregulation, internationalisation and globalisation, there is a lack of thorough knowledge about 'the others' and their commitments to higher education.

This lack of knowledge may be said to be relevant to a number of higher education relations; it is relevant to situations concerning the funding of higher education, that is, whether higher education institutions (HEIs) can rely on the long-term commitments of those funding the sector, or whether those funding the sector can rely on the commitments of the HEIs to provide the agreed results. Trust is also of relevance concerning relations within HEIs, for example in human resource management policies, student admission processes, resource allocations and governance and management issues (see also Maassen & Olsen 2007).

However, within Europe and following the key objective of the Bologna Process of creating an open European Higher Education Area (EHEA), trust has been more associated with issues related to quality. While new degree structures, credit systems (ECTS) and other structural aspects were meant to stimulate increased mobility of students and improved transferability of skills and labour, it soon became clear that trust in these new degrees and study programmes were not obtained by the structures as such. The explanation for this is closely related to the intangible nature of higher education and the difficulties associated with delivering hard facts about the quality of the products higher education deliver.

The main objective of this paper is to outline two ideal types (in a Weberian sense of the term) of trust and use them to shed light on different aspects of trust in higher education. The main point of our argument will be that current attempts of systemic integration involved in the EHEA process bring to the surface some fundamental issues of how to handle trust and distrust. In the remaining part of the chapter, we will first sketch out the theoretical understandings of trust and how trust can be developed accordingly. This will then be contrasted by a more forward-oriented look on how issues of trust will appear and develop in the period up to 2020 followed by a discussion on the possible critical factors to account for in the future. In the final sections of the chapter we will identify the strategic room for manoeuvring when attempting to build trust before closing our discussion with an attempt to outline some realistic objectives and instruments for the future.

THE THEORETICAL FEATURES OF TRUST AND THEIR APPLICATIONS IN MODERNISING WELFARE STATES

Trust can be defined as a relationship between two parties where one of the parties will trust the other one if (s)he thinks the other is trustworthy in relevant circumstances (Honderich 1995: 881). Whether the other one is seen as trustworthy depends on the knowledge one has of the other's future commitments to behave as one trusts. This is not the only definition of trust as a number of disciplines employ an array of definitions. Lane (1998: 3) argues that all these perspectives still share three common elements. First, there is a degree of interdependence between the trustor and the trustee. Second, trust is a way to deal with risk and uncertainty in exchange relationships. Third, there is an assumption that the vulnerability caused by taking risk in trusting the other will not be taken advantage of by this actor. Hence, since almost all perspectives share these assumptions, what separates them are their views on how a trusted relationship between the trustor and the trustee can develop. From a more economic perspective, developing trust is then a matter of rational calculations of whether it is advantageous to trust others. From more sociological perspectives, trust can be established either by a moral belief that trusting others is the right thing to do or by various forms of cognitive processes, for example social similarity or cultural congruence (Zucker 1986). However, while normative and cognitive forms of trust may be analytically separable categories, this distinction is more difficult to maintain empirically since there is no critical test available to empirically resolve whether trust follows from 'cultural scripts or internalised norms, or both at varying times' (Hirsch 1997: 1720).

Agreeing with Hirsch, we will as a consequence argue for the existence of only two basic distinctions in how the issue of trust is perceived and how to achieve trust – a calculative/rational perspective and a normative/cognitive perspective.
- The rationalist-instrumental perspective on trust: The basic assumption is that individuals will follow the logic of consequentiality. If otherwise not induced to it, the individual will pursue his or her own self-interest and maximise its utility. Social order and predictability can be achieved through making sure that behaviour can be controlled and incentives are in place that will make it in the actors' self-interest not to cheat, lie and engage in free-riding (Olson 1965). Others can be trusted to the extent that there are effective mechanisms of control or the incentives are "right", especially to regulate the behaviour of individuals when the rational pursuit of individual gains might produce outcomes that are collectively undesirable. Without sticks and carrots others cannot be trusted to

act in trustworthy ways. Social order is thus based on rationality and exchange (March and Olsen 1989, 1995). Trust is established through the existence of independent actors and auditors that can be trusted by all parties involved in a relationship and then are assigned to check the quality of higher education. Procedures, standards, rules and regulations established by the independent auditors are then the proxies of trust. Trust is established on the basis of thorough analysis of how procedures, standards, etc., are followed. Trust can be established through "contracts" devised to fit self-serving instrumental actors and as a result of more or less free transactions between various parties in a market-like situation. Trust is dependent on the outcome of these relations i.e., those institutions, study programmes or offerings that become popular, are proven to be effective or relevant are also those that will enjoy trust.

– Normative/Cognitive perspective on trust: Trust is established by the existence of strong norms and expectations as to what is appropriate behaviour of various parties involved in a relationship. Such strong norms are internalised by all actors creating trust because it is taken for granted that everybody should and will follow norms and rules. Relatively stable sets of norms, values and rules underpin social relations and they create a sense of belonging to a community. Social order is based on common history, obligation and reason (March and Olsen 1989: 117–119). It involves the socialisation in values and norms but also the accumulated tacit knowledge based on experience-based learning. Norms, values and experiences are carried and embodied in social institutions and trust is established through the existence of institutions at which trust is directed. Trust is achieved when institutions, over time, demonstrate accountability through the results and outcomes produced. The reputation a given university achieves will then become a proxy for trust. Whereas the problem of trust is seen as an issue of control and incentive from the rational-instrumental perspective, it is from a norm-based institutional perspective seen as a question of appealing to common identity and socialisation and acting according to what is appropriate. More than a matter of a social contract, trust is embedded in a pact (Olsen 2007). That implies also that there are limitations to which trust is subject to design, negotiation, "command and control".

These two perspectives and their variants can be combined in various ways; they are sometimes blurring and overlapping, but can also be read as the historical journey of how the notion of trust has developed in recent years. Concerning the former, Christensen and Røvik (1999: 177) have pointed out that behaving according to norms in a modern society often implies to behave rationally since rationality and instrumentality are strong ideologies in most Western societies influencing both our moral values and cognitive schemes. Hence, a trustor will normally not engage in 'blind trust' but will use a combination of calculative (if available) and norm-based judgements pointing to the indication that trust is a 'hybrid phenomenon' between calculation and predictability on one hand and goodwill and voluntary exposure to risk on the other (Bachmann 1998: 303). Also time and resources are limited and hence also overcoming distrust by information seeking and checking the accuracy of information incurs heavy costs. Trusting may be risky but rational if the cost of distrust weighs heavier than its gains.

To further complicate the clear distinction between the two perspectives, Hardy et al, (1998: 83) have argued that cooperative relations that appear to reflect trust can hide asymmetrical power relationships where one of the actors is forced to trust the other because of the potential negative sanctions the other actor controls. In this way power can, at least in some situations, be seen as a way to replace trust in coordinating social interaction.

However, the distinctions between normative/cognitive and rational/ instrumental perspectives still make sense if we employ a retrospective look at how trust has been dealt with in the modernisation of Western welfare states in the last couple of decades. Although empirical studies suggest a rather surprising stability concerning political trust in Western societies during the last decades (Dalton and Klingemann 2007), one can still identify a shift in the ways in which trust is sought and sustained. As Power (1997) has argued we have seen a transformation of professional exchange relationships from being based on a tacit (normative) pact to increasingly being based on explicit (rationalistic) audits and other accountability measures. Zucker (1986) has described this transformation in a similar way, but by using other labels. According to her, trust can be found in different versions. Process-based trust is gained through an incremental and often time-consuming process of knowing the other actor in a relationship. Characteristics-based trust is based on social coherence and similarity between two or more actors in a relationship. However, Zucker (1986) claims that these versions of trust are more difficult to accomplish in culturally more complex and rapidly changing societies. Hence, it is her notion of institutional-based trust, trust that is based on impersonalised structures, arrangements and practices, that she thinks is most appropriate for developing trust in more advanced societies. Although the label may suggest otherwise, this version of trust comes close to what we in the introduction termed the rational-instrumental perspective on trust.

The typical sign of the latter form of trust is found in the establishment of independent or quasi-independent agencies responsible for checking whether the behaviour of an actor is in accordance with the agreed contract. Still, as pointed out by Hardy et al, (1998) these establishments often hide asymmetric power relations as such agencies seldom control both actors in a relationship, but rather are set up by one actor to control the behaviour of the other.

Closely related to this change is the increase in the belief in information as a basis for creating trust. This belief is linked to the rational/instrumental perspective because of the assumption that well-informed people make decisions based on calculations and stringent analysis of various alternatives. Hence, the growth of various forms of performance indicators, consumer-tailored databases, consumer tests, benchmarks and a number of ranking lists can be found in all service sectors of a modern welfare state. At the same time, information is also a basis for the normative/cognitive perspective as knowledge about the 'correct' moral or cognitive decision is not easy to determine as social complexity increases. Interestingly, and observed in several sectors of society, actors in the private sector often function as new providers of information about exchange relationships in the public sector. This trend can especially be found in sectors with intangible products and with various electronic and mass media as central actors.

Finally, the rising popularity of the rational/instrumental perspective can also be indicated by the increase in the use of legal instruments and various forms of contracts, standards and rules in the modern welfare state (Brunsson et al. 2000). These instruments are used in different settings not least when engaging in social exchange situations between providers and buyers of services and products. However, standards and rules may also be interpreted as a form of contract although this type of 'contract' can be regarded as more unspecified and related to more general social exchange situations within a larger sector or a system than between two defined parties. Also, standards not only provide a yards-stick for assessing one's performance according to a quality benchmark, but in many instances they are also a prerequisite for interaction. Setting up common standards means that actors and entities can interact using the same "language", with no necessary implication whether one set of standard is better than another set.

POSSIBLE EUROPEAN DEVELOPMENTS 2010 – 2020

Recent history and current indications suggest that higher education is following the same path as sketched above and that developments in the period towards 2020 will be highly influenced by the path already embarked upon. While European cooperation in the form of exchange programmes such as Erasmus and Socrates was established on the basis of mutual ("blind") trust between the participating countries and HEIs (Kehm 2003: 110), higher education witnessed a development during the latter decades where traditional forms of (norm-based) trust were partly deinstitutionalised at the national level, and instrumental means to accomplish trust were becoming more prevalent. An example is the mutual recognition of degrees based on the Lisbon Convention that forms a much stronger legal basis than the Bologna Process' attempts at creating a comparable degree system. Another example is the changing of public funding regimes across Europe. In the traditional trust-based regime, the state paid the costs and the universities performed the teaching (Sorlin 2007). In the new regime performance- and incentive-based funding schemes are rapidly becoming the new norm. A similar change has occurred with respect to teaching and research. A tacit understanding and informal assessment of the quality of education and research have been made formal and subject to more "rationalised" and formally regulated regimes (Salter and Tapper 2000). As Power (1997) has pointed out, the whole notion of trust has changed – it is not taken for granted anymore – it has to be demonstrated.

However, a change towards more rational/instrumental ways to define and secure trust may have implications far beyond the emergence of new procedures and instruments. This change affects a number of other issues including governance, the relationship between public and private actors in higher education, control over how quality should be defined in education and research and tensions between individual states and supranational initiatives. Although a thorough discussion of these implications is beyond the scope of this paper, some important issues are highlighted below.

Trust: An Issue Solved Through New Governance Arrangements?

Following the initial Bologna Declaration, with its emphasis on a joint degree structure and credit transfer system (ECTS), the subsequent policy initiatives, including standards and guidelines for quality assurance, qualification frameworks and the recent register for recognised agencies dealing with evaluation of higher education, could all be interpreted as ways to improve the trust when establishing a common higher education area. However, when studying how these initiatives have come to the fore, one could also argue that these initiatives signal a considerable struggle in achieving trust. While quality assurance in the 1990s was a national responsibility with international cooperation only taking place in more ad-hoc pilot projects, the establishment of European standards and guidelines can be seen as a way to increase the trustworthiness of the national agencies established in the field and as a first step in trying to come to terms with the many different and contested interpretations of quality throughout Europe. The process is marked by a process of agencification across Europe, i.e. letting this subject area in the hands of semi-independent national agencies. This in itself is subject to questions of how and to whom such agencies are accountable. In turn, such agencies are heavily involved in transnational networks that we most certainly should see as efforts to create trust "among agencies" in different higher education systems. A main consideration in these agency networks is to promote information about each other's QA systems and whether they are "up to standards". The main problem facing the European standards and guidelines was that the issue of quality was not addressed. As Westerheijden (2007: 89) points out, the standards are not at all concerned with the content of education.

On this basis, the "tuning projects" leading to the formulation of a European Qualification Framework were understandable next steps in trying to build trust within the European Higher Education Area. The "tuning projects" are also mainly in the hands of the academic disciplinary communities that we assume are accountable to their respective academic disciplines. While this process is still underway, one could question whether qualification frameworks will be the ultimate answer. The main problem is perhaps that it is unclear which problem qualification frameworks actually solve. Given the many purposes and intensions attached to qualification frameworks, and what seem to be quite general descriptions given of the structures and content of the education, qualification frameworks may easily be yet another (symbolic) planning device for higher education institutions (and students), with far less relevance for employers and other stakeholders in society.

An indication that the attempts to build trust have not ended with the launching of qualification frameworks was the establishment of a European register for quality assurance agencies in London in 2007. While one could imagine that the existence of European standards and guidelines would be a sufficient instrument for improving the accountability of European quality assurance agencies, there is seemingly not enough trust in these standards and guidelines opening up for a new meta-agency aiming at controlling the controllers. Of course, the question to be raised is whether this is the last structure established for meta-control.

Trust: A New Contestation between Public and Private Actors?

It is perhaps on the background that 'more governance' apparently is not sufficient to secure and build trust within the EHEA that one can notice the emerging influence of private actors in the process of creating trust in European higher education. However, interestingly enough, this is not framed as an issue of trust, but as an issue of "transparency" and information. The high-profiled ranking schemes of universities popping up both in Europe and the rest of the world is perhaps the most noticeable indication that mass media and independent research and/or consultancy organisations are fast becoming major players in defining an alternative way and providing alternative means as to how trust should be created in higher education. While most governance-related arrangements have been focusing on process-related criteria (standards, procedures, rules and regulations), university rankings claim to address quality issues more directly – through the identification of output criteria such as the numbers and quality of research publications, employment ratios and salaries of university graduates, reputation of HEIs, etc. While it is debateable whether quality, at least within education, actually is addressed through these criteria, the rankings are nevertheless successful as an agenda-setting device for both politicians and for the higher education sector. The attention that such private rankings have received in European and international media have created somewhat of a public sphere around higher education institutions whereby universities and other higher education institutions are publicly held accountable for their "performance". The problematic aspects of these rankings notwithstanding, they are explicit indications of the substantial differences that exist between universities and also within the EHEA. As such they can be seen to unveil questions about the comparability and compatibility of degrees offered between the European institutions that are at the top and bottom of the ranking. Whether this is conducive to or unsettling for the trust that the general public has in these higher education institutions is another matter.

However, the interesting point concerning rankings is not their design but that trust, by private actors, is seen as a commodity from which profit can be made. This represents a shift concerning the foundations of trust. While trust within the public sphere usually is related to expenditure of time and resources, it seems that trust within the private sphere is seen as more of a service for which there is a price to pay by those using or being exposed to it. Thus, depending on the success of the emerging enterprises one could expect a growth in this market in the years to come. Whether this will result in a downscaling of public means to create trust or a more intense contestation between public and private actors as the 'trustworthy' agents remains to be seen.

Trust: Who will become Legitimate Actors in Defining Quality?

Whether the dominant actors in the trust-creating business will belong to the public or private sphere may mean less for the staff and students of higher education. Although staff and students are represented frequently in both public and private trust-building schemes, either as those providing information and input to these schemes or as those targeted as recipients of the knowledge provided by the systems, staff and students are only allowed to provide their views on externally defined issues and problems. As such there is a growing paradox concerning the role staff and students play in such schemes. While their participation is often underlined as crucial for the legitimacy of any scheme with the ambition to create trust in higher education, staff and students are on the other hand losing influence due to an increasing weight given to the use of indicators, various performance measures and stakeholders within society, industry and business as alternative sources of legitimacy.

One should still be careful in being too deterministic concerning the diminishing power of staff and students. First, the emerging interest in excellence in research and teaching could represent a renewed weight given to more traditional and scholarly ways of assessing quality as quality assessment based on more standardised indicators and procedures may have difficulties addressing excellence issues. Second, the current introduction of student fees in many European countries may cause a strengthening of student power providing them with a stronger voice also in issues of legitimacy and trust. A shift from the public to the private purse in paying for higher education may have consequences in terms of how students (and their parents) view the accountability of higher education and create a push more in the direction of trust ensured by a "contract" rather than a "pact" between them and higher education institutions. It is for instance telling when students and graduates take their disappointment and grievances with respect to the quality of the education offered to the Ombudsman for consumer affairs rather than to the Ministry of Education or to a national quality assurance agency.

Trust: Towards Universal Standards?

This brief sketch of possible developments in the decade to come indicates that trust is not an easy task to achieve. It may also be that trust is among those phenomena that are notoriously recalcitrant to attempts to bring them about intentionally and by design (Elster 1993:249) – the more control, oversight and material inducement are introduced to actors in order for them not to misrepresent themselves, lie and cheat about their actions and performance, the less trusted they become. Furthermore, there seems to be a lack of universal standards and an instrument for agreeing on what grounds judgements on quality in higher education should be made. However, we might soon be experiencing the first attempt of creating such a universal standard. If the OECD initiative of creating a PISA test for higher education is successful, this might represent an important step towards agreeing on the means of creating trust. One should still be warned against being too optimistic. The initiative might even backfire as "name-and-shame" is not the most favourable hotbed for growing trust and confidence "among strangers". If one follows the national debates concerning the already existing PISA tests in primary education, an observer would not be impressed by a high level of agreement on what this test is actually measuring. The reception that the PISA results have generated in different national contexts has also questioned whether such tests can be trusted as an accurate measure of educational performance across diverse educational systems. Still, the agenda setting capabilities of the PISA tests do suggest that these new initiatives are more and more disconnected from national standards and politics and are to be found beyond national borders.

Whether such a development is acceptable for governments within the Europe of Knowledge is another matter. For many countries their system of higher education is highly intertwined with their national identity and with a political culture which might mean a possible enforcement of a classic tension between culture and economy when attempting to build a more integrated Europe.

Risks and Opportunities in Building Trust in European Higher Education

The developments described above are to some extent exposed to deliberate design attempts by national governments being part of the Bologna Process or by the EU. Whether or not such manipulation should be attempted is still another question. As underlined by Zucker (1986), trust is partly a 'path-dependent' concept – often shaped as a result of a number of interactions between two or more parties that over time are engaged in a relationship. Interfering or disturbing such relationships by organisational, legal, financial or other forms of intervention imply both risks and opportunities.

Turning to the risks, one could argue that radically changing what seems to be a recipe for success is perhaps the greatest danger. How Bologna has moved forward in the period from the signing of the initial agreement until today is in many ways remarkable (Neave & Maassen 2007). The systematic way in which political decisions are reached through a complex web of meetings, dialogues and informal negotiations can in many ways be seen as a triumph for those with much sympathy for incrementalism. And although not all groups and stakeholders have been included in the process, changing what seems to be a very proven and effective way to reach political agreements could have unforeseen consequences. Trust is here not only a matter about the future quality of European higher education as such, but it is also in the political process that is to bring us forward to the next phase. If we relate the whole Bologna follow-up structure to the conceptual framework of Zucker (1986), we could argue that this structure fits both the process-based trust and the institutional-based trust schemes. Most of the actors playing the game have done so for years and know each other and the game very well. The system of reaching decisions is also well known, almost emerging as being institutionalised not only by those within the inner circle, but also by the higher education sector as such. Since a major challenge related to trust is that it usually takes a long time to create while it is easy to break down, there are obvious risks associated with changing the current decision-making structure – even though it may be far from perfect. Stability and a long-term strategy for creating trust is probably a key to stimulate trust in European higher education. One fundamental advantage with the current setup is that it allows the combination of long-term strategies with short-term adjustments. For example, the developments of qualification frameworks, schemes for quality assurance and so forth have been in the pipeline of several ministerial meetings before final endorsements are reached.

Breaking away from this setup can also be met with protest and contestation. Trust is, as quality, a concept defined in many different ways by different stakeholders. What some value, others do not. Turning to a process by which decisions are reached in a more streamlined fashion would at some point still have to go through a phase of negotiation and persuasion – processes that the current decision-making structure handle rather well as part of the setup of meetings, seminars and informal negotiations. Critical issues would then be how alternative processes should be organised and what should be defined as the appropriate standards and procedures meant to create trust in alternative ways (see also Gornitzka et al. 2007: 204).

It is nevertheless possible to turn the coin and argue that there are also risks in continuing down the same path as before. An important issue here is related to the possibility that a rather high level of trust can also hinder creativity and innovativeness (Bachmann 1998). The argument is that there are fewer incentives for producing the unexpected in a blind-trust relationship as this relationship is based on a tacit mutual understanding of what should be exchanged and the characteristics of the exchange. In a process towards establishing the EHEA, sustained attention to a predictable agenda is probably more relevant than supporting a decision making structure that produces the innovative and unexpected.

There is also another argument that is worth bringing into play concerning risks. In a period of rapid change in higher education, institutionalised practices and ways to produce trust might not be the mode for handling such challenges. Institutionalised practises and routines are ways to deal with the normal and standardised situation – not with the unexpected and with a more dynamic environment.

However, besides the risks there are also opportunities associated with building trust for the coming decade. One such opportunity lies in the close and interchanging relationship between trust and power. Although some may view power as the opposite of trust, one could also argue that power is an important facilitator or even a precondition in the creation of trust (Bachmann 1998: 313). The point is that power can create a more binding relationship as illegitimate behaviour could run the risk of being sanctioned by one or both of the parties. For those controlling important resources in higher education, this could represent a possibility to increase the level of trust in the system as a whole. As such, this is an argument in favour of a more interventionist and proactive approach in creating trust. Of course, the relationship between trust and power is a delicate one where the actual use of power also could have a negative impact on the level of trust. The dilemma for those with power is then that having power without using it fuels trust, while an active use of power may have the opposite effect.

One could also argue that a more legalistic approach in structuring the relationship between different actors within higher education is an option not fully explored until now. Within this approach one could again differentiate between 'hard' and 'soft' versions of legal instruments. For example, although structuring relationships through various forms of contracts are gaining popularity within the sector, there are few examples of 'hard' contracts being established (see for example, Gornitzka et al,.

2004). So far, contracts appear to be softer and more developmental tools, often strongly related to strategic ambitions. This soft approach may have its advantages, not least in that this type of contracts may strengthen technical and more pragmatic cooperation between two or more actors; the contracts may for example be an instrument to improve communication and planning and be an initial step in securing a more long-term relationship (see also Bachmann 1998: 315). Hence, a legalistic approach should not necessarily be interpreted as an alternative to trust. It can also be seen as a basis for developing a stronger sense of trust in the future.

In the 'hard' version, a more legalistic approach resembles the characteristics between trust and power. The difference is that the power in a 'hard' legalistic version is not (only) in the hands of the actors involved, but very much held by a third actor that controls resources and/or can instigate sanctions with dramatic consequences. Again, the 'hard' version is faced with the same dilemma as a relationship solely based on power; if, for example, disputes are taken to the court, a contract has mainly failed to do the job. As long as the transfer of legal competencies to supranational institutions that can act as the third party enforcer is not a viable option within the Bologna Process, this option will be off-limits within the EHEA.

TRUST AS SOCIAL ENGINEERING? POSSIBLE STRATEGIES AND TARGETS TOWARDS 2020

Given the risks and opportunities mentioned above, maintaining and improving the notion of trust in European higher education is no easy task. Due to the size of the sector, the number of actors and the increased competition within the sector, the most likely answer is that it is very difficult to imagine a 'one-size-fits-all' strategy to achieve trust in the European higher education sector as a whole.

What is more likely is that trust will operate in certain strata within the Europe of Knowledge. Hence, as in the US, one can imagine that arrangements intended to create trust or that have trust enhancing consequences will be differentiated and given to certain groups of actors and institutions defined geographically, economically or academically. Whether this is a politically acceptable solution at the national level is another issue.

Another challenge related to trust is the costs and benefits related to obtaining it. An essential characteristic of trust is that when trust exists transaction costs associated with maintaining a relationship between two or more parties are low. When trust is absent, transaction costs are high. A key factor for the future is therefore the willingness and capacity to pay for the procedures associated with creating trust. But given the fact that The Europe of Knowledge is created at various speeds in different countries following somewhat different political agendas (Neave & Maassen 2007: 137), is this willingness shared by all countries and HEIs? On the other hand, can they afford not to pay if the risk is a lack of trust? The simple observation is that the EHEA covers countries with enormous differences in the level of trust citizens have in public institutions (cf. Eurobarometer 2007). Again, this might make a 'one-size-fits-all' approach less relevant.

The specific issues that come to the surface when trying to balance unity and diversity in Europe's higher education have so far implicitly and in practice been handled by 1) formal agreements ("blind trust") such as the Lisbon Convention on the Recognition of Qualifications concerning Higher Education in the European Region that might be seen, in the name of "polite" deference to national differences, to have understated them, 2) attempts to reduce structural differences by introducing structural compatibility 3) dodging the issue of systemic differences by basing the EHEA on an understanding that performance and learning outcomes are of great importance and that those can be measured according to a European standard that is trustworthy (EQF or discipline-based Tuning). From a theoretical point of view, these initiatives resemble what Zucker (1986) has labelled "institutional-based" trust arrangements, which by Zucker are regarded as the most needed to create trust in a complex and modern society.

This brings us back to our two original perspectives on trust, i.e., the rationalistic-instrumental perspective and the normative/cognitive perspective. As shown in our discussion, the rationalistic-instrumental perspective can be said to fit many of the initiatives in the Bologna Process. The weight given to evaluation, meta-evaluation, checks and performance are all in line with this perspective. It seems that a normative/cognitive perspective on trust has lost its momentum at the Pan-European as well as at the national level.

However, given the fact that trust is a hybrid phenomenon, one could argue that a normative/cognitive approach to trust still has much to offer. When considering the issue of sources and implications of applying the principle of mutual recognition where one tries to integrate systems and institutions with very different traditions and where there are at best limited knowledge, information and history of inter-action between the actors, how can one obtain the balance between autonomy and connectedness, between deference for each other's particularities and intervention based on power and legalistic instruments, without emphasising issues related to norms, values, and the historical legacy of higher education? One can create formal agreements that spell "blind trust" through the signing of conventions and agreements, but these will remain superficial unless there exists some social and institutional "glue" of binding trust (Nicolaidis 2007).

Communication, interaction and dialogue are essential processes in creating stronger social and institutional coherence (Witte 2006: 530-531) and could be seen as one way forward. However, it should be underlined that such dialogue should aim at both vertical and horizontal integration where representatives from different interest groups could meet without necessarily aiming at a specific policy outcome or political recommendation. As such, the recently launched annual European Forum for Quality Assurance is an interesting initiative. While problems and prospects related to the area of quality assurance is at centre stage of this gathering, one should not underestimate the side effects such meeting places have on creating trust. Similar initiatives aimed at creating more academic and professional meeting places in other areas of interest to the EHEA should be considered.

While initiatives such as these hold few promises as "quick-fix" solutions, there are not that many other options. Given the characteristics of the higher education, trust inducing arrangements operate in a delicate balance; the very means of formal arrangements fashioned according to a control/incentives based perspective might undermine the mechanisms that sustain trust based on a sense of community and moral commitment. Furthermore, it is reasonable to assume that trust is developed at an uneven pace at different levels; – political commitment based on mutual trust and understanding between ministers of education and European level associations representing academic communities and institutions is removed from the trust that institutions, academics, students and potential employers have when faced with the consequences of the EHEA. To conclude, what is needed is to find a more proper balance between the instruments available to create trust and opportunities for developing stronger normative trust in the system. Needless to say, this is indeed a challenging task of social engineering. A key and remaining condition for trust in higher education – among academics, students, parents, employers, governments, funders and the range of those who hold stakes in higher education – is that the academic community and the institutions that house them adhere to professional academic standards. This is a condition that has not changed even if the world has become more complex and modern. Stimulating this fundamental building block of trust in higher education will also stimulate the building of a European Higher Education Area.

LITERATURE

Bachmann, R. (1998) Conclusion: Trust – conceptual aspects of a complex phenomenon. In Lane, C. & Bachmann, R. (eds.) (1998) *Trust within and between organizations. Conceptual issues and empirical applications.* Oxford: Oxford University Press.

Brunsson, N., Jacobsson, B., and associates (2000) *A world of standards.* Oxford: Oxford University Press.

De Boer, H. (2002) Trust, the essence of governance? In Amaral, A. Jones, G.A. & Karseth, B. (eds.) *Governing higher education: National perspectives on institutional governance.* Dordrecht: Kluwer Academic publishers.

Dalton, R,J, & Klingemann, H-D. (2007) *The Oxford handbook of political behaviour.* Oxford: Oxford University Press.

Eurobarometer (2007) *Perceptions of Higher Education Reforms. Survey among teaching professionals in higher education institutions, in the 27 Member States, and Croatia, Iceland, Norway and Turkey.* Flash Eurobarometer Series, The Gallup Organization.

Gornitzka, Å. & L. Langfeldt (2005) The role of academics in the Bologna process – a survey of participation and views Results from a survey among EI-member organisations in Europe. Oslo: NIFUSTEP Workning Paper 1/2005

Gornitzka, Å., Maassen, P., Olsen, J.P. & Stensaker, B.(2007) "Europe of Knowledge": Search for the new Pact. In Maassen, P.A.M. & Olsen, J. P. (eds.) *European integration and the dynamics of university organisation.* Springer. Dordrecht, pp. 181–214.

Gornitzka, Å., Smeby, J-C., Stensaker, B. & De Boer, H. (2004) Contract arrangements in the Nordic countries: solving the efficiency – effectiveness dilemma? *Higher Education in Europe,* 29, pp. 87–101.

Hardy, C., Phillips, N. & Lawrence, T. (1998) distinguishing trust and power in interorganizational relations: Forms and facades of trust. In Lane, C. & Bachmann, R. (eds.) (1998) *Trust within and between organizations. Conceptual issues and empirical applications.* Oxford: Oxford University Press.

Hirsch, P.N. (1997) sociology without social structure: neoinstitutional theory meets brave new world. Review essay. *American Journal of Sociology,* 102, pp. 1702–1723.

Honderich, T. (ed.) (1995) *The Oxford companion to philosophy.* Oxford: Oxford University Press.

Kehm, B, (2003) "Internationalisation of Higher Education". In Begg, R. (ed) *The dialogue between higher education research and practice*. Dordrecht: kluwer Academic Press.

Lane, C. (1998) Introduction: Theories and issues in the study of trust. In Lane, C. & Bachmann, R. (eds.) (1998) *Trust within and between organizations. Conceptual issues and empirical applications.* Oxford: Oxford University Press.

Lane, C. & Bachmann, R. (eds.) (1998) *Trust within and between organizations. Conceptual issues and empirical applications.* Oxford: Oxford University Press.

Maassen, P.A.M. & Olsen, J. P. (eds.) *European integration and the dynamics of university organisation.* Springer. Dordrecht,

March, J. G. and J. P. Olsen (1989) *Rediscovering institutions: the organizational basis of politics,* New York: Free Press.

March, J. G. and J. P. Olsen (1995) *Democratic governance,* New York: Free Press.

Neave, G. & Maassen, P. (2007) "The Bologna Process: an intergovernmental policy perspective". In Maassen, P.A.M. & Olsen, J. P. (eds.) *European integration and the dynamics of university organisation.* Springer. Dordrecht, pp. 181–214.

Nicolaidis, K. (2007) 'Trusting the poles? Constructing Europe through mutual recognition', *Journal of European Public Policy,* 14(5): 682–698.

Olsen, J. P. (2007) *Europe in Search of Political Order. An institutional perspective on unity/diversity, citizens/their helpers, democratic design/historical drift, and the co-existence of orders.,* Oxford: Oxford University Press.

Olson, M. (1965) *The Logic of Collective Action: Public Goods and the Theory of Groups.* Cambridge, MA: Harvard University Press.

Power, M. (1997) *The audit society: rituals of verification.* Oxford: Oxford University Press.

Sako, M. (1998) Does trust improve business performance? In Lane, C. & Bachmann, R. (eds.) (1998) *Trust within and between organizations. Conceptual issues and empirical applications.* Oxford: Oxford University Press.

Salter, B. and T. Tapper (2000) 'The politics of governance in higher education: the case of quality assurance', *Political Studies,* 48(1): 66–87.

Sorlin, S. (2007) Funding Diversity: Performance-based Funding Regimes as Drivers of Differentiation in Higher Education Systems, *Higher Education Policy,* 20(4): 413–440.

Stensaker, B., Rosa, M.J. & Westerheijden, D.F. Conclusion and further challenges. In: Westerheijden, D.F. Stensaker, B. & Rosa, M.J. (eds) *Quality Assurance in Higher Education.* Springer. Dordrecht, pp. 247–262.

Westerheijden, D.F. (2007) States and Europe and quality of higher education. In Westerheijden, D.F. Stensaker, B. & Rosa, M.J. (eds) *Quality Assurance in Higher Education.* Springer. Dordrecht.

Witte, J.K. (2006) *Change of Degrees and Degrees of Change: Comparing Adaptations of European Higher Education Systems in the Context of the Bologna Process.* University of Twente/CHEPS, Enschede.

Zucker, L.G. (1986) Production of trust: Institutional sources of economic structure, 1840–1920. *Research in Organizational Behaviour,* 8, pp. 53–111.

JOHN BRENNAN, RAJANI NAIDOO AND KAVITA PATEL

8. QUALITY, EQUITY AND THE SOCIAL DIMENSION: THE SHIFT FROM THE NATIONAL TO THE EUROPEAN LEVEL

INTRODUCTION

In recent years, policy bodies at both national and European levels have given increasing emphasis to the role of higher education in addressing issues of social equity and cohesion. While the argument presented for social equity has often been linked to the economic 'wastage of talent' argument, a social justice dimension has also been evident. Such arguments have also been linked to issues of social cohesion, crime reduction, democracy, citizenship and the well-being of society as a whole.

However, although there is considerable rhetoric expended on such topics, the evidential base for policy making and practice is relatively limited. This paper will review our current state of knowledge of higher education's contribution to social equity and the achievement of a just and fair society. In the first section below we will summarise different perspectives to be found in the academic literature on the balance between higher education's contribution to extending opportunities and enhancing mobility on the one hand and to protecting privilege and reproducing inequalities on the other. In the next section we review some policy assumptions prevalent in the European context before turning to an analysis of access and participation, including the wider benefits of higher education. With the expansion of higher education has also come increasing differentiation of higher education's institutional forms and so we attempt to assess the extent to which differentiation and diversity of higher education may work to reinforce or limit wider social diversities. We conclude the paper by turning to policy implications at the European level.

THEORETICAL ASSUMPTIONS

Theoretical accounts of the role of higher education in relation to social equity can be characterised along a continuum with the 'liberal' and the 'elite reproduction theorists' comprising opposite ends of the spectrum. Moore (2005:38–39) provides a useful outline of the perspectives of such theorists. In general, liberal social theorists assign progressive social change to higher education which is perceived to:
- produce the 'human capital' required by an increasingly high-skill, science-based economy;
- promote the 'civic' values and behaviour appropriate to advanced liberal democracy;

B.M. Kehm, J. Huisman and B. Stensaker (eds.), The European Higher Education Area:
Perspectives on a Moving Target, 141–161.

- develop a 'meritocratic' selection system whereby people can achieve social status by virtue of their actual abilities and contributions rather than having it merely 'ascribed' by the accident of birth;
- facilitate an 'open' society characterised by high levels of social mobility reflecting the relationship between ability and opportunity.

Moore contrasts such accounts with those of the elite reproduction theorists who see educational processes in terms of how they:

- reproduce the privileges and dominance of the ruling class (e.g. through access to educational advantages leading to elite jobs and social positions);
- secure the legitimacy of capitalist social relations through the inculcation of the dominant ideology;
- block the development of a counter-hegemonic working-class consciousness that could effectively challenge capitalism;
- systematically prepare pupils for their differentiated future positions within the capitalist economy and social structure.

Clearly the two positions are extreme ones and are not necessarily contradictory. A limitation of the reproduction theorists is that they focus on the 'elite' – both educational and social – and have rather neglected what is going on in perhaps 90% of 'mass' systems of higher education. Second, their work cannot be easily applied to contexts characterised by social conflict and change where a range of external and internal socio-political and economic forces may be in play. More importantly, the question that needs to be posed is the extent to which such theories remain relevant in the context of current developments in higher education. Much of the work of the reproduction theorists was developed in the context of a 'social compact' that evolved between higher education, the state and society over the last century and which led to the insulation of universities from direct market pressures. In the current context, it may well be argued that the juxtaposition of elite institutions with social class may be displaced by a closer relationship between elite institutions and business interests. While the perspectives of the 'liberal' or 're-allocation' theorists have generally proved to be the more palatable to policy interests – and the higher education community itself – there may also be a certain element of 'wishful thinking' in some of their conclusions.

It is important to point out that these are *theoretical* positions, not necessarily supported by the results of empirical research. The latter paints a rather more complex picture. Altbach for example has summarised some of the achievements arising from expanded higher education systems as (i) increased opportunities for social mobility, (ii) increased income levels associated with higher education, (iii) academe opened up to women and "historically disenfranchised groups worldwide" (Altbach, 2000, p2). Both the extent and the details of these achievements differ between societies but can be found to some extent virtually everywhere.

However, while the accumulation of educational credentials has been a major route to upward social mobility for many in modern industrial societies, some have questioned the extent to which this remains so and express doubt about whether the children of the upwardly mobile generation of the 1960s and 1970s will be able to cling onto the social positions of their parents (Brown and Hesketh, 2004). Of course, the acquisition of credentials may become as crucial to 'clinging on' to social status as it once was to being upwardly mobile. These authors and others also point out that access even to elite institutions may not be enough to ensure access to 'good jobs', especially for students from lower socio-economic groups.

In the final analysis, we would tend to agree with Altbach who concludes that "inequalities remain, but progress has been impressive" (Altbach, 2000, p2). We also believe that current theories need to be suitably modified so as to broaden the scope of analysis to encompass a wider notion of *social* mobility, embracing opportunities for access to middle-ranging positions in society as well as to elites. And finally, in this, as in much else, we need also to be alert to the possibility of important country differences.

The above theoretical positions are essentially about the 'selection' function of higher education, about who gets the credentials and how lives are changed as a consequence. In a recent article, Craig Calhoun has raised the important question of what higher education contributes to social justice for the majority of people who do not participate in it directly, who do not themselves go to university or college (Calhoun, 2006). At an individual level, of course, the answer must be that their opportunities and life chances are reduced in a major way. For them, the 'contest' – for all sorts of 'goods' and 'positions' within society – is effectively over with the 'failure' to enter higher education. Although in this context, however, we must be alert to the 'second chance' opportunities and lifelong learning provisions which are being increasingly emphasised across Europe.

However, Calhoun's question directs us to consider a much wider range of social and educational issues than those of individual educational achievement. We will discuss some of these issues in the later section on the wider benefits of higher education.

In considering these and other points, the research evidence is likely to prove to be both limited and contradictory. Contradictions, though, should not worry us. Higher education as a whole, as well as individual institutions and individual academics, may well be performing contradictory functions – for example, bolstering and reproducing privilege and inequality at the same time as they are creating new knowledge of benefit to all. In this context, some attention must surely also be given to the increasing differentiation of higher education systems. In later sections we will illustrate how differentiation seems to be an important way by which higher education can pull off the 'trick' of simultaneously achieving both elite and mass functions.

POLICY ASSUMPTIONS

Higher education has received heightened policy attention all over the world in recent decades. There are several reasons for this. A central one is the belief in the importance of the so-called 'knowledge economy', and the related expansion of most higher education systems (with increased costs to the public purse) bringing heightened visibility and accountability requirements. Globalisation is part of the story, with international competitiveness at the heart of much policy thinking – at the level of individual institutions as well as of national governments.

At its simplest, the policy message is two-fold:
- Higher education is important to the development of successful economies (regional as well as national)
- Higher education is important in providing opportunities for all individuals in a society to participate in and benefit from a successful economy.

Quite often, the second 'social equity' argument is subsidiary to the first and economic argument. Opportunities must exist for all in order to avoid a 'waste of talent' to the detriment of the economy and the interests of all. Thus 'employability' and 'widening participation' become central and linked policy themes. But more recently issues of social equity have come more to the fore, as the foci of several international conferences over the last year have demonstrated.

The meeting of OECD education ministers in June, 2006 referred to the 'dual mandate' of higher education: (i) to promote democracy, tolerance and social cohesion, and (ii) to fuel economic development through the creation of knowledge and skills (OECD, 2006). The same meeting highlighted the problems being encountered in meeting this mandate, noting that virtually all countries were struggling to ensure equitable provision of higher education, commenting that "access to and completion of higher education typically varies widely, most importantly by social background, minority or immigrant status, or disability" (OECD, 2006, p5).

Policy statements are frequently aspirational as the 2005 'Glasgow Declaration' by the European Universities Association on the Bologna Process illustrates:

> "In refocusing the Bologna Process, universities undertake to give higher priority to the social dimension as a fundamental commitment, to develop policies in order to increase and widen opportunities for access and support to under-represented groups, and to promote research in order to inform policy and target actions to address inequality in higher education systems." (EUA, 2005, p3)

Perhaps unsurprisingly, many international organisations place much of their emphasis on cross-border higher education. For example, the International Association of Universities emphasises the benefits to equity, access and quality of higher education that can come from increased international mobility of students. A statement issued in 2005 refers directly to higher education's responsibilities to "instil in learners the critical thinking that underpins responsible citizenship at local, national and global level" (IAU, 2005, p2).

That international mobility tends to be the preserve of students from already advantaged social backgrounds is one of the many inconvenient pieces of data that sit uncomfortably with policy intentions.

The Council of Europe is an organisation with a long history and mandate of concern with issues of human rights and citizenship. At a recent Council of Europe Higher Education Forum, the participating higher education leaders and policy makers affirmed a number of commitments. The report of the meeting stated that higher education had a role to play in, and a responsibility for developing a democratic culture by educating the new generations in the values of democracy. It regarded it as being higher education's responsibility to foster the commitment of citizens to sustain public actions aimed at the well-being of society at large rather than to be concerned solely with the benefits to the individual. It concluded that higher education must promote the values of democratic structures and processes, active citizenship, human rights and social justice, environmental sustainability and dialogue (Council of Europe, 2006).

It is worth noting that the above set of statements go well beyond a widening participation agenda to address directly issues of democracy, citizenship and human rights. At a previous Council of Europe meeting, participation agendas were addressed more directly and the conference report provides a good summary statement of the state of play across Europe:

"Higher participation rates have not removed inequities based on socio-economic, racial or ethnic origins of students, and significant gaps remain within many countries and between countries in Europe." (Egron-Polak, 2004, p3)

The different senses of equality in terms of higher education policy and practice are summarised in the report of an International Association of Universities conference in 2004. The IAU distinguished between (i) equity of access or equality of opportunity, (ii) equity in terms of learning environment or equality of means, (iii) equity of achievement, (iv) equity in using the results of education or equality of application (IAU, 2004).

The many brave and aspirational statements made by policy bodies in recent years may succeed in influencing agendas at national and institutional levels to a certain degree but they do not face up to the wider structural social inequalities which exist and the part being played by higher education, not in removing them but in helping to sustain them.

What is clear is that there are significant national differences in the attention given to equity and social justice issues in respect of higher education. As well as differences in the importance attached to the subject, the literature suggests that we should take into account differences in

- the perceptions of the scale and nature of the problem;
- the groups that are focused on (class, ethnic, gender, regional etc);
- where responsibility is seen to lie (i.e. within or beyond higher education, with governments, within the family, within other parts of the education system, with the values and aspirations of the non-participants);
- pre-higher education educational structures (and routes into higher education);
- admissions policies and practices (for example, the use of SATs and of special entry procedures for certain groups);
- the extent and nature of the differentiation of the higher education system;
- whether the main focus is on admission, retention or outcomes;
- the quality of the student experience and the role of fees and financial support mechanisms;
- higher education traditions – with regard to factors such as professional training, elite reproduction etc;

– the existence and effects of larger processes of social change (for example, in the former communist countries).

It may be noted that most of the above factors concern widening participation and social access to higher education rather than the broader agenda of the social impacts of higher education. In the next section, we examine the participation issue in more detail.

ACCESS AND PARTICIPATION ISSUES

Previously we noted that much of the research literature is concerned with the 'import' into higher education of equity and social justice issues current in the wider society. In this case, higher education institutions are no different from other large organisations. They should give consideration to disadvantaged groups and must show concern for gender and racial equality among their staff and students and seek ways of improving it. There is a regional dimension to social equity in many countries and this also is likely to be reflected within higher education agendas. Research can be critical of higher education's performance in some or all of these respects – whether at system or institutional level or both – and the reasons for higher education's failings may be found inside or outside higher education itself. And there is an appropriate set of technical questions to pose about the relative success of the various policy interventions to improve the performance of higher education in extending access.

There was considerable growth in higher education participation during the last decades of the 20th century. Enrolments increased significantly between 1970 and 2000 and there has been further expansion in recent years. For example, Clancy and Goastellec's (2007) 27-country comparison showed significant improvements in access and participation in most places (Table 1). The highest levels of participation were in the USA (84.6%), Finland (87.5%) and Korea (96.2%). Norway, Sweden, Belgium and Greece were in the top one-third of participation levels, ranging between 72%-77% (Clancy and Goastellec, 2007). Although some countries were expanding at a slower pace than others, they were still expanding.

widening. In all developed countries, there are significant differences in participation rates according to factors such as social class, ethnicity and region (Thomas, 2001, Gorard et al., 2007, Clancy and Goastellec, 2007). It should always be remembered, however, that these factors interact, both with each other and with additional factors such as gender, age and disability. Nor should it be forgotten that many of the categories used are simply aggregates which hide considerable variations between sub-groups. In some countries, for example, many ethnic minority groups enjoy considerably better chances of entering higher education than do a majority of the population. However, whatever their source, differences in opportunities to enter higher education have major consequences for the life chances of individuals and they also may represent a significant 'waste of talent' with consequences for society as a whole.

Table 1. Access to and Participation in Higher Education in Selected Countries.

Country	Gross enrolment rates	Index of participation in higher education
Austria	49	42.1
Belgium	61	74.9
Denmark	67	69.8
Finland	86	87.5
France	56	66.1
Germany	51	51.1
Greece	68	72.6
Hungary	51	48.7
Iceland	55	60.8
Ireland	50	66.0
Italy	57	46.5
Korea	85	96.2
The Netherlands	58	61.1
Norway	81	76.8
Poland	60	55.0
Portugal	53	46.0
Spain	62	69.7
Sweden	76	76.6
Switzerland	49	53.5
United Kingdom	64	65.0
United States	81	84.6

However, expansion of participation in higher education does not mean that it is
While participation rates vary considerably between European countries (Otero
and McCoshan, 2005, Kaiser et al., 2005), there is some disagreement in the
research literature about whether expanding enrolments in themselves do anything
for social equity. Some authors have pointed out that in most countries recent
increases in higher education participation rates among young people from lower
socio-economic groups have actually been less than the overall rate of increase
(Blondal et al., 2002, Galindo-Rueda and Vignoles, 2003).

However, some recent studies have indicated that inequalities in access and
participation are in fact reducing as a result of the overall expansion of higher
education (Clancy and Goastellec, 2007). That said, such inequalities remain large.
A recent UK study (Gorard et al., 2007) reported that the social class advantage in
gaining access to higher education had declined from 10:1 in favour of the middle
class to 6:1 in their favour. Progress certainly, but a large social equity problem
still remains.

There are differences in the progress in extending access to higher education
between countries, in part because they are attempting to widen participation from
a very different base. A 13-country study by Shavit and Blossfeld (1993) reported

substantial equalisation of participation rates between socio-economic groups in Sweden and the Netherlands. A more recent 15-country study by Shavit, Arum, and Gamoran (2007) indicated maintenance of this trend. They report that the expansion of tertiary education has coincided with a reduction in social selection, reflecting progress in both expansion *and* inclusion within higher education (Clancy and Goastellec, 2007).

To a considerable extent, long-term life chances are dependent on one's education. This is an important part of higher education's role in the *'export'* of equity and social justice to the wider society. Getting into higher education is also about getting a better job and a better life. This reflects an underlying assumption that 'unequal treatment' on the basis of possession of educational credentials is both legitimate and required. Inequality of inputs is of concern but inequalities of output are regarded as necessary, even essential. This is fundamentally a functionalist belief in the need to get the 'right people' into the 'right social positions', to the general benefit of all.

Observing the larger society and higher education beyond the elite sectors, one finds international differences in the importance of educational credentials but the following points are probably all more or less true:
- Credentials are getting more important in the determination of life chances.
- There is unequal access to credentials.
- Credentials are a vital route to social mobility – although this requires certain labour market conditions: the possibility of 'status congestion' (Brown and Hesketh, 2004) remains.
- Credentials combine with other social and cultural factors to determine life chances and may disguise the continuing importance of these other factors.
- Mass systems and their credentials are increasingly differentiated – elite sectors remain, new vocational sectors and qualifications are created for the masses; different 'classes of higher education' come to serve different social classes.
- There may be a larger 'social order' function within increasingly unstable societies where the 'appearance' at least of opportunity structures for all is essential to the maintenance of order.
- In other words, 'it's your own fault if you don't succeed' – difference and inequality are thus legitimised.

Authors differ in the extent to which they find inequalities in participation in higher education to be the fault or responsibility of higher education or to lie elsewhere in society. It has been argued that universities come far too late in a potential student's educational and social experience to overturn or compensate for accrued disadvantage (Hale, 2006).

On the other hand, the argument is also heard that higher education institutions must themselves change if they are to meet the needs of new kinds of students. Barriers to equitable access within the higher education sector itself include "the cost of participation; entry qualification requirements; a lack of flexible learning opportunities (including curricula); limited availability of support services and an institutional culture" (Thomas, 2001, p365).

We might summarise the current European position on widening participation by saying that there is evidence that inequalities are reducing in some countries but that overall very large inequalities remain, in spite of the considerable expansions in enrolments. However, the fact that a few countries are making progress proves that change is possible and that "enlightened educational and social policy is capable of reducing but not eliminating inequality" (Clancy and Goastellec, 2007, p152). Clearly, there are opportunities for learning from the differences in experiences and policies of different countries. Where the effectiveness of particular policies can be evidenced, the case for policy transfers between nation-states becomes potentially quite powerful, always bearing in mind caveats about national traditions and circumstances.

Considering future developments of the European Higher Education Area, we can expect higher education to continue to expand but not that this expansion will of itself remove social inequalities in access. Expansion will, however, provide opportunities for increased social mobility, although a downside could be the growth of an 'underclass' of those excluded who would be unequipped to play a full and constructive role in modern society.

As greater proportions of national populations become educated to the level of a first degree, it may be anticipated that the focus of differentiation may shift to postgraduate levels and to lifelong learning. Here, the fate of the harmonisation objectives of the Bologna process will be significant, especially the status to be accorded to the bachelors qualification in continental Europe. It remains to be seen in practice whether employers and students will be prepared to use this as the initial entry to the labour market.

Also relevant to the future will be the question of student mobility, both before, during and after higher education. As with anything which provides the potential for a greater degree of choice, it is possible that it will become another source of inequality with some students enjoying a much wider range of options than others. And at a technical level, significant increases in student mobility (outside of existing arrangements such as ERASMUS) will pose challenges to admissions arrangements and to the balance between supply and demand of places in particular subjects. It remains to be seen whether it is possible to harmonise some things without also harmonising others, e.g. fees and student support arrangements.

The opportunity, therefore, is for the European Higher Education Area to be a source of greater choices and options for students and thereby to stimulate greater demand and access. The risk is that this would just add a further layer of inequality to the inequalities which already exist, with disadvantaged groups limited to a small number of local institutions while students from more advantaged backgrounds would be able increasingly to utilise the full richness of opportunities across the whole of the European Higher Education Area.

Strategic objectives for the period 2010 to 2020 might therefore include:

– the equalisation of opportunities for students to be mobile across the full European Higher Education Area;

– involving further steps towards harmonisation of things such as admissions arrangements, fees and student support;

– an increase in attention to access and participation beyond the first degree and over the life-course;

– as a way of addressing current cycles of social advantage/disadvantage as well as meeting changing economic and employment needs.

HIGHER EDUCATION'S WIDER SOCIAL IMPACT

This section focuses on the question of whether and how higher education contributes to social justice for the majority of people who do not participate in it directly. This leads us beyond questions of higher education as a measure of individual achievement or as the appropriation of a private good to the question of higher education's wider contribution to society. This wider function of higher education is often encapsulated in the notion of higher education as a public good and is also closely related to concerns over who pays for higher education. Contemporary discussions on these issues are also frequently linked to debates in higher education about the role of market forces, new systems of management and accountability, and the perceived erosion of academic autonomy.

These are issues that are being debated more widely at the present time (see, for example, the Council of Europe initiatives mentioned above). This debate however is informed by little substantial research literature as yet. In particular, the identification and measurement of 'wider benefits' of higher education present major challenges for research.

We can, however, identify a strand of literature on education's effects on personal change and development – and through these on society more generally. In the UK, there is a government-funded research centre that investigates the 'wider benefits of learning', mainly focusing on the analysis and re-analysis of data from large longitudinal cohort studies (Bynner et al., 2004; Bynner and Egerton, 2001; Bynner et al., 2003, with the last two focusing specifically on higher education). Various publications arising from this work suggest a number of positive outcomes from participating in higher education. For example, it was found that graduates tend to live longer, are less likely to be involved in crime, more likely to be engaged in politics and in their local communities, and tend to be less racist or sexist. Insofar as graduates possess such characteristics, there are implications for the whole of society.

There are a number of possibilities to extend the wider benefits of higher education to those who do not directly participate in it. Calhoun makes the point that as well as delivering private benefits through the award of credentials, higher education also produces public benefits through, for example, the development of new technologies and contributions to local industries but also through "value-rational claims about the inherent virtues of knowledge, culture or religious inquiry or non-economic accounts of public contributions, such as individual self-development or improved citizenship" (Calhoun, 2006, p12).

On the research function of higher education, Calhoun makes the important distinction between those subjects which are essentially specialist and inaccessible to the majority of people (e.g. theoretical physics or mathematics) and those which are potentially relevant and accessible to all (e.g. electoral politics or social welfare). Hence a broader distinction between 'knowledge for experts' (closed) and 'public knowledge' (open) is important when discussing social equity in respect of access to 'authoritative knowledge' (Calhoun, 2006, p23).

"We store knowledge in inaccessible academic journal articles written for the approbation of a handful of colleagues or simply for a line on a vita. We treat our opportunities to do research not as a public trust but as a reward for previous studies, and we treat the research itself too often as a new examination to pass in order to enjoy additional career benefits than as an opportunity to benefit others.....Too often we invest heavily in the autonomy of disciplines at the expense of both the advance of knowledge in interdisciplinary projects and the circulation of knowledge more widely." (Calhoun, 2006, p31)

Developments such as the 'open sourcing' of knowledge on the web and collaborations between higher education with the mass media are contemporary examples of the 'circulation of knowledge more widely'.

There are also references in the literature to higher education functioning as a critical and independent space to appraise knowledge claims and to provide intellectual resources for citizens to contribute to a balanced and rational public discussion and debate on contested issues. Standing alongside this expectation one can also find references to the 'moral' responsibilities of academics in exercising a critique of society. Clearly there are tensions between these different functions, particularly between higher education as a site of disinterested scholarly activity and the call for academics to act in the role of 'public activists'.

The capacity of higher education to function as a critical space tends to be bound up with arguments for the protection of academic autonomy, guaranteed public funding and insulation from corporate forms of governance (see, for example, Van Ginkel 2002). The implementation of funding and regulatory frameworks which are introducing neo-liberal forms of market funding and governance mechanisms are reported to be undermining academic autonomy. The common critique is that this erodes the critical space and disempowers academics. However, there is also a post-structuralist literature which draws on the work of Rose (1999) to develop an analysis of how neo-liberal systems, rather than removing academic autonomy, actually re-shape academic autonomy and harness it to the idea of the entrepreneurial university (Marginson, 2007).

Moreover, it is rather unclear whether higher education has always acted as a critical space in previous decades when academics were perceived to be more autonomous. Research on the role of universities has indicated that universities have played multiple roles, sometimes advocating democracy and taking 'truth to power' and at other times colluding in the maintenance of unequal social and political relationships (Brennan et al., 2004).

These themes direct us towards a literature concerned with higher education and the 'public good'. The term 'public good' is often deployed with little clarification as to its meaning. It is often not entirely clear what is meant by 'public' (is there one or many publics?) and what is meant by 'good'. One definition that tends to be used is Samuelson's (1954) political economy definition which defines public goods as non-rivalrous (consumption by one person does not impair its value for another) and 'non-excludable' (no one can be excluded from the benefits of the good). Other related concepts include 'externalities' which refer to the actions of an individual 'economic agent' which result in positive consequences or spill over effects to other members in society (Marginson, 2004). While such definitions are useful, there appears to be limited development of these early political economy definitions. A further difficulty reflected in the literature is the assumption that public goods are outcomes of public universities while private and 'for profit' institutions provide 'private goods' (an assumption recently questioned by Calhoun, (2006)). Clearly, publicly funded institutions have the potential to produce both public and private goods and governments may develop regulatory mechanisms to steer private institutions towards the public good. This is an area that requires greater research attention, as does the relationship between the public and private outcomes of higher education in relation to different forms of funding and governance frameworks. An example of how new pressures towards market competitiveness in the steering of higher education can entail changes to basic functions is made by Calhoun; noting the tensions between 'excellence' and 'access', he states that the former has recently been transformed from 'the quality of doing well' into a positional good of 'being seen to be better than others' (Calhoun, 2006, p9).

There are a number of points that surface through this discussion:
— First, discussions of equity and social justice cannot be reduced to questions of who participates in higher education and what individual benefits they gain.
— Second, academic autonomy of itself does not necessarily deliver much by way of equity and social justice and indeed may itself be part of processes of elite reproduction.
— Third, and relatedly, higher education's contribution to the achievement of equity and social justice may well require both cultural change within the academic profession and new forms of relationship between institutions of higher education and the societies of which they form a part.

In looking ahead to developments in the European Higher Education Area, we might initially note that even a timescale of fifteen years may be too short to assess the wider impacts of the expansion of higher education. Even on the purely economic considerations, a typical graduate will spend around 40 years in the labour market. And it will be in this sort of timescale that the increased proportions of the population entering higher education will be matched by a similar rise in the proportions of graduates in the labour market.

Looking beyond the economic considerations, similarly long timescales can be envisaged. Any contribution which increased enrolments in higher education might have on factors such as integration and social cohesion is likely to occur only gradually. All of this creates problems for the policy maker, especially since the wider impacts of expanded higher education systems cannot automatically be assumed to be entirely positive. Positive and negative impacts are to be expected and the drawing up of a balance sheet will not be easy.

However, based on the arguments set out above and further insights from the literature, some predictions can be risked:

- graduates tend to be more mobile than non-graduates and future mobility is likely to transcend national borders;
- accordingly, we can envisage much larger population flows across Europe in future decades;
- elite and mass functions will continue alongside each other; elite reproduction functions may occur increasingly at an international level while mass functions of up-skilling the workforce may be carried out locally;
- concerns about intellectual property will become more important in relation to the research function of higher education, with implications for social equity with regard to access to knowledge;
- the increased size and expense of higher education will continue to attract political attention with new forms of accountability and management;
- there may also be a growth in private forms of higher education provision and/or greater diversity of funding sources for nominally 'public' institutions.

The risks that can be envisaged would be of a Europe increasingly divided between the haves and the have-nots with the graduate majority enjoying benefits in terms of health, prosperity and general quality of life denied to their fellow citizens. The opportunities might include a growth in active citizenship at a European level along with a wide variety of social and economic benefits which would be enjoyed by all, whether or not they had participated in higher education.

Much is claimed for the wider impacts of higher education but the evidence base with which to evaluate them is very limited. Thus, one of the objectives for policy makers will be to find better ways of monitoring the impact of expanded higher education systems. A related objective would be to separate evidence on impact from the interests of the various stakeholders who have direct engagement with higher education, either as producers or consumers. By so doing, it may be possible to develop governance and management arrangements which reflect wider public interests than those of the more immediately interested parties. The identification and implementation of such governance and management arrangements –whether they be market-led or state-led or some combination thereof – would be a further objective for the coming decade.

DIVERSITY, QUALITY AND EQUITY

With expansion has come increasing differentiation of higher education's institutional forms. A consequence of this is that more importance may attach to 'where' one studies in comparison to 'what' one studies. In some countries, the access debate therefore comes to centre on widening access to so-called 'top universities'.

We can distinguish between 'horizontal' or functional differentiation and 'vertical' or hierarchical differentiation, especially as different European countries seem to be characterised by one rather than the other of these (Teichler, 2007). Vertical differentiation tends to come with increasing power of markets and is more likely to be found in Anglo-American systems and those influenced by them. The greater state control found in many continental European systems seems to be associated with flatter hierarchies and functional differentiation in terms of the social and economic roles of different institutional types or sectors.

Differentiation certainly seems to be an important way by which higher education can pull off the 'trick' of simultaneously achieving both elite and mass functions. The social elite possess a mechanism for the reproduction and legitimisation of their positions and privileges by effectively preserving space at a distinctive and privileged set of educational institutions. It might be argued that the elite needs the support of the state to maintain this differentiation by ensuring the continuous flow of reputational data and the demonstration of 'difference' and 'hierarchy' between what might otherwise be seen as equivalent institutions and experiences; a key function of quality assurance? For the 'mass' – or at least the expanded middle class – there is at least the promise of opportunities of 'something better' for their offspring, whether an entry route into the elite or, more probably, positional advantage within the expanded and dynamic 'knowledge economy'. But the key to simultaneously pulling off both elite and mass functions must be that different forms and institutions of higher education cannot be regarded as 'all the same'. Where once entry to higher education was the passport to power and privilege, today it may only be entry to a relatively small number of institutions that can provide equivalent opportunities. But this should not hide the fact that entry to *any* form of higher education is likely to maintain or improve a person's life chances and that this is especially the case for people from disadvantaged social groups.

While we can identify system differentiation in terms of vertical and horizontal dimensions, we must also note some instability and change in particular countries. Teichler has distinguished between collective movement, for example, the wholesale 'promotion' of the English polytechnics to university status, and individual movement, for example, where an individual institution 'climbs' the national and/or international league tables (Teichler, 2007). It is particularly in relation to the latter possibility that evaluation systems come to play a role, especially those which involve or lend themselves to quantitative outputs and rankings. External evaluation lends itself, in principle, to the provision of 'promotion' or 'relegation' opportunities for individual institutions or, if a subject-based evaluation is in place, for individual academic departments.

Through the European Network of Quality Assurance (ENQA) agencies, national evaluation systems are now in place in most European countries. Questions arise about the extent to which there will be convergence and equivalence of quality standards driven by the ENQA approval process and indeed whether ENQA might lead to the development of cross-national evaluations, especially for those institutions which consider themselves to be part of an international elite. There are already examples to be found at subject level within some of the professional evaluation bodies in subjects such as engineering and business.

Considering evaluation and quality assurance processes at both national and international levels, one needs to ask whether they are predominantly concerned with ensuring commonality and comparability of standards or whether they are concerned with the highlighting of differences and, in the case of the latter, whether these differences reinforce or threaten existing reputational hierarchies (Brennan and Singh, 2008).

The balance between 'comparability' and 'difference' becomes particularly important at the European and international levels. The Bologna process represents an attempt at harmonisation across national systems yet must take account of the increasing differentiation of those systems. The extent to which the 'public good' is best served by increasing standardisation or by increasingly competitive and differentiated higher education systems would seem to be a key question at the present time. Within all differentiated systems, whether vertical or horizontal, there are very real questions about how differentiated higher education systems map onto wider social diversities and about whose interests are being served by the differentiation.

Where equivalences between the courses and qualifications of formally similar institutions cannot be assumed in practice, there are large implications both for the mobility of students and for the mobility of graduate labour. One distinct possibility is for an elite of internationally referenced research universities to emerge which would possess a degree of autonomy from nationally regulated systems with the latter comprising more regional and teaching-focused institutions. Access to these elite institutions and the existence of opportunities for mobility between them and other types of higher education providers would then become key factors in achieving social equity.

A further issue concerns whether the need for expanded higher education systems to become increasingly multi-functional is in fact being undermined by pressures towards standardisation on the one hand and by trends towards increasingly competitive behaviour in relation to single functions and success criteria on the other. If different types of higher education are needed in order to meet the different needs of different groups in society, they may require new forms and combinations of external regulation and market responsiveness.

Thus, a key question for the European Higher Education Area will be the extent to which differentiation of higher education institutions maps onto, and thereby reinforces, wider forms of social differentiation. And where these differences take a vertical form, it seems likely that social inequities which previously related to differential access to higher education as a whole will be replaced by inequities in access to particular institutions and sectors.

Another aspect to diversity, however, concerns the diversity of traditions and forms of higher education that can be found across the countries of Europe. There is surely a risk that many of these will not survive the pressures of globalisation and market competition to succeed against criteria which are alien to many of higher education's traditional values. On the other hand, the maintenance of many of these diverse traditions coupled with the expected growth in student mobility may lead to greatly expanded choice and a richness of horizontal diversity that may serve to meet future needs that are currently unknown.

Strategic objectives therefore may be to:
— ensure an appropriate balance of horizontal and vertical differentiation in higher education's institutional forms;
— in so doing, protecting the diversity and richness of traditions of European higher education;
— seek to avoid too rigid a separation of elite and mass functions and institutions and too close a relationship between social and educational diversities;

- at the same time, to develop realistic formulations of the functional mixes which can be achieved in individual higher education institutions – the extent of diversities 'within' and diversities 'between' institutions;
- ensure the development of evaluation and quality assurance systems which provide well-founded evidence on the qualities of different providers of higher education and are not biased or manipulated to reinforce existing reputational hierarchies.

POLICY IMPLICATIONS AT EUROPEAN LEVEL

The classic model for the co-ordination of higher education proposed by the American sociologist Burton Clark located national systems at different points within a triangle of forces representing the state, the market and the academic oligarchy (Clark, 1983). Today, many of the elements of this model need review. First, there is the question of whether higher education systems are best seen as 'national' – or as 'regional' within international (e.g. Europe) or national boundaries. And for some institutions, global reference points may seem more important than system ones, however the latter are defined. Second, there is the related question not just of the authority of the state and how it is exercised but of whether the nation-state remains the only or the main level of authority. Third, there is a question of the scope of the market, the ever-widening range of 'consumers' and the ever-widening range of higher education's products. Finally, there is a question of the possible demise of an academic oligarchy and its replacement by a new higher education management class.

Various factors have therefore come together to disrupt both the focus as well as the locus of governance and authority away from the nation-state to the regional (European) and global arenas. Many researchers have discussed the extent to which the modern European university developed as an adjunct of the modern state and was instrumental in the state projects' of social selection and national cultural integration. Clearly, in the context of contemporary developments associated with globalisation, the relation between these components is beginning to break down. Influential commentators state that the perceptions of higher education as an industry for enhancing national competitiveness and as a lucrative service that can be sold in the global marketplace has begun to eclipse the social and cultural objectives of higher education generally encompassed in the conception of higher education as a 'public good' (Gumport, 2000). In this sense, many states may be thought of as beginning to exhibit the characteristics of what Cerny (1990) has termed the 'competitive' state. The competitive state is described as one that defines its primary objective as one of fostering a competitive national economy. Policies are shaped to promote, control and maximise returns from market forces in international settings while abandoning some of the core discourses and functions of the welfare state.

Global competition in higher education brings with it international league tables, rankings, benchmarks and other comparisons of the performance of higher education institutions which act as new modes of governance in the age of globalisation. They invite the creation of new groupings of institutions whose reference points will be the need to maintain global reputations rather than to contribute to local and national needs. For the richer research universities, the attractiveness of such opportunities may be irresistible. But for the majority of institutions of higher education, the pursuit of such goals would be a distraction from more important purposes. The latter include the economic roles but they also comprise roles in relation to social equity, social mobility, social cohesion, citizenship, democracy, cultural engagement and much else. It is these which form the various potential 'public goods' which flow from investment in higher education. They are achieved less by competition and more by co-operation. They are likely to require horizontal rather than vertical differentiation. And in order to achieve them, institutions may need some protection from market forces and from the pressures of a wide variety of interest groups aiming to utilise higher education for sectional or positional advantage.

Global competition has been seen as a threat not merely to individual countries but to Europe as a whole resulting in a call for a response co-ordinated at the European level. The message emanating from many of the documents, speeches and communiqués coming out of organisations such as the European Union Commission, for example, is that Europe is lagging behind the rest of the world, particularly the United States of America (although India and China are also increasingly seen as threats) and that these challenges are not mainly national ones but are common European challenges. An important sign of potential intervention in the sector at regional level can be seen in the European Commission communication 'Mobilising the Brainpower of Europe: enabling universities to make their full contribution to the Lisbon Strategy' (CEC 2005:10) which notes that higher education is not just the sum of its education, training and research activities: "[It is] also a fundamental economic and social sector in its own right in need of resources for redeployment". The document goes on to indicate that "[t]he EU has supported the conversion process of sectors like the steel industry, or agriculture; it now faces the imperative to modernise its 'knowledge industry' and in particular its universities". Issues related to competitiveness therefore appear to be moving between the national and the global-market arena and between the national and the regional European levels.

The role of a European level of policy intervention in offering encouragement and support for the wider social benefits of higher education may also be important, not least in maintaining a balance between the economic and social functions of higher education. Policy at the European level may be more distant from the pressures of local interest groups and hence more democratic. Nor does it rest with any single monolithic body. The European Universities Association, the European Science Foundation, the European Network of Quality Assurance agencies, the European Research Council and the Council of Europe are just some of the organisations that sit alongside the European Commission in possessing a potential authority to shape policies and practices within higher education.

Some of the long-term benefits that could be delivered by such organisations might include:

- providing recognition for wider forms of 'excellence' than those dominated by the research elite and which could serve to encourage and reward new and different models of higher education';
- encouraging innovation through provision of funding streams, information and quality assurance which complement rather than duplicate national provision;
- monitoring the levels of social equity and impact achieved by student mobility schemes;
- investigating the diversity and differentiation of higher education across Europe in order both to spread good practice and to protect the valuable and the unique where this may be under threat;
- helping to ensure that there is equitable access to the full range and diversity of European higher education.

Leaving aside the question of where authority lies in European higher education, there is arguably the larger question of the issues it has to address. This paper has examined themes related to equity, quality and diversity and has identified a number of issues which have implications at a European level. In summary, they are:

- continued expansion of national systems will not necessarily lead to social equity in participation;
- greater opportunities for student mobility across Europe may produce new forms of social inequality;
- greater harmonisation of higher education structures and processes across Europe may improve both student and labour mobility but at the same time it may reduce the diversity and potential choice available from different national and cultural traditions;
- the benefits from mobility when higher education is everywhere 'much the same' may be limited;
- within mass-enrolment higher education systems, some aspects of inequality may be transferred to access to postgraduate levels of education;
- relatedly, access to learning across the full life-course becomes more important within the knowledge economy; yet such access can become another source of inequality;
- while much is claimed about the wider social benefits of higher education, the evidence base for them is quite limited; comparative research and monitoring at a European level can inform decision-makers and users about 'what works and what does not' more convincingly than purely national and local studies;
- the balancing of producer and consumer interests, together with those of an ever-increasing range of stakeholders, is likely to bring further questions about governance and funding of higher education, including the role of any private sectors;
- quality assurance procedures at the European level – whether based on peer review or performance indicators – have the potential to achieve levels of independence and authority that may be more difficult at local and national levels;
- it may be anticipated that greater differentiation of higher educational institutional forms will occur across Europe, bringing with them opportunities

for individual institutions to 'opt out' in whole or in part from their respective national systems.

We might also note that European higher education is frequently the destination point for international students. This is often viewed largely in revenue terms – the additional student fees paid are valuable to universities. But the impact of international students upon the experiences of all students may also be important, and potentially a source of greater mutual respect and understanding. At the same time, the role which international higher education plays in supporting the reproduction of elites in developing countries has also to be acknowledged. Once again, we find a tension between higher education's potential positive contribution to equity and social justice and its role in maintaining and legitimising existing inequalities.

It is perhaps important to conclude by stating two points. First, despite the existence of numerous analyses indicating that the nation-state is coming under increasing pressure from global and regional pressures, it may nevertheless be important to emphasise the usefulness of a historically, culturally and theoretically informed approach to developing policy on social equity. National specificities still play a major role in mediating global and regional pressures and discourses and it may be as important to focus on a European higher education space constituting various cultures and histories as it may be to create a marketised higher education European arena consisting of European consumers. Second, it may also be important to look outside Europe at a range of policy regimes that are more diverse than the Anglo-American neoliberal one towards ones, such as the Nordic social democratic model, components of which might better achieve the goals of economic competitiveness and social cohesion.

REFERENCES

Altbach, P.G. (2000) What Higher Education Does Right. *International Higher Education*, Available from: http://www.bc.edu/bc_org/avp/soe/cihe/newsletter/News18/text1.html (accessed April 2008).

Barnett, R. (2000) *Realizing the University in an Age of Supercomplexity*, Buckingham: Open University Press & SRHE.

Blondal, S., Field, S. & Girouard, N. (2002) *Investment in Human Capital through Post-Compulsory Education Efficiency and Equity Aspects*, Paris: OECD, Economics Department Working Papers No 333, http://www.olis.oecd.org/olis/2002doc.nsf/43bb6130e5e86e5fc12569fa005d004c/efdc39066d09357 4c1256bf3005a7d85/$FILE/JT00129531.PDF (accessed August 2006).

Broadfoot, P.M. (1996) *Education, Assessment and Society*, Buckingham and Philadelphia: Open University Press.

Bourdieu, P. (1996) *The State Nobility*, Cambridge: Polity Press.

Brennan, J., King, R. & Lebeau, Y. (2004) *The Role of Universities in the Transformation of Societies: Synthesis Report*, London: Association of Commonwealth Universities and the Open University.

Brennan, J and Singh M, (2008 forthcoming) Playing the quality game – whose quality and whose higher education? in Calhoun C and Rhoten D (eds), *The Transformation of Public Research Universities*, New York: Columbia University Press.

Brown, P. & Hesketh, A. (2004) *The Mismanagement of Talent: Employability, Competition and Careers in the Knowledge-driven Economy*, Oxford: Oxford University Press.

Bynner, J., Brassett-Grundy, A., Hammond. C., Preston, J., & Schuller, T. (2004) *The Benefits of Learning. The Impact of Education on Health, Family Life and Social Capital*, London: Taylor and Francis, p225.

Bynner, J., Dolton, P., Feinstein, L., Makepeace, G., Malmberg, L., & Woods, L. (2003) *Revisiting the Benefits of Higher Education*, London: Institute of Education, University of London, 70p.

Bynner, J. & Egerton, M. (2001) *The Wider Benefits of Higher Education*, London: Higher Education Funding Council for England, HEFCE 01/46, p18.

Calhoun, C. (2006) The University and the Public Good, in *Thesis 11* (84), pp7–43.

Cerny, P.G. (1997) Paradoxes of the Competition state : The Dynamics of Political Globalisation *Government and Opposition* 32 (2) pp251–274

Clancy, P and Goastellec, G (2007) *Exploring Access and Equity in Higher Education: Policy and Performance in a Comparative Perspective*, Higher Education Quarterly, Vol 61, No 2, pp136–154

Commission of the European Communities (CEC) (2005) 'Mobilising the Brainpower of Europe: enabling universities to make their full contribution to the Lisbon Strategy. http://ec.europa.eu/education/policies/2010/doc/comuniv2005_en.pdf. Accessed 30 July 2008

Clarke, B R, (1983), *The Higher Education System: Academic Organisation in Cross National Perspective*, Berkeley, CA: University of California Press.

Collins, R. (2002) 'Credential Inflation and the Future of Universities' in Brint, S. (ed) *The Future of the City of Intellect*, pp23–46, Stanford, CA: Stanford University Press.

Council of Europe (2006) Declaration on Higher Education and Democratic Culture: citizenship, human rights and civic responsibility, Strasbourg, 22–23 June 2006, http://dc.ecml.at/contentman/resources/Downloads/Declaration_EN.pdf (accessed April 2008).

Egron–Polak, E. (2004) Public Responsibility for Higher Education and Research, Conference final report, 23–24 September 2004, Council of Europe www.coe.int/T/DG4/HigherEducation/PublicResponsibility/FinalReport.pdf (accessed March 2008).

EUA (2005) Glasgow Declaration. Strong Universities for a Strong Europe, Brussels: The European University Association, http://www.eua.be/eua/jsp/en/upload/Glasgow_Declaration.1114612714258.pdf (accessed April 2008)

Galindo-Ruenda, F. & Vignoles, A. (2003) *Class Ridden or Meritocratic? An Economic Analysis of Recent Changes in Britain*, London: London School of Economics, Centre for the Economics of Education.

Goldthorpe, J. (1996) Problems of 'Meritocracy', in Erikson, R. and Jonsson, J.O. (eds) (1996) *Can Education be Equalised? The Swedish case in comparative perspective*. Westview Press, pp255–287.

Gumport P.J. (2000) Academic Restructuring: Organisational Change and Institutional Imperatives. *Higher Education, 39(1) pp,*67–91

Gorard, S. Adnett, N. May, H. Slack, K. Smith, E and Thomas, L (2007) *Overcoming the Barriers to Higher Education* Staffordshire: Trentham Books

Hale, S. (2006) Widening Particpation, Equalising Opportunity? Higher Education's Mission Impossible. *Politics*, 26 (2), pp.93–100.

IAU (2005) Sharing Quality Higher Education Across Borders: a statement on behalf of higher education instituions worldwide, nternational Association of Universities, http://unesco.org/iau/p_statements/index.html (accessed March 2008).

Kaiser, F., Hilligers, H. & Legro, I. (2005) *Lining Up Higher Education. Trends in Selected Higher Education Statistics in Ten Western Countries*, Higher Education Monitor Trend Report, Enschede: Centre for Higher Education Policy Studies, p74.

Lynch, K. & O'Riordan, C. (1998) Inequality in Higher Education: A Study of Class Barriers. *British Journal of Sociology of Education*, 19 (4), pp445–478.

Mayor, F. (1998) Foreword. *Higher Education in the Twenty-first century. Vision and Action*. UNESCO World Conference on Higher Education, Paris.

Marginson, S. (2004) 'Global Education Markets and Global Public Goods' Keynote address. ANZCIES conference, Australian Catholic University, Melbourne, 3 December 2004.

Marginson, S. (2007) Freedom as control and the control of freedom: F.A.Hayek and the academic imagination. Prepared for Kayrooz, Akerlind and Tight (eds.) *Autonomy in Social Science Research.*

Moore, R. (2004) *Education and Society: issues and explanations in the Sociology of Education*, Cambridge: Polity Press

OECD (2006) Summary by the chair M. Giannakou, Minister of National Education and Religious Affairs, Greece, Meeting of OECD Education Ministers *Higher Education: Quality, Equity and Efficiency*, 27–28 June 2006, Athens, http://www.oecd.org/dataoecd/62/21/37032873.pdf (accessed August 2006).

Otero, M. & McCoshan (2005) *Study on Access to Education and Training*. Final Report for the European Commission, Birmingham: ECOTEC Research and Consulting Ltd.

Reay, D., Davies, J. David, M. & Ball, S. (2001) Choices of Degree or Degree of Choice? Class, Race and the Higher Education Choice Process, *Sociology*, Vol 35, pp855–874.

Rose, N. (1999) *Powers of Freedom: Reframing political thought*, Cambridge: Cambridge University Press.

Samuelson, P. (1954) The Pure Theory of Public Expenditure. *Review of Economics and Statistics*, 36 (4), pp387–389.

Shavit, Y. and Blossfeld, H.P. (1993) *Persistent Inequality: Changing Educational Attainment in Thirteen countries*, Boulder: Westview Press

Shavit, Y., Arum, R. and Gamoran, A. (eds.) (2007) *Expansion, Differentiation and Inequality of Access to Higher Education: A Comparitive Study*, Stanford, CA: Stanford University press

Schomburg H and Teichler U, 2006, *Higher Education and Graduate Employment in Europe*, Dortrecht: Springer

Schuetze, H. G. & Slowey, M. (2002) Participation and Exclusion: A Comparative Analysis of Non-traditional Students and Lifelong Learners in Higher Education. *Higher Education*, 44, pp309–327.

Teichler, U, 2007, *Higher Education Systems: Conceptual Frameworks, Comparative Perspectives, Empirical Findings*, Rotterdam: Sense Publications

Thomas, L. (2001) Power, Assumptions and Prescriptions: A Critique of Widening Participation Policy-Making. *Higher Education Policy*, 14 (4), pp361–376.

Van Ginkel, H. (2002) Academic Freedom and Social Responsibility – the Role of University Organisations. *Higher Education Policy*, 15 (4), pp347–351.

Vincent, C. (2003) *Social Justice, Education and Identity*, London: Routledge/Falmer.

Woodrow, M. (1999) Advocates for Access: Do We Really Need a European Access Network? *Higher Education in Europe*, 24 (3), pp337–343.

DAVID WATSON AND PAUL TEMPLE

9. THE UNIVERSITY COMMUNITY IN A EUROPEAN COMMUNITY: INVESTIGATING THE NOTION OF AN ENGAGED UNIVERSITY

INTRODUCTION: KEY FEATURES

All over the world, universities and colleges are working strategically on their relationships with their immediate communities. In this contribution, we describe how and why this is so, including the extent to which the priority reflects rediscovery of the institutions' founding purposes. In short, "engagement" is at the heart of the drive for higher education to contribute to national and regional prosperity as well as to social identity and cohesion.

Defining "University Engagement"

For the purposes of this paper we have decided to use the definition of higher education's civic and community engagement set out by the Association of Commonwealth Universities (ACU) in a seminal document in 2001.

> Engagement implies strenuous, thoughtful, argumentative interaction with the non-university world in at least four spheres: setting universities' aims, purposes and priorities; relating teaching and learning to the wider world; the back-and-forth dialogue between researchers and practitioners; and taking on wider responsibilities as neighbours and citizens (ACU, 2001: i).

This document and the global consultation which it inspired could be said to have stimulated the renewal of interest in this particular topic, which has returned to the top of the agenda of both policy and strategic management interests within higher education systems and institutions.

Foundations

A strong case can be made for the University as a quintessentially European institution. With the exception of idealized views of the Socratic dialogues and the Aristotelean *peripetea*, as well the Library of Alexander (there remains a case that what is common to all conceptions of a university – in all eras – is a library), the models of a university most regularly appealed to as cultural icons are the late medieval foundations of Bologna, Paris, Oxford, and Cambridge. What is more,

B.M. Kehm, J. Huisman and B. Stensaker (eds.), The European Higher Education Area:
Perspectives on a Moving Target, 163–180.
© 2009 Sense Publishers. All rights reserved.

these models – properly understood – were anything but "ivory towers," set apart from the societies which founded them.

Here is Elizabeth de Burgh, Lady Clare, founder of Clare College, Cambridge in 1359 setting out a "mission statement":

> through their study and teaching at the University the scholars should discover and acquire the precious pearl of learning so that it does not stay hidden under a bushel but is displayed abroad to enlighten those who walk in the dark paths of ignorance (Shaw-Miller, 2001).

And here is the Papal bull establishing the University of Aberdeen in 1495:

> In the northern parts of the kingdom the people are ignorant and almost barbarous owing to their distance from a university. The city is near these places and suitable for a university, where all lawful faculties could be taught to both ecclesiastics and laymen, who would thus acquire the most precious pearl of knowledge, and so promote the well-being of the kingdom and the salvation of souls (see http://www.neadvent.org/cathen/01042a.htm).

Lady Clare and Innocent VIII were thus not only patrons of scholarship but also early advocates of "service," or, as it is now inelegantly called, "the third leg." The "pearl of knowledge" was always intended to benefit the community.

If we then fast-forward to the early twenty-first century, European governments (like those on every other continent) see universities as vital parts of modern, competitive knowledge economies. The context has changed, but the expectations of communities that founded and maintain institutions of higher education remain constant.

In between these chronological points, higher education has developed differently in differing regional and national contexts, but a broad pattern can be discerned, in which, again, Europe took a lead. Watson (2010) sets out the pattern, as in the following paragraphs.

The early foundations were specialist communities, such as the late medieval colleges for poor scholars in England (Oxford and Cambridge) and for urban professionals (such as Bologna and Paris in continental Europe). Three centuries later, a similar trajectory was followed by the American colonial seminaries (many of which subsequently became expensive private schools in the US, including the heart of the Ivy League). Stephen Lay points out that what distinguished all of these foundations from their ancient predecessors was the presumption of independence from the state, or what has subsequently become termed autonomy (Lay, 2004: 109).

After a further fallow period, the next significant wave of foundations took place in the nineteenth century. These grew similarly out of perceived social and economic needs, but in the radically different context of industrializing societies. Examples are the University of Berlin in 1810, the national universities founded by newly-created European states, the late-nineteenth century "civic" universities in the UK and the Land Grant universities of the American West and mid-West. These were leavened by specific, primarily research-based institutions on the German Humboldtian model, such as Johns Hopkins.

In the next wave of development, the twentieth century saw the development across Europe of technical university or college systems, sometimes regionally planned as with the English polytechnics and American state systems (of which the archetypes are Wisconsin and the Californian Master Plan). These were equally specifically tied to expectations about relevant education and training, with a new element of ensuring both access by groups previously under-represented, and well as ensuring their progression.

In many countries, the result was to create what came to be known as binary systems of higher education: a group of traditional university institutions contrasted with a more local, apparently more locally-accountable, and apparently more responsive pattern of provision. In his 2008 lecture for the Higher Education Policy Institute in London, Yves Mény, President of the European University Institute, sees this division as largely constructed around the separate realms of research and teaching. It reached its highest form (and one of the rare instances in which teaching is seen as more significant than research in reputational terms) in France:

> In fact, in most continental countries this strict division of labour was put in place rather late and mostly after the Second World War. Indeed in France for instance, where the Napoleonic model was imposed in a radical way, the fundamental division was not so much between teaching and research but between the university system on the one hand and the professional schools in charge of educating and training the future civil servants of the State (Mény, 2008: 2–3).

Around the turn of the twenty-first century, this juxtaposition posed real dilemmas for policy-makers dealing with the advent of mass higher education. Those with binary systems felt that they had run their course; those without them felt that the only way to re-inject mission diversity was to try to create a polytechnic-style counterpoint to unresponsive autonomous universities; others who had tried the change decided they needed to change back.

These were followed by late twentieth century experiments in curriculum, pedagogy, and a further drive towards accessibility (such as, notably, the pioneering of open access, or admission of adults without formal qualification by the UK's Open University and New York's City College system, and their imitators around the world). At the same time, developing nations began to establish the mega-universities, as analysed by John Daniel, making use of open and distance learning technologies (ODL) to speed up participation, and to cut costs. The Indira Gandhi National Open University, founded in 1985 had 1.4m enrolments in 1996, and the Islamic Azad University had 1.2m (Daniel, 1996). The notion of community interest is thereby dramatically expanded. However, even the experiments in ODL built upon traditional foundations. In 2008, the University of London's external degree scheme (which is celebrating 150 years of such business) supports 43,000 students in 183 countries (Kenyon Jones; 2008: 35–50).

Finally, the latter part of the twentieth and the beginning of the twenty-first centuries have seen significant action on the frontier activity between compulsory education, optional tertiary provision, and the initial rungs of higher education. Examples are the UK phenomenon of "higher education in further education" and the vitally important American Community College network: the former especially in the provision of intermediate qualifications such the Higher National Certificates and Diplomas and Foundation Degrees, and the latter through two-year (when taken full-time) Associate Degrees. The latest descriptor of activity in this borderland is that of "dual sector" provision (Macfarlane and Garrod, 2008). There are not yet significant Continental versions of this model, although it is under consideration in parts of Germany.

These latter two waves of developments illustrate that as communities have changed – most recently in response to global communications – not only have existing universities had to respond, but also the acts and intentions of foundation of new institutions have also adapted.

Contemporary University Engagement: a Typology

The contemporary outcome for university engagement is set out in Watson 2007 (134–42). As a result of this history, it is suggested that universities relate to their communities in three main ways.

First order engagement arises from the university simply being there. One of the primary roles for universities is to produce graduates who go to work (perhaps in areas completely unconnected with those they have studied); who play their parts in civil society (where the evidence suggests they are likely to contribute more than if they had not been to university); who have families (and read to their children); who pay their taxes (and return a proportion of their higher-than-average incomes as graduates through progressive taxation); and who support their universities through gifts and legacies. An analysis of national cohorts in the UK has securely established that graduates are not only wealthier, but also happier, healthier, and more democratically tolerant than their non-graduate peers (Schuller et al., 2004).

Also in this first domain, universities guard treasures (real and virtual) in their museums, galleries, and archives. They provide a safe place for the exploration of difficult issues or challenging ideas. They can supply material for a branch of popular culture (the campus novel, film, and television series).

Together these features add resonance to the university as a social institution in its own right: at its best a model of continuity and a focus of aspiration for a better and more fulfilled life; at its worst a source of envy and resentment.

First order considerations also imply that universities should strive to behave well, to be ethical beacons. Universities can choose to behave well or badly in a number of different directions, in relation:
− to applicants (and their families);
− to students (and their sponsors);
− to staff (of all kinds);
− to the local community (or neighbours);
− to the institutions of civil society;
− to investors and supporters;
− to government (in their role as a commentator and contributor to policy, as well as a deliverer of a public service);

- to global citizenship (e.g. by progressive engagement with political, economic, social and environmental issues); and
- to groups of other higher education institutions (locally, regionally, nationally and internationally) (see Watson, 2008 [b]).

Some of the sticking points include the following. Universities can offer misleading advice – to staff, students, and potential students – about their real performance and intentions. As powerful institutions, they can undermine and intimidate their members, their partners, and their clients. They can perpetuate self-serving myths. They can hide behind specious arguments (narrow constructions of academic freedom, *force majeure*, and the like). They can displace responsibilities, and blame others. They can fail the stewardship test (e.g. by not assessing and responding to risk, by cutting corners, or by failing to safeguard their assets). They can be bad neighbours. Above all, they can fail to tell the truth to themselves at least as easily as failing to tell the truth to others.

Second order engagement is generally structured and mediated by contracts. In this domain the university produces graduates in required disciplines and professional areas (whether directly or indirectly required to do so). It responds to perceived needs for particular skills, or for professional updating, or to more general consumer demand for courses in particular subjects. It supplies services, research and development, and consultancy at either a subsidized or a for-profit rate. The university may run subsidiary businesses – some as spin-outs or joint ventures, others in the "service" sector of entertainment, catering, conference organizing or the hotel business.

Also in this domain the university is often an important local and regional economic player. It supplies employment – from unskilled occupations to the highly skilled ones. It provides an expanded consumer base, as students and staff are attracted to the institution and its locality. The university offers a steady, well-indemnified customer for goods and services. It is a source of development, such as of buildings, amenities, office space, and green spaces, although this has its downsides, like controversy over planning, car-parking, congestion, or "studentification" (the perceived take-over by temporary student residents of neighbourhoods, as well as the potential displacement of local residents from low-paid jobs).

The first domain affects the second in some complex and significant ways. The university, as a kind of moral force, is expected to behave better than other large organizations (which are similarly concerned about the bottom line).

Third order engagement relates to commitments between the university and its members.

Universities are voluntary communities: around the world they are rarely part of the compulsory educational infrastructure of the state. Thus, they should not be regarded as agents of the state in creating citizens or subjects. This is not to say, following the precepts of first order relationships, that universities do not play a role in ensuring social cohesion, in promoting community solidarity, and in problem-solving for policy makers and practitioners of all kinds.

University members have a similar set of obligations as individuals; this is the dimension of academic citizenship. To be a full member of a university requires more than completing basic, obvious tasks. For traditional academics this has meant collective obligations: to assessment, to committee membership, and to strategic scoping. The guidance offered by *The European Charter for Researchers* (European Commission, 2005) to researchers and their employers on acting "responsibly and as professionals within their working environment" forms part of this tradition. There is a growing body of literature about professional academic practice.

Since the late twentieth century, such practice has been recognized as no longer belonging exclusively to the ranks of the faculty. The teaching, research, and service environments are increasingly recognized as being supported and developed by university members with a variety of expertise (e.g. finance, personnel, estates, libraries, and information and communications technology), each with their own spheres of professional competence, responsibility, and recognition.

At the heart of academic citizenship is the concept of membership. As consumers, students have entitlements and expectations. Both students and staff have responsibilities, along with all of their rights, within the community. Such responsibilities include the following:

– A special type of academic honesty, structured most clearly around scientific procedure.
– Reciprocity and honesty in expression, for example, avoiding plagiarism by accurately and responsibly referring to other people's work within one's own.
– Academic manners, such as listening to and taking account of other people's views.
– Self-motivation and the capacity for independent learning, along with learning how to learn.
– Submission to discipline (most clearly in the case of assessment – for both assessors and the assessed).
– Respect for the environment in which members of the college or university work.
– Adherence to a set of collectively arrived at commitments and policies (on equalities, grievances, harassment, etc.).

National "Systems" and Their Influence on Engagement

The influence of the European nation state on the evolution of "systems" of higher education has been well documented (Teichler, 2007: 2–4; 55–68). From the point of view of university engagement the differing jurisdictions and legal frameworks have proved to offer both opportunities and constraints. Most recently the fall of the Iron Curtain and the accession of new states to a European Higher Education Area has posed major challenges of reform (Jarab, 2008). Meanwhile, the "autonomy" referred to by Lay as characteristic of European universities has always operated within a context: of national or provincial law; of conditions of public funding; or of recognition and accreditation. A good example is the Swedish Higher Education Act, which specifies three main activities for universities: "higher education, research, and collaboration with the surrounding society" (Bladh, 2007).

To take a vital "worked case," Humboldt's famous *memorandum* of 1810 was about the university in support of the state, although paradoxically he saw the university most effectively serving the state when it was allowed to be wholly independent (Elton, forthcoming). Two decades later, Hegel, in the *Philosophy of Right*, presented the historicist logic of the state as an all-encompassing "ethical idea." In the early twentieth century, the independence of the university from the apparatus of the state seems more important than ever, as eloquently argued by Michael Daxner in his account of "society-making not state-making" (EUA/ACE 2004: 68). The engaged university can, of course, serve the state critically and supportively, but it is wise to retain both a wider and a deeper vision, and one which can survive political vicissitudes. Most seriously, it should avoid co-option into state crusades, for example, of a nationalistic or ethnic nature.

International and Pan-European Initiatives on Engagement

Higher education – as is well known – is not a European Commission sphere of competence. It is, however, widely recognized as a critical influence upon both economic competitiveness and social cohesion. As a consequence, two broad approaches have been developed to draw it into the wider European project. The first has been through coordinated national political initiatives: an example would be the Bologna Declaration to create a European Higher Education Area (1999). Essentially this has been achieved through ministerial signature of agreed protocols. The second has been through explicit drawing-in of higher education to policy fields that do have a treaty source. Examples would be research (as in the Lisbon Declaration, development of both a European Research Area and Funding Council, and the foundation of the European Institute of Innovation and Technology [EIT]), Lifelong Learning (as in the European Year of Lifelong Learning in 1996), and the Year of Intercultural Learning in 2008. There have also been treaty adjustments such as the inclusion of targets for access to higher education in the Treaty of Amsterdam (1999).

These have been supplemented by coordinated institutional initiatives. In 1998, a thousand university representatives gathered to celebrate the ninth centenary of the University of Bologna by signing the Magna Charta Universitatum, a declaration of enduring principles of university organization and life. Three such principles were reaffirmed: institutional autonomy leading to "freedom of teaching and research"; the essential interdependence of teaching and research; and a vision that "transcends geographical and political frontiers." In his anniversary volume, Stephen Lay suggests the addition of a further principle, consonant not only with successive waves of university foundations but also their historical ability to respond and adapt to differing circumstances: "the maximising of reason in all human societies" (Lay, 2004: 105). For him, this leads inevitably to a "concept of civil service as a fundamental principle of the Magna Charta":

> instead of being perceived as a monolithic structure dispensing degrees and obscure, little-read publications, the university should be valued as an

intellectual resource of inherent social usefulness and admired as the model of a reasoned approach to life (*Ibid*, 107–8).

Subsequent gatherings and signings have pushed these commitments further into connections with civil society, with supranational concerns such as sustainability, and in particular with democratic citizenship. In September 2005, Tufts University brought together leading figures from universities across the world at their conference centre in Talloires, south-west France. The meeting resulted in another draft declaration "on the civic roles and responsibilities of higher education." In June 2006, 150 university and government leaders in Strasbourg under the aegis of the Council of Europe Forum on Higher Education and Democratic Culture, met and affirmed a statement on "Higher Education, Civic Responsibility and Democracy" (Watson, 2007: 4–7; Weber, 2008: 239–41; Huber and Harkavy, 2007).

EXPECTED DEVELOPMENTS WITHIN THE EUROPEAN HIGHER EDUCATION AREA, 2010–2020
CURRENT DEVELOPMENTS LIKELY TO INTENSIFY

Universities in most European countries have changed considerably over the last decade or so; and the indications are that the rate of change is increasing. These changes may be thought of as both *exogenous* – caused by external pressures from various directions, and being most apparent in the ways in which public funding is provided to institutions – and *endogenous*, caused by changed understandings coming from within the university itself. But this way of classifying change cannot be pressed too far. What may appear to be essentially internal (like academic choices about the organization of teaching and learning) will reflect changed understandings in society about the roles of students and their teachers. Similarly, external forces will often reflect ideas coming from within the university about, for example, the organization of research. That is to say, the university can only be understood by examining its engagement with the societies to which it relates.

Teaching and Learning

In a Europe where mobility, especially among younger people, is increasingly taken for granted, and where language barriers are becoming less significant, new approaches to teaching and learning which are attractive to students are likely to spread, driven by student demand. These approaches will be more student-centred than have been the case in some higher education traditions, involving more project and group work, perhaps being more employer-oriented, with varying assessment methods (e.g. the wider use of "formative" assessment followed by "summative" assessment) replacing traditional written or oral examinations. The impact of such changes on community engagement will vary: but there is a danger that universities that do not adjust to changing demands may find themselves in difficulty generally, and as a result be less able to engage with their communities.

Charging students tuition fees is currently controversial in many European countries, but is likely to become less so. The English experience (arrangements in other parts of the UK differ) may offer a guide: currently, fees for undergraduate students of about €4000 a year are charged, paid to the university by government and recovered through the tax system once the student starts work. This higher fee level, introduced in 2006, does not seem to have had a negative effect on participation (although there is strong debate about how much further it can be pushed). It should be noted that variable fees for postgraduates have been charged in the UK for many years, set mainly in relation to market conditions. Despite (or because of) this, postgraduate admissions, from within the EU and internationally, have generally increased at a faster rate than for undergraduates.

Significant levels of tuition fees do, however, open debates about "the student as customer," and may lead to new types of relationships between students and their universities. There are potentially positive aspects to this (students taking a closer interest in institutional governance, or perhaps choosing between institutions in part because of reports on the quality of teaching). There are also potential downsides (students coming to believe that their relationship with the university is in essence a conventional commercial one). These changes may have significant effects on how universities engage with students (and perhaps their parents) and, through them, with the wider community. In UK universities, it is widely believed that middle-class parents – at least – are becoming more assertive on behalf of their legally-adult student children, perhaps coming to see their relationship with the university as no different to that with any other service provider. Their nature of their engagement with the university, then, changes. However, the American experience suggests that it is possible to operate a marketized system while retaining a sense of "ownership" by its users.

While distance learning in its "pure" forms has not had the impact that was predicted by some of its promoters around the end of the last decade (Daniel, 1996), "e-universities" have not generally prospered in Europe, and the once-expected threat to the European university from US distance-education providers has not materialized. Blended learning (a mix of face-to-face and online teaching and learning) is developing rapidly. Often involving "learning at a short distance" – that is, using a university's online facilities while actually on or near the university's premises – this use of virtual learning environments (VLE) offers students greater flexibility in when and where they work, and allows good use to be made of the fast-growing range of digital resources becoming available. The availability of affordable laptops, wifi networks, and now 3G mobile phone internet access has greatly facilitated this. More sophisticated systems can allow lectures to be transmitted in forms that allow interactions between teachers and remote students, and for scientific experiments or rare artefacts and so on to be observed remotely. There are opportunities here for universities in relatively remote regions to offer at least some of the facilities once only available in large cities. Involvement in such activities opens the way for wider community engagement, as the university becomes a portal (in the both the "IT" and the conventional sense) to the wider world. We should note that the university library, while increasingly being a site for access to remote digital resources, remains at the physical and intellectual heart of every university: digital demands appear to be increasing the demand for library space (albeit partly of new types), not reducing it. There is a wider lesson here for the engaged university: the traditional needs to be cherished by modern means.

There will be some implications here for the built environment of universities, with requirements for specialist spaces for "highly-interactive virtual environments" (HIVE). The most likely physical requirement, though, will be flexibility is space design ("future-proofing"), allowing institutions to modify their buildings easily to suit changing use patterns.

The Framework 6 project EUEREK studied how universities in a number of European countries have engaged, through their academic programmes and consultancy and other activities, with particular regional needs (Shattock 2008). The University of Lapland, in Finland, for example, has tried to tailor its teaching, research, and consultancy activities around the needs of its very remote communities and their traditional arts and crafts. It has engaged local companies in its work, provided support services to them, and facilitated links among them.

Patterns of engagement can be encouraged in various ways. National funding mechanisms based on student numbers (rather than being intended to fund a staff establishment, or to support an historic cost base) have encouraged the recruitment of students from backgrounds without experience of higher education. The EUEREK study showed, for example, how Plymouth University, in the relatively deprived south-west of England, has been encouraged by the funding mechanism to develop innovative means of student recruitment in its largely rural catchment area. The University has deepened its engagement with its region through building links with the secondary schools and vocational (Further Education) colleges from which it recruits; indeed, it has encouraged the colleges in its region to consider themselves as forming a faculty of the University. In order to protect its recruitment base (among other policy goals), it has created a structure of closer engagement.

Knowledge Production and Use

Changes in the organization of knowledge production will also affect universities' engagement. There is the risk of some regions, and nations, becoming research-poor as research funding concentrates on a few leading centres, where firms and research facilities are clustered, limiting the possibilities of certain forms of engagement. (In the UK, about half of all R&D spending and resulting employment is located in the south-east of the country.) It seems likely that high-cost research in science and technology will become increasingly concentrated in a relatively small number of centres of excellence. CERN is the classic example.

But there are opportunities for applied research, related to particular industries, to develop. The EUEREK study gave the example of R&D supporting the regional ceramics industry developing at the University of Castellon-Jaume in the Valencia region of Spain. The strong higher education role of regional governments in Spain is an important factor in ensuring focused engagement of this kind. Variations in costs across Europe may lead corporations to site research facilities in low-cost regions which possess good educational infrastructures (as is happening to an extent with R&D outsourcing from the US and Europe to India), and so support university-based research in these areas. However, the current rapid economic development of the newer member states suggests that purely cost-advantages will be short-lived; enduring advantage is likely to come from high-quality research units.

Patterns of public funding will determine significantly whether universities have the flexibility to respond to emerging community needs. In many countries, governments are increasingly expecting public universities to respond to market signals, and this provides scope to develop new modes of engagement. Finland and Romania offer examples of governments introducing competitive funding strategies into what had been strongly egalitarian systems, where all institutions considered themselves as equals. This approach, it can be argued, is part of a wider trend, driven in part by globalization (Rinne and Koivula, 2005).

Universities within the same country have different origins (e.g. elite national, regional technological), resulting in different present-day missions. The EUEREK project found that public, research-oriented, multi-faculty universities appeared to be the most "entrepreneurial," in terms of generating non-core income, as they were able to take the (relatively modest) risks in developing new teaching, research or service activities that smaller, or private, institutions typically felt unable to support. Much of this "entrepreneurialism" was in fact related in different ways to community engagement: in Sweden, Umeå University's policy of developing programmes about what the EUEREK study described as "the great outdoors" both supported the University's student recruitment and, through its impact on the local economy, arguably reduced depopulation in its remote region. There are several examples in this study of public investment in universities leading not merely to their engagement with their communities, but also becoming a fundamental means of support to them through their subsequent attraction of people, their ideas, and investment.

However, the increasing competitiveness in national higher education funding systems noted above, and increasing trans-national competitive pressures, will support some modes of engagement (the example of Plymouth's regional recruitment), but may weaken others, where the institution sees no advantage deriving from it. Institutions may point to national quality and credit processes (including the Bologna 3+2 model) as demonstrating national/international comparability, regardless of local conditions. Certain modes of engagement will look to international league-table rankings, rather than local or regional demands, for validation; transnational accreditation may also develop.

One important way in which community engagement is likely to be enhanced is through the blurring of boundaries between universities and enterprises, public and private. This has always existed in teaching hospitals, for example; now more industrial research centres in university laboratories and tailored master's degrees will appear. Universities will increasingly develop long-term relationships with companies, or local industries, and involve them in teaching, research, and consultancy activities. In the UK, various publicly-funded initiatives have encouraged moves in this direction, with some apparent success – as measured, for example, by steadily increasing numbers of patent applications and licensing agreements arising from engagement with enterprises.

The physical (and organizational) integration of universities into urban re-developments, with shared facilities, will become more common, with shared library, social, recreational, sporting, and cultural facilities.

POTENTIAL NEW DEVELOPMENTS

Globalization and Institutional Differentiation

In late-modern society, one of the traditional roles of the university, of providing a local repository of global knowledge, will become more important as globalization becomes ever more significant, economically and socially, in Europe. The university will play a key role in embedding ideas and developments from elsewhere in the domestic social and economic culture. The "internationalised university" – one rooted in a national culture yet comfortable with a wide range of other, possibly contradictory, cultures – will become a key institutional form. It remains uncertain whether truly global higher education brands will emerge: in effect, images not identified with a particular national educational culture. Were this to happen, the role of national institutions would be challenged, with consequences for patterns of local engagement.

It is likely that national "apex" institutions (and, increasingly, institutions which see themselves as serving an elite European market) will continue to set global standards (Cowen, 2002). This small number of elite institutions will not grow substantially, nor will they individually expand in size greatly, but they will continue to set academic standards on the basis of their research; and they will continue to recruit the most able students from across Europe. It is likely that many countries will strive to create one, or a few, arguably world-class universities within their own national systems, where the increasingly influential international rankings of universities find that none currently exist. This will be a remarkable testimony to the significance placed in universities both as motors of national prosperity and as symbols of national prestige. Institutions of this type will be increasingly international in tone and outlook, and will create new opportunities for scholars and researchers with international reputations – so it may actually become harder to create a new "apex" institution on an essentially national platform. There will thus be benefits for some kinds of engagement – with enterprises seeking high-quality research, for example – but local people may find them increasingly out of touch with their needs, and turn to institutions in "lower" tiers.

The language of instruction will be increasingly significant, and universities in small countries will increasingly teach in English or another widely-spoken language (not least so that they can recruit international students). There will be issues here about local engagement: on the one hand, the university will be able to offer local access to a wider range of written and spoken materials; on the other hand, the university may be seen as distancing itself from local needs and local culture. The university may, then, play a role in defining (or undermining) ideas of national culture in global, multicultural societies.

Mode 2 "Service"

"Mode 2 research" is now a well-understood term, describing research undertaken in the context of its application, involving typically researchers from a university and an enterprise planning to apply the research (Gibbons *et al.,* 1994). Similarly, "Mode 2 learning and teaching" may be thought of as learning and teaching undertaken, and assessed, in the context of its application – in the workplace, for example, using examples and materials from the work setting. "Mode 2 service" activities may now emerge as an important university activity. These will be so-called "third leg" functions which have always in a sense been undertaken in the context of their application – like consultancy – but where now the university becomes closely engaged, on a continuing basis, with an enterprise or public agency. The result might be the blurring of boundaries between the university and its partner organizations. There will be various legal issues arising here, such as intellectual property rights, employment rights, and legal liabilities, and legislation will probably be needed to allow otherwise productive partnerships to flourish.

Relationships of this kind may develop into clusters of innovative activities, either in the same industry, or in different industries but drawing on similar sets of skills. These may be cross-border clusters in a Europe where national boundaries make increasingly less economic (and eventually less social) sense. These may not be R&D centres in the usual sense, but looser groupings of people, focused around a university: some of them being university staff, others postgraduate students, people in companies spun-out from universities, consultants working on a succession of research or consultancy contracts, and others employees of firms. Individuals will move easily between these roles as demand or personal inclinations change. The creative industries, which will play an increasingly significant role in Europe's economy, will favour this model. The development of clusters of this type will probably be initially unplanned and bottom-up, but will then come to be supported by infrastructure investment by local governments, firms, and universities.

Universities will be especially important in these clusters, by adding an element of institutional stability to the mix, by offering good research facilities, but also by being able to risk funding projects, using money gained from previously successful enterprises. They will increasingly work with private venture capital firms on the larger projects – the Silicon Valley model. This form of engagement will, as noted earlier, probably come most easily to mid-sized research-focused universities, with a degree of financial flexibility and which are less concerned about annual student recruitment targets. Although there has been a trend for specialist institutions to merge to create multi-faculty institutions (with the inter-disciplinary benefits this can bring), both the growth in size of institutions generally, and the clustering effect, will mean that high-quality specialist institutions can gain a comparative advantage. The demerger of some large institutions to create smaller institutions, more able to address the needs of particular client groups, may take place. Technological advances will mean that equipment costs in some fields are no longer prohibitive for smaller institutions (e.g. because of computer simulations replacing actual machines). This narrower, sharper focus may assist engagement with enterprises and other partners.

RISKS AND OPPORTUNITIES

Universities and the "Public Good"

The opportunities for the engaged university over the coming decade greatly outweigh the potential risks it faces. As we have noted, the "organisational DNA" of the university form has enabled it to adapt rapidly to changing environments over the centuries, in a way that firms have not, and we expect this evolution to continue. The continuing development of the knowledge society and economy will help to ensure that the university becomes increasingly influential, and will be able significantly to set the terms of national and international debates. Its influence will be economic, political, and social. Even universities mainly dependent on public funding – particularly if they are large, and/or of high status – will be in increasingly strong positions to resist political or other demands. Set against this is the university's traditionally internally fissiparous tendencies, and the resulting risk that it might be unclear about what it wants to achieve, and how. It is likely that universities will develop more forceful presence and leadership in order to take advantage of new opportunities for engagement: the traditional "leading scholar" approach to university leadership, found in some European countries, is likely to be seen as less appropriate.

Universities are likely to find new avenues for engagement as new funding streams develop; and as a wider range of social actors comes to appreciate the knowledge that the university can make available – such as smaller enterprises, municipalities, or regional bodies of various kinds. The opportunities here for the university from these types of engagement are both financial and academic – for example, in being able to apply theoretical ideas to practical problems. The major risk is that the "public good" mission of the university in knowledge production – one that no other institution is able to undertake – may come to take second place to commercial activities. University governance needs to be closely aware of this dilemma.

The trend is likely to be that more research and consultancy work from public bodies is tendered for, rather than being simply awarded to, say, national research institutes. This will be in line with the general European trend towards output-based (rather than input-based) funding of higher education and public bodies, and seeking value for money in public spending generally, and will provide further opportunities for the more effective universities to pursue new forms of engagement. We may expect to see more universities undertaking work for public bodies in other countries, in the same way that they currently undertake bespoke teaching or research for companies across national boundaries. The larger, research-intensive universities, with strong international reputations, will have many advantages in these respects, though high-quality specialist institutions will continue to thrive – the latter, in particular when science-based, may become increasingly European, rather than national, in character.

Beyond Europe

A further set of engagements will be found beyond Europe, in terms of the recruitment of international students, collaborative research with universities in fast-industrializing countries such as India and China, and support for various European initiatives in these and other areas of the developing world. Opportunities and risks abound here. UK universities are, next to the US, the largest international student recruiters, and while there are important financial and academic benefits, there is also a risk of destabilization through sudden fluctuations in student numbers from particular regions, normally as a result of financial or political turbulence. As universities in other European countries move into these markets, they will need to assess risks carefully. UK universities have also been in the lead in Europe in establishing, with local partners, campuses in East Asia and the Gulf states. Again, such developments open up a range of engagement opportunities, but reputational and financial risks need to be assessed and, as far as possible, mitigated. It remains to be seen how sustainable these initiatives become.

It is particularly important that universities are able to set their own priorities and methods for engagement. Any form of standard template – as distinct from the sharing of successful practice – could be unfortunately restrictive, and could prevent universities from responding to perceived local needs as quickly as they otherwise might.

Ethical Considerations

With power and authority comes responsibility, and (as suggested) higher standards of behaviour are normally expected from universities than from other organizations. This reflects the role that universities are seen as playing in civil society – neither driven (it is believed, at least) by the profit motive, regardless of whether their formal status is public or private, nor subject to rapidly-changing political whims. The university is therefore seen as standing for stability, integrity, and attachment to a set of values not determined by the seeking of short-run advantages. The risk here, clearly, is that a badly-mistaken judgement, in a situation of developing opportunities, could bring lasting harm to a university's reputation. As we noted in our introductory section, this places a special duty of care on university leaders.

Another risk may be that the increasing demands on the university will encourage it to pursue simply too many initiatives and thereby to lose a sense of strategic focus. The sense of what a particular university stands for – usually a difficult matter to define in any case – will become even harder to understand if its engagements appear random. An important role for a university's management will be to determine what the university can do well, and to do it, and to prevent its energies being used in a large number of marginal activities, which others may do better. This is easy to determine in principle: the difficulty, of course, is in spotting the difference when new ideas are presented, and not rejecting what could turn into an important new activity for the university.

The European university's historic role as a guardian – and critic – of cultural heritage must not be forgotten as universities develop new entrepreneurial functions and global vision. These roles are likely to remain dependent on public, or possibly philanthropic, funding, and must be carefully defined and supported.

SELECTED STRATEGIC OBJECTIVES AND TARGETS, 2010–2020

The most basic objective for universities in relation to civic engagement should be to do it well. The following specific options are recommended in Watson (2007).

> Some of these will be simply about perceived *civic duty*, as when students and staff work as volunteers. Often the specific areas in which they do volunteer will draw upon the intellectual capital of the institution, as when students tutor school pupils or run homework clubs in areas connected with their studies, or when staff members take on governance responsibilities in sectors where they have direct expertise.

> Others will be directly embedded in the *curriculum*, as when credit can be earned for structured volunteering, or more programmatically when work-based learning has a civic or community application. The American model of service-learning represents the fullest development of this theme. Community-based projects and dissertations can also be negotiated.

> More broadly the institution's programme of *research, development, and business support* can be strategically orientated to serve civic and community needs.

> Across all three of these core domains (personal civic duty, curriculum development, and research, development and "third-leg" activity) there is likely to be a special set of relationships which develop with other parts of the public sector: schools; further education; medicine and health; police and probation services; youth and community. In many local authority areas this will tie higher education intimately into the development of integrated children's services.

> Meanwhile there is the important dimension of *shared and open access facilities*, in areas like sport, the arts, libraries, and information technology.

> Finally, the university or college has a direct influence upon both the *physical and business* environment (Watson, 2007: 107).

More broadly, lessons for policy and practice in the future would seem to include the following:
- appreciating the historical pattern in each country is essential;
- the engaged university has to serve civil society, and may be distracted as well as led by the state;
- varied income streams are necessary to allow effective engagement;
- universities should identify their true stakeholders in the sense of sharing risk, and to build alliances;
- they need to deploy their intellectual resources to achieve social ends;
- to mobilize their members living in the community;

- to be a good neighbour, in various senses; and
- to try to act ethically (Watson 2008 [a]).

University engagement with society throws up many tensions and contradictions. Autonomy and independence – as eloquently endorsed by Lay (*op. cit.*) can sit uneasily with political and market forces. It may also be seen as internally competitive with the drivers for university contributions to business and community development, for which more secure metrics and more immediate financial returns are apparent. Too often a drive for "third mission" activity across the spectrum of "business and the community" can be seen as heavily weighted towards the former (Watson, 2007: 107–13).

However, managing these strains has been possible historically, and may prove to be so in future, by restoring and relying on some key themes of our shared intellectual inheritance, not least a "liberal" notion of higher education as the "critic and conscience of society" going back to Newman, and Humboldt's conviction that autonomy (defined as "loneliness" [Einsamkeit] as well as "freedom" [Freiheit]) is necessary for effective service of society (Elton, forthcoming). The "engaged university" has been thrown a challenge by contemporary society. It remains to be tested as to whether it can live up to the weight of legitimate expectation. One response has to be that it has succeeded in this endeavour in the past, and there is no reason why it cannot do so again.

REFERENCES

Association of Commonwealth Universities (2001) Engagement as a Core Value for the University: A Consultation Document (http://www.acu.ac.uk/policyandresearch/research/engagement.pdf)

Bladh, A (2007) Institutional Autonomy with Increasing Dependency on Outside Actors. *Higher Education* Policy, 20, 243–59.

Cowen, R. Comparing and Transferring: vision, politics and universities, in Bridges, D. *et al.* (2007) *Higher Education and National development: universities and societies in transition*,13–29. London and New York: Routledge.

Daniel, J. (1996) *The Mega-Universities and Knowledge Media*. London: Routledge.

Elton, L (forthcoming) *Collegiality and Complexity: Humboldt's relevance to British Universities today*. University of Manchester: Centre of Excellence in Enquiry-based learning.

European Commission (2005) *The European Charter for Researchers*. Brussels, European Commission, Directorate-General for Research.

European University Association (EUA)/American Council on Education (ACE) (2004) *Charting the Course between Public Service and Commercialisation: prices values and quality*. Turin: conference proceedings (3–5 June).

Gibbons, M., Limoges, C., Nowotny, H., Schwarzman, S., Scott, P. and Trow, M. (1994) *The New Production of Knowledge: the dynamics of science and research in contemporary societies*. London, Sage.

Huber, J. and Harkavy I. (eds.) *Higher Education and Democratic Culture: citizenship, human rights and civic responsibility*. Strasbourg: Council of Europe.

Jarab, J. (2008) Reforming systems and institutions of higher learning: towards the creation of a European and global higher education area. *Education, Citizenship and Social Justice*, 3:1 (March), 85–96

Kenyon Jones, C. (2008) *The People's University: 150 years of the University of London and its external students* London: University of London.

Lay, S (2004) *The Interpretation of the Magna Charta Universitatum and its Principles.* Bologna: Bononia University Press.

Macfalane, B. and Garrod, N. (2008) *Challenging Boundaries: managing the integration of post-secondary education.* New York and London: Routledge.

Mény, Yves (2008) *Higher Education in Europe: National Systems, European Programmes, Global Issues. Can they Be Reconciled?* Higher Education Policy Institute Annual Lecture. 15 January.

Rinne, R., and Koivula, J. (2005) "The changing place of the university and a clash of values: the entrepreneurial university in the European knowledge society". *Higher Education Management and Policy,* 17(3), 91–123.

Schuller, T., Preston, J., Hammond, C., Brassett-Grundy, A., and Bynner, J. (2004) *The Benefits of Learning: The Impact of Education on Health, Family Life and Social Capital* London: Routledge Falmer.

Shattock, M (ed.) (2008) *Entrepreneurialism and the Knowledge Economy: Diversification and Organisational Change in European Universities.* Maidenhead: McGraw Hill/Open University Press.

Shaw-Miller, L. (ed.) (2001), *Clare Through the Twentieth Century.* Lingfield, Surrey: Third Millennium

Teichler, U. (2007) *Higher Education Systems: Conceptual Frameworks, Comparative Perspectives, Empirical Findings.* Sense publishers: Rotterdam.

Watson, D (2007) *Managing Civic and Community Engagement.* Maidenhead: Open University Press.

Watson, D (2008a) "The university in the modern world: ten lessons of civic and community engagement." *Education, Citizenship and Social Justice.* 3:1 (2008), 46–57.

Watson, D. (2008b) Universities Behaving Badly? In *Higher Education Review,* 40:3.

Watson, D. (2010) Universities' engagement with society, in *Elsevier International Encyclopedia of Education.* 3rd edition.

Weber, L. (2008) The Responsibilities of Universities to Promote a Sustainable Society, in Weber, LE.E. and Duderstadt, J.J. (eds.) *The Globalization of Higher Education.* London, Paris and Geneva: Economica, 229–43.

Part III: Mobility and Human Resources

ULRICH TEICHLER

10. STUDENT MOBILITY AND STAFF MOBILITY IN THE EUROPEAN HIGHER EDUCATION AREA BEYOND 2010

INTRODUCTION

The increase of student mobility within Europe is generally viewed across Europe as one of the most impressive or even the most impressive "success stories" of higher education since the 1980s – a trend initiated in 1987 by the establishment of ERASMUS, the support programme for temporary student mobility. The ministers from European countries signing the Bologna Declaration in 1999 obviously wanted to keep the momentum of this success story or even to carry student mobility to more impressive levels of success. The Bologna Declaration underscores the aim of enhancing student mobility more strongly than any other aim, whereby two directions are specified: making European higher education more attractive for students from other regions of the world and facilitating intra-European student mobility.

One could assume, therefore, that the Bologna Process in the first decade of the 21st century is just a continuation of the policies and actual developments already underway one or even two decades earlier. If there was such a continuity of aims and growth of involvement and impact, this could allow us to forecast a continuation of aims and trends beyond 2010. The subsequent analysis, however, will show that *student mobility in Europe from the 1980s until the present cannot be viewed as a linear process which can be extrapolated into the future.* There were substantial shifts of public attention, policies and activities. And there are various problems visible now which deserve attention in the discussion of possible future scenarios.

Academic staff mobility was not a "success story" similar to that of student mobility. Certainly, mobility of academic staff for the purpose of research and exchange of information in general is a well-established feature; the Science Directorate of the European Commission has supported intra-European mobility and cooperation, for research purposes in various respects, among others through one-year or two-year fellowships for young researchers. Closely linked to student mobility, efforts were made as well under the leadership of the Education Directorate to support staff mobility for teaching purposes. Available figures show an impressive quantitative increase of teaching staff mobility within ERASMUS. But this did not affect the scene of teaching in higher education in Europe in a similarly impressive way as student mobility. It remains an open question whether teaching staff mobility has a chance to be promoted to a priority area of European

B.M. Kehm, J. Huisman and B. Stensaker (eds.), The European Higher Education Area:
Perspectives on a Moving Target, 183–201.

higher education policy when decision-makers take stock of the developments of the EHEA up to 2010 and set new priorities for the future. Therefore, staff mobility will be addressed only briefly in the following considerations.

PAST POLICIES AND TRENDS

Student mobility became an important issue of higher education policy shortly after World War II. A shock was felt widely in regard to how inhumanly people had treated each other. International mobility of staff and students was expected to serve as a countermeasure to hatred and mistrust, to further universal and cosmopolitan values and to enhance mutual understanding across boundaries. This was reflected in the U.S. policies of that time of promoting a *"junior year" abroad of U.S. students* and of providing fellowships for foreign students and academics to spend some period of study and research in the United States (see Altbach/ Teichler, 2001). Already during the 1950s, the Council of Europe followed similar lines and initiated *conventions on the recognition* of entry qualifications, periods of study and degrees. These activities subsequently were intensified and spread all over Europe, when UNESCO and the European Commission got involved in these activities (see Deloz, 1986). They culminated in the Lisbon Convention of 1997 calling for mutual recognition of educational achievements across Europe strongly based on mutual trust. Educational achievements abroad prior to higher education, during the course of study and at graduation should be recognized, "unless substantial differences can be shown" (Council of Europe, 1997).

Many individual European countries as well supported mobility in various respects. During the 1970s, when the consequences of expanding student enrolment were a key issue, various European countries decided to extend the promotion of student mobility in order to assure that it did not remain confined to a small elite. Also, increased support for students from developing countries was viewed as an essential means of development aid.

The predecessor institution of the European Union became a key actor of higher education policy not before the 1970s. In the search of taking over tasks not fully covered by national higher education policies, a decision was taken in the mid-1970s to establish a pilot scheme of temporary student mobility in Europe between cooperating departments. Both the success and the limitations of the *Joint Study Programmes* (1976-1986) eventually triggered off the idea of establishing a large-scale scheme of temporary student mobility. Within the ERASMUS programme, established in 1987, students obtained means aimed to cover the additional costs for study in another European country for up to one year provided that home and host institutions agreed on curricular and administrative cooperation and took care of the recognition of study achievements (see European Commission, 1994).

ERASMUS did contribute not only to quantitative growth but also to a paradigmatic shift in the area of student mobility. In the past, mobility comprised mostly the total period of study and had primarily a "vertical" character: mobile students went to institutions and countries with an academic quality superior to that at home and had to immerse themselves completely into the study conditions and provisions abroad. ERASMUS, however, underscored the value of seeking for experiences different from those at home, the potentials of reciprocity and the virtues of "horizontal" mobility, i.e. student exchange "on equal terms" – benefits which could be expected from temporary student mobility within Europe. Though ERASMUS never outweighed other mobility quantitatively, it had a profound *impact on the internationalisation policies* of European higher education at least until the mid-1990s. It certainly helped that the value of cooperation and mobility on equal terms was highly appreciated and that the higher education institutions moved towards a systematic higher education policy. Thereby, international activities were increasingly embedded into the core activities of higher education and the core activities were designed increasingly to be beneficial to international cooperation and mobility (see Teichler, 1997).

MOBILITY WITHIN THE BOLOGNA APPROACH

Mobility – a Priority Aim, not a Priority Action in the Bologna Process

In operational terms, mobility is not the first priority of Bologna Process. Rather, a process of *structural convergence* of study programmes and degrees across Europe is most indicative. This structural change is bound to have an enormous impact on curricula in all the countries involved. Additionally, the debates on curricular changes in the Bologna Process are pre-occupied with two wider issues: the consequences of structural and curricular reforms for quality in higher education and for "employability", i.e., the links between the competences acquired on the various degree levels and the subsequent graduate employment and work.

But mobility was a dominant issue in the rationales. The *Sorbonne Declaration* of 1998 expressed the potential international value of a new "harmonized" system of study programmes and degrees as follows:
– As regards the *intra-European* mobility and cooperation: "An open European area for higher learning carries a wealth of positive perspectives, whilst of course respecting our diversity, but requires on the other hand continuous efforts to remove barriers and to develop a framework for teaching and learning, which would enhance mobility and ever closer cooperation".
– As regards *world-wide* mobility: "The international recognition and attractive potential of our systems are directly related to their external and internal readabilities".

The *Bologna Declaration* of 1999 refers to *intra-European mobility* in various instances. Mobility should be promoted by overcoming existing obstacles. A credit system should be established "as a proper means of promoting the most widespread student mobility", whereby the reference to ECTS underscores that the authors have temporary mobility and intra-European mobility primarily in mind with this recommendation.

As regards *world-wide mobility*, the Bologna Declaration points out: "We need to ensure that the European higher education system acquires a world-wide degree of attraction equal to our extraordinary cultural and scientific traditions ... we engage in co-ordinating our policies to reach ... the following objectives, which we consider of primary relevance in order to establish the European area of higher education and to promote the European system of higher education world-wide …".

Obviously, the prime aims of the structural reform of study programmes and degrees were to make higher education in Europe more attractive for students from other parts of the world and to facilitate intra-European student mobility. Moreover, several accompanying measures suggested, such as the introduction of a credit system and the award of a Diploma Supplement, are expected to reinforce student mobility.

Renewed Attention to Incoming Students from Other Parts of the World

In one respect, these formulations clearly signal a shift of attention since the early years of ERASMUS. Since about the mid-1990s, in Europe increasing attention has been paid to worldwide student mobility. The *increasing use of the term "globalisation"* gradually challenged or even substituted the use of the term "internationalisation". Governments had become aware of the fact that continental Europe was hardly on the agenda when a growing number of Asian students chose a host country for study abroad. In France and Germany, this triggered off lively debates and rapid measures to make higher education more attractive for students from other parts of the world even before these countries signed the Sorbonne Declaration in 1998. It is certainly justified to argue that the enormous efforts to establish convergent stage structures of study programmes and degrees never would have made it, if this was just for the purpose of facilitating intra-European student mobility.

The two objectives of facilitating short-term student mobility in Europe and of making degree study in Europe more attractive for students from outside Europe, notably from less economically advanced countries, cannot be pursued together without *substantial tensions*:
– the debate on worldwide attractiveness of European higher education focuses on the *import of students* from other continents, while *reciprocal mobility* is advocated within Europe;
– inward mobility from other parts of the world is understood primarily as *"vertical"* mobility, i.e. from countries with a lower educational level to countries with an advanced level, while intra-European mobility is interpreted primarily as *"horizontal"* mobility, as exchange on equal terms which might be stimulating through the substantive contrast of the programmes abroad and at home;
– as a consequence, students from other parts of the world are primarily expected to *adapt* to the environment of their host institutions, while students mobile within Europe might *challenge established practices* and contribute to educational innovation;
– *degree mobility*, i.e. mobility for studying the whole degree programmes, is prevalent among students coming to Europe from other parts of the world, while *temporary mobility* is widespread within Europe;

– as a consequence, the *granting of credits for transfer*, one of the accompanying measures of the Bologna Process, is most important for intra-European mobility, while the Diploma supplement, the other accompanying measure, is more likely to be important for intercontinental mobility;
– last but not least, the composition of students vary across fields of study: temporary "horizontal" student mobility in Europe is on average over-proportionally opted for by students in *humanities and social sciences*, while "vertical" degree-mobility across continents is more widespread among students in *science and technology* (cf. Teichler, 2007a).

Therefore, it is interesting to note what role these different thrusts of mobility played in the early years of the Bologna Process and to consider the relevance of these experiences for possible future options.

INCREASE OF STUDENT MOBILITY: DOES BOLOGNA MATTER?

Overall Increase of Student Mobility

It is possible to describe the "success story" of ERASMUS in quantitative terms: about 10,000 students were supported in the second year of the programme, more than 80,000 in the tenth year, i.e. shortly prior to Sorbonne Declaration and about 150,000 in the 20th year. When ERASMUS was embedded into the new Life Long Learning Programme of the European Union in 2007, a target was set of about 300,000 ERASMUS students by the year 2013.

The absolute number of foreign students worldwide, according to UNESCO statistics, was about 200,000 in the mid-1950s. It surpassed 500,000 in 1970 and reached about 1.2 million, when the ERASMUS programme was established in 1987. Thereafter, the number of foreign students more than doubled, whereby the growth rate has increased since the late 1990s; it reached about 2.5 million in 2004 (UNESCO, 2006).

The Limits of Available Statistics

For various reasons, however, these general trend data do not help us establish whether the Bologna Process contributes to student mobility in the expected way. First, the statistics are not strong and valid sources. International educational statistics collected by UNESCO, in recent years together with OECD and EUROSTAT, have the following drawbacks:
– They do not inform us primarily about *"inward mobile"* and *"outward mobile"* students, but rather about *"foreign students"* and *"students studying abroad"*. Ironically, the more internationally mobile people have become, the less the nationality is an indication of mobility which just has happened. "Mobile students" differ from "foreign students", because, on the one hand, some foreign students have not been mobile for the purpose of study, but rather have lived and learned in the country of study before they have started to study; on the other hand, some persons move from elsewhere to the country of their citizenship for the purpose of study;

- They are in various respects *incomplete*: some countries do not deliver data, and some deliver according to other definitions; data on those sectors of "tertiary education" are not considered "higher education", and data on doctoral candidates sometimes are lacking or incomplete. Finally, some countries do not include temporarily mobile students at all or not completely, e.g. ERASMUS students (see Kelo/Teichler/Wächter, 2006).

Second, we have to be cautious in hoping that we can measure the impact of Bologna to a substantial extent already through stocktaking before 2010. Evaluation studies of the Bologna Process have shown that it takes time to make the new stage structure of study programmes and degrees the dominant feature all over Europe and it takes even more time to make this known worldwide for students intending to study abroad. Moreover, statistical data potentially measuring the changes occurring in student mobility are not available quickly: it takes two to three years as a rule.

Incoming Students from Other Parts of the World: Only "Push Effects"?

Third, as regards students from other regions of the world, we still might employ statistics of foreign students as an approximation for mobile students. In fact, we note an increase of students in Europe from other parts of the world during the early years of the 21st century. But we have to ask whether this is due to Bologna. A first glance suggests that the growth rate of non-European students in Europe does not differ considerably from the overall growth rate of non-European students studying abroad. Thus, the increase in Europe seems to be dominantly a push effect of a rising absolute number of students from China, India and other countries studying abroad, while the *"pull effect" of Europe might be small*.

It is worth remembering in this context, as pointed out above, that the number of foreign students has not increased faster for about 50 years than the overall number of students; thus, the study abroad rate remained more or less constant at about two percent. We might estimate, though, that the proportion of foreign students in Europe increased during this period from less than three percent to more than seven percent – primarily because the absolute number of students grows more substantially in the developing countries than in the economically advanced countries. It is also worth noting that, contrary to widespread rumours, the percentage of foreign students opting for study in non-English-speaking economically advanced countries had not been on a decline during the two decades prior to Bologna.

Intra-European Mobility – the Future Will Tell

Fourth, the available statistics are too deficient to allow us to draw conclusions about trends of intra-European temporary mobility in the wake of the Bologna Process. More detailed statistics available in a few countries show that numbers of "foreign" students clearly differ from numbers of "mobile" students; temporary mobility is not even covered in the statistics of some countries, and the international statistics do not differentiate between bachelor and master students.

First data available on Italian graduates (according to Alma Laurea studies) and on German students shortly before graduation (according to HIS surveys) suggest that the proportion of Bachelor students studying temporarily abroad is moderately smaller than that of students of long study programmes prior to the implementation of Bologna, but we do not know whether mobility in the Master programmes leads to altogether lower, similar or even higher mobility rates.

In recent years, the European Parliament as well as the supranational agencies in charge of educational statistics recommended the European governments to improve student statistics in a way that student mobility for the purpose of study can be measured in addition to foreign students. Also, the progressing implementation of Bachelor and Master programmes in Europe will eventually lead to such a state of affairs that impact of the Bologna Process on student mobility can be assessed with a higher degree of certainty than this can be undertaken now.

ISSUES OF CURRICULA AND RECOGNITION

The Bachelor-Master Structure – Not a Key Factor for Intra-European Mobility

According to the Sorbonne Declaration and the Bologna Declaration, the establishment of a stage structure of study programmes and degrees should facilitate intra-European mobility. However, the introduction of a Bachelor and Master structure per se could hardly be expected to serve any breakthrough regarding the frequency of student mobility. Within Europe, years of study had served relatively well as an "exchange rate" irrespective of the varying numbers of years required up to a degree in different countries, types of higher education institutions and field of study.

In-depth evaluation studies of ERASMUS pointed out other possible causes for incomplete recognition and for the need to prolong the overall period of study as a consequence of temporary study in another European country. There are notable limits in the readiness of institutions to consider courses abroad to be equivalent in level and matching in substance to those at home; differences in the modes of certifying and counting study achievements; lower numbers of courses taken abroad than at home; and gaps in foreign language proficiency as well as various problems of adaptation to the host country and institutional environment (see Teichler, 2002).

The Potentials of Accompanying Measures

One could not expect, therefore, that the introduction of the Bachelor-Master structure as such is a magic tool to increase recognition. One could expect, however, that accompanying measures and a growing favourable mood as regards student mobility might lead to increased recognition. Notably, five measures are worth noting in this respect.
- First, the Bologna Declaration called for a spread of the use of *credits* in order to facilitate recognition. A prior evaluation study of ERASMUS, in fact, had

shown that the extent of recognition was higher if achievement abroad was certified in terms of credits than otherwise (Teichler, 2002).

- Second, the Diploma Supplement aiming to provide an internationally readable certification of the national setting, the study programme and the study achievements of the individual graduate are expected to enhance the mobile students' and graduates' chances of being appropriately treated by potential employers. As a consequence, more students might be mobilized to opt for study abroad.
- Third, the willingness to establish *joint degree programmes* between networks partner departments in various European countries seems to have increased in recent years.
- Fourth, the European Commission, not the formal driver but in various respects involved in the Bologna Process, established the *ERASMUS Mundus* programme which provides for students from outside Europe the opportunity to experience more than a single European higher education system in the course of their Master study. It will be interesting to note how this programme will develop qualitatively and quantitatively in the future. Certainly, it does not fit the obvious expectations from other parts of the world. As a survey of students from a select number of countries outside Europe showed, there are well-established images worldwide of higher education in various individual European countries, but not of Europe as a whole (European Commission, 2006).
- Fifth, in order to attract more students from other parts of the world, *English* is increasingly employed *as the language of instruction and communication* at institutions of higher education in non-English-speaking countries in Europe. Surveys undertaken suggest that the number of courses taught in English might have tripled from 2002 to 2007, but still remained a minority phenomenon, i.e. estimated to comprise at least 2 % and at most 7 % of all study programmes (Wächter/Maiworm, 2008).

The spread of the Diploma Supplement and of English as the language of instruction might serve both the attractiveness of Europe for students from other parts of the world and smooth conditions for intra-European mobility. Joint degree programmes and the spread of credit systems notably are relevant for temporary intra-European mobility. ERASMUS Mundus is designed to attract students from other parts of the world.

Short and Dense Curricula – a Detriment to Intra-European Mobility?

In contrast, we cannot exclude detrimental effects of the Bologna Process on student mobility. According to a survey undertaken in 2005 (Bürger et al., 2005), some experts are convinced that the Bologna Process *discourages intra-European mobility* and create new barriers. About one quarter each of the experts and actors on the central level and about one sixth each of the experts and actors on departmental level surveyed believe that

- the *short duration* of the new study programmes will lead to a decrease of mobile students,

- the *curriculum is too dense* to enable students to go abroad temporarily, and
- the *curricula are not flexible enough* to take some of the courses abroad.

These concerns might be surprising at first glance: if universities are really willing to recognise periods of study at a European partner university as equivalent to corresponding study periods at their own institution, why should shorter periods of overall study and more highly structured curricula be impediments to recognition? These arguments, rather, reveal that recognition has been shaky in the past. Often, students were recommended to forego at home the softer parts of the curriculum, e.g. self-study, electives and other elements are not considered the core of the curriculum, or they even were advised to accept an overall longer period of study in order to incorporate a period of study abroad with little concern about recognition. Many British universities even defined the period abroad as an additional period of the overall study programme, thus making a longer study period mandatory for all intending to spend a period abroad.

Thus, the shorter (Bachelor) and often more highly structured study programmes in the Bologna Process seem to be barriers against assuring recognition "the cheap way", i.e. without really accepting core parts of curricula of the partner university as equivalent to core parts of one's own curricula. It will be interesting to note whether this phenomenon will turn out to be frequent in the future or whether it will succeed to challenge the universities to pave the ground more consistently for "real" recognition.

A Growing Emphasis on Curricular Convergence in Europe?

In comparing the communiqués of the follow-up conferences in Prague, Berlin, Bergen and London with the initial Sorbonne Declaration and the Bologna Declaration, we note an increasing direct or indirect emphasis on curricular matters: *"Quality assurance", "learning outcomes", "employability" and "qualifications frameworks"* are some of the terms employed which underscore this trend. Possibly the hope has faded among politicians initiating and implementing the Bologna Process that the core measure, i.e. the establishment of convergent structures of study programmes and degrees, as such could elicit an impressive impact commensurate to all the objectives called for, notably the enhancement of student mobility. The multitude of curriculum-related measures recently addressed in key Bologna documents might even indicate a hidden agenda: that a certain degree of curricular convergence has to be strived for now in order to achieve the goals initially associated solely with structural convergence. One has to bear in mind, though, that the formulations chosen in the follow-up communiqués are not very clear and certainly could not be very clear in that respect because the issue of persistence of curricular variety *versus* curricular convergence remained controversial.

But we certainly can assume that the direct and indirect measures taken within the Bologna Process to affect the curricula in higher education will have, if successfully implemented, the result of contributing to a certain degree to curricular convergence. Therefore the question in place is how this affects intra-student mobility. On the one hand, curricular coordination is likely to reduce barriers to recognition; similar courses abroad might be more easily recognised as equivalent to courses at home than contrasting ones. On the other hand, one of the major elements of the ERASMUS "success story" has been undoubtedly that learning from contrasts was viewed as highly valuable. If the Bologna Process contributes in the long run towards a decline of substantive variety of teaching and learning within Europe, it would undermine one of the key benefits of study temporarily in another European country.

STUDENT MOBILITY AND THE PATTERNS OF THE HIGHER EDUCATION SYSTEM

As already pointed out, the growing reciprocal student mobility and increasing cooperation on equal terms was accompanied around 1990 by a paradigmatic shift in the internationalisation policies of national governments and respective strategies of higher education institutions in Europe. Not only did student mobility move from an exceptional choice towards a normal option, but steps were also undertaken towards systematization of international activities and towards their integration into the mainstream of the higher education activities.

Since about the mid-1990s, however, the term *"globalisation"* has spread in Europe depicting a paradigmatic notion of the conditions in which higher education operates as well as of the imperatives higher education should opt for in their worldwide oriented activities (see Teekens/de Wit, 2007; Teichler, 2004). According to these views, knowledge generation becomes increasingly driven by imperatives of technological and economic utility *expecting higher education to compete globally and on a commercial basis.* Accordingly, international academic and institutional interaction would be shaped predominantly by a *notion of rivalry* while only select "strategic alliances" might be based on a cooperative approach; *knowledge is seen as commodity* which can be traded through attracting high-fee-paying students or through *"transnational education"*, e.g. setting up branch campuses abroad or "franchising" programmes. Finally, the institutions of higher education are expected according to this approach to put all their energy on enhancing their international reputation and visibility in order to excel as a *"world-class university"*. Often, advocates of such a paradigmatic shift claim that higher education has the option of either remaining "traditional" in underscoring cooperation and open knowledge transfer or becoming increasingly "competitive" in terms of the worldwide "rankings" of universities (see Sadlak/Liu, 2007).

In various respects, "globalisation"-oriented higher education policies and strategies seem to be conflicting with those underlying the Bologna Process or reinforced by it, even though the Bologna Declaration refers to global competition. First, strategies of gearing international activities towards *income generation* collide with those of promoting intra-European mobility along worldwide mobility, for educational provisions can be sold more easily to foreign students from countries not on equal terms as far as the quality of higher education is concerned. Moreover, the major promotion scheme of intra-European mobility, ERASMUS, requires hosting institutions *not to charge tuition fees.*

Second, strategies of commercialising higher education, as a rule, aim to increase *import of foreign students* or to sell programmes internationally. They are hardly interested in the *internationalisation of their own students.*

Third, and most importantly, there is a conflict between the underlying notions of a desirable pattern of the higher education system. It is widely assumed that rivalry-oriented international activities of higher education institutions and competitive behaviour in order to be visible in rankings of "world-class universities" contribute towards a growing *vertical stratification* of national higher education systems. The initiatives in several European countries to strengthen notably top universities and many debates and activities associated with the Lisbon Process of taking research as a main tool to make Europe "the most competitive economy of the world" are all factors pushing towards increased vertical stratification of the national higher education systems in Europe. As a consequence, temporary student exchange is likely to be confined to small sets of institutions of higher education belonging to the same stratum. In contrast, the Bologna Declaration seems to be based on the rationale that student mobility within Europe should be as open and wide as possible. Wide *"zones of mutual trust"*, however, can be expected only in flat institutional hierarchies.

The Declining Exceptionality of International Experience through Study Abroad

Available analyses on the careers of graduates from European institutions of higher education having been mobile during their course of study allow us to conclude cautiously that formerly mobile students are somewhat superior to nonmobile students in their *competencies relevant for employment and work* and are more successful in their *early career*. But the findings are not consistent and the advantages found here and there are small on average.

Striking differences between formerly mobile and formerly nonmobile students, however, are consistently observed regarding *visibly international and intercultural competences and related employment opportunities and work assignments*. Formerly mobile students are on average clearly superior to nonmobile ones in foreign language proficiency, knowledge on other countries and cultures as well as in understanding and communicating with people from other countries. They are by far more often employed abroad or sent by the employers abroad for some period, and they take over a much higher proportion of assignments implying international knowledge, cooperation or communication with persons of another cultural background within one's country.

If one compares studies undertaken at different points of time over the most recent two decades, the comparative *advantage of formerly mobile students in taking over work assignments with an international component seems to decline in some respects*. In a recent study on the Professional Value of ERASMUS, this decline is pointed out (Teichler/Janson, 2007). The authors conclude that this is primarily due to the fact that study abroad is becoming less and less exceptional as a consequence of the fact that all students, also the nonmobile ones, live in an increasingly international societal environment and that they study at universities which have become more international beyond mobility. Studying abroad as such therefore adds less than previously to the experiences most students have anyway. As a consequence, the authors suggest that stronger curricular efforts should be made within ERASMUS in order to make teaching and learning during the study period abroad more meaningful.

VARIATIONS ACROSS EUROPEAN COUNTRIES

Varying Rates of Participation

The observations presented above have to be specified. We have to take into account an enormous diversity by country.

Although the available statistics are deficient in various respects, they can serve to indicate the varying conditions. Leaving aside very small European countries with incomplete systems of higher education (Cyprus, Iceland, Liechtenstein, Luxembourg and Malta), we note substantial differences in the rates of foreign students and study abroad.

In the academic year 2002/2003, the *rate of foreign students* among all students was
- 10-20% in Switzerland, Austria, United Kingdom, Belgium, Germany and France,
- only 2% or less in Estonia, Italy, Latvia, Lithuania, Poland, Romania, Slovenia, Slovakia and Turkey.
- In the same academic year, the *students studying abroad* corresponded to
- 5-10% in Bulgaria, Greece, Ireland, Slovakia, Norway, Austria and Switzerland, but
- less than 2% in Poland, Spain and United Kingdom (Kelo/Teichler/Wächter, 2006).

This indicates on the one hand that higher education in some European countries is strongly affected in its daily life by large and growing proportions of foreign students. On the other hand, we note that some countries have ample room to catch up as far as student mobility is concerned. This might vary between foreign students and study abroad: the rate of foreign students is low, but the study abroad rate is high in the case of Slovakia; in contrast, the United Kingdom has a high rate of foreign students, but a low rate of study abroad.

The Value of Mobility for Students of Central and Eastern European Countries

Intra-European student mobility currently is viewed as *more interesting and valuable for students from Central and Eastern European countries* than for those from Western Europe. Available statistics, though deficient in various respects, clearly indicate that students from Central and Eastern Europe opt more frequently for "degree mobility", i.e. for studying the whole study programme in another European country, whereby they mostly go to Western Europe. And according to ERASMUS evaluation studies, students, teachers, programme coordinators and employers agree in stating that ERASMUS students from Central and Eastern

Europe are an academically more select group than those from Western Europe. The ERASMUS experience turns out to be more valuable for them in enhancing their personality and competences, and the professional impact is more impressive (see Bracht et al., 2006).

The stronger motivation to study in another European country on the part of students from Central and Eastern Europe and the higher value of study in another European country for them clearly can be attributed to the fact that the Central and Eastern European higher education systems are not yet considered to be on equal terms with the West and are clearly driven since the political changes around 1990 by efforts to "catch up" and to get more similar to the West. If this is successful, the differences in the mobility patterns and their impact might diminish in the future.

Variations of Policies and Strategies in Europe

Neither the "success story" of the ERASMUS programmes nor the subsequent attention paid to challenges of "globalisation" nor the involvement in the Bologna Process has led to similar internationalisation trends, policies and strategies across Western European countries. This is not only obvious from the above named statistics. But this is demonstrated as well by a study on globalisation, internationalisation and Europeanisation policies of governments and respective strategies of higher education institutions in select European countries in the early stage of the Bologna Process (Huisman/van der Wende, 2004, 2005). On the one hand, we observe that higher education in the United Kingdom operates under regulatory conditions which stimulate efforts to take in large numbers of fee-paying students from outside Europe and to embark strongly in transnational education, while hardly encouraging their own students to study abroad and hardly hosting students from other European countries. On the other hand, Norway puts a strong emphasis on cooperation and mobility as regards developing countries as part of a development aid policy.

TEACHING STAFF MOBILITY

Academic staff in Europe often is temporarily mobile for research purposes. Moreover, some academics are employed at major stages of their career or the whole academic career in a country different from that of their nationality. This notably holds true for teachers of foreign languages as well as for all academics within country groups or regional groups sharing common languages, cultures or politically supported cooperation, e.g. within French-speaking, within German-speaking countries or regions, among the Nordic countries or within the persistent ties between the Czech Republic and Slovakia; moreover, the English language as a *lingua franca* opens up diverse channels of academic staff mobility. It is obvious, however, that academics wishing to be mobile in Europe for a whole career stage or permanently face many risks and barriers. Enormous changes of the career models, employment conditions and social benefit systems would be needed to make mobility of academics a matter of routine.

Temporary mobility for teaching purposes never was as high on the agenda in Europe as temporary student mobility within Europe. In the framework of the ERASMUS programme, however, temporary teaching staff mobility becomes the second biggest action line, and recent data of more than 20,000 persons teaching in another European country in the framework of ERASMUS are certainly impressive. Also, teaching staff mobility is often praised as beneficial for enhancing the conditions of student mobility and as contributing to the internationalisation of non-mobile students. A recent ERASMUS evaluation study also shows that the formerly mobile teachers consider these relatively short periods of teaching abroad as highly valuable for creating awareness of the different educational systems, for initiating long-term ties of cooperation in teaching and research, for the formerly mobile teachers' careers and sometimes even for paving the way for long-term employment in another European country (cf. Bracht et al., 2006).

Yet, teaching mobility can be viewed as having remained marginal. Most teachers mobile in the framework of ERASMUS teach at most for two weeks one or two compact courses at a partner institution. They might have some institutional support here and there, but as a rule, this is an occasional, additional teaching activity beyond the usual teaching assignments. There seem to be relatively *few cases* of

- *regular agreements between partner departments* to have certain mandatory courses of their study programmes regularly taught by incoming mobile teachers,
- *reservation of funds or positions* for inviting regularly temporary mobile teachers,
- *incorporation* of temporary teaching abroad *into the regular teaching assignments and loads* of teaching at home and
- *teaching mobility for a whole semester* (or term).

In the 1990s, the European Commission funded expert studies and arranged conferences to explore the opportunities of ensuring a stronger role of teaching staff mobility. It became clear that this would imply funds for mobility for a whole semester, regular cooperation contracts as well as integration of teaching mobility into the regular work assignments of academic staff. This obviously implies more than what could be expected to be funded for large numbers of persons within ERASMUS. One could ask, however, whether new activities in that direction were appropriate in the future.

PERSPECTIVES OF STUDENT MOBILITY BEYOND 2010

Quantitative Growth of Student Mobility

All experts agree in predicting a further growth in student mobility. Even a doubling of foreign students in Europe from other parts of the word until about 2020 seems to be likely.

As regards intra-European mobility, a substantial growth of the ERASMUS programme is envisaged. In various European countries, moreover, strong efforts are made to stimulate a further growth of intra-European student mobility. *The ambitious aims of the Sorbonne Declaration might remain out of reach, but a substantial growth is underway.* Concerns about various barriers, e.g. through curricular overcrowding of the Bachelor programmes, are by no means trivial, but they are not likely to revert the growth trend.

It is more uncertain, though, whether the *differences by country* as regards involvement in student mobility will continue, become smaller or even increase. No clear signs of convergence in this respect could be observed in the past, and joint involvement in the Bologna Process does not guarantee any convergence in this respect in the future.

Languages of Instruction

The trend towards offering more study programmes in the English language is likely to continue. European institutions of higher education can attract students from other parts of the world more easily, and temporary study in another European country can be extended more easily if study programmes are taught in the English language. As teaching and learning of English is customary in secondary education in many countries of the world, students are likely to study successfully in the host country where the programmes are provided in English. Moreover, English seems to have become increasingly important in recent years as a language of professional communication for large numbers of university graduates all over the world.

Yet, it will be interesting to note *how far this trend will progress*. Will small countries in the West and in the North of Europe move completely to English as the language of instruction, and if so, what would be the side effects of such an all-out policy? Will the increased use of English be realised without losses in quality of study provisions and learning outcomes? Will the ongoing move towards English as the language of instruction be linked to increased curricular convergence, or will this, on the contrary, facilitate the opportunities of mobile students to learn from contrasts, and what does this imply for the attractiveness of intra-European mobility? Finally, will the growing use of English as the *lingua franca* of mobile students in Europe be compatible with increased *learning and communication in other foreign languages*, or will the use of other languages decline?

CONSEQUENCES OF INCREASED PROPORTIONS OF STUDENTS FROM OTHER REGIONS OF THE WORLD

In most European countries, our systematic knowledge is very limited about the effect of increasing enrolment rates of students from other countries. We certainly note not only examples of improving academic and administrative support, but examples of less desirable consequences as well.

We note less about other salient issues:
– What is the *academic quality* actually provided for students from other parts of the world? And how do they actually fare academically? For example, in some countries, available information suggests that drop-out among these students is clearly higher than among home students. It is widely assumed as well that students from other countries are assessed more leniently than home students in order to avoid disappointments.

- To what extent did *curricula change in response to the increasing number of foreign students*, for example in terms of increasing remedial education or of counteracting the "Eurocentrism" of the study provisions?
- What is the *impact* of the increasing number of students from other regions *on the European* home students and on students mobile within Europe?

Will the higher education institutions in Europe address these potential consequences of the increasing number of students from other regions of the world more openly in the future, or will they boast the successes and hide the problems in those respects? Will these issues be reflected in the higher education policies of the individual European countries, and will there be supra-international initiatives to monitor the consequences and take action for improvement?

We cannot predict the major directions. However, we predict without risk that issues like the ones named above will be more visibly on the agenda in Europe beyond 2010.

Increasing Stratification of Higher Education or Broad Zones of Mutual Trust?

Many experts predict that higher education systems in European countries move towards increasing vertical stratification in the future. There is a widespread notion that expansion of enrolment leads to a growing diversity of talents, ambitions and career prospects of students and this is best served by a growing diversity of institutions and programmes. However, we observe that "vertical diversification" according to "quality" and "reputation" outweighs "horizontal diversity" through substantive profiles. Moreover, the trend towards "globalisation", accompanied by a stronger sense of rivalry and by stronger vertical stratification as the outcome of fiercer competition, is viewed by many observers as inevitable or as an imperative of "modernisation". Last but not least, policies of research promotion seem to favour vertical stratification of the higher education and research systems more strongly than educational policies; this tension is mirrored in various distinctions undercurrent to the Bologna Process and the Lisbon Process (see van Vught/van der Wende/Westerheijden, 2002; Teichler, 2004). A closer view, however, reveals that *higher education can choose between varied options in responding to the trends of economic globalisation*. For example, efforts to commercialize student mobility and transnational education are not more or less the automatic responses, but rather most likely to be chosen within regulatory systems of individual countries aimed at promoting such types of commercialisation of higher education. And we also note efforts to counterbalance the "imbalances" likely to result from globalisation (see van der Wende, 2007). It will be interesting to note whether the Bologna Process will have enough support for the aim of enabling intra-European student mobility across a broad range of higher education institutions or whether intra-European mobility will be forced by increasing vertical stratification to be *concentrated within smaller zones of mutual trust* in similar quality and in productive interrelationships between the profiles of the partner institutions.

Intra-European Student Mobility and Equal Opportunity

Traditionally, student mobility was seen as a prerogative of financially well-off students or of academically superior students who might be awarded a fellowship. ERASMUS, however, was initiated as a "mass" programme supposed to be open for all students irrespective of socio-biographic background, and the "social dimension" of student mobility is increasingly underscored in the Bologna Process.

The ERASMUS programme had an above average participation of women. It is only marginally selective in terms of social origin. But available information suggests that certain groups face difficulties in being involved in intra-European mobility: *"adult students", students with responsibilities for family and child-rearing, physically handicapped students and students with migration background.* What will happen in the future? Will targeted measures be taken to facilitate mobility for these students, and will they gain as well from increasing "internationalisation at home"?

Emphasis on Curricular Reforms

There are many convincing reasons to assume that *curricular issues will play a major role in efforts to increase and enhance student mobility beyond 2010.*
– As already pointed out, the *Bologna Process* moved over the years from a strong emphasis on quantitative-structural changes to a strong emphasis on curricular issues. This is likely to continue and likely to affect issues of student mobility.
– The *higher the proportion of students from other parts of the world* will be, the less likely it is that the European countries will succeed to absorb them by providing only select services and otherwise expect these students to adapt. Curricular strategies will have to be chosen so as to cope strategically with the needs of a growing heterogeneity of student backgrounds.
– The more the *daily life internationalizes*, the less "experiential learning" in another country will guarantee to "make a difference". More ambitious curricular approaches have to be spread so that students can learn more consciously from contrast.
– Internationalisation of the daily life seems to grow in many respects faster than numbers of students studying abroad. Therefore, already in the 1990s discussions started on how to improve international and European learning of nonmobile students. We might predict that *"internationalisation at home"* has to grow faster than mobility.

The last point might be explained further. We could argue anyway that internationalisation through student mobility is not the best possible option. Higher education, in principle, claims to offer successful and efficient provisions arranged deliberately in separation from the "real life" spheres in order to prepare students well for the world of work and other life spheres. Experiential learning through internships, from this perspective, can be viewed as indicating insufficiencies of higher education to prepare their students through their own genuine modes to the world of work. Similar, the widespread experiential learning during the study period abroad can be viewed on the one hand as a successful means to understand a variety of academic cultures and paradigms, but on the other hand as an indication of the weakness of higher education to provide international education and to help them to understand a variety of cultures and academic paradigms through the normal courses at home. Thus, we could argue that higher education should always do three things concurrently – offering study opportunities abroad, offering a substitute at home for the nonmobile students and making study abroad "superfluous" by offering a functional equivalent to experiential learning abroad.

CONCLUDING OBSERVATIONS

Our knowledge of the effect of the Bologna Process until 2010, the target year for establishing the European Higher Education Area, is limited. Some highly informative studies on select aspects of the Bologna Process have been undertaken (e.g. Reichert/Tauch, 2005; Alesi et al., 2005; Teichler, 2007b; see Kehm/Teichler, 2006), but many aspects were only addressed in passing, and information processes cannot follow the speed of actual events under conditions of dynamic reforms. Analyses on international mobility are constrained in some respects; even no consensus has been reached among governments to produce appropriate statistics on student mobility all over Europe. However, the quality and the thematic range of research on internationalisation of higher education in recent years are quite impressive (see the overview in Kehm/Teichler, 2007).

Altogether, student mobility has not shown stable trends in the past other than that of a mere quantitative overall growth. As a consequence, we hardly can predict the future on the basis of extrapolation.

Obviously, the Bologna Process wants to serve a balance between a growing intake of students from other parts of the world and an increase of intra-European student mobility. And there is ample room as well for interpretations of how these two objectives could be served best. We have to expect conflicting interpretations and actions in the future regarding the following: whether intra-European student mobility will turn out to be more beneficial amidst a certain degree of curricular convergence or through preservation of the existing degree of diversity, whether the increasing number of students from other parts of the world requires curricular adaptation or is served best through nonadaptation, how the growing student mobility ought to be funded, whether increased stratification of the higher education is beneficial for the mobile students or undermines their range of opportunities, what curricular reforms are needed to make study abroad a more valuable experience in the future and what role physical mobility will play in the future as compared to "internationalisation at home". But this weakness, as far as valid prediction is concerned, underscores the leeway for and the relevance of strategic decisions.

REFERENCES

Alesi, B. et al. (eds.). Bachelor and Master Courses in Selected Countries Compared with Germany. Bonn/Berlin: BMBF, 2005.

Altbach, P.G./Teichler, U. (2001): "Internationalisation and Exchanges in a Globalized University", Journal of Studies in International Education, 5 (1), 5-25.

Bracht, O. et al. (2006). The Professional Value of ERASMUS Mobility. Brussels: European Commission (http://www.ec.europa.eu/education/programmes/Socrates/Erasmus/evalcareer.pdf).

Bürger, S. et al. (2006). "International Study on Transnational Mobility in Bachelor and Master Programmes". In Deutscher Akademischer Austauschdienst (ed.), Transnational Mobility in Bachelor and Master Programmes. Bonn: DAAD, pp. 1-65.

Council of Europe (1997). Convention on the Recognition of Qualifications Concerning Higher Education in the European Region. Strasbourg.

Deloz, M. (1986). "The Activities of the Council of Europe Concerning the Recognition of Studies and Diplomas of Higher Education and Academic Mobility", Higher Education in Europe, 9 (1), 2-27.

European Commission (1994). Cooperation in Education in the European Union 1976-1994. Luxembourg: Office for Official Publications of the European Communities.

European Commission (2006). Perceptions of European Higher Education in Third Countries. Luxembourg: Office for Official Publications of the European Communities.

Huisman, J./van der Wende, M. (eds.) (2004). On Cooperation and Competition I. Bonn: Lemmens.

Huisman, J./van der Wende, M. (eds.) (2005): On Cooperation and Competition II. Bonn: Lemmens.

Kehm, B.M./Teichler, U. (2006). "Which Direction for Bachelor and Master Programmes? A Stocktaking of the Bologna Process", Tertiary Education and Management, 12 (4), 269-282.

Kehm, B.M./Teichler, U. (2007). "Research on Internationalisation in Higher Education", Journal of Studies in International Education, 11 (3/4), 260-273.

Kelo, M./Teichler, U./Wächter, B. (eds.) (2006). EURODATA: Student Mobility in European Higher Education. Bonn: Lemmens.

Reichert, S./Tauch, C. (2005). Trends IV: European Universities Implementing Bologna. Brussels: European University Association.

Sadlak, J./Liu, N.C. (eds.) (2007). The World-Class University and Rankings: Aiming Beyond Status. Bucarest and Cluij-Napoca: UNESCO-CEPES and Presa Universitara Clujeana.

Teekens, H./de Wit, H. (2007). "Special Issue on the Occasion of 10 Years of the Journal of Studies in International Education: Challenges and Opportunities for the Internationalisation of Higher Education in the Coming Decade", Journal of Studies in International Education, 11 (3/4).

Teichler, U. (ed.) (2002). ERASMUS in the SOCRATES Programme: Findings of an Evaluation Study. Bonn: Lemmens.

Teichler, U. (2004). "The Changing Debate on Internationalisation of Higher Education", Higher Education, 48 (1), 5-26.

Teichler, U. (2007a). Die Internationalisierung der Hochschulen. Frankfurt a.M./New York: Campus Verlag.

Teichler, U. (2007b). Higher Education Systems: Conceptual Frameworks, Comparative Perspectives, Empirical Findings. Rotterdam/Taipei: Sense Publishers.

Teichler, U./Janson, K. (2007). „The Professional Value if Temporary Study in Another European Country: Employment and Work of Former ERASMUS Students", Journal of Studies in International Education, 11 (3/4), 486-495.

UNESCO Institute for Statistics (2006). Global Education Digest 2006. Montreal.

Van der Wende, M. (2007). "Internationalization of Higher Education in the OECD Countries: Challenges and Opportunities for the Coming Decade", Journal of Studies in International Education, 11 (3/4), 274-289.

Van Vught, F./van der Wende, M./Westerheijden, D. (2002). "Globalisation and Internationalisation: Policy Agendas Compared". In Enders., J./Fulton, O. (eds.), Higher Education in a Globalising World. Dordrecht: Kluwer Academic Publishers, pp. 103-120.

Wächter, B./Maiworm, F. (2008). English-Taught Programmes in European Higher Education. Bonn: Lemmens.

JULIEN BARRIER AND CHRISTINE MUSSELIN

11. THE RATIONALIZATION OF ACADEMIC WORK AND CAREERS: ONGOING TRANSFORMATIONS OF THE PROFESSION AND POLICY CHALLENGES

During the last two decades, the reforms led by national governments across Europe and the policies developed at the European level have transformed the organization of universities and their relations to public authorities. But they have also deeply affected the situation of the academic profession. This paper aims at looking at these transformations and is organized into two parts. The first one deals with the key features of the academic profession in Europe and presents the main results which have been highlighted by different research and approaches. The second part identifies some potential developments between 2010 and 2020 and the main issues which will have to be dealt with.

While this paper is about the academic profession in Europe, most empirical evidence is drawn from national studies. It is not a choice, but a limitation imposed on us by the existing literature and the relatively low numbers of international comparisons on work processes and careers at the European level. Therefore, the aim of this paper is to identify common trends at the European level from a set of mainly national-based studies.

KEY FEATURES ABOUT THE ACADEMIC PROFESSION IN EUROPE

In terms of change, two main domains have to be distinguished. First we will look at the transformations of academic work and the increase in organizational control. Then, we will turn to the evolutions experienced by academic labor markets. In a last point, the relationships between these changes will be discussed.

De-professionalization or Rationalization of the Academic Profession?

Since the early 1990s, higher education and research have experienced far-reaching changes in terms of governance, organization, and funding. These changes have affected the organization of academic work. However, they cannot be equated with de-professionalization, but rather by a formalization of the division of labor and new forms of control among peers.

The changing conditions of academic work. Among the multiple evolutions faced by universities, four have most significantly contributed to change academic work conditions.

B.M. Kehm, J. Huisman and B. Stensaker (eds.), The European Higher Education Area:
Perspectives on a Moving Target, 203–221.
© 2009 Sense Publishers. All rights reserved.

First, facing rising financial constraints, governments have diminished the share of block grants and core funding in the budgets of academic institutions, and have implemented competitive project or performance-based formula funding in universities. These pressures developed market-like mechanisms in the competition for resources, what Slaughter and Leslie (1997) refer to as "academic capitalism". In this more competitive environment, academics develop new practices to attract resources. For instance, in the US, distant education – and especially online programs – is becoming a major source of revenue for universities and course materials are copyrighted (Rhoades and Slaughter, 2004). Academics engage in entrepreneurial activities, such as contracting with industry, and transform their teams into "quasi-firms" (Etzkowitz, 1992, 2003) competing for external collaborations and funding opportunities to produce science. Of course, the effects of academic capitalism on work may be less salient in disciplines removed from immediate market opportunities, like the humanities, but the latter are also concerned by this evolution (Ylijoki, 2003). Thus, academic capitalism means more competition, but also changes in the contents of work.

A second, overlapping dimension of change in the conditions of academic work has to do with the rise of managerialism, i.e. the introduction of management discourses and instruments from the for-profit sector (Deem, 2001, p.8). The UK system represents an exemplary case. Since the late 1980s, the British government has developed a set of evaluation tools under the framework of the *Research Assessment Exercise* in order to allocate core funding selectively to departments on the basis of their performance. In parallel, universities started to monitor the costs of teaching and research units, while departments adopted strategic plans to attract prospective students and professors. Managerialism prompts academics to formalize and to report on the distribution, costs, and outputs of their professional practices. Such reforms pushes towards the specialization of academics and the differentiation between professionalized "manager academics" and rank-and-file "knowledge workers" (Deem et al., 2007).

The third dimension of change concerns more specifically research activities. It lies in the growing hybridization of institutions producing knowledge, such as universities, government labs, and industrial R&D centers (Gibbons et al., 1994; Etzkowitz and Leydesdorff, 1998). Since the 1980s, it has been progressively assumed that fostering collaborations across different institutional settings was critical to the performance of innovation and research systems. Subsequently, science policies have promoted new regulations for intellectual property, boosted research contracts with industry, and encouraged the development of science parks and technology transfer offices. These evolutions have been accelerated by the emergence of new fields, i.e. computer science or nanotechnology, radically different from older disciplines: these new sciences "require the mobilization of cognitively heterogeneous teams and of formalized collaboration between academia and other institutions, such as hospitals, government laboratories, regulatory agencies, or industry" (Bonaccorsi, 2007, p. 309). The involvement of scientists in such "heterogeneous networks" is nothing but new (Latour, 1987), but the management and the design of such networks has become an objective of science policy.

Fourth, the internationalization of higher education has urged universities to develop new institutional strategies to attract international students and follow international standards. The proper effects of internationalization on academic work are still ambiguous (Enders, 2004, p. 376), and recent studies suggest that internationalization may mostly amplify existing national trends. Nevertheless, getting involved in international arenas is growingly critical to compete for funds, collaborations, and students. Likewise, in the exemplary case of business education and research, international standards have been diffused and enforced by accreditation agencies, but their direct effects on the day-to-day activities of academics are uncertain (Muller-Camen and Salzgeber 2005; Cret, 2007).

More constraints on academic work, yet an enduring professional autonomy. Beyond changes in the conditions of academic work, authors like Ziman (1994) announce a radical shift in the very nature of academic work, corresponding to the rise of new norms: profit-oriented behaviours, private appropriation of knowledge and managerial control over professionals. However, sound empirical evidence suggests to relativize the notion of radical change (Deem, 2001). We argue that the core values of academics remain stable, but that changes increase differentiation in practices and values.

First, the profession is much more diverse and fragmented than it used to be, thus raising inequalities and conflicts among faculty members. Under academic capitalism, the hierarchy of disciplines is partly redefined according to their relative position to the market, prestige being associated to external market resources, whether they are drawn from research, teaching, or consulting (Slaughter and Leslie, 1997; Rhoades and Slaughter, 2004). Market forces may accentuate the unequal distribution of resources among individuals as exemplified by science-industry relations. Indeed, industrial relations and contracts do not automatically have a skewing effect on scientific output (Gulbrandsen and Smeby, 2005): Van Looy et al. (2004) even demonstrate that academics who have more industrial contracts may also display higher publication records, which amplifies the traditional "Matthew effect" in science (Merton, 1968)[1]. Commercialization also contributes to the emergent differentiation of practices, career orientation, and professional values (Owen-Smith and Powell, 2001). Whereas some professors interpret commercialization opportunities as threats, others consider them as resources to advance research and provide a better access to graduate students on the job market. The coexistence of traditional "mertonian" academics with "entrepreneurial" professors might raise diverging interpretations about professional roles and expectations, and end up in internal conflicts.

However, it should not be concluded that academics passively accept external changes. These changes are mediated by organizational structures and enduring professional values, as illustrated by the resistances encountered by managerialism in the UK. Managerialism embodies a severe threat to the professional autonomy, for instance, in the allocation of their time or their ability to define their research agendas. Nonetheless, several studies indicate that academics in the UK have managed to protect their autonomy, even though their working conditions have deteriorated (Bryson, 2004). Morris and Rip (2006) show how UK life scientists have developed strategies to fit with national priorities and funding programs without altering the core of their scientific agenda. Similarly, Cohen et al. (1999) show that the accountability measures introduced in UK public research institutes did not radically affect work processes: researchers turned their previously informal agenda-setting processes into "mission statements" documents, to facilitate negotiation with patrons and prevent modifications in research-planning.

Eventually, several studies indicate that although academics have unquestionably changed their management practices, they have not embraced managerialist values (Henkel, 2000, 2005; Bryson, 2004). They remain loyal to the mertonian ideals of open science and their identity as teachers and researchers is still deeply anchored in the traditional disciplinary system. In a study of research activities in Finland, Ylijoki (2003) draws very similar conclusions. The changes are mediated by local conditions and disciplinary cultures. Academics might engage in entrepreneurial ventures, yet they still adhere to traditional norms and strive to protect them. Has nothing changed then? The answer is negative: while the basics of academic identity have remained largely untouched, autonomy is not taken for granted any longer. Autonomy has to be defended and constantly redefined in the relations between academics, external audiences (Henkel, 2005, p.173). Therefore, claims that academics are being "de-professionalized" might be slightly overstated.

Academic work rationalized. In spite of the numerous challenges, we argue that academic work has not been de-professionalized, drawing on the framework developed by Freidson (1994). Freidson contends that the growing integration of professionals into organizational structures means the demise of professional power. Since substantial evidence indicates that professionals in a large number of sectors still enjoy high levels of autonomy, power, and expertise, Freidson argues that the issue is not about de-professionalization, but about the changing nature of professional control. According to Freidson, there is a growing formalization and differentiation of relations among peers: professions are not likely to disappear, but they might become more stratified with the emergence of a specialized, distinct "professional elite", controlling the work of other professionals. Following Freidson, we argue that the main transformation of academic work concerns the formalization of tasks and the increasing division of labor.

First, academic activities have diversified and are more formalized into evaluation criteria and organizational rules. Since the Humboldtian revolution, academic work has traditionally been distributed between teaching and research. With the growth and bureaucratization of higher education systems since the 1960s, administrative and managerial tasks have expanded. Since the mid 1990s, academics are also more and more expected to contribute to economic development, innovation, and diffusion of knowledge. Even if academics have engaged in a variety of entrepreneurial activities well before the emergence of debate about the "third mission" (Shinn, 2000; Auger, 2004), what is new is that these activities are now integrated in the formal mission of universities, with a shift from individual to organizational responsibility (Krücken and Meier, 2006, p. 250). Similarly, expanding activities related to research and teaching – such as developing contracts, finding internships for students, elaborating e-learning programs – are no longer considered as peripheral.

These changes bear consequences for academic careers and the internal segmentation within disciplines has amplified. Traditionally, the role of an academic in the division of labor depends highly on career stage and position in the internal hierarchy of the discipline (Shinn, 1988; Etzkowitz, 1992), but when the specialization of tasks augments, the differentiation among academics performing those tasks is likely to increase. In a study of work patterns in physics and life sciences in French universities, Becquet and Musselin (2004) show that experiments are generally carried out by doctoral students and post-docs under the supervision of junior professors, while seniors raise funds, develop contacts, and write project proposals. This increasing share in project management, administrative responsibilities, and maintenance of partnerships to secure external resources which comes with seniority is again not new, but it has become more explicit.

Second, academic work has become more and more embedded in complex organizational arrangements spanning institutions and disciplines, as exemplified by the evolution of research. Bibliometric studies reveal a striking rise in multi-authored papers as well as multi-institutional and international collaborations in the last 30 years. These results indicate a vast increase in the specialization and division of scientific labor. In the US, Adams et al. (2005) found out that the average size of research teams in a set of 12 scientific fields, as reflected by the number of authors in publications, rose by 50% between 1981 and 1999. During the same period, the rate of domestic inter-institutional collaborations has doubled, while the rate of international collaborations was multiplied by 5. While the humanities lag well behind this trend, it significantly affects both the natural and the social sciences (Larivière et al., 2006). Despite the absence of an equivalent, systematic study, the literature points to similar conclusions for European countries, confirming the growth of the size of teams and the expansion of inter-institutional and interdisciplinary collaborations (Hicks and Katz, 1996a; Grossetti and Milard, 2003; Sandström and Wadskog, 2005).

As collaboration between universities, government labs, and industry develop, the articulation of multi-institutional projects and networks results in higher coordination costs (Cummings and Kiesler, 2005). In addition to funding programs supporting collaborative networks (Corley et al. 2006), universities have set up structures to optimize collaborations across organizations, institutional sectors, and/or disciplines. These changes go beyond the creation of interface structures, such as technology transfer offices, and affect the core organization of academic work: the departments. Problem-oriented organized research units, have been created to supplement traditional discipline-oriented departments (Geiger, 1990; Boardman and Bozeman, 2003). In some cases, research centers may represent little more than a strategy to attract funds from external sponsors (Groenewegen et Peters, 2002; Mignot-Gérard, 2003). However, research centers correspond to a "collectivization of research" that allows for economies of scale in experimental work. They also encourage the specialization of academics, a dynamic reinforced by the capacity of centers to hire technical and administrative personnel or casual contract researchers (Etzkowitz and Kemelgor, 1998).

The Transformations of Careers and Employment Agreements

The transformation of work goes hand in hand with a transformation of academic labor markets. First, the relationships between permanent and casual occupations are moving as the later are increasing. Secondly, recruitment procedures and practices are evolving. Finally the link between academics and their institution has been transformed and internal labor markets developed.

A strongly grounded assessment of these transformations would require studies based on empirical data which are not always available today. Moreover, the still rather high diversity in career patterns and procedures among European countries makes general assessments very fragile. Nevertheless, some general trends seem to develop over European nations and more broadly over industrialized countries.

The expansion of secondary labor markets. Following the seminal work of Piore (1969 and 1975), it is useful to distinguish between primary and secondary markets in order to account for the ongoing transformations. Primary labor markets are characterized by long-term employment relationships and organizational career while on secondary labor markets short-term employment and market-like mechanisms prevail. Tenured, on tenure track[2] and civil-servant positions in higher education institutions characterize the academic primary market, while assistantships, doctoral and post-doctoral positions, part-time and adjuncts jobs are typical for the secondary market.

In many countries the latter is expanding to the detriment of the former. This is a well documented trend in the US for instance. In the recent years, only about 40% of the positions opened were tenured or on tenure track positions. As a result the share of full-time faculty members holding such positions steadily decreases: in 1969, it reaches 96.8%, against 85.5 in 1998, and 65.2% in 2003. Simultaneously, the share of part-timers increases: within the research institutions, they represented 15% of all positions in 1969, against 25% in 1998, and 46% in 2003 (Schuster et Finkelstein 2006, pp. 44–45).

Such a trend is also observable in Europe. In the UK for instance, the fixed-term contracts represented 39% of the academic staff in 1994 (Court, 1998) and 44.8% in 2003, while part-timers reached 12% in 1995 and rose to nearly 18% in 2002. In France, a similar evolution can be observed: the fixed-term staff among university teachers reached 9.4% in 1994 (Note d'information 95–40) but 15% in 2006 (Note d'information 07–46). But this only reflects one part of the reality as post-doctoral positions also developed during the same period of time but are not included in the official data on faculty members produced by the ministry because they have no teaching duties.

In Germany, according to Janson, Schomburg, and Teichler (2007, p. 53), the share of the professors (who are almost always on long-tem contracts) reached almost 25% in 1995 but only 23% in 2004 among the academic staff of German higher education institutions. While on this period of time the number of professors rose from 2%, the number of fixed-terms assistants rose from 10%.

An important element to add to this panorama concerns the worsening possibilities for access to the primary market. The traditional career path which consisted in waiting a period of time[3] on the secondary market before accessing to the primary one does not work as well as it used to. An increasing share of the academic staff remains part of the academic profession but never succeeds in getting access to the primary market. In the US, Erhenberg (2005) observed that some institutions began developing specific career path for their not on tenure track academic staff while Schuster and Finkelstein (2006) remark that 61% of the *part-timers* holding a doctorate have always been part-timers and only 14% of the full-time staff previously were part-timers. We unfortunately miss comparative figures on European countries, but similar trends as in the US are expected to be observed.

Shifting norms and practices in recruitment. While access to the primary market seems to become more difficult and uncertain, it is at the same time more standardized. The criteria to meet in order to have a chance of getting a permanent job have been more precisely defined. In Europe, for instance, holding a PhD has become the rule. But this is a minimal pre-requisite. In order to get a maître de conférences position in France, or a lecturer in the UK it is also often required to have some teaching experience, to publish papers in peer-reviewed journals, and to participate in international conferences.

This also impacts recruitment procedures. For permanent staff, the information provided by the applicants is always more variable. Nowadays, they may be asked to prepare synopsis for specific courses in order to test their teaching capacities. The candidates invited for a visit on campus are not only interviewed by the hiring committee, they may also be asked to give a seminar or a lecture. Some universities even introduce psychological tests and interviews with the person in charge of the human resources department. This increasing investment in procedures is also observable for the non-permanent academic staff. It is not rare to launch a recruitment procedure for post-doctoral positions where networking previously often prevailed.

This rising formalization reflects a more general shift. In some European countries the access to a position depended on a national competition aimed at identifying "the bests". It increasingly becomes a recruitment, i.e. a procedure which is specific to each institution and by which the specific needs of this institution have to be met. The job advertisements featured by universities show they are looking for multi-sided profiles: almost none is solely defined by scientific objectives and they all provide information about the teaching duties which will be expected, about the classes to teach, and about whom and what subjects they will address. They even often ask for managerial skills or capacity in getting grants, managing research contracts and the like.

A final shift concerns the disqualification of inbreeding. Such practices were rather common in many European countries. In French Belgian universities, most teachers were promoted where they are recruited. This was also usual in Portugal,

Spain, Norway, etc. and rather frequent in France. Inbreeding in these countries was seen as normal and satisfying: there was less uncertainty about the quality of the recruited colleagues as he/she was already known and had proven his/her capacities, their loyalty to the group is expected to be higher, etc. Countries like Germany and Austria where professors cannot get a position where they passed their *Habilitation* were rather exceptional. This is no more the case. Inbreeding is now considered as a threat for scientific quality and institutional mobility is becoming the norm. The same holds true for international mobility: in evaluation procedures or activity reports, indicators on the number of international staff are more and more important and are convincing incentives to recruit externally and even abroad.

The development of internal labor markets. A last point documenting the transformation of academic labor markets, deals with the increase in instruments developed at the national or institutional level to assist higher education institutions in managing their staff.

In many European countries, with the exception of the UK and Belgium for instance, academic positions and/or staff were managed at national or regional levels. During the last two decades, the management of positions and/or staff have been delegated to the institutions in countries where it was not the case yet. This affected the nature of the relationships between each academic and his/her institution and pushed towards more employer–employee like relationships. It also transformed the relationships between academics and academic leaders, as the latter could no longer behave as pure *primus inter pares* and have to endorse rather hierarchical and managerialist attitudes.

As they now are responsible for their staff and/or positions, higher education institutions developed instruments aimed at creating or reinforcing internal labor markets (Doeringer and Piore, 1971). In other words, they introduced tools, devices, procedures, or rules enabling them to manage their academic careers by themselves (Musselin, 2005). In some cases, they rely on the results of national procedures in order to make their own decisions. In the UK for instance, the Research Assessment Exercise provides the institutions with information they can use to reward their staff, to allocate reduction in teaching duties, etc. In this country too, getting grants from external bodies such as the research councils is used as an indicator for academic quality. All this is reinforced by the local devices institutions may develop themselves in order to evaluate their own staff on a regular basis. Academics may be regularly asked to provide reports about their activities, or even in some cases to fulfil time-sheets.

Such evaluation devices are used as a basis for decisions about promotion, salary increase, and allocation of work. They provide institutions with capacities to manage their human resources. What happened in Germany by the beginning of the 2000s is typical for this evolution: merit-salary has been introduced, thus allowing universities to define objectives and indicators during the recruitment of professors and then to reward them (or not) according to their performances. By the same token, the resources[4] negotiated by the professors when they are recruited are no longer allocated for ever but for a fixed period of time at the end of which they can be renewed or not[5].

As the increase in casual employment and the increasing formalization of recruitment procedures, the creation and expansion of internal labor markets deeply transform the academic labor markets and career developments.

How the Transformations of Work and the Transformation of Careers Work Together

The transformation of academic work and the transformation of the academic labor market described in the previous section are coupled processes. The specialization of individual academics is paralleled by a differentiation in statuses and career tracks, so that specific activities are allocated to particular types of manpower.

The increasing share of academics belonging to the secondary labor market are not only employed on fixed-term contracts: they are also mostly allocated on specialized tasks. It is thus frequent for post-doctoral staff to achieve only research activities, while adjuncts and part-timers often concentrate on teaching to large classes of undergraduate students. The increasing number of contingent staff allows for a specialized distribution of activities as well as for flexibility in an uncertain and moving environment. The remarkable increase in post-docs in the US (Ehrenberg, 2005) and in many other countries (with regards to Australia, see Robinson, 2005) is not only a consequence of a depressed job market for PhD graduates, but also a response to the needs of senior scientists to develop their team in order to apply to competitive grants. It allows adjusting to the research as well as to the teaching workload. It furthermore reintroduces more hierarchical relationships, while horizontal relationships mostly prevail among peers[6]. This allows for more direct control on work while performances are easier to evaluate because the tasks are more specialized.

On the primary academic labor market, simultaneous evolution of work and careers are leading to more differentiation among peers. While teaching and research were considered as the core tasks of academics in most European universities, the development of evaluation and the equipment of universities as internal labor markets are challenging these traditional representations. Distinct groups of academics achieving different tasks are emerging and are always more formally identified. On the one hand academics elected or appointed on management positions (chairs, deans, presidents…) belong to the specific group of academic managers which is characterized by the tension they experience between their academic identity and their managerial activities. On the other hand, the ever stronger distinction introduced between publishing and not-publishing staff sustains the recognition of different ways of being an academic, different allocation of work, different career paths. In some countries (such as the US, the UK, the Netherlands, and Germany recently), the trend towards specialization leads to a reconsideration of the link between research and teaching and to the segmentation of the permanent professoriate between those specialized in research and holding a position as research professors, and the others.

KEY PUBLIC POLICY CHALLENGES FOR THE ACADEMIC PROFESSION IN THE
EUROPEAN RESEARCH AREA

The transformations of the academic profession imply new challenges for policy making in the European Research Area. Drawing on the analysis of ongoing changes, we have identified four issues that may prove critical for national governments and European institutions in the management of academic work and the regulation of careers. First, the problems raised by the ongoing transformations of the control and the evaluation of academic work. Second, the challenge of heightened pressures on academic work in the context of further institutional hybridization. The third issue concerns the growing role of universities as employers. The fourth challenge is the construction of a European academic labor market.

The Challenges of Control and Evaluation of Academic Work: Effectiveness, Efficiency, and Legitimacy

Although academics are not likely to be de-professionalized, the rationalization of academic work is expected to progress in the next decade. Systems of control and evaluation of academic work shall continue to expand and refine. However, if professional power is to remain robust, one may wonder about the possibly ever-increasing discrepancies between attempts at control on the one hand and unintended consequences due to professional resilience on the other hand. This problem raises three challenges: the effectiveness, the efficiency, and the legitimacy of control and evaluation systems.

The first challenge concerns effectiveness, i.e the ability of institutions and governments to monitor, assess, and control academic work. Formal organizational structures and processes can be good tracer of the new forms of the division of scientific labor, but they may also prove ineffective and have little grasp on actual practices. A first example can be drawn from university technology transfer policies. Specialized offices dedicated to this function in universities have been generalized worldwide to provide help in the negotiation of intellectual property rights and diffuse entrepreneurial norms. However, it is not clear whether they have deeply affected the views and practices of academics on technology transfer, which depend less on organizational incentives than on individual experience (D'Este and Patel, 2007; Bercovitz and Feldman, 2008). Academics may also prefer to rely on their personal informal networks with industry rather than resorting to a university office to set up a collaboration (Krücken, 2003). A second example is provided by quality assurance processes. Hoecht (2006) argues that quality assurance often result in procedural, self-referential "rituals of verification" (Power, 1997), that do not actually enhance the control of external stakeholders on academics nor guarantee substantive quality. Thus, the potential development of formal compliance strategies may hinder the effective control over academic work.

The second challenge has to do with the efficiency of the evaluation of academic outputs, i.e. the direct and indirect costs of these processes in regard to their benefits. Direct costs mainly concerns the time spent by academics on assessment-related work (e.g. filling out evaluation forms, writing proposals, or peer-reviewing the work of others). Academics in Europe complain less about accountability than about the efficiency of assessment procedures. In the UK for example, voices are raising to complain that at the aggregate level the time spent in preparing and carrying out of the Research Assessment Exercise might be out of proportion to its benefits (House of Commons, 2004). The same sort of critiques is often addressed to quality assurance for teaching and learning (Hoecht, 2006; see also Bornmann et al., 2006, pp. 688–689). For this reason, one may expect the further rationalization of assessment processes in order to lower their direct costs. For instance, the assessment of management-related costs, e.g. the time spent by experts peer-reviewing a program, might be improved. Standardizing peer-review and relying more on quantitative indicators to lower costs has also been one of the reasons for the recent reform of the Research Assesment Exercise in the UK, (House of Commons, 2004; DfES, 2006). However, the rationalization of evaluation procedures may not be free of indirect costs through unintended effects. Evaluation criteria can impact the measurable practices of academics, e.g. publication outputs, at the detriment of non measurable dimensions of work, e.g. the involvement in collegial tasks or what Losego (2004) labels "invisible work". The generalization of scientometric methods in the evaluation of scientific productivity in the context of Evaluation Based Funding (i.e. formulas to calculate funding according to indicators) may have inadvertent, detrimental consequences on research: "under a regime of evaluation-based funding scientists have been found to publish more but less riskful, mainstream rather than borderline papers and try to place them in lower quality journals as long as they are in the ISI journal index" (Weingart, 2005, p. 126). Subsequently, hot debates are expected to emerge around the production and the use of performance indicators, especially if policy makers uncritically rely on them.

One last question can be asked regarding evaluation and control: the legitimacy of both performance criteria and assessors. The creation of new intermediate positions in evaluation and control might blur the boundaries between administrators and academics, and thus raise legitimacy issues. And yet legitimacy is a central issue in the acceptance and diffusion of standards of evaluation, especially when several standards are in competition (Durand and McGuire, 2005). Then, how to guarantee the quality of standards, or to put it more sharply, who is going to watch the watchmen? The competition between national traditions, accreditation agencies, quality insurance systems, and definition of performance might represent a major challenge to the construction of the European Research Area.

A Continuing Institutional Hybridization Resulting in Pressures on Individuals and Differentiation Among Academics

The rise of multi-institutional collaborations, the hybridization of higher education and research, and the resulting differentiation between academics involved in diverse social networks and sharing different systems of value – exemplified earlier by the divergences in careers and practices among life scientists – should continue and expand in the next decade. These evolutions raise at least two challenges in terms of management of academic work.

First, one can wonder how much institutional diversity and hybridization universities can absorb as organizations. As stakeholders (e.g. charities, industrial firms, local governments) and intermediary organizations (e.g. funding agencies, quality assurance, and evaluation bodies) will expand in numbers and diversify in the field, tensions may arise between actors pursuing divergent rationales and strategic objectives. From a principal–agent perspective on science and higher education policy (Van der Meulen, 1998; Braun and Guston, 2003), stakeholders and intermediary organizations can be seen as principals in competition for the control of academics. Thus, more principals mean more coordination work on the side of the agents between their multiple, potentially conflicting demands. Consequently, administrators and academic leaders at the university level might have to intervene more frequently to solve emerging conflicts, at least on a punctual basis (e.g. intellectual property litigations with industry), and to participate more actively in the building of coalitions to minimize divergences among stakeholders (e.g. initiatives to create centers of excellence in teaching and research). Nevertheless, one might expect them to relay a large share of external pressures on individual academics and departments, because administrators and academic leaders mostly deal with external stakeholders on general matters or to formalize projects which have been already initiated at the departmental or the individual level. Moreover, they often act as diffusers of "management fads" within academia, as illustrated by the introduction of industrial or business-inspired governance methods (Kleinman and Vallas, 2001). In other words, one might expect the rising "coordination costs" of the system to be borne by individual academics.

A second related question concerns the experience of growing external pressures on the academic profession. To protect from these pressures, academics might engage in a variety of tactics. The first type of response deals with adaptation at the individual level. According to the principal–agent perspective, one may expect learning effects to occur as academics develop coping strategies to resist the agendas of their principals and policy schemes. For instance, Morris and Rip (2006) point out academics can engage in industrial relations to comply with government innovation policy, but actually carry out non-innovative, routine research with industry in order to fund basic research in parallel. In a sense, a higher number of stakeholders and more collaborative practices across institutions and sectors can undermine the ability of institutions to master their agenda (Hicks and Katz, 1996b). However, the ability to retain autonomy will probably not be equally distributed among academics. On the contrary, inequalities are likely to expand with the specialization of academic into particular tasks: the generalization of casual workers would allow for a quicker adaptation to policy changes and institutional priorities. A second type of response could lie in the further development of "buffer" organizational structures to mediate the demands of their principals. This trend is already visible in the growing role of departments in the UK (Morris, 2002) or research centers in the US (Bozeman and Boardman, 2007): although they relay managerial pressures on individuals, they simultaneously play a supportive role. These organizational arrangements provide collective resources (e.g. information or strategic positioning) increasing the bargaining power of individual academics vis-à-vis external audiences. They may also allow facilitate decoupling between formal structures and actual work practices (Meyer and Rowan, 1977). Similar remarks can be made about intermediary organizations in research and higher education, such as funding councils or quality assurance agencies. Because of their simultaneous position as agents of the government and emanation of the academic community, they can be used by academics to push their own agenda and defend their interests (Morris and Rip, 2006; King et al., 2007). In consequence, conflicts and tensions resulting from changes in the institutional environment are likely to manifest at the organizational level, within departments, research centers, and intermediary organizations, accelerating the ongoing division of the profession.

Universities as Employers

These reconfigurations in the internal balance of power of academic organizations are developing at the very moment when these organizations are increasingly engaging into employers–employees" relationships with their faculty members and developing more individualized forms of career management. Thus, they have to deal with the tension raised by the management of a group of autonomous professionals who have a status of employees. This further challenges the internal balance in power as it affects both the role of academic and administrative leaders and the relationships between academics and their university.

The delegation of the management of academic staff and positions to the university level first confronts academic leaders with major decisions, which were previously in the hand of public authorities. From a rather technical point of view, it requires a profound evolution of the administrative staff in universities, for them to acquire the skills needed by the management of human resources at the institutional level. From a more strategic point of view, it means that choices such as where should positions be cut or developed have to be handled by universities themselves. These are very complex decisions because an internal consensus among the different disciplines seems difficult to obtain – each and everyone trying to get more and refusing to give positions back. Academic leaders are never considered as legitimate to make such choices. One may therefore expect them to increasingly rely on external assessments (scientific evaluation of a department for instance) or environmental pressures ("demands from the students") to argument and legitimize their strategies. This means that the role and the impact of evaluation bodies will probably grow. If they remain in the hand of the peers, they will become very central levels of professional regulation. Rather than a regression of professional power, one might expect an increasing professional influence exercised by the academics who participate in these evaluation bodies, allowing for interfaces between professional and institutional forms of control.

Second, one can expect some paradoxical transformations in the university/ academics relationships. On the one hand, the development of contractual agreements closer to employer–employees relationships, increases the commitment expected from academics. The latter must display a stronger institutional affiliation and feel concerned by the strategic statement of their institution. This results from the construction of universities into organizations (Brunsson and Sahlin-Anderson, 2000; Musselin, 2006). According to Brunsson and Sahlin-Anderson this process first relies on the construction of stronger frontiers and identity to which academics are expected to adhere. Following the two authors, this process also relies on the construction of hierarchy. This implies a transformation in the nature of the relationships between each academic and its institution: they are now regulated by employment arrangements and work relationships. But, on the other hand, institutional affiliation is challenged by the increased pressure in favor of institutional and international mobility and the construction of research networks bypassing the organizational frontiers university are trying to build. In a way, academics are asked to behave at the same time as cosmopolitans and as locals (Gouldner; 1958a and 1958b) and to manage the internal contradiction between these two different roles.

Towards a European Academic Labor Market?

A last point to address deals with the potential emergence of a European labor market. Until now, academic trajectories still remain mostly national. Despite the different devices promoting mobility and the overall discourses in favor of internationalization, the weigh of foreign academics in most European higher education institutions remain rather low. Among them the share of foreigners coming from European countries is not very high either.

Many reasons may explain this phenomenon. First the rules regulating the academic profession are still very national. Career paths, status, and recruitment procedures remain different from one country to another. Second because of the informal implementation of national rules, looking at the latter is not enough for an applicant to discover what is expected from him/her: many implicit rules and practices are better known by the national candidates than by the others, unless the foreign applicants previously spent some time in the concerned country. A further reason comes from the varying social security and pensioning regimes. Going from one country to another with a family is still an administrative challenge. Last but not least, national actors may give a preference to national candidates because they better trust their national degrees or because of the language used by teaching.

Despite these rather pessimistic conclusions, some factors plea for the development of a more international academic labor market. First recruiting international staff has become a positive criteria in many countries and higher education institutions try to meet it. Moreover, the development of an international market for doctors and post-docs has clearly expanded. In some disciplines (like life sciences) a post-doc abroad has become the norm. It may thus be expected that an increasing number of young academics will know about the national rules and implicit norms of other countries, thus improving their chances to be recruited. The other way round, this should help the diffusion of information about each system and push towards more coherence.

Nevertheless, will this expected increase in foreign recruitments be European or international? In other words, will a global academic labor market prevail or will a European academic labor market comparable to the US develop, i.e. a territorial space (the US/the EU) sharing rather similar norms and rules and considered by the applicants has the "natural place" where to apply?

This raises at least two further range of questions. First: what conditions should be achieved for Europe to become the relevant academic marketplace? Can these conditions be achieved? Is the emergence of this European labor market a necessary condition for the existence of the EHEA and ERA or, one the contrary should the EHEA and the ERA first become a reality for this European labor market to be predominant over the nation-states?

But, and secondly, should a European marketplace be favored to a global labor market? In very concrete terms, what will be the consequences of predominantly recruiting within the EU borders versus predominantly recruiting from everywhere? Answering these questions go far beyond the scope of this paper as they are closely linked to the construction of the European Union as a legitimate supra-national political entity.

CONCLUSION

Rationalization of work as well as the differentiation and the formalization of career tracks are expected to continue and generalize. Policy makers should recognize the challenges raised by the differentiation of work and careers, especially in terms of growing inequalities and tensions. They could pay closer attention to the design of reward systems in order to limit negative effects, for instance in pushing forward evaluation criteria that would better fit the ever growing diversity of academic tasks and career paths (e.g. recognizing the involvement in collegial tasks or "invisible work"). Changes have been thorough, yet incremental in most cases, so the academic profession in Europe is not likely to experience a radical shift in the next decade. Change may instead derive from the addition and combination of evolutions that have already been set in motion within national systems of higher education and research. Future changes in the profession may still be rather dependent on national institutional trajectories, policies, and reforms than on European initiatives.

That is not to say that European-level institutions and policies will not play a role in the evolution of the academic profession, or that there will not be similar developments between countries. Parallel or at least comparable changes in EU countries could be indirectly induced or accelerated by European institutions and policies, for instance through research funding instruments or education policy schemes carrying implicit or explicit rationales and organizational arrangements. Evolutions may also occur indirectly through international exchanges: the internationalization of careers might foster the transfer of management practices or career schemes from one country to another. Similarly, countries might emulate reforms implemented abroad, as New Public Management in the UK has inspired the reorganization of academic institutions in other EU countries. In order to grasp these evolutions, research on academic work, following the studies already at hand in the UK, should develop in all other European countries.

NOTES

[1]   The Matthew effect initially refers to the fact that scientists who already have a high credit are more likely to be credited for discoveries than others, so "the rich get richer at a rate that make the poor become relatively poorer" (Merton, 1968, p. 62)

[2]   Because the chance to get a tenure is very high when one is on a tenure track position, we will consider "on tenure track" positions as part of the primary market.

[3]   The length of this period of time may vary a lot from one country to another. It is rather short in France (the average age of access to a first tenured assistant position is 33). In Germany by contrast the average age of access to a tenured position was 42 (Mayer 2000)!

[4]   A certain number of assistant positions, budget for books, the acquisition of equipment, etc.

[5]   This is also the case in the UK.

[6]   In France, for instance, the maîtres de conférences are tenured and not the subordinate of the professors while in Germany the assistants are not permanent and are dependent on "their" professors.

REFERENCES

ADAMS, James D., BLACK, Grant C., CLEMMONS, J. Roger and STEPHAN, Paula E., (2005), "Scientific teams and institutional collaborations: Evidence from U.S. universities, 1981-1999", *Research Policy*, vol. 34, no. 3, p. 259–285.

AUGER, Jean-François (2004), "Le régime de recherche utilitaire du professeur-consultant au cours de la Seconde Révolution industrielle », *Annals of Science*, vol. 61, no.3, p. 351–374.

BECQUET, Valérie and MUSSELIN, Christine (2004), *Variations autour du travail des universitaires*. Ministère de l'Enseignement Supérieur et de la Recherche, Rapport pour l'Action Concertée Incitative Travail.

BERCOVITZ, Janet and FELDMAN, Maryann (2008), "Academic Entrepreneurs: Organizational Change at the Individual Level".,*Organization Science*, vol.19, p. 69–89.

BOARDMAN, Craig and BOZEMAN, Barry (2007), "Role strain in university research centers", *The Journal of Higher Education*, vol. 78, no. 4, p. 430–463.

BONACCORSI, Andrea (2007), "Explaining poor performance of European science: institutions versus policies", *Science and Public Policy*, vol. 34, no.5, p. 303–316.

BORNMANN, Lutz, MITTAG, Sandra and DANIEL, Hans-Dieter (2006), "Quality assurance in higher education - meta-evaluation of multi-stage evaluation procedures in Germany", *Higher Education*, vol.52, no.4, pp. 687–709.

BRAUN, Dietmar and GUSTON, David H. (2003), "Principal-agent theory and research policy: An introduction", *Science and Public Policy*, vol. 30,no. 5, p. 302–308.

BRUNSSON, Nils and SAHLIN-ANDERSSON, Kerstin (2000), "Constructing Organizations: The Example of Public Sector Reform", *Organization Studies*, vol. 21, no. 4, p. 721–746.

BRYSON, Colin (2004), "What about the workers? The expansion of higher education and the transformation of academic work", *Industrial Relations Journal*, vol. 35, no.2, p.38–57.

COHEN, Laurie, DUBERLEY, Joanne and MCAULEY, John (1999), "Fueling Discovery or Monitoring Productivity: Research Scientists' Changing Perceptions of Management", *Organization*, vol. 6, no.3, p. 473–497.

CORLEY, Elizabeth A., BOARDMAN, Craig and BOZEMAN, Barry (2006), "Design and the management of multi-institutional research collaborations: Theoretical implications from two case studies", *Research Policy*, vol. 35, p. 975–993.

COURT, Stephen (1998), "Academic Tenure and Employment in the UK", *Sociological Perspectives* vol. 41, p. 767–774.

CRET, Benoît (2007), *L'Émergence des accréditations : origine et efficacité d'un label*, Thèse de doctorat en sociologie de l'Institut d'Etudes Politiques de Paris.

CUMMINGS, Jonathon N., Sara KIESLER (2005), "Collaborative Research Across Disciplinary and Organizational Boundaries", *Social Studies of Science*, vol.5, p. 703–722.

D'ESTE, Pablo and PATEL, Parimal (2007), "University-industry linkages in the UK: What are the factors underlying the variety of interactions with industry?", *Research Policy*, vol. 36 no. 9, p. 1295–1313.

DEEM, Rosemary (2001), "Globalisation, New Managerialism, Academic Capitalism and Entrepreneurialism in Universities: Is the Local Dimension Still Important?", *Comparative Education*, vol. 37, no.1, p. 7–20.

DfES (2006), *Reform of higher education research assessment and funding: Summary of results*, UK Department for Education and Skills, last accessed online on 03/19/2008 at http://www.dfes.gov.uk/consultations/conResults.cfm?consultationId=1404

DOERINGER Peter D. and PIORE, Michael J. (1971), *Internal Labour Markets and Manpower Analysis*, Heath: Lexington Books.

DURAND, Rodolphe and MCGUIRE Jean (2005), "Legitimating agencies facing selection: the case of AACSB", *Organization Studies*, vol. 26, no.2, p.113–142.

EHRENBERG, Ronald G. (2005), "The changing nature of the faculty and faculty employment practices", working paper, Cornell Higher Education Research Institute.

ENDERS, Jürgen (2004), "Higher education, internationalisation, and the nation-state: Recent developments and challenges to governance theory", *Higher Education*, vol. 47 no. 3, pp. 361–382.

ETZKOWITZ, H. (2003): Research groups as 'quasi-firms': the invention of the entrepreneurial university. *Research Policy*, vol. 32, no.1, p.109–121.

ETZKOWITZ, Henry (1992), « Individual Investigators and their Research Groups », *Minerva*, vol. 30 no. 1, Spring, pp. 28–50.

ETZKOWITZ, Henry and LEYDESDORFF, Loet (1998), "The Endless Transition: A 'Triple Helix' of University-Industry-Government Relations" Introduction to a Theme Issue, *Minerva* vol. 36, p. 203–208.

FREIDSON, Eliot (1994), *Professionalism Reborn: Theory, Prophecy, and Policy*, Chicago: University of Chicago Press.

GEIGER, Roger (1990), "Organized Research Units: Their Role in the Development of University Research, *The Journal of Higher Education*, vol. 61, no. 1, p. 1–19.

GEIGER, Roger L. (1990), "Organized Research Units - Their Role in the Development of University Research", *Journal of Higher Education*, vol. 61, no.1, p.1-20.

GIBBONS, Michael, LIMOGES, Camille, NOWOTNY, Helga, SCHWARTZMAN, Simon Schwartzman, SCOTT, Peter and TROW Martin (1994), *The New Production of Knowledge: The Dynamics of Science and Research in Contemporary Societies*. London: Sage.

GOULDNER, Alvin W. (1958a), "Cosmopolitans and Locals : Toward an Analysis of Latent Social Roles 1", *Administrative Science Quarterly*, vol. 2, pp. 281–306.

GOULDNER, Alvin W. (1958b), "Cosmopolitans and Locals : Toward an Analysis of Latent Social Roles 2", *Administrative Science Quarterly*, vol. 2, pp. 440–480.

GROENEWEGEN, Peter and PETERS, Lois (2002), "The Emergence and Change of Materials Science and Engineering in the United States", *Science Technology and Human Values*, vol. 27, no.1, p.112–133.

GROSSETTI Michel and MILARD Béatrice (2003), « Les évolutions du champ scientifique en France à travers les publications et les contrats de recherche », *Actes de la recherche en sciences sociales*, no.148, pp.47–56.

GULBRANDSEN, Magnus and SMEBY, Jens-Christian (2005), "Industry funding and university professors' research performance", *Research Policy*, vol. 34, no.6, p. 932–950.

HANNEY, Steve, HENKEL, Mary, von WALDEN LAING, Dagmar (2001), "Making and implementing foresight policy to engage the academic community: health and life scientists' involvement in, and response to, development of the UK's technology foresight programme", *Research Policy*, vol. 30 no. 8 pp. 1203–1219.

HENKEL, Mary (2000), *Academic Identities and Policy Change in Higher Education*, London : Jessica Kingsley.

HENKEL, Mary (2005), "Academic identity and autonomy in a changing policy environment", *Higher Education*, vol. 49, no. 1–2, p. 155–176.

HICKS, Diana M. and KATZ, J. Sylvan (1996a), "Where Is Science Going?", *Science, Technology and Human Values*, vol. 21: 379–406.

HICKS, Diana M. and KATZ, J. Sylvan (1996b), "Science Policy for a Highly Collaborative Science System", *Science and Public Policy*, vol. 23, no. 1 pp. 39–44.

HOECHT, Andreas (2006), "Quality assurance in UK higher education: Issues of trust, control, professional autonomy and accountability", *Higher Education*, vol. 51, no. 4, pp. 541–563.

HOUSE OF COMMONS (2004), *Research Assessment Exercise: A re-assessment*, report of the Science and Technology Committee, London: The Stationery Office.

JANSON Kerstin, SCHOMBURG Harald and TEICHLER Ulrich (2007), *Wissenschaftliche Wege zur Professur oder ins Abseits? Strukturinformationen zu Arbeitsmarkt und Beschäftigung an Hochschulen in Deutschland und den USA*, Munster, Waxmann.

KING, Roger, GRIFFITHS, Paul and WILLIAMS, Ruth (2007), "Regulatory intermediation and quality assurance in higher education: the case of the auditors", *Oxford Review of Education*, vol. 33, no. 2, pp. 161–174.

KRÜCKEN, Georg (2003), "Learning the 'New, New Thing': On the role of path dependency in university structures", *Higher Education*, vol. 46, no. 3, p. 315–339.

KRÜCKEN, Georg and MEIER, Frank (2006), "Turning the University into an Organizational Actor", in Gili Drori, John Meyer, and Hokyu Hwang (Eds), *Globalization and Organization: World Society and Organizational Change*, Oxford University Press, Oxford, pp. 241–257.

LARIVIÈRE, Vincent, GINGRAS, Yves, ARCHAMBAULT, Eric (2006), "Canadian collaboration networks: A comparative analysis of the natural sciences, social sciences and the humanities", *Scientometrics*, vol. 68, no. 3, pp. 519–533.

LATOUR, Bruno (1987), *Science In Action: How to Follow Scientists and Engineers through Society*, Cambridge, MA: Harvard University Press.

LOSEGO Philippe (2004), « Le travail invisible à l'université : le cas des antennes universitaires », *Sociologie du travail,* vol. 46, pp. 184–204.

MAYER, Karl-Ulrich (2000), « Wissenschaft als Beruf oder Karriere? », contribution presented at the conference "*Wissenschaft zwischen Geld und Geist*", Max-Planck-Institut für Wissenschaftsgeschichte, Berlin, 16 – 18 november, 2000.

MERTON, Robert K. (1968), "The Matthew Effect in Science", *Science*, vol. 159, no. 3810, p. 56–63.

MEYER, John W. & ROWAN, Brian (1977), Institutionalized Organizations: Formal Structure as Myth and Ceremony, *American Journal of Sociology*, vol. 83, no.2, p.340–363.

MORRIS, Norma (2002), "The Developing Role of Departments", *Research Policy*, vol. 31, no. 5, p. 817–833.

MORRIS, Norma (2002), "The developing role of departments". *Research Policy*, vol. 31, no 5, p. 817–833.

MORRIS, Norma and RIP, Arie (2006), "Scientists' coping strategies in an evolving research system: the case of life scientists in the UK", *Science and Public Policy*, vol. 33, no. 4, p. 253–263.

MULLER-CAMEN, Michael and SALZGEBER, Stefan (2005), "Changes in Academic Work and the Chair Regime: The Case of German Business Administration Academics", *Organization Studies*, vol. 26, no. 2, p. 271–290.

MUSSELIN, Christine (2005), "European academic labor markets in transition", *Higher Education*, 49, p. 135–154.

MUSSELIN, Christine (2006), "Are Universities specific organisations ?", in KRÜCKEN G., KOSMÜTZKY A. and TORKA M. (ed.), *Towards a Multiversity? Universities between Global Trends and national Traditions*, Bielefeld: Transcript Verlag, p. 63–84.

OWEN-SMITH, Jason Walter W. POWELL (2001), "Careers and Contradictions: Faculty Responses to the Transformation of Knowledge and its Uses in the Life Sciences", *Research in the Sociology of Work*, vol. 10 pp. 109–40.

PIORE, Michael J. (1969), "On-the-Job Training in a Dual Labor Market", *in* WEBER, A.R., CASSELL, F. H. and GINSBERG, W. L. (Ed.), *Public-Private Manpower Policies*, Madison: Industrial Relations Research Association.

PIORE, Michael J. (1975), "Notes for a Theory of Labor Market Stratification", REICH M., GORDON D. and EDWARDS R. (Ed.) *Labor Market Segmentation*, Heath: Lexington Books.p.125–150.

POWER, Michael (1997), *The Audit Society: Rituals of Verification*, Oxford: Oxford University Press.

RHOADES, Gary and SLAUGHTER, Sheila (2004), *Academic Capitalism and the New Economy: Markets, State and Higher Education*, Baltimore: The Johns Hopkins University Press.

RIP, Arie et VAN DER MEULEN, Barend (1996), « The post-modern research system », *Science and Public Policy*, vol. 23, no. 6, p. 343–352.

ROBINSON, David (2005) "The Status of Higher Education Teaching Personnel in Australia, Canada, New Zealand, the United Kingdom and the United States", (paper presented at the International Higher Education and Research Conference, Melbourne, December 2005).

SANDSTRÖM, Ulf and WADSKOG, Daniel (2005), "A Decade after Hicks and Katz: Interdisciplinary Research Re-Examined", *Paper presented at the ISSI Conference, Stockholm*.

SCHUSTER, Jack H. and FINKELSTEIN, Martin J. (2006), *The American Faculty: The Restructuring of Academic Work and Careers*, Baltimore: Johns Hopkins University Press.

SHINN, Terry (1988), "Hiérarchie des chercheurs et formes des recherches", *Actes de la recherche en sciences sociales*, no. 74, p. 2–22.

SHINN, Terry (2000), « Formes de division du travail scientifique et convergence intellectuelle. La recherche technico-instrumentale », *Revue française de sociologie*, vol. 41 no. 3, p. 447–73.

SLAUGHTER, Sheila and LESLIE, Larry (1997) *Academic Capitalism: Politics, Policies and the Entrepreneurial University*, Baltimore: The Johns Hopkins University Press.

VAN DER MEULEN, Barend (1998), "Science Policies as principal-agent games: Institutionalization and path dependency in the relation between government and science", *Research Policy*, vol. 27, p. 397–414.

VAN LOOY, B. RANGA, M. CALLAERT, J. DEBACKERE ,K. and ZIMMERMAN, E. (2004), "Combining Entrepreneurial and Scientific Performance in Academia: Towards a compound Matthew Effect encompassing both activity realms?", *Research Policy*, vol. 33, no. 3, p. 425–441.

WEINGART, Peter (2005), "Impact of bibliometrics upon the science system: Inadvertent consequences?", *Scientometrics*, vol. 62, no. 1, p. 117–131.

YLIJOKI, Oili-Helena (2003), "Entangled in academic capitalism? A case-study on changing ideals and practices of university research", Higher Education, vol. 45, no. 3, p.307–335.

ZIMAN, John (1994), *Prometheus Bound: Science in a Dynamic Steady State*, Cambridge University Press, Cambridge.

BARBARA M. KEHM

12. NEW FORMS OF DOCTORAL EDUCATION AND TRAINING IN THE EUROPEAN HIGHER EDUCATION AREA

THE DOCTORATE IN THE CONTEXT OF EUROPEAN HIGHER EDUCATION REFORMS

Doctoral education is currently high on the higher education policy agenda in Europe. It does not only represent the most important interface between two major reform processes, the Bologna Process to create a European Higher Education Area and the Lisbon Strategy to create a European Area of Research and Innovation; it is also a focal point in national and regional policies vis-à-vis the emerging knowledge societies and economies. Doctoral education is no longer mainly geared towards recruitment into the academic profession. Rather it is increasingly concept-ualized as research training for knowledge intensive economic sectors outside academia. Needless to say that these developments have led to the fact that doctoral education has become an object of policy making at institutional, national and – in the EU – also supra-national level and is deemed to be a valuable resource which should not be left exclusively in the hands of the disciplinary and scientific communities.

Concerns about weaknesses in doctoral education can be found in other regions of the world as well. Maresi Nerad (Nerad 2004: 185) summarized the main criticism of doctoral education and training in the United States as follows:

"Doctoral students are believed to be:
– educated and trained too narrowly,
– lacking key professional skills, such as collaborating effectively and working in teams, and lacking organizational and managerial skills,
– ill-prepared to teach,
– taking too long to complete their doctoral studies and in some fields many are not completing their degrees at all,
– ill-informed about employment outside academia,
– having too-long a transition period from PhD completion to stable employment."

Basically, these criticisms hold true for doctoral education in most of the European countries as well. The European University Association (EUA 2005) emphasized the following problems:
– long duration of doctoral education and high drop out,
– no proper regulation of full-time and part-time doctoral education,
– lack of transparency in recruitment, selection, and admission of appropriate candidates,

B.M. Kehm, J. Huisman and B. Stensaker (eds.), The European Higher Education Area:
Perspectives on a Moving Target, 223–241.

– unclear status of doctoral candidates (e.g. students or salaried junior researchers),
– funding of doctoral education.

In Europe, there is currently an ongoing debate whether young people in the phase of getting their doctoral degree should be regarded as students or as junior researchers at the beginning of their professional career. This is not only a question of status but also determines whether they pay tuition fees and are treated as trainees or whether they receive a salary and are treated as employees of the university with tasks in research and teaching. Despite the attempt to harmonize higher education structures and degrees in Europe in the framework of the Bologna Process, these issues are treated rather differently in the European countries.

To summarize the main points it can be stated that status, quality of supervision, funding, duration, and successful completion as well as appropriate skills and competences for professional research careers inside and outside academia are issues in doctoral education which are under close scrutiny and found to be problematic.

Therefore, new concepts of doctoral education recently have been and currently are being developed which also take into account that the increase in doctoral students which could be observed over the last ten years and is envisaged to increase even further in the coming years in the framework of the Lisbon Agenda will lead to a much larger diversity of motives and purposes of getting a doctoral degree.

CONCEPTS OF DOCTORAL EDUCATION IN EUROPE

During the last few years it could be observed that the traditional forms of doctoral education are changing. The notion "traditional forms" refers here to the "master–apprentice model" prevalent in continental Europe which is characterized by individual supervision and research work for the thesis but hardly any coursework and mostly no programme or structure. This particular model has been criticized increasingly

– as having a high degree of dependence on the supervisor (exploitation) and lacking quality,
– for its high drop-out due to lack of regulation and registration,
– for its long duration and increasing age at successful completion.

In continental Europe a solution for these problems has been seen in recent years in establishing doctoral programmes which have a more formalized structure and include a certain amount of course work. However, there seems to be no solid evidence that doctoral programmes can actually provide such a solution since dropout rates in the USA are known to be high and there are also problems of attrition despite the fact that doctoral education is much more formalized and structured there. And Germany with its very traditional mode of doctoral education has always produced a very high number of doctorates.

In other European countries as well concerns increased in the course of the 1990s about the quality, efficiency, and effectiveness of doctoral education. At first the issue was less an increase in numbers of doctoral degrees awarded as that could be observed for some time already. Rather there were questions about the appropriateness of doctoral education and training in the face of the growing heterogeneity of doctoral students (or candidates as they are called in those countries which did not consider the student status appropriate) themselves, a fact closely related to the growth in numbers. Many doctoral students did not embark on getting this degree in order to remain in academia and possibly join the academic profession. Instead, many saw the degree as providing them with an opportunity for a boost in their professional career. In the United Kingdom the distinction between a "research doctorate" and a "professional doctorate" was thus introduced. The first served (possibly among other things) as a pool for recruitment into academia, the second was developed as an upwardly mobile qualification for professionals who were working already and often studied part-time for their degree. Despite the fact that an equivalent of the "professional doctorate" has existed in other European countries as well for quite some time, no terminological and conceptual differentiations were introduced. Existing differences were rather attributed to various disciplinary cultures.

In general, the United Kingdom has turned out to become something like a trendsetter for the differentiation and diversification of models in doctoral education and has by now established a number of different pathways to the doctorate. For the time being it must remain an open question whether these models will be adopted by other European countries and in which way they are transferable. We can note, however, that the distinction between a "research doctorate" and a "professional doctorate" is increasingly applied in other European countries as well. Among other things this trend might be an indicator for academic drift of non-university institutions wanting to gain the right to award doctoral degrees themselves (so far a privilege of universities only in the majority of European countries) and arguing that applied sciences could or should culminate in a "professional doctorate".

The following paragraphs will describe in more detail the various models of doctoral education which can be found.

The Research Doctorate

For the research doctorate the dissertation is central and expected to be an original contribution to the knowledge base of a discipline or a research domain. Independent of the fact whether the degree (or title) is acquired within the framework of a structured programme including course work or in the framework of a master–apprentice relationship, the research doctorate as a rule is an entrance ticket to the academic profession who – by being responsible for the training – also has a gatekeeper function. Using the example of six disciplines, Golde and Walker (2006) have characterized the main purpose of doctoral education in the research doctorate as developing students to be "stewards of the discipline". The goal of such a training is a scientific or scholarly ideal type characterized as someone "who can imaginatively generate new knowledge, critically conserve valuable and useful ideas, and responsibly transform those understandings through writing, teaching and application. A steward is someone to whom the vigor, quality, and integrity of the field can be entrusted" (Golde/Walker 2006:5). This rather normative image contrasts starkly with the image generated by Slaughter and Leslie (2000) of the successful academic as "capitalist entrepreneur" who has recognized the demands and challenges of market orientation, competition, and globalization in the emerging knowledge societies and knows how to draw advantages from these developments.

The Taught Doctorate

By definition, the taught doctorate consists of a substantial proportion of course work. Typically there will be a fixed curriculum and learning outcomes will be graded and weighted for the final grade. As in the research doctorate students are supposed to contribute to the generation of new knowledge but they do this in the framework of a research project the results of which are summarized in a project report. The report is presented in the framework of an oral examination and is graded as well. In contrast to the two-phase doctorate in the United States (course work first, then research and writing of thesis), the course work of the taught doctorate is spread over the whole period of degree training (predominantly offered in the United Kingdom). The oral examination and the grade of the research project report are regarded as an equivalent to a dissertation and its defence.

PhD by Published Work

The model of the PhD by published work is known in Germany since the 19th century (it is called "cumulative dissertation"). From there it spread to other parts of the world, mainly the United States but also to Belgium, to the Netherlands and to Sweden. At second glance the British model of the PhD by published work differs to some extent from the German model of a "cumulative dissertation". Both models are basically characterized by combining several articles which have appeared in peer reviewed scholarly or scientific journals into a book and providing them with a coherent framework. But while this option is open for many candidates in Germany, the PhD by published work is awarded in the United Kingdom almost exclusively to members or alumni of the university awarding the degree (cf. Green/Powell 2005:72).

This model has frequently been criticized for:
− its lack of consistency and weak demarcation to other forms of the doctorate,
− differences in the definition of what constitutes a publication and which time frame should be taken into account,
− its threat to undermine other forms of doctoral education,
− the difficulty in allowing for adequate supervision.

Furthermore, in this model of the doctorate it is predominantly a product which is evaluated and graded and not the process of getting the degree itself. Therefore, most countries which provide this opportunity have regulations in place which determine the character and the content of the dissertation and possibly also the question whether and in which form a programme of additional studies has to be taken (cf. Green/Powell 2005:71).

The Professional Doctorate

A number of European countries have by now picked up the British trend to explicitly distinguish between a research doctorate and a professional doctorate. The professional doctorate is not awarded in all disciplines but restricted to subjects like business administration, medicine and health care, education, engineering, social work etc., i.e. to subjects which have a relatively demarcated field of professional practice. In professional doctorates the title usually includes an indication of the professional field (e.g. DBA or EdD). Quite a number of publications have appeared in recent years on the professional doctorate (cf. Bourner/Bowden/Laing 2001, Park 2005, and Green/Powell 2005). To some extent this seems to be related to the fact that in academic circles the professional doctorate is often looked down upon as a second class doctorate so that pressure for legitimation increased.

The professional doctorate is defined as a programme of advanced studies which – apart from fulfilling university criteria for the award of the degree – is geared towards satisfying a particular demand from a professional group outside the university and towards developing research skills needed within a professional context (Bourner/Bowden/Laing 2001:219). In the United Kingdom, professional doctorates are typically taken up by people who are pursuing a professional career and are employed. Therefore, professional doctorates are frequently offered as part-time programmes and usually require several years of professional experience. Tuition fees are often covered fully or in parts by the employer. The target group wants to gain the degree in order to be eligible for promotion in their professional field. Consequently the research work carried out for the dissertation is regarded less as a contribution to the knowledge base of a discipline but more as a contribution to the development of a professional domain. The dissertation then has a focus on the generation of new but more applied knowledge and the topic is often generated from the respective professional practice. In some areas, e.g. in engineering the dissertation can also have the form of a larger or a series of smaller projects which are carried out in the framework of actual professional practice.

Apart from aspects of the subject or discipline, the course work involves training in research and research methods with which problems of professional practice can be solved and a familiarization with research results and their utilization or relevance for professional practice. There is also an emphasis on career management skills. Course work is usually graded separately from the dissertation. In the United Kingdom study programmes of professional doctorates are frequently accredited by the relevant professional organizations (cf. Green and Powell, 2005:86ff.).

The Practice Based Doctorate

The practice based doctorate is a terminological specificity of the British university system as well but it is also awarded in Australia. It denotes the award of doctoral degrees in the Arts and in Design. While German universities, for example, award a doctoral degree in musicology or art history, the highest degree in the various arts as such (e.g. painting, sculpting, acting) is called "*Kuenstlerische Reife*" (which can be translated literally as "artistic maturity"). No doctoral degree is awarded in these fields.

The practice based doctorate increased in importance with the integration of colleges of art into the universities in the 1990s in the United Kingdom. The degree is awarded as a result of course work in the framework of which students are familiarized with theories and research methodologies and the presentation of a work of art or a performance as a substitute for the dissertation. The presentation or performance is accompanied by a text in which the candidate explains how he or she has arrived at the result or product by applying research methods. This is regarded as generating new knowledge through practice. Successful candidates are also expected to demonstrate how their work of art is related to other works of art in the same field (theoretical, historical, critical, or visual context) and to evaluate possible effects. In the field of composition frequently not just one work is presented but a whole portfolio. In the oral examination the work of art will be presented or performed and the candidate demonstrates on the basis of the accompanying text that he or she has sufficient knowledge and appropriate skills to independently generate new knowledge.

The practice based doctorate is contested in the United Kingdom because – compared to all other models of the doctorate – it shows the least proximity to the traditional notion of a dissertation. However, about half of all British universities offer such a doctorate (cf. Green/Powell 2005:100ff.).

The "New Route" Doctorate

The model of the "new route PhD" (also called integrated doctorate) was developed by ten British universities as a form of brand name in 2001 with the purpose of attracting international students. In the meantime it is offered by more than 30 British universities. The programme basically consists of three (integrated) elements: a taught component in the area of research methods and subject specialization, another taught component in the area of transferable skills and the work on a dissertation (disciplinary or interdisciplinary). Admission can be granted right after having completed a Bachelor degree. The taught components are frequently offered in the framework of related Master programmes and accompany the whole four years envisaged for getting the degree. For the taught components 240 credit points are awarded. Requirements for the dissertation are similarly high as for the research doctorate.

However, in comparison to the research doctorate the taught elements are more important and also prescribed in more detail with respect to the qualifications and competences to be acquired. Often there is also the possibility after having finished all the course work to write a master thesis instead of a doctoral dissertation and finish with a master degree.

In Germany, this model has become known as "fast track PhD" and is offered in specific subjects at some universities. Although the Master degree in Germany is required for admission into doctoral programmes or acceptance as doctoral candidate this model offers transition into the doctoral phase for particularly talented students right after their Bachelor degree.

Basically the new route PhD as well the fast track PhD follow the American model of an integrated postgraduate education in which the master level and the doctoral level are combined in terms of course work to be done. However, the American model clearly separates the course work phase from the phase of writing a thesis which follow each other in sequence and are not integrated. This American two-phase approach results in high dropout rates after having finished the course work or (compared to Europe) a rather long time to degree (between six and nine years). Despite the fact that a fast track to the doctoral degree is possible in exceptional cases in many European countries, the European University Association has recommended that the Master degree should constitute the rule for access into doctoral programmes or the doctoral qualification phase.

Two Models of the Joint Doctorate

The model of the joint doctorate is characteristic for doctoral programmes jointly offered by two or more universities which may be located in the same region, the same country or different countries. A study carried out by EUA (EUA 2005) about changes in doctoral education in Europe included a survey among member institutions. Eighteen per cent of responding universities confirmed that they offer joint doctorates. Leading countries in terms of the number of joint doctoral degree programmes are Germany, Spain, France, Italy, the United Kingdom, and the Netherlands.

In the EUA study (EUA 2005:28ff.) the joint doctorate is characterized as follows:
- a joint curriculum for the taught components which has been developed in close cooperation among the participating institutions; the doctoral students take courses at several universities;
- an agreement signed by all participating institutions clarifying funding issues and other matters (e.g. mobility, quality assurance).

Certification of a joint doctorate is regulated in various ways: from award of the degree from the university at which the candidate is enrolled, to a double degree on the basis of joint supervision (i.e. co-tutelle arrangements) and a joint degree.

Joint doctorates are predominantly awarded by universities (or more exactly by faculties and departments) cooperating in transnational networks. The advantages for doctoral students are that in most cases phases of mobility are built into the programme, that they often have more than one supervisor and additionally access to further experts in their field who are members of the network. However, the actual practice differs from this ideal type. Joint doctorates have a higher degree of internationalization and more opportunities for mobility but they are often not based on a joint curriculum of the participating partner institutions.

A particular variant of the joint doctorate is the "European doctorate" which does, however, not yet exist in practice. The idea and an informal initiative came up at the beginning of the 1990s during a meeting of the Confederation of

European Rectors' Conferences (an organization which has merged with the former CRE to become EUA). The "Doctor Europaeus", as the planned title was to be, is contested until today, although there is a consensus about promotion and improvement of European cooperation in doctoral education and mobility of doctoral students (or candidates). Currently another initiative in this direction is undertaken by the European Commission offering funding for joint doctoral programmes emerging from partner universities of an Erasmus Mundus Programme. The difficulty of putting the idea into practice is due to the fact that within Europe there is an increasing competition for best talent among institutions and on the national level a more competitive research policy and innovation strategy. Thus, best talent is not easily "shared". Still, the discussion about the "Doctor Europaeus" has been revived in the context of the Lisbon Strategy to create a European Research and Innovation Area.

THE MULTITUDE OF MODELS AS AN ANSWER TO THE MULTITUDE OF PURPOSES AND MOTIVES?

This proliferation of types and models for doctoral education certainly does not provide the impression of contributing to more transparency which is one of the goals of the Bologna Process reforms. Indeed the growing variety of degrees and programmes has already triggered some criticism (cf. overview in Park 2005:201). The four main points of criticism can be summarized as follows:
– Other models than the research doctorate tend to be regarded as second class doctorates. The quality of the dissertation as well as the quality of the process of getting the degree are often ranked lower than those of the research doctorate.
– External examiners have noted – in particular with respect to practice based doctorates – a lack of intellectual depths, of cohesion, of discussing existing literature, of originality and generalizable results of the work. In addition, they have criticized methodological weaknesses and bad presentation.
– Bourner, Bowden, and Laing (2000) criticized that the new types of doctorates often lack clarity and coherence.
– Some experts have also voiced concern about the growing proliferation of titles and the increasing differentiation of types and models.
Supporters of the growing differentiation of models of the doctorate argue, however, that the increase of doctoral students which can be observed since the 1980s in many European countries has also led to a growing heterogeneity of interests and motives among the students or candidates. Getting a doctoral degree does no longer serve almost exclusively as a preparation for entrance into the academic profession but is also used increasingly as a qualification for non-academic labour markets and professional career boosts. These goals and purposes must be taken into account when shaping this phase of qualification.

In more general terms then the question arises "what is a PhD?", i.e. what are the particular cognitive and personal characteristics of doctoral degree holders? Analysing the models and purposes that have been introduced here it is possible to distinguish between three concepts which are of paradigmatic importance because they are mutually exclusive. As long as there is a consensus that there should be many pathways to a doctoral degree and that the knowledge society poses quite different demands and challenges to doctoral degree holders, all three concepts have a certain amount of legitimacy (cf. for this and the following McCarty/Ortloff 2005:17).

The first concept is predominantly based on the traditional ideas about the competences and skills to be acquired in the process of getting a doctoral degree. It is characteristic for doctoral education in the traditional disciplines. These in turn are characterized by an established epistemological core and a pronounced disciplinary culture. Furthermore, there exists a widely shared view among the members of the scientific community about the core curriculum. In this concept getting a doctoral degree consists predominantly in the acquisition and critical discussion of highly specialized knowledge. The character of the dissertation is mostly geared towards establishing and conserving the core knowledge of that discipline (interpretation and exegesis are core methodologies).

The second concept is based on the idea that the phase of doctoral education and training should be reformed in order to prepare students for professional careers as researchers. Doctoral education in this concept is focused on the acquisition of skills and competences to apply research methods in order to generate new knowledge. Conservation, expansion, and transmission of existing knowledge are more peripheral in this concept. The process of getting a doctoral degree consists in the expansion of a knowledge domain or a discipline by discovering new knowledge which is being validated through scientific methods. Apart from the methodological tool box (e.g. to generate hypotheses, to analyse data, to carry out experiments) this concept also has a normative side which is the development of intellectual curiosity, scientific or scholarly honesty, and the ability to treat the objects of research in an adequate manner. Knowledge in this concept is used as an instrument to generate new knowledge. The intellectual world is not the comprehensive library which contains already all the knowledge but a labyrinth of problems and riddles which can be solved. Doctoral education takes the form of an apprenticeship under the masters of the scientific community and is the first phase in the career of an academic.

The third concept finally is based on the idea that the doctoral degree is the door opener for a professional career or for a promotion in one's professional job. This concept of doctoral education is not about new or old knowledge and also less about conservation or acquisition of knowledge. Getting a doctoral degree rather prepares for taking over a multitude of responsibilities and tasks. In the process of getting the degree, candidates acquire competences in various areas of their future job and possibly also an entrepreneurial spirit. Learning outcomes and acquisition of knowledge are assessed according to the criterion how useful they are to achieve specific career goals. The degree is the door opener for a particular job.

THE TENSION BETWEEN DIVERSITY AND TRANSPARENCY

I have so far tried to open up a field of tensions between the poles of differentiation and national as well as European transparency. In order to prevent diversity turning into intransparence European and national qualifications frameworks have been developed (or are currently being developed) to assure transparency and recognition.

The European Qualifications Framework (EQF) was formally adopted by the European Council in April 2008 and member states of the EU are expected to eventually relate their National Qualifications Framework (NQF) to the European one. The framework is supposed to serve as a reference tool to compare the qualification levels of different countries and different education and training systems. It consists of altogether eight levels describing "what a learner knows, understands and is able to do" (EQF 2008). Accordingly, the EQF distinguishes between knowledge, skills, and competences at eight different levels of learning outcomes. With regard to doctoral education (Level 8) learning outcomes in terms of knowledge are defined as "knowledge at the most advanced frontier of a field of work or study and at the interface between fields". Learning outcomes in terms of skills are defined as "the most advanced and specialized skills and techniques, including synthesis and evaluation, required to solve critical problems in research and/or innovation and to extend and redefine existing knowledge or professional practice". Learning outcomes in terms of competences are defined as "demonstrate substantial authority, innovation, autonomy, scholarly and professional integrity and sustained commitment to the development of new ideas or processes at the forefront of work or study contexts including research" (EQF 2008, Annex 4, p. 4).

These definitions may suffice to show that they are rather generic and do not distinguish between a doctorate and other forms of acquiring the qualifications deemed appropriate for the highest level. This means that qualifications acquired through experience and on the job might be established as equal to a doctorate. Furthermore, the wording together with the establishment of levels implies a clearly stratified system of levels and degrees. Whether this helps to achieve a general consensus about the characteristics of a doctorate and the holder of the degree, i.e. what kinds of qualifications and qualities a person with a doctoral degree should have, still remains to be seen. Equally open is the question whether sufficient transparency and comparable qualification levels in doctoral education can be achieved to include all the meanwhile 45 Bologna signatory states and in the face of national tendencies to keep open a multitude of pathways to a doctoral degree. The observation of a diversification of models and purposes of the doctorate due to the growing heterogeneity of people interested in getting the degree provides evidence that a functional differentiation rather than a stratified differentiation of doctoral might be appropriate.

However, it can be expected that the increasing competition for talented doctoral students and highly qualified young researchers as well as a stronger vertical stratification of universities within national higher education systems and within Europe on the basis of rankings and the quest for excellence will lead to an end of the paradigm of recognition based on trust and equivalence. Instead, recognition will increasingly follow a new paradigm based on proven (and measured) equivalence along hierarchical scales. Thus, recognition and possibly exchange might increasingly take place only in "zones of mutual trust", i.e. universities will only cooperate with each other if they are in the same "league". This in turn might have unintended effects for the accreditation of doctoral programmes and cause a shift from functional or horizontal differentiation of a variety of models for doctoral education and training to new forms of vertical and stratified differentiation. The tension between diversity and transparency tends to be solved by substituting the horizontal dimension of differentiation into a hierarchical order.

VISIBLE TRENDS AND FIELDS OF TENSION

From what has been said so far at least five fields of tension can be derived which will be discussed in the following paragraphs.

Increasing Numbers and Selecting Best Talent

The first field of tensions opens up between the intention to increase the numbers of doctoral degree holders in Europe and the trend to only recruit best talent, be it from within, be it from without Europe. This changes first of all the traditional European notion of temporary mobility to degree or programme mobility. Second, an increase in doctoral degree holders will require not only a more efficient organization of the process of getting the degree but also has to take into account the growing heterogeneity of potential candidates interested in the degree. This trend will favour the implementation of more structured doctoral degree programmes. However, such an expansion contradicts to some extent the idea to recruit only the very best and most promising graduates into doctoral training. Can we expect the emergence of an elite sector within doctoral education and training? Typically expansion is followed by differentiation. Differentiation can take place in horizontal and functional forms or in vertical and stratified forms. It will be an issue of policy in the coming years whether differentiation of doctoral education will move towards functional or stratified forms. This issue is closely related to a second field of tensions.

Access and Admission

The more structured the phase of qualifying for a doctoral degree, the more regulations will be necessary for access and admission. In the future, potential candidates for a doctoral degree will increasingly have to apply for admission into graduate schools, doctoral programmes, etc. In order to create transparent and fair procedures for access and admission general criteria and regulations have to be defined. What has been rarely discussed until now is the tension between access and admission itself when designing policies for shaping the transition from one cycle to the next.

As at the beginning of studies or at the point of transition from Bachelor to Master studies, the regulations of access to doctoral education are linked to criteria or conditions which define entitlement. How open or closed should access into doctoral education be? Who can apply for access into doctoral education? What are the preconditions for access? Should it be successful completion of a Master degree or is successful completion of a Bachelor degree sufficient? The general regulation of access is an issue of national or even European level policy making. Admission must be distinguished from access. It defines the eligibility of applicants for a certain programme of graduate school and depends on local circumstances like capacity, availability of appropriate supervision, the fit between topic and programme or profile of the candidate and profile of the programme, institutional selectivity, etc. For admission, institutional and even departmental policies have to be developed in order to establish fair and transparent procedures to select from among the pool of applicants who fulfil the access requirements. It can be expected that there will be highly selective and less selective programmes for doctoral education and training in the future.

The Link between the Second and the Third Cycle

Currently there is a majority of higher education experts and practitioners in the European higher education area who share the view that successful completion of a Master degree is required in order to go into doctoral education and training. However, this condition is beginning to erode at the margins. Based on the American model of graduate education there is a growing number of doctoral programmes in which the taught elements are offered for Master degree students together with doctoral students. The British "new route" or integrated doctorate and the German "fast track PhD" are examples for this trend. Once the taught components have been completed the student must make a decision whether to opt for a doctoral thesis or a Master thesis. Increasingly, highly promising Bachelor graduates with excellent grades are admitted into doctoral programmes directly without having to do a Master degree first. This destabilizes the link between the second and the third cycle of studies and might pose a threat to the Master degree level by turning it into a degree for weaker students who did not succeed in getting a doctoral degree. Policies are needed here to design and shape the transition between the three cycles as a sequence for the majority of students, despite that fact that exceptions might be possible. It seems to be important to uphold the character of the second cycle (Master level studies) as a valid and worthwhile qualification.

Funding

A further issue is funding of doctoral education which is handled quite differently in the European countries and is closely related to decisions about the status of doctoral students or candidates. Are they in fact students who should pay fees for the teaching and training services they require? Or are they young researchers who contribute with their work to the teaching and research performance of their institutions and should receive a salary for that? From the perspective of the universities the question is whether their available budget is sufficiently high to be able to finance doctoral education and the required infrastructure or whether the costs incurred should be covered by the students or candidates? Whose responsibility should it be that doctoral students have sufficient financial means to concentrate full time or part time on their qualification? Despite that fact that the different status of doctoral candidates in the Bologna signatory countries can not be unified currently, the issue of funding requires policies in two respects: (a) funding of the institutions to establish and run doctoral programmes and (b) funding of doctoral students or candidates to be able to devote an appropriate amount of time to their research work and thesis production.

Critical Mass

A final issue is "critical mass". The origin of this concept can probably be found in the British Research Assessment Exercise (RAE). The RAE does not only serve to identify the best and most research-intensive departments and research groups and provide legitimacy for their promotion and additional public funding. It also serves to pave the way for a process of concentration of research training with the argument that this will be a more effective and efficient use of public money. It also enables a simplification of priority setting in terms of national research, development, and innovation policy. Where critical mass is achieved – and whether this means five or twelve or twenty professors in a given discipline or subject area is a question of definition since critical mass is relative – doctoral students have more opportunities to discuss their work with experts beyond their individual supervisor and thus are confronted with a broader range of knowledge and specializations. Furthermore, doctoral students can learn from each other and larger programmes or graduate schools offer better opportunities for that than the master–apprentice model with individual supervision. Often it is proposed that several universities within one region should cooperate in the establishment and running of doctoral programmes and/or graduate schools in order to achieve critical mass (examples can be found in the Netherlands and in France). It is expected that the German Excellence Initiative will trigger similar developments. Concentration and critical mass will re-enforce competition for best talent. As a result we might not only end up with an even starker stratification of higher education institutions but with whole regions or even countries having no doctoral education at all. This possible scenario has been characterized as the emergence of "research free zones".

FURTHER DEVELOPMENTS, STRATEGIC OBJECTIVES, POSSIBLE TARGETS

As has been indicated, in particular in the previous section that there are a number of trends and tensions emerging from the processes and policies to reform doctoral education and training in Europe which require attention. In order to achieve the goal of the Lisbon Strategy to create a European Research Area and make Europe competitive on a global scale in terms of its research and innovation systems and in order to achieve the goal of the Bologna Process to create a European Higher Education Area which is also attractive for students from countries beyond Europe a multitude of pathways to the doctorate should be established rather than concentrating doctoral education and training in highly selective centres of excellence, thus indirectly supporting the emergence of "research free zones and regions".

Further Developments

Anticipating the further developments of doctoral education in the European Higher Education and Research Area it can safely be said that the two main trends will most possibly be (a) an increasing internationalization in the composition of doctoral students and candidates based less on temporary mobility than on degree mobility; and (b) an growing heterogeneity of this group due to the fact that further expansion will be accompanied by a larger variety of purposes and motives in getting a doctoral degree. These developments will contribute to a diversification of the models and modes of doctoral education as well as an increasing integration of this phase of qualification into structures like programmes, schools, centres, or graduate colleges. To some extent the focus will shift away from the end product (thesis) and concentrate more on shaping the process (education and training for research). The growing multitude of models and motives will make it difficult to provide transparency and good information. For the time being, the European Qualifications framework is too generic to serve transparency, rather it will contribute to further diversification if recognition mechanisms will accept qualifications towards a doctoral degree which have been acquired on the job or in other non-formal settings. The idea to have many pathways to a doctorate is to some extent appealing but will have impacts on the income and job related rates of return of a doctoral degree. Of importance in this context will be efforts to achieve transparency and equity of access. The former can be achieved by establishing a good European wide information basis on options and opportunities for getting a doctoral degree, the latter can be achieved by emphasizing functional rather than stratified diversity.

Strategic Objectives to Accomplish Sustainability

As has been pointed out before, a multitude of models of doctoral education is appropriate to the increasing multitude of purposes of and motives for the doctorate. That implies functional differentiation rather than highly selective concentration. However, there are a few other issues which should be considered as potential strategic objectives as well.

The creation of a European Higher Education and Research Area has been closely linked to its attractiveness and competitiveness on a global scale on the one hand and to its support of the emerging European knowledge societies and economies on the other. Frequently this link has been characterized as being determined by the concept of relevance. It is important, however, to define relevance in a broader manner than often seems to be the case. Just as there are many forms of quality and excellence, there are many forms of relevance as well. Getting a doctoral degree means generating new knowledge which can be relevant for society, for economy, for the cultural sphere, or for the knowledge base of a given discipline or knowledge domain. Commodification and reification of new knowledge should be prevented as much as possible. Access to knowledge is also an issue in the context of equity. Universities which mostly have the exclusive right to award doctoral degrees are local repositories of global knowledge and should provide as far as possible free access to it. Only in this sense they can be global, national, and local institutions at the same time.

Last but not least it will be important to foster a culture of innovation and creativity in doctoral education. Too much regulation and emphasis on cost effectiveness will prevent risk taking and open inquiry. The possibility of curiosity driven or "free" research is in many cases a better predictor of innovative results than research embedded in programmes. The openness of the European Research Council for such applications will be an important indicator for this.

Possible Targets

A number of possible targets can be derived from this analysis of the changes in doctoral education and training in Europe so that a sustainable future for the European Higher Education and Research Area may be accomplished. The proposals being made here should be regarded as an orientation rather than a definitive list. Certainly a promising beginning has been made by EUA in establishing a Council for Doctoral Education (EUA-CDE) to develop and advance doctoral education and research training in Europe. "The objectives of the new Council include:
– Enhancing the quality of doctoral education in Europe by fostering debate and promoting the exchange and dissemination of good practice;
– Encouraging and supporting the development of institutional policies and strategies as well as the introduction of effective leadership and management practices;
– Strengthening the international dimension of doctoral programmes and research training through improved cooperation among its members and by establishing dialogue with partner organizations in other world regions;
– Identifying and monitoring emerging trends in doctoral education inside and outside Europe;
– Promoting the doctorate as a key professional qualification and underlining the importance of young researchers for a knowledge-based society" (EUA Newsletter 2/2008).

Furthermore, a European-wide debate is proposed about the doctorate and its future in order to see whether responsible policy makers and practitioners will be able to agree on a joint definition of the particular form of "graduateness" a doctoral degree holder should possess. Not only could the European Qualifications Framework serve as a basis for this but a joint definition can also contribute to creating more transparency in the face of the growing diversification and differentiation of doctoral education in Europe.

Such a debate and ensuing potential policy guidelines should be evidence based and there is a need to initiate and fund comparative research on the diversification of types and modes of doctoral education which might result in a database providing information on opportunities for doctoral education in Europe not only for potential candidates from countries having signed the Bologna declaration but possibly worldwide. A better knowledge about the many and continuously increasing opportunities for doctoral education and training in Europe might also contribute to increase the attractiveness of European research training for potential candidates worldwide.

Finally, the administrative and content related coordination of all the newly established doctoral programmes, schools, and centres as well as the coordination of those existing already for some time seems to be the breeding ground for a new type of higher education professional. Coordinators of these structures often have themselves a doctoral degree and take over managerial functions with their responsibilities for such programmes, schools, or centres. A European network of these coordinators should be established in order to exchange information and learn from examples of good practice.

LITERATURE (INCLUDING FURTHER READING)

Bartelse, Jeroen (1999): Concentrating the Minds. The Institutionalisation of the Graduate School Innovation in Dutch and German Higher Education. Enschede: CHEPS and Utrecht: Lemma.

Berlin Communiqué (2003): http://www.aic.lv/ace/ace_disk/Bologna/maindoc (accessed 7 October 2005).

Berning, Ewald, Falk, Susanne (2005): "Das Promotionswesen im Umbruch". In: Beiträge zur Hochschulforschung, Vol. 27, No. 1, pp. 48–72.

Bologna Declaration (1999): http://www.aic.lv/ace/ace_disk/Bologna/maindoc (accessed 7 October 2005).

Bourner, Tim, Bowden, Rachel, Laing, Stuart (2000): "Professional Doctorates: The Development of Researching Professionals." In: Bourner, T., Katz, D. Watson (eds.): New Directions in Professional Higher Education. Buckingham: SRHE and Open University Press, pp. 214–225.

Bourner, Tim, Bowden, Rachel, Laing, Stuart (2001): "Professional Doctorates in England". In: Studies in Higher Education, Vol. 26, No. 1, p. 65–83.

Busquin, Philipe (2000): Presidency Conclusions of the Lisbon Summit. URL: http://www.bologna-berlin2003.de/pdf/PRESIDENCY_CONCLUSIONS_Lissabon.pdf (accessed 16 June 2007).

CIRGE (2005): http://www.depts.washington.edu/cirgecon Council of Graduate Schools (2006): "A Transatlantic Dialogue on Doctoral Education." In: Communicator, Vol. 9. No. 8, October, pp. 1–2 and 5. URL: http://www.cgsnet.org/portals/0/pdf/ comm_2006_10.pdf (accessed 14 June 2007).

De Weert, Egbert (2004): "The Netherlands". In: Sadlak, Jan (ed.) (2004): Doctoral Studies and Qualifications in Europe and the United States: Status and Prospects. Bucarest: UNESCO-CEPES, pp. 77–97.

Dill, David D., Soo, Maarja (2005): "Academic quality, league tables, and public policy: A cross-national analysis of university ranking systems." In: Higher Education, Vol. 49, pp. 495–533.

Enders, Jürgen, Bornmann, Lutz (2001): Karriere mit Doktortitel? Ausbildung, Berufsverlauf und Berufserfolg von Promovierten. Frankfurt/M., New York: Campus.

Enders, Jürgen (2005a): "Brauchen die Universitäten in Deutschland ein neues Paradigma der Nachwuchsausbildung?" In: Beiträge zur Hochschulforschung, Vol. 27, No. 1, pp. 34–47.

Enders, Jürgen (2005b): "Wissenschaftlicher Nachwuchs in Europa." In: 50. Beiheft der Zeitschrift für Pädagogik. Weinheim, Basel: Beltz, pp. 158–169.

EQF (2008): The European Qualifications Framework. URL: http://ec.europa.eu/education/policies/ educ/eqf/index_en.html (retrieved 5 April 2008).

EUA (2005): Doctoral Programmes for the European Knowledge Society. Brussels. URL: http://www.eua.be/ eua/jsp/en/upload/Doctoral_Programmes_Project_Report.1129278878120.pdf (accessed: 1 November 2005).

EUA (2007): Call for Case Studies for DOC-CAREERS Project. URL: http://www.eua.be/index. php?id=48&no_cache=1&tx_ttnews%5Btt_news%5D=335&tx_ttnews%5BbackPid%5D=1 (accessed 16 June 2007).

EUA Newsletter 2/2008 from 28 January: EUA launches new membership service: Council for Doctoral Education. URL: http://www.eau.be/index.php?id=604 (retrieved 9 March 2008.)

European Commission (2003a): Communication from the Commission: The role of universities in the Europe of knowledge. Brussels (COM(2003) 58 final).

European Commission (2003b): Communication for the Commission to the Council and the European Parliament: Researchers in the European Research Area: One profession, multiple careers. Brussels (COM(2003) 436 final).

Golde, Chris M., Walker, George E. (eds.) (2006): Envisioning the Future of Doctoral Education. Preparing Stewards of the Discipline. Carnegie Essays on the Doctorate. San Francisco: Jossey-Bass.

Green, Howard, Powell, Stuart (2005): Doctoral Education in Contemporary Higher Education. Maidenhead, New York: Society for Research into Higher Education and Open University Press.

Guth, Jessica (2006): The Bologna Process: The Impact of Higher Education Reform on the Structure and Organisation of Doctoral Programmes in Germany". In: Higher Education in Europe, Vol. 31, No. 3, pp. 327–338.

Hüfner, Klaus (2004): "Doctoral Degrees in Germany." In: Sadlak, Jan (ed.): Doctoral Studies and Qualifications in Europe and the United States: Status and Prospects. Bucarest: UNESCO-CEPES, pp. 51–61.

Johnston, Bill, Murray, Rowena (2004): "New Routes to the PhD: Cause for Concern?" In: Higher Education Quarterly, Vol. 58, No. 1, pp. 31–42.

Kehm, Barbara M. (1999): Higher Education in Germany. Developments, Problems and Perspectives. Bucarest: UNESCO CEPES and Wittenberg: Institute for Higher Education Research.

Kehm, Barbara M. (2004): "Developing Doctoral Degrees and Qualifications in Europe. Good Practice and Issues of Concern." In: Sadlak, Jan (ed.): Doctoral Studies and Qualifications in Europe and the United States: Status and Prospects. Bucarest: UNESCO-CEPES, pp. 279–298.

Kehm, Barbara M. (2005): "Promovieren in Europa: Strukturen und Konzepte im Vergleich". In: Hochschule Innovativ, No. 14, pp. 2–3.

Kehm, Barbara M. (2006): Doctoral Education in Europe and North America. A Comparative Analysis. In: Teichler, Ulrich (ed.): The Formative Years of Scholars. Wenner-Gren International Series Vol. 83. London: Portland Press.

Kehm, Barbara M. (2007): Quo Vadis Doctoral Education? New European Approaches in the Context of Global Changes". Manuskript eines Vortrag auf der RIF-EDSE Konferenz "Le doctora(n)t en sciences de l'éducation: enjeux, défies, perspectives". Universität Genf, 8./9. Juni.

Kehm, Barbara M. (2008): "Germany". In: Nerad, Maresi, Heggelund, Mimi (eds.): Toward a Global PhD? Forces & Forms in Doctoral Education Worldwide. Seattle and London: University of Washington Press, pp. 19–35.

Kivinen, Osmo, Ahola, Sakari, Kaipainen, Päivi (eds.) (1999): Towards the European Model of Postgraduate Training. Research Report 50. Turku: University of Turku, Research Unit for the Sociology of Education (RUSE).

Kupfer, Antonia (2007): DoktorandInnen in den USA. Eine Analyse vor dem Hintergrund des Bologna-Prozesses. Wiesbaden: Deutscher Universitäts-Verlag.

Kupfer, Antonia, Moes, Johannes (2003): Promovieren in Europa. Ein internationaler Vergleich von Promotionsbedingungen. Frankfurt/M: GEW and Hans Böckler Stiftung.

Kwiek, Marek (2004): „Poland". In: Sadlak, Jan (ed.): Doctoral Studies and Qualifications in Europe and the United States: Status and Prospects. Bucarest: UNESCO-CEPES. S. 119–133.

Lemerle,Jean (2004): "France". In: Sadlak, Jan (ed.): Doctoral Studies and Qualifications in Europe and the United States: Status and Prospects. Bucarest: UNESCO-CEPES. S. 37–50.

LERU (2007): LERU Statement on Doctoral Training and the Bologna Process. URL: http://www.leru_statement_on_doctoral_training_february_2007.pdf (accessed: 17 June 2007.

Lisbon Summit (2000): http://www.bologna-berlin2003.de/pdf/PRESIDENCY_CONCLUSIONS_Lissabon.pdf (accessed 17 June 2007).

London Communiqué (2007): "Towards the European Higher Education Area: responding to challenges in a globalised world." 18 May. URL: http://www.dfes.gov.uk/bologna/uploads/documents/ LondonCommuniquefinalwithLondonlogo.pdf (accessed: 17 June 2007).

Mähler, Helena (2004): "Sweden". In: Sadlak, Jan (ed.): Doctoral Studies and Qualifications in Europe and the United States: Status and Prospects. Bucarest: UNESCO-CEPES. S. 201–230.

Maki, Peggy L., Borkowski, Nancy A. (eds) (2006): The Assessment of Doctoral Education. Emerging Criteria and New Models for Improving Outcomes. Stirling, Virginia: Stylus.

Manifesto (2006): "Manifesto of European Doctoral Students in Literature and the Humanities." URL: http://www.univ-bpclermont.fr/IMG/pdf/manifeste-doctorant.pdf (accessed: 17 June 2007).

McCarty, Luise P., Ortlof, Debora H. (2005): "Reforming the Doctorate in Education: Three Conceptions." In: Educational Perspectives, Vol. 37, Issue 2, S. 10-19.

Mitchell-Kernan, Claudia (2005): "Doctoral Education: Reform on a Weakened Foundation." In: Communicator, Vol. 38, No. 10, December. URL: http://www.cgsnet.org/portals/0/pdf/Mitchell% 20Kernan%20article.pdf (accessed 16 July 2007).

Moscati, Roberto (2004): "Italy". In: Sadlak, Jan (ed.): Doctoral Studies and Qualifications in Europe and the United States: Status and Prospects. Bucarest: UNESCO-CEPES. S. 63–76.

National Science Foundation (ed.) (2000): Graduate Education Reform in Europe, Asia and the Americas and International Mobility of Scientists and Engineers. URL: http://www.nsf.gov/statistics/ nsf00318/pdf/c2.pdf (accessed 15 June 2007).

Neave, Guy, Blückert, Kjell, Nybom, Thorsten (eds.) (2006): The European Research University. An Historical Parenthesis? New York, Basingstoke: Palgrave Macmillan.

Nerad, Maresi (2004): "The PhD in the US: Criticism, Facts, and Remedies." In: Higher Education Policy, Vol. 17, No. 2, pp. 183–199.

Nerad, Maresi (2008): United States of America". In: Nerad, Maresi, Heggelund, Mimi (eds.): Toward a Global PhD? Forces & Forms in Doctoral Education Worldwide. Seattle and London: University of Washington Press, pp. 278–299.

Nyquist, Judy D. (2002): "The PhD: A Tapestry of Change for the 21st Century." In: Change, Vol. 34, No. 6, November/December, p. 12–20.

Park, Chris (2005): "New Variant PhD: The changing nature of the doctorate in the UK." In: Journal of Higher Education Policy and Management, Vol. 27, No. 2, July, pp. 189-207.

Paul, Jean-Jacques (2002): "Postgraduate Training and Postdoctoral Careers : Recent Reforms and Experiences in France." Paper delivered at the International Conference "Science, Training and Careers. Changing Modes of Knowledge Production and Labour Markets. CHEPS, University of Twente October. URL: http://www.u-bourgogne.fr/labo-IREDU/2002/0205.ppt (accessed 27 June 2007.

Pechar, Hans, Thomas, Jan (2004): "Austria". In: Sadlak, Jan (ed.) (2004): Doctoral Studies and Qualifications in Europe and the United States: Status and Prospects. Bucarest: UNESCO-CEPES, pp. 13–35.

Powell, Stuart, Long, Elizabeth (2005): Professional Doctorate Awards in the UK. UK Council for Graduate Education. URL: http://www.ukcge.ac.uk/OneStopCMS/Core/CrawlerResourceServer.aspx? resource=8793819F-95F4-4E23-96B0-7B12757BB1B6&mode=link&guid=a57997aa5a9f4450bb1411 44a86634e6. (accessed: 15 June 2007).

Recotillet, Isabelle (2003): "Availability and Characteristics of Surveys on the Destination of Doctorate Recipients in OECD Countries." OECD Science, Technology and Industry Working Papers, 2003/9, Paris: OECD Publishing. Doi:10.1787/245308553443.

Sadlak, Jan (ed.) (2004): Doctoral Studies and Qualifications in Europe and the United States: Status and Prospects. Bucarest: UNESCO-CEPES.

Scott, David, Brown, Andrew, Lunt, Ingrid, Thorne, Lucy (2004): Professional Doctorates. Integrating Professional and Academic Knowledge. Buckingham: SRHE and Open University Press.

Slaughter, Sheila A., Leslie, Larry L. (2000): Academic Capitalism: Politics, Policies and the Entrepreneurial University. Baltimore: Johns Hopkins University Press.

Sorbonne Declaration (1998): http://www.aic.lv/ace/ace_disk/Bologna/maindoc (accessed 7 October 2005).

Stewart, Debra, W. (2003): Current Issues in Doctoral Education in the U.S.: Change and Response. A paper delivered at the Deutsche Forschungsgemeinschaft (DFG) Meeting on Graduate Research Training in Würzburg, Germany, 1 July. URL: http://www.dfg.de/wissenschaftliche_karriere/focus/2003/promotionsfoerderung/download/stewart.pdf. (accessed: 17 June, 2007).

Sverker, Sörlin et al. (2006): A Public Good: PhD Education in Denmark. Report from an International Evaluation Panel. Danish Ministry of Science, Technology and Innovation. URL: http://videnskabsministeriet.dk/site/forside/publikationer/2006/a-public-good---phd-education-in-denmark/phd.pdf (accessed 16 July 2007).

Teichler, Ulrich (2005): "Future Challenges for Doctoral Education in Germany." Unpublished manuscript of a paper presented at a Conference in Kassel, in June

Trends V (2007): Trends V: Universities shaping the European Higher Education Area. Written by Crosier, David, Purser, Lewis, and Smidt, Hanne. Brussels: EUA. URL: http://www.eua.be/fileadmin/user_upload/files/Publications/Final_Trends_Report_May_10.pdf (accessed 17 June 2007).

UK Council for Graduate Education (1995): Graduate Schools. Warwick: KCGE. URL: http://ukcge.ac.uk (accessed 17 June 2006).

UK Council for Graduate Education (1996): Quality and Standards of Postgraduate Research Degrees. Warwick: UKCGE. URL: http://www.ukcge.ac.uk/OneStopCMS/Core/CrawlerResourceServer. aspx?resource=6B22F9C5-DC02-4633-9964-579846D4B3A4&mode=link&guid=a57997aa 5a9f 44 50bb141144a86634e6. (accessed: 17 June 2007).

UK Council for Graduate Education (1997): Practice-based Doctorate in Creative and Performing Arts and Design. Warwick: UKCGE. URL: http://www.ukcge.ac.uk/OneStopCMS/Core/Crawler ResourceServer.aspx?resource=CD25644D-0D5A-41DA-8CC4-EEFADA55DB31&mode=link&guid=a57997aa5a9f4450bb141144a86634e6. (accessed: 17 June 2007).

UK Council for Graduate Education (2002): Professional Doctorates. Warwick: UKCGE. URL: http://www.ukcge.ac.uk/OneStopCMS/Core/CrawlerResourceServer.aspx?resource=53BE34C8-EBDD-47E 1-B1C7-F80B45D25E20&mode=link&guid=a57997aa5a9f4450bb141144a86634e6. (accessed 27 June 2007.

Weissinger Ellen (2003): Diffusing Graduate Reform Initiatives in the Sciences: How Might "Institutionalisation" Really Work? A paper presented at the Merrill Conference in the Series: The Research Mission of Public Universities, June. URL: http://merrill.ku.edu/PDFfiles/weissinger2003.pdf (accessed: 16 July 2007).

Williams, Garth (2008): "Canada". In: Nerad, Maresi, Heggelund, Mimi (eds.): Toward a Global PhD? Forces & Forms in Doctoral Education Worldwide. Seattle and London: University of Washington Press, pp. 249–277.

Wulff, Donald H., Austin Ann E., & Associates (2004): Paths to the Professoriate. Strategies for Enriching the Preparation of Future Faculty. San Francisco: Jossey-Bass.

Part IV: Diversity

JEROEN HUISMAN

13. THE BOLOGNA PROCESS TOWARDS 2020: INSTITUTIONAL DIVERSIFICATION OR CONVERGENCE?[1]

INTRODUCTION

Diversity is generally considered as an "inherent good" in higher education, implying that it is a characteristic of higher education systems and institutions which everybody would support. A quote of the 1980s is still relevant today: "We have in this country a rich array of institutions that serves a variety of needs. We celebrate the diversity, acknowledging that our system of higher education is the envy of the world ... [O]ur goal must be continuously to promote both excellence and diversity in higher education" (Carnegie Foundation for the Advancement of Teaching, 1987, 2). Stakeholders like the Carnegie Foundation, but more importantly governments across the globe have typically endorsed diversity and have paid considerable attention to developing policies and instruments to take care that diversity would be protected.

Not only at the national levels is the issue of diversity important as will be evident as we look closer at supranational developments. It may have been a shock to those endorsing diversity to read that the 1998 Sorbonne Declaration was a declaration on the "harmonisation of the architecture of the European higher education system", which may hint at decreasing the heterogeneity across systems. But a close reading of the Declaration reveals that it was not so much the intention to create a European higher education system[2], but to create a "European area of higher education, where national identities and common interests can interact and strengthen each other". The 1999 Bologna Declaration echoes this intention by stressing to construct a European Higher Education Area to achieve greater compatibility and comparability of the systems of higher education, but that this should be realized "within the framework of national competences and taking full respect of the diversity of cultures, languages, national education systems and of university autonomy" (see also Witte, 2008). Likewise, communications from the European Commission (EC) stress the idea of diversity within the overall need for comparability/compatibility to "constitute an effort to organise that diversity within a more coherent and compatible European framework, which is a condition for the readability, and hence the competitiveness, of European universities both within Europe itself and in the whole world" (European Commission, 2003, 5).

Although the threat of harmonization – in the English meaning of standardization and unification – has been reassuringly discarded, the Bologna and EC documents easily seem to step over the tension between achieving compatibility/comparability

B.M. Kehm, J. Huisman and B. Stensaker (eds.), The European Higher Education Area:
Perspectives on a Moving Target, 245–262.

and preserving diversity. And the observation of one of the reports presented just before the Bologna Declaration that there was "a high degree of convergence towards a duration of five years for master-level studies" (Haug, Kirstein, & Knudsen, 1999, 10) – even though it turned out to be a rather preliminary observation, given results from later studies – gave further input to expectations that diversity was on the decrease. One could even argue (as Witte, 2007 does) that the preliminary observation had the effect of a self-fulfilling prophecy: stakeholders have considered the trend towards the 3+2 model as a safe policy option. The question therefore remains how diversity can be maintained or increased within a political context that puts pressure on comparability and compatibility. The idea of compatibility and comparability – almost by default – denotes that systems and institutions have to adapt structures and processes to realize the objectives. And, the documents seem to be clear about priorities: comparability and compatibility come first; diversity – second order – should be protected as much as possible. And although adaptations can take shape in various ways, the vision of achieving the European Higher Education Area implies – in one way or another – that higher education institutions and systems have to move in a certain direction.

This leads us to the main questions to be addressed in this contribution:
– What do studies on the Bologna process tell us about current changes in diversity?
– How can we explain the current outcomes of the Bologna process? Which factors have affected the process?
– What does the above imply for institutional diversity in higher education towards 2010?
– What are risks and opportunities regarding institutional diversity in the future decade and which strategies seem appropriate to preserve or increase institutional diversity?

Before embarking upon these questions, it is important to bring about some clarity regarding the terminology and it is worthwhile to pay attention to the importance of diversity.

THE CONCEPT OF DIVERSITY

Terminology

To come to terms with what is meant with diversity (in higher education), first a few fairly recent examples of "diversity policies" are presented. In 2004, the Higher Education Funding Council for England (HEFCE) produced guidance for managers regarding monitoring staff and student diversity and equality within higher education institutions (HEFCE, 2004). Also the 2003 White Paper *The future of higher education* of the Department for Education and Skills (DfES, 2003) addressed the issue of diversity, but focused on another form of diversity. It addresses the idea of a diversified institutional landscape, in which the department would "[r]ecognise and encourage diversity of role, with universities and colleges proud to be different and to play to their individual strengths" (DfES, 2003, 96). In a similar vein, the Australian Department for Education, Science and Training

(DEST) addressed institutional diversity in one of its recent policy documents *Our universities. Backing Australia's future* (DEST, 2003). The document states: "Australia needs a high quality higher education sector with a range of institutions servicing different communities and varied requirements. It is neither necessary nor desirable for all universities to be the same. A more diverse system will be achieved by institutions forging distinct missions within the overall system and through greater collaboration between individual universities and other education providers, industry, business, regions and communities" (DEST, 2003, 11). As a final example, the German *Exzellenzinitiative* are mentioned. The German government announced in 2005 to invest about 1.9 billion Euro for a five-year period to promote top-level research, aiming to strengthen science and research in the country, to improve the international competitiveness and raise the profile of the top performers in German universities. Whereas the concept of diversity is not explicitly mentioned, obviously the aim is to create more qualitative variety (*Spitzen im Universitäts- und Wissenschaftsbereich*) within the higher education system.

Despite the importance of the topic and the variety of government-led initiatives developed, the academic literature and often the policy documents have been rather imprecise when it comes to defining diversity. As it becomes clear from the examples above, diversity may refer to staff and student composition within higher education institutions, general variety in the institutional landscape, or more specifically variety with respect to research quality in a higher education system.

Birnbaum's (1983, 37–56) classification may be helpful to distinguish forms of diversity. His main concerns relate to external or institutional diversity. He identified seven forms:
- Systemic diversity refers to differences in institutional type, size, and control found within a higher education system.
- Structural diversity refers to differences resulting from historical and legal foundations, or differences in the division of authority within institutions.
- Programmatic diversity relates to the degree level, degree area, comprehensiveness, mission and emphasis of programmes and services provided by the institutions.
- Procedural diversity describes differences in the ways that teaching, research and/or services are provided by institutions.
- Reputational diversity communicates the perceived differences in institutions based on status and prestige.
- Constituential diversity alludes not only to differences in students served, but also to other constituents (faculty, administration).
- Values and climate diversity is associated with differences in social environment and culture.

Based on this classification, the HEFCE example above would be a case of constituential diversity (bearing in mind that HEFCE speaks about internal diversity), the Australian and English governments' proposals refer to systemic (and structural) diversity, the German example also relates to systemic diversity, but particularly links to reputational diversity. Following Birnbaum (1983), institutional diversity – in this chapter – is defined as the variety of types of institutions within a higher education system (or area) (see also Huisman, 1995).

Whereas diversity refers to a static situation, terms like diversification, hetero-genization, convergence and homogenization refer to processes of change. Diversific-ation and heterogenization denote processes of increasing diversity, terms like convergence and homogenization refer to processes of decreasing diversity (Huisman, 1995, 51–52).

The Importance of Diversity

By depicting diversity as an inherent good, the reasons to maintain or increase diversity often remain implicit, but it is relevant to pay some attention to this. Various authors (see e.g. Birnbaum, 1983; Stadtman, 1980; Van Vught, 1996) have set out why diversity is important and what its benefits are. I am following Van Vught (2008) in his adaptation of Birnbaum's arguments. First, a diversified system is better able to cater for the wide variety of students seeking access to higher education. Second, a diversified system is deemed (more) flexible when it comes to mobility from one institution to another. If, for whatever reason, the student's first choice may not be the right one, there are plenty of opportunities for him or her to find another – hopefully more suitable – place elsewhere in the system. A third argument is taken from the perspective of the labour market. Given the needs of highly diversified labour markets in modern society, it is a good thing that the offerings are varied as well. It is more likely that there is a good match between supply and demand in diverse systems. Or in slightly different words: the risks of a mismatch are smaller in diverse systems than in homogeneous systems. The fourth argument is that a diverse system is better able to cope with a variety of needs of certain interest groups. Think of interest groups (either political, religious or ethnic) that would like to have their "own" higher education institutions, defending their views and values. In less diversified systems, such needs may be unaddressed. Fifth, in a diverse higher education system, both mass and elite higher education can be catered to. Or, in the words of Trow (1979), the survival of elite institutions is dependent on being surrounded by a comprehensive set of non-elite institutions, catering for mass education. Finally, in a diverse system higher education institutions more effectively can experiment with innovations, which allows for a high – and necessary – level of dynamism in higher education systems.

One counter argument must be mentioned. One may posit that a relative homogeneous system with fairly large institutions, internally strongly diversified, may as well meet the needs from the various stakeholders. If such institutions are spread adequately across a country, students may find their choice in relative proximity and the labour market would be ensured of a variety of graduates because the institution is internally diversified. A further argument would be that such internally diversified institutions are inhabited by a diverse set of students and staff, supporting the idea of exchange and communication between various cultures. Interest-groups may be less satisfied with such an outcome, for they may find it difficult to find a higher education institution that clearly represents their values and views. What is important to bear in mind is that such a homogeneous system is very likely to be less efficient. A more specialized institution is better able to focus its energy on that specialist function, whereas in large, internally diversified institutions the chances of being less effective are higher. And here a system argument enters the debate as well. A homogeneous system is much more vulnerable to shocks in the system. Following a biological metaphor, climate change quite often does much more harm in less diverse areas and systems than in areas of rich variety, such as the tropics. The chances of an extinction of higher education systems – if they would be homogeneous – seem unlikely, but the threat of sincere damage in case of an external shock (a sharp decline in resources) will affect the whole system. In a diverse system only a limited number of higher education institutions will be affected, admitting that the effect can be that serious that some institutions are not able to survive.

THE BOLOGNA PROCESS

Outcomes of the Process so Far

The EUA trend reports contain valuable information on changes in higher education systems during the Bologna process (Crosier, Purser, & Smidt, 2007; Reichert & Tauch, 2003, 2005). We skip the two first trends reports (1999 and 2001) for these were mainly based on information provided by national governments, leading to a rather biased picture of developments, i.e. stressing the policies and policy intentions and not so much the actual changes within higher education and its institutions. From the third report on, one can see the pattern of further implementation and institutionalization of the elements of the Bologna process. Whereas in the third report (Reichert & Tauch, 2003, 7) maintained that the "reforms have yet to reach the majority of the HE grass-roots representatives who are supposed to implement them and give them concrete meaning", the 2005 report concludes that "many institutions have made great efforts to "internalise" the reform process, incorporating Bologna issues into their own institutional strategies and activities" (Reichert & Tauch, 2005, 4). A central theme in the trends reports is that much of the implementation relates to structural changes, such as the implementation of two or three cycles, the adoption of the European Credit and Transfer System (ECTS) and issuing a Diploma Supplement, whereas "[s]tructural change must be matched with proper redevelopment of the curricula, and often this has not been completed" (*ibid.*, 4) and – with regard to ECTS and the supplement – "the challenge of providing clear information about learning outcomes remains" (*ibid.*, 5). A second theme running through the documents is that – for various reasons – the implementation is less straightforward than possibly expected. It is not only about operationalizing the elements of the process at the basic levels as such, it is also about implementing change in particular historical, political, and cultural contexts. The 2005 report (Reichert & Teich, 2005, 4) states that "the process ... is a highly complex cultural and social transformation that has set off a chain of developments with their own dynamics in different contexts" and the latest report (Crosier, Purser & Smidt, 2007, 7) refers to "the different national interpretations of the nature and purpose of the three cycles, and whether these different national interpretations will prove to be compatible" (see also Witte,

2006). In a similar vein the Eurydice report (2005) emphasizes the structural elements being in place in many of the signatory countries, while at the same time it becomes obvious that behind the common trends the devil is in the detail: when it comes to the actual implementation of reforms, countries have found specific national solutions to challenges of the Bologna agenda. This is made even more explicit in a report on Bologna developments in the fields of law, teacher training, medicine, history, and engineering (Huisman, Witte, & File, 2006, 18): "Most of the 32 countries have in general the 'hardware' in place. By this we refer to the general structural regulations and conditions regarding a two-cycle degree structure, regulations regarding the diploma supplement and a credit transfer system. Behind this general picture however, we find a huge variety of mechanisms and procedures as well as great diversity in terms of implementation … And, importantly, the level of implementation is only partial for initiatives at the system level. Implementation at the level of individual institutions ranges from full conceptual development and implementation (but this is seldom the case) to fragmented experiments and pilots". At the level of the discipline – the length of engineering programmes is taken as an example (see e.g. Witte & Huisman, 2008 forthcoming) – a myriad of operationalizations of the two-cycle structure can be found across signatory countries: the length of first cycles ranges from three to four-and-a-half years, and the length of the second cycle ranges from one to two years. And in some countries, the undivided structure is still in place or hybrid situations can be found.

The picture that emerges is that at the macro-structural level, there are patterns of convergence: two or three cycles, ECTS, Diploma Supplement, quality assurance regimes. These changes indicate – in Birnbaum's terminology – mainly convergence when it comes to structural and, to some extent, programmatic diversity (see also Witte, 2006, 2008). But when looking closer at the actual manifestations at the level of individual institutions, disciplines or departments, there is considerable variety in the length of cycles, the organization of access to the cycles, Diploma Supplement automatically supplied or only at the request of the student, quality assurance regimes stressing quality control versus regimes stressing enhancement, etc. Note that the studies mentioned above stress that there is diversity at these meso- and micro-levels, but the reports do not – or cannot – inform us about an increase or decrease of structural and programmatic diversity at these levels or whether it is a different kind of diversity. If we, however, consider diversity in the European context, one could convincingly argue that – given the uneven development and implementation across signatory countries – micro-level diversity has increased.

The phenomenon of the combination of some macro-level convergence and micro-level diversity comes close to what Vaira (2004) terms *allomorphism*, borrowing a term from linguistics. Although he primarily addresses the impact of globalization on higher education organizations, he argues that the concept and the accompanying framework may also be applicable to the Bologna process. The concept of allomorphism implies that there may be converging patterns at the macro-level of the higher education system(s), but that at the meso- (national) and micro-level (organization) there may be a fair amount of local variation: "higher education institutions are neither becoming strictly homogeneous and isomorphic at a global level, nor are highly differentiated and polymorphic at the local-organizational level, but rather they could be conceived as local variants (*not* different forms) of the same institutional archetype" (Vaira, 2004, 503). This perspective comes close to what Marginson and Rhoades define as glonacalisation (Marginson & Rhoades, 2002, see also Douglass, 2005 and Ahola, 2005), a concept that emphasizes that global, national, and local dimensions and forces are *all* significant in change processes in higher education and that globalization does not have an unidirectional impact on nation-states and organizations: these impacts are mediated by national and institutional contexts.

Whereas such approaches are enlightening, it does not yet yield an explanation for the process. There are various explanations that can be listed under the following disciplinary headings: policy sciences, sociology, political sciences. The set of explanations is not exhaustive, but sufficiently elaborated given the aim of this chapter: to set the stage for our forward looking exercise.

Explaining the Outcomes of the Bologna Process (so far)

Let us start of with a set of explanations with a long tradition in policy sciences and public administration. In the 1960s, public administration and policy theories gradually stepped away from the then dominant rationalist approach to policy-making. From then on, many authors contented that policy-making is much more a case of "muddling through" (Lindblom, 1959, 1979); that the idea that policy and implementation should be seen as interdependent (Pressman & Wildavsky, 1973); and that historical and cultural contexts play an important role in policy implementation (see e.g. Steinmo, Thelen, & Longstreth, 1992). Such theoretical and conceptual notions are reflected in research on higher education policy and policy implementation[3]. Noteworthy is the work of Cerych and Sabatier (1986) on policy reform in higher education and mixed outcomes of the policy processes and the work of Van Vught (1989) on the complex relationships between governmental policies and instruments and innovation (see also Beverwijk, 2005; Gornitzka, Kogan, & Amaral, 2007; Gornitzka, Kyvik, & Stensaker, 2002; Theisens, 2004).

Whereas these perspectives might differ – either in detail or more profound – the basic tenet of the state of the art in the policy analysis literature is that much may change in the process from the drafting of the policy to the actual implementation within higher education. Quite often reference is made to the "bottom-heaviness" (Clark, 1983) of higher education institutions, indicating a fair amount of autonomy of the professionals when it comes to responding to policies. In addition, there is a fair amount of goal ambiguity in higher education, high levels of (potential) conflicts between either academics and managers or between disciplines, all leading to less rosy expectations about straightforward implementation according to the intentions of the policy-makers (see e.g. Van Vught, 1989). Looking at the specific characteristics of the Bologna process one could add that in the policy chain from supranational-level policy formation to grass-root implementation the distance is even longer than from national policies to implementation, creating space for "distortion" of the initial policy ideas (see the Europeanisation literature: e.g. Hanf & Soetendorp, 1998; Menon & Hayward, 1996; Mény, Muller, & Quermonne, 1996; Olsen, 2002). And, adding to this, the Bologna policy agenda does not come very close to the ideal-type model of policy-making as in: achieving certain objectives within a certain period of time through specified policy instruments. Indeed, the time-span is mentioned but it is a rather long-term perspective of a decade, not causing any pressure for urgent action. Moreover, the objectives are rather abstract and policy instruments to reach the objectives are hardly mentioned, neither is it clear whether there are sanctions when objectives are not met. And, through time the Bologna agenda underwent changes as well: new elements were added, initial elements were changed, etc. Here again, much distortion can take place from policy to implementation. Furthermore, the declaration came more or less out of the blue, without the involvement of important stakeholders. In this approach, there is a risk that stakeholders might conceive of the declaration as being alien leading to a lack of commitment or even hostile reception. Later in the process, stakeholders were given a more prominent role.

A second explanation – rooted in organizational sociology, but not necessarily at odds with the arguments from the policy literature set out above – takes the idea of *translation* as a point of departure. Basically, work following this concept (e.g. Czarniawski & Sevón, 1996) argues that ideas are transformed while they travel. This is in sharp contrast to theories that emphasis diffusion of ideas/innovations, which assume that the central idea will be accepted (or not). The translation of ideas can take place because of different interpretations of the idea, but also because the idea has to be fitted into the particular institutional context. National cultures and ideologies and local policy processes are likely to affect the idea, which lead to the transformation/translation. Furthermore, following garbage can theory (Cohen, March, & Olsen, 1972; see also Kingdon, 1995), there is not always a one-to-one relationship between problem and solution. In the context of Bologna, the national policies may not (only) be a response to the Bologna agenda, but (as well) a solution to existing national problems. As such, the translation concept bears resemblance to the literature on policy borrowing and policy transfer (Dolowitz & Marsh, 1996, 2000; Phillips & Ochs, 2003). To some extent policy transfer can – in the context of Bologna – be seen as a horizontal dimension of the top-down process. That is, national governments ponder about how to translate the challenges of the Bologna process at the national level, while at the same time they may be looking across borders for examples, lessons to be learnt and best practices. Policy transfer may occur to different degrees. Dolowitz and Marsh (2000) discern copying, emulation, mixtures, and inspiration, indicating a scale of full acceptance to the limited travel of an idea.

Gornitzka (2006; see also Välimaa, Hoffman, & Huusko, 2006) has applied the "travel of ideas" concept and set out how the Bologna idea travelled in Norway. In Norway, the Bologna process and the Quality Reform process – an encompassing reform process not solely focusing on quality, but also on governance, funding, degree structures, financial support for students, and internationalization – more or less ran parallel. She convincingly argues that the European agenda has been used as a "menu of solutions for domestic problems" (Gornitzka, 2006, 35) and as such proved to be a political leverage in a national policy change process.

A third explanation stresses the political elements of policy–and decision-making. The work of Scharpf and Mayntz (Mayntz & Scharpf, 1995; Scharpf, 1997) – under the heading of *actor-centred institutionalism* – may be taken as an example. Their approach focuses particularly on the role of actors in an institutional context in the policy process. Scharpf (1997) argues that actors have perceptions, preferences, and capabilities, the latter particularly determined by the institutional context in which the actors "play their games". When actors play their game, the role of actor constellations and modes of interaction are important elements in the policy process. The basic argument is that – through the interaction of multiple actors in policy networks (of a multi-level nature in the case of the Bologna process) – the policy process is open to somewhat unexpected turns (because of changes in power constellations or changes in interests) but also affected by historical legacies and path dependencies. Path dependencies are looming largely because of the impact of institutions on actor perceptions, preferences, and capabilities. As such, the outcome of the policy process is less predictable than it might seem at first hand. This is very nicely illustrated in Witte's (2006) work. Combining the actor-centred institutionalism of Scharpf and Mayntz with notions of North's institutional theory (North, 1990), she analyses the higher education policy process since the 1998 Sorbonne Declaration in the Netherlands, France, UK, and Germany. Indeed, she demonstrates that preferences, perceptions, capabilities (particularly of national ministries responsible for higher education), and the national institutional settings (including their constraints, see also Huisman et al., 2005 on the impact of ERASMUS) worked out differently in the four systems. Taken together, the factors explain the amount of change in the four countries. Moreover, the analysis showed that there was weak convergence between the countries, but this was mostly visible at the structural and formal level. The latter implies that the agreement on formal aspects hides many different national meanings and interpretations.

It can be concluded that the three perspectives can adequately explain the outcomes of the Bologna process (so far). The outcomes can briefly be summarized as: some convergence with respect to the structural elements of the systems, but behind this macro-level convergence a pattern of great variety emerges at the micro-levels. The perspectives differ in their emphasis, but not radically, on the role of characteristics of the policy (process), the role of actors and their interests, and the role of the institutional context and historical legacies in which the changes are introduced.

But what does this tell us about institutional diversity? One could argue that – despite some convergence trends that obliged higher education institutions to adapt their curriculum structures somewhat (cycles, Diploma Supplement, ECTS) – there is no reason to assume that organizations would respond differently to the Bologna process and that, consequently, the general convergence patterns hides a great amount of institutional variety. Also reminding that there are considerable differences between the nation states regarding to what extent they have fully adopted the Bologna agenda and the differences between frontrunners and laggards, one could even argue that diversity has increased at the organizational level. An increase that could be temporary if the currently dynamic and not so transparent situation – with many Bologna elements still "under construction" in many countries – gradually changes to more clarity and less ambiguity.

Other Factors Explaining the Developments

The above conclusion is unsatisfactory however. First, we have no clear insights in which respects there is more organizational diversity. The contention is based on an extrapolation and does and cannot tell us whether programmatic diversity increases, whether there is an impact on procedural or reputational diversity, etc. Second, and this is a methodological point, looking at the potential impacts of the Bologna process blinds us to a considerable extent for other factors that seriously could impact institutional diversity (see also Huisman, Luijten-Lub, & Van der Wende, 2005; Huisman & Van der Wende, 2004 for similar arguments). The literature informs us that it is worthwhile to address the role of governments and markets in sustaining diversity and to drift processes, including the impact of rankings, and globalization. It may lie at hand also to look at demographic patterns, but elsewhere (Huisman, Kaiser, & Vossensteyn, 2000) we have argued on the basis of comparative research that there is no clear relationship between access mechanisms and participation levels on the one hand and institutional and programmatic diversity on the other, reason enough not to address this factor.

The role of governments and markets. Our current knowledge on diversity informs us that it is neither the market nor the government solely that drives higher education diversity (Huisman, Meek, & Wood, 2007; Meek, Goedegebuure, & Huisman, 2000; Meek, Goedegebuure, Kivinen, & Rinne, 1996; Taylor, Ferreira, Machado, & Santiago, 2008). There are clear indications in the literature that governments to some extent – through regulation – inhibit diversity. If governmental regulations state that certain types of institutions can carry out research and offer the PhD and others cannot, this clearly sets limits to the scope of activities of certain institutions. At the same time, creating much freedom for institutions in a market environment does not automatically imply that higher education institutions each will strive for the highest level of distinctiveness. Although distinctiveness – or even uniqueness – will be claimed by many higher education institutions, research has indicated that there is a considerable pressure to imitate practices and structures in highly institutionalized fields such as higher education (DiMaggio & Powell, 1983; Gioia & Thomas, 1996). Research in higher education has pointed out that the model of the research-intensive university has many attractions, and may be worthwhile to aspire (Aldersley, 1995; Huisman & Kaiser, 2001; Meek et al., 1996; Neave, 1979; Van Vught, 2008). Processes of academic drift may lead to a decrease of diversity, unless governments are able to demarcate the boundaries for (groups of) higher education institutions, actually preventing them to imitate other institutions in certain respects. This leads to the current state of knowledge that a mix of steering and market mechanisms may be the best solution to preserve diversity and to offer sufficient incentives to have dynamic growth in diversity: the more diverse the (incentives in the) environment, the more diversity. Recently it has been argued (Van Vught, 2008), referring to the situation and developments in California and Hong Kong, that it may be wise to rely more on (national) policy instruments, such as contracts between governments and individual higher education institutions and sophisticated funding mechanisms, than on the market. Also Horta, Huisman, and Heitor (2008) argue that funding mechanisms can play an important role in stimulating diversity.

Globalization. The increasing global interconnectivity and the blurring of national boundaries make the concept of distance almost illusive. In the flat world (Friedman, 2006), opportunities to learn from or to copy each other and to cooperate may lead to adjustments of organizational structures. But here again the arguments of the "glonacalists" can be repeated: the impacts of global forces are mediated by national and institutional histories and contexts. And, at the same time, increasing competition – as a concomitant of globalization – and the opportunities opened by increasingly sophisticated technologies (e.g. distance education) may as well lead to niche-seeking and distinctive positioning of higher education institutions (see also Teichler, 2007).

Rankings, league tables, and drift. Rankings and league tables are of all times, but only since the 1990s we see more attention to this phenomenon in Europe (Hazelkorn, 2008). More recently, the debate focuses on developing adequate methodologies that really reflect the genuine qualities of the higher education institutions being "measured". It indicates a general acceptance that league tables are here to stay (Yorke & Longden, 2005). In its current imperfect state, rankings do not live up to the expectations. The main reason is that compilers of rankings are looking for relatively easy to collect data that might reflect qualities of higher education institutions. This implies that there is a considerable measurement bias in favour of research (citations, impact scores, prizes won, research grants acquired) at the detriment of teaching. There are attempts to measure added value in the area of teaching and findings from student satisfaction surveys are included in the institutions' scores, but there are still many methodological shortcomings. An important question is e.g. whether we can be assured that students use the same yardstick in their evaluations?

The current state of the art indicates that research performance, mainly in the hard sciences is the dominant indicator in league tables and thus yielding at best a partial understanding of institutional quality. This leaves aside whether it is really relevant for e.g. students and employers to have insight in the overall quality of an institution; information on the quality of programmes or departments is likely to be much more useful and relevant. A good example of sophisticated ranking are the CHE rankings at level of study programmes (see www.che-ranking.de).

Given the growing importance of rankings, it implies that higher education institutions have basically three options, nicely reflecting Hirschman's (1970) concepts of loyalty, voice, and exit. Loyalty would imply playing the ranking game and trying to score better on indicators. Obviously this strategy fits best for institutions that already perform above average and seems less appropriate for an institution currently on position 991. Voice would imply that those responsible within higher education institutions would have critically judged ranking positions and measurement, and that they would present and use alternative indicators of the institution's qualities in their profiling and marketing strategies. The exit option would imply that league tables are largely ignored (Brown, 2006).

The research of Hazelkorn (2008, 199) indicates that managers/leaders of higher education institutions are of the opinion that rankings "helped establish a hierarchy which did little to promote or value institutional diversity or differentiation or represent the complexity of higher education activities". Moreover, national governments are pushing their universities to perform better in the rankings (Marginson, 2007) and even do this by implementing supportive policies to achieve this (see e.g. the German *Exzellenzinitiative*). This seems to indicate that institutions are most likely to follow the loyalty and (small) voice strategies. The challenge to try to mimic the model of the prestigious research-intensive university seems to be much stronger than the challenge to be unique, or at least different.

This brings us to the broader topic of drift. Various authors have argued that drift is inherent in higher education (see e.g. Meek *et al.*, 1996 and special issue of *Higher Education Policy*, volume 13, no. 4, 2000) and that the "less noble" (Neave, 1979) will try to emulate the "noble" institutions, the latter term referring to the traditional research universities. These notions of drift – based on status and prestige seeking being the drivers of such processes – are clearly visible in European binary systems (Huisman & Kaiser, 2001; Kyvik, 2004; Taylor et al., 2008). In the discussions on structural reform in the context of Bologna, it was noteworthy that stakeholders representing the "non-university" sectors saw the Bologna process as a window of opportunity to lever the status of their institutions. Examples are: Dutch *hogescholen* claiming the right to offer Master programmes, to be funded by the government and Finnish *ammattikorkeakoulu* suggesting they could offer professional doctorates (see also Witte, Van der Wende, & Huisman, 2008). It should be added, however, that emulation might take place within certain sub-systems, e.g. within the *hogescholen* or *ammattikorkeakoulu* sectors. That is, institutions may be driven by the challenge to be the best among their peers, instead of trying to copy the research-intensive university model. Despite this, the trend of emulating the latter model seems dominant.

The above seems to indicate that relatively strong incentives of government through regulation and funding are needed to maintain structural diversity to prevent institutions from following their status-seeking instincts and consequently potentially harm (this form of) diversity.

IMPLICATIONS FOR INSTITUTIONAL DIVERSITY IN HIGHER EDUCATION TOWARDS 2020

From the sections above, we can deduce – with a certain risk, for we cannot tell with certainty how things will develop – future developments regarding institutional diversity in the upcoming decade. To prevent falling into the pitfalls of forecasting, the future developments will be cast in the form of propositions and accompanying arguments. Let us first summarize what the point of departure for this forward-looking exercise is.

Wrapping up the arguments above, the Bologna process and other developments such as globalization, rankings, league tables, governmental steering, and market mechanisms, have brought about some structural convergence across signatory countries, but at the same time have increased (reputational) diversity or at least sustained the levels of diversity at the micro-level of programmes, processes, and procedures. Explanations for the current outcomes can be found with reference to (a) the policy science perspective: the "distance" between policy development at the supranational level and implementation at the faculty and departmental level; (b) the sociological perspective: the idea that ideas travel and that things get lost or are changed "in translation"; and (c) the political science perspective: the notion that preferences and capabilities of actors in the policy process in particular institutional contexts to a large extent determine the outcomes of such a policy process. But factors largely unrelated to the Bologna process should be taken into account as well. Striking a balance between government steering and market mechanisms seems to be a sound strategy to preserve institutional diversity, although it – unfortunately – is not yet fully clear how this mix exactly should look like. What is clear however is that either a strongly regulated or a fully marketized higher education system would seriously damage the level of institutional diversity. The impact of globalization forces is not fully clear, but it seems the arguments for increasing diversity – competition, niche seeking, global impacts – are mediated by national and local institutional contexts and are stronger than those for decreasing diversity – more opportunities to copy or to learn from other experiences in a "flat world". The rise of rankings and league tables seems to trigger institutions to play the game, despite an undercurrent of dissatisfaction with the current measurement practices. Drift processes are strong as ever and will continue to challenge the "less noble" institutions to emulate their "noble" counterparts.

How do these factors evolve in the coming decade? Again, it is impossible to predict this. Therefore these evolutions will be presented in the form of "ifs". This will also allow us to better address the potential risks and opportunities in the near future.

– If the follow-up to the Bologna process – i.e. the post-2010 agenda – is as ambiguous and abstract as the Bologna process, there will be no further macro-level convergence. The more concrete and directive the policies, the more convergence will take place.

According to this proposition, the vagueness and abstract level of the objectives and the lack of strong controls on achieving objectives will not challenge nation states and higher education institutions to go beyond the current levels of structural convergence. If the post-2010 process is much clearer in terms of objectives, achievements, and "strong" policy instruments, convergence is more likely.

– If the same conditions (as under 1) apply, micro-level diversity will be maintained.

Some, if not most, of the turmoil of the current dynamics and unevenness of translation efforts – in terms of countries and institutions being at different stages of the process, including the co-existence in one country or institution of pre- and post-Bologna structures simultaneously – will be overcome in due time. This may indicate more convergence at the micro-level. But it is argued here that there is still considerable leeway for nation states and higher education institutions' management to translate the vague and abstract objectives to fit their own interests, leaving much room for local variety.

– If globalization factors continue to affect higher education, these impacts will (continue to) be mediated by local and national circumstances.

Following the glonacalisation perspective, globalization will not have a sweeping unifying impact, but globalization factors will be adapted in local and national settings.

– If national governments (and supranational agencies, see also 1) strike the "right" balance between governmental steering and market mechanisms, diversity will be maintained or increased.

Acknowledging that the qualification "right" needs further substantiation, the proposition actually denotes that neither a full reliance on governmental steering nor a full focus on market mechanisms will suffice to maintain or increase diversity. Market forces, sufficiently bound by governmental regulation or quality assurance and funding mechanisms seem the right ingredients for such a balanced mix.

– If rankings continue to be "underdeveloped", drift tensions will be dominant and lead to less institutional diversity.

Underdevelopment relates to a biased focus on the measurable, leading to an unwarranted reliance on (partly dubious) research output indicators. This exacerbates a focus of national governments and higher education institutions on the ideal–typical image of the (comprehensive) research university and governmental focus on establishing and supporting centres or institutions of research excellence, leading to mission drift and decreased institutional diversity. Hazelkorn's (2008) finding that two-thirds of the institutions surveyed actually take actions in response to ranking is illustrative, not only with respect to the amount of attention rankings get, but also in setting institutional directions. Looking at the responses to rankings, actions to improve the position on the rankings (upward drift) apparently dominate the discourse among institutional leaders.

– If rankings become more sophisticated, measuring adequately the quality of the higher education institutions (in various domains), drift tensions will be suppressed and diversity will be sustained or will increase.

This proposition is based on the expectation that initiatives like the CHE rankings and sophisticated work of academics on improving the reliability of data, and developing a more balanced set of indicators reflecting the full range of higher education institutions' portfolio create a context in which each higher education institution can develop a "genuine" profile. That is, a profile that fits the preferences of internal and external stakeholders allowing them to arrive at a good position in a particular ranking. And, thus take away the fear of a focus on a one-dimensional hierarchy of institutions based mostly on research reputation.

It is – given our current understanding of mechanisms impacting diversity – impossible to develop a clear-cut scenario for developments in the next decade. But, with the propositions above in mind, one can make up his or her mind about the most appropriate supranational, national, and institutional strategies to achieve or maintain a certain level of institutional diversity. Barriers to diversity are "relatively easy" to circumvent by balancing a fair mix of incentives from government policies and market mechanisms. The most serious risk seems to be an unsound focus and reliance in strategy-setting and policy-making on rankings that disproportionately stress and value the characteristics of the classical research-intensive university. Mechanisms that contribute to transparency, such as multi-dimensional classifications, may counterbalance such biases.

NOTES

[1] Thanks to Frans van Vught (Center for Higher Education Policy Studies, University of Twente, the Netherlands) and Johanna Witte (*Bayerisches Staatsinstitut für Hochschulforschung und Hochschulplanung*, Germany) for valuable comments on the draft version of this paper.

[2] Witte (2006, p. 128) points at linguistic issues at stake as well. The French were the initial leaders of the drafting process and used the term harmonisation, which has different meanings and connotations in French and English: convergence versus standardisation/unification, respectively.

[3] To be clear: We do not think that the Bologna process should be conceived of as a "classical" implementation study, but "[l]essons from implementation analysis can however serve to shed light on crucial features of the Bologna process ..." (Witte, 2006, 18).

REFERENCES

Ahola, S. (2005). Global and local priorities in higher education policies: A headache at the national level? *Tertiary Education and Management, 11*(1), 37–53.

Aldersley, S. F. (1995). 'Upward drift' is alive and well. Research/doctoral model still attractive to institutions. *Change*(september/october), 51–56.

Beverwijk, J. (2005). *The genesis of a system. Coalition formation in Mozambican higher education, 1993-2003.* Enschede: CHEPS.

Birnbaum, R. (1983). *Maintaining diversity in higher education.* San Francisco: Jossey-Bass.

Brown, R. (2006). League tables - do we have to live with them? *Perspectives, 10*(2), 33–38.

Carnegie Foundation for the Advancement of Teaching. (1987). *A classification of institutions of higher education.* Berkeley: Princeton University Press.

Cerych, L., & Sabatier, P. A. (1986). *Great expectations and mixed performance: the implementation of higher education reforms in Europe.* Trentham: Trentham books.

Cohen, M. D., March, J. G., & Olsen, J. P. (1972). A garbage can model of organizational choice. *Administrative Science Quarterly, 17*, 1–25.

Crosier, D., Purser, L., & Smidt, H. (2007). *Trends V: Universities shaping the European Higher Education Area.* Brussels: EUA.

Czarniawski, B., & Sevón, G. (Eds.). (1996). *Translating organizational change.* Berlin/New York: Walter de Gruyter.

DEST. (2003). *Backing Australia's future.* Canberra: DEST.

DfES. (2003). *The future of higher education.* London: HMSO.

DiMaggio, P. J., & Powell, W. W. (1983). The iron cage revisited: institutional isomorphism and collective rationality in organizational fields. *American Sociological Review, 48*(April), 147–160.

Dolowitz, D., & Marsh, D. (1996). Who learns what from whom: A review of the policy transfer literature. transfer literature. *Political Studies, 44*(2), 343–357.

Dolowitz, D., & Marsh, D. (2000). Learning from abroad: The role of policy transfer in contemporary policy-making. *Governance, 13*(1), 5–24.

Douglass, J. A. (2005). How all globalization is local: countervailing forces and their influence on higher education markets. *Higher Education Policy, 18*, 445–473.

European Commission. (2003). *Researchers in the European Research Area: One profession, multiple careers.* Brussels: European Commission.

Eurydice. (2005). *Focus on the structure of higher education in Europe 2004/05. National trends in the Bologna process.* Brussels: Eurydice.

Friedman, T. L. (2006). *The world is flat.* New York: Farrar, Straus and Giroux.

Gioia, D. A., & Thomas, J. B. (1996). Identity, image and issue interpretation: Sensemaking during strategic change in academia. *Administrative Science Quarterly, 41*, 370–403.

Gornitzka, Å. (2006). What is the use of Bologna in national reform? In V. Tomusk (Ed.), *Creating the European Area of Higher Education. Voices from the periphery* (pp. 19–41). Dordrecht: Springer.

Gornitzka, Å., Kogan, M., & Amaral, A. (Eds.). (2007). *Reform and change in higher education. Analysing policy implementation.* Dordrecht: Springer.

Gornitzka, Å., Kyvik, S., & Stensaker, B. (2002). Implementation analysis in higher education. In J. C. Smart (Ed.), *Higher education: handbook of theory and research* (Vol. XVII, pp. 381–423).

Hanf, K., & Soetendorp, B. (Eds.). (1998). *Adapting to European integration. Small states and the European Union.* London/New York: Longman.

Haug, G., Kirstein, J., & Knudsen, I. (1999). *Trends in learning structures in higher education I.* Copenhagen: Danish Rectors' Conference.

Hazelkorn, E. (2008). Learning to live with league tables and rankings: The experience of institutional leaders. *Higher Education Policy, 21*(2), 193–215.

HEFCE. (2004). *Equality and diversity monitoring in higher education institutions. A guide to good practice.* Bristol: HEFCE.

Hirschman, A. O. (1970). *Exit, voice, and loyalty: Responses to decline in firms, organizations, and states.* Cambridge: Harvard University Press.

Horta, H., Huisman, J., & Heitor, M. V. (2008). Does competitive research funding encourage diversity in higher education? *Science and Public Policy, 35*(3), 146–158.

Huisman, J. (1995). *Differentiation, diversity and dependency in higher education.* Utrecht: Lemma.

Huisman, J., & Kaiser, F. (2001). *Fixed and fuzzy boundaries in higher education. A comparative study of (binary) systems in nine countries.* The Hague: AWT.

Huisman, J., Kaiser, F., & Vossensteyn, H. (2000). Floating foundations of higher education policy. *Higher Education Quarterly, 54*(3), 217–238.

Huisman, J., Luijten-Lub, A., & Van der Wende, M. (2005). Explaining domestic responses to European policies: The impact of the Erasmus programme on national higher education policies. In M. Tight (Ed.), *International perspectives on higher education research: International relations.* Amsterdam: Elsevier.

Huisman, J., Meek, V. L., & Wood, F. Q. (2007). Institutional diversity in higher education: a cross-national and longitudinal analysis. *Higher Education Quarterly, 61*(4), 563–577.

Huisman, J., & Van der Wende, M. (2004). The EU and Bologna: Are supra- and international initiatives threatening domestic agendas? *European Journal of Education, 39*(3), 349–357.

Huisman, J., Witte, J., & File, J. M. (2006). *The extent and impact of higher education curricular reform across Europe.* Enschede: CHEPS.

Kingdon, J. W. (1995). *Agendas, alternatives and public policies* (2nd ed.). New York: HarperCollins.

Kyvik, S. (2004). Structural changes in higher education systems in Western Europe. *European Journal of Education, 29*(3), 393–409.

Lindblom, C. E. (1959). The science of "muddling though". *Public Administration Review, 19*, 79–88.

Lindblom, C. E. (1979). Still muddling not yet through. *Public Adminstration Review, 39*(6), 517–526.

Marginson, S. (2007). Global university rankings: Implications in general and for Australia. *Journal of Higher Education Policy and Management, 29*(2), 131–142.

Marginson, S., & Rhoades, G. (2002). Beyond national states, markets, and systems of higher education: A glonacal agency heuristic. *Higher Education, 43*(3), 281–309.

Mayntz, R., & Scharpf, F. W. (Eds.). (1995). *Soziale Dynamik und politische Steuerung.* Frankfurt: Campus.

Meek, V. L., Goedegebuure, L., & Huisman, J. (2000). Editorial: diversity, differentiation and the market. *Higher Education Policy, 13*(4), 1–6.

Meek, V. L., Goedegebuure, L. C. J., Kivinen, O., & Rinne, R. (Eds.). (1996). *The mockers and mocked: Comparative perspectives on differentiation, convergence and diversity in higher education.* Oxford: Pergamon.

Menon, A., & Hayward, J. (1996). States, industrial policies and the European Union. In H. Kassim & A. Menon (Eds.), *The European Union and national industrial policy* (pp. 267-290). London/New York: Routledge.

Mény, Y., Muller, P., & Quermonne, J.-L. (Eds.). (1996). *Adjusting to Europe. The impact of the European Union on national institutions and policies.* London/New York: Routledge.

Neave, G. (1979). Academic drift: some views from Europe. *Studies in Higher Education, 4*(2), 143–159.

North, D. C. (1990). *Institutions, institutional change and economic performance.* Cambridge: Cambridge University Press.

Olsen, J. P. (2002). The many faces of Europeanization. *Journal of Common Market Studies, 40*(5), 921–952.

Phillips, D., & Ochs, K. (2003). Processes of policy borrowing in education: Some analytical and explanatory devices. *Comparative Education, 39*(4), 423–438.

Pressman, J. L., & Wildavsky, A. (1973). *Implementation: how great expectations in Washington are dashed in Oakland.* Berkeley: University of California Press.

Reichert, S., & Tauch, C. (2003). *Trends 2003: Progress towards the European Higher Education Area.* Geneva/Brussels: EUA.

Reichert, S., & Tauch, C. (2005). *Trends IV: European universities implementing Bologna.* Brussels: EUA.

Scharpf, F. W. (1997). *Games real actors play. Actor-centered institutionalism in policy research.* Boulder: Westview Press.

Stadtman, V. A. (1980). *Academic adaptations: Higher education prepars for the 1980s and 1990s.* San Francisco: Jossey-Bass.

Steinmo, S., Thelen, K., & Longstreth, F. (Eds.). (1992). *Structuring politics: Historical institutionalism in comparative analysis.* Cambridge: Cambridge University Press.

Taylor, J. S., Ferreira, J. B., Machado, M. d. L., & Santiago, R. (Eds.). (2008). *Non-university higher education in Europe.* Dordrecht: Springer.

Teichler, U. (2007). Changing views in Europe about diversification of higher education. In U. Teichler (Ed.), *Higher education systems. Conceptual frameworks, comparative perspectives, empirical findings* (pp. 107–117). Rotterdam: Sense.

Theisens, H. (2004). *The state of change. Analysing policy change in Dutch and English higher education.* Enschede: CHEPS.

Trow, M. (1979). *Elite and mass higher education: American models and European realities.* Stockholm: National Board of Universities.

Vaira, M. (2004). Globalisation and higher education organizational change: A framework of analysis. *Higher Education*(48), 483–510.

Välimaa, J., Hoffman, D., & Huusko, M. (2006). The Bologna process in Finland. Perspectives from the basic units. In V. Tomusk (Ed.), *Creating the European Area of Higher Education. Voices from the periphery* (pp. 43–67). Dordrecht: Springer.

Van Vught, F. (1996). Isomorphism in higher education? Towards a theory of differentiation and diversity in higher education systems. In V. L. Meek, L. C. J. Goedegebuure, O. Kivinen & R. Rinne

(Eds.), *Mockers and the mocked. Comparative perspectives on differentiation, convergence and diversity in higher education* (pp. 42–58). London: Jessica Kingsley.

Van Vught, F. (2008). Mission diversity and reputation in higher education. *Higher Education Policy, 21*(1), 151–174.

Van Vught, F. (Ed.). (1989). *Governmental strategies and innovation in higher education.* London: Jessica Kingsley.

Witte, J. (2006). *Change of degrees and degrees of change. Comparing adaptations of European higher education systems in the context of the Bologna process.* Enschede: CHEPS.

Witte, J. (2007). *European and US-American higher education: The Bologna Process between internal and external aspirations.* Paper presented at the ASHE International Forum, Louisville, Kentucky, US, 7-10 November.

Witte, J. (2008). Aspired convergence, cherished diversity: Dealing with the contradictions of Bologna. *Tertiary Education and Management, 14*(2), 81–93.

Witte, J., & Huisman, J. (2008). Disciplines in the Bologna process: curriculum reconstruction by German engineers. In L. Purser, L. Wilson, E. Froment & J. Kohler (Eds.), *EUA Bologna Handbook.* Stuttgart: EUA/Raabe.

Witte, J., Van der Wende, M., & Huisman, J. (2008). Blurring boundaries: How the Bologna process changes the relation nship between university and non-university higher education in Germany, the Netherlands, and France. *Studies in Higher Education, 33*(3), 217–231.

Yorke, M., & Longden, B. (2005). *Significant figures - performance indicators and 'league tables'.* London: SCOP.

KURT DE WIT AND JEF C. VERHOEVEN

14. FEATURES AND FUTURE OF THE NETWORK SOCIETY: THE DEMOGRAPHIC, TECHNOLOGICAL AND SOCIAL CONTEXT OF HIGHER EDUCATION

INTRODUCTION

The network society is an amalgam of technological, economic, political, social, and cultural developments that, taken together, form a new context for our European societies and for higher education within these societies. The idea of a network society, it can be said, captures 'the spirit of our age', that is, it is an attempt to make sense of the changes of which we are in the midst of (Barney 2006).

In this chapter, we first explain Manuel Castells' theory of the network society, and then we go into some basic features of European societies that form the context in which the network society develops. More in particular, we discuss demographic, technological, and social developments. Throughout, we point out their consequences for higher education. Then we will discuss the European Area for Higher Education (EHEA) in the context of the network society. Finally, we will draw some conclusions regarding the future development of the EHEA in view of the network society and its basic features.

THE NETWORK SOCIETY AND ITS CONSEQUENCES

The network society, according to Castells, is the social structure of the Information Age (Castells 1996, 1997, 1998, also 2000). In the Information Age, our societies are increasingly being organized on the basis of a new technological paradigm with technical, organizational, and managerial innovations. As a result, 'dominant functions, social groups, and territories across the globe are connected' (Castells 1996: 34). The network society consists of both the technology to make all kinds of networks work and the network as an organizational form that penetrates the entire social structure. In other words, if we want to characterize our societies, the metaphor of a network, rather than that of a structure, seems to be more appropriate. A shift is taking place from national societies based on a social structure towards global flows or networks of signs, money, information, technology, and people (Lash & Urry 1994). Of course, global flows or networks are not entirely new (indeed, trade and religion have been 'larger than national' for centuries). But a number of features make the current age stand out against earlier phases. The network society is an ideal type with particular economic, social/ cultural, and political characteristics.

The new *economy* is informational and global. An informational economy is based on the capacity of economic units to generate, process, and apply knowledge.

B.M. Kehm, J. Huisman and B. Stensaker (eds.), The European Higher Education Area: Perspectives on a Moving Target, 263–280.

It is characterized by technological innovation, organizational flexibilization, and the use of ICT-based knowledge, even in industrial production, to enhance the knowledge production itself. The dominant strategy of companies has become to seek profit rather than improve productivity. This leads them to concentrate on searching for new markets or market segments, which in turn requires better mobility and better communication. This has become possible through market deregulation and the new ICT. In this way, the key elements and processes of the economy become global: capital, the labour market, science and technology, goods and services, and management (Castells 1996: 93–96). This strategic core becomes networked on a global scale in a global economy (Castells 1996: 92; 2000: 10). Economic decisions can be made immediately, continuously, and globally by means of electronic communication. However, while capital is becoming extremely volatile, labour remains more static as it is curtailed by cultures, institutions, borders, and the like. But even with regard to labour, global interdependence is increasing as a result of the multinationals, international trade, and global competition. Labour is becoming increasingly exchangeable throughout the globe in so far as the work itself consists more and more of information processing. What the informational economy needs is 'self-programmable labour' (Castells 1996). These autonomous, trained labourers show their informational capacity in that they can lead large parts of the labour process, can constantly retrain themselves, and can continuously adapt to new tasks, new processes, and new sources of information, thereby analysing and solving problems creatively and in communication with others. On the other end of the spectrum is 'generic labour', the unqualified labourers throughout the world. Their jobs are replaceable and disposable, not unlike machines, and their only good fortune is still to be part of the network. If no longer networked, they become 'switched-off labour', (Castells 1998). In the global informational economy, successful organizations are the ones that are network organizations, that is, have new organizational forms (in production, in management, in cooperation, etc.) based on networks between organizations, within organizations, between people, and between computers (Castells 1996: 165–166).

The impact of informationalism in the *social and cultural domain* is defined by Castells as the emergence of a 'culture of real virtuality' (Castells 1996, 2000). Increasingly, we are living in an audio-visual multimedia environment. We see the world as a succession of electronic signs that not only *represent* reality but increasingly *become* reality. In this way, what is created is 'a multifaceted semantic context made of a random mixture of various meanings' (Castells 1996: 371). It is, in a sense, a homogenized culture. Receivers still interpret this cultural context but individually, not starting from common cultural codes, or do so to a lesser degree. This generates fragmentation but at the same time leaves room for collective actors to communicate and participate in the system, as no single actor, not even large companies or governments, can completely control this system. Unfortunately, this emancipatory power of the new system is only realized in principle because computer-mediated communication is unevenly distributed and the prosperous, the wealthy, and the skilled are far more likely to participate in it (see below) than are others.

This brings us to a third aspect of the network society, that is, *power relations*. Networks lack a single centre and have no clear-cut hierarchy. Networks are clusters of relations that can change in number and intensity, unbound by a fixed space or time in the interaction with changes in their environment. Networks are, therefore, at odds with territorial and hierarchical organizations such as nation states, churches, and schools (Castells 2000: 19). As far as the nation state is concerned, it loses some of its power in a network society because of the aggregation of interests and policies at a supranational level and the tendencies towards decentralization (Castells 1997). As a result, national identities are waning and new identities are being built on the basis of other cultural, ethnic, social, or geographical elements. This can lead both to a rejection of the globally networked society and a turn towards local, narrow cultures or to new forms of democracy embracing local democracy, electronically stimulated participation, and communication and political mobilization (Castells 1997).

The ideal type of the network society will take on a different form in specific societies because each society has its own history, its own culture, and its own institutions. Therefore, we will now consider some of the basic demographical, technological, and socio-cultural features of European societies.

DEMOGRAPHIC CHALLENGES

In the network society, both personal development and economic development depend on the skills and competencies of individuals. These are acquired by means of higher education. But for higher education to retain its quality, a minimum enrolment is needed – if only to ensure the replacement of teachers and researchers. Demographic challenges lie ahead for the EHEA. The population is decreasing and ageing, and participation in higher education can be expected to stagnate or even decline in the medium term.

With regard to the general population trend in the EHEA, the situation is clear. The European population is not achieving the minimum birth rate needed to reproduce itself and will decrease over the next 50 years (Mizikaci & Baumgartl 2007).The population pyramid is rapidly inversing, with an ever smaller proportion of 18-24 years olds and an ever greater proportion of people above 50 (Klemenic & Fried 2007). Given this demographic development alone, the potential number of students in higher education can be expected to decline. But this general picture has to be qualified somewhat. Social factors also play a role in enrolment rates (see below) and the number of pupils completing secondary education. Gender and age differences also define participation in higher education in general and in specific sectors of higher education in particular (full-time vs. part-time, humanities vs. sciences, etc.). This is why, generally speaking, participation in higher education in the EHEA is still expanding (European Commission (EC) 2007). In academically oriented programmes at ISCED level 5A[1], the number of students is increasing. In vocationally or practically oriented programmes (ISCED level 5B) participation rates are stable or slightly decreasing. At ISCED level 6 (advanced research programmes) enrolment is strongly increasing but account for only a small part of the students in higher education (only 2.9% of all students in the EU) (EC 2007: 38).

In short, overall student numbers are growing. In the European Union, the higher education participation rate in the 18-19 year-old age group now amounts to 11% on average, but there is large variation between countries from less than 5% in Lithuania to more than 18% in Finland (EC 2007: 41).

Women are slightly higher in number at ISCED levels 5A and 5B but are underrepresented at level 6 (EC 2007: 44). However, this overall figure masks large differences regarding the fields of study. If we look at the EU only, the fields of study populated by a clear majority of women are education, health, and the humanities and arts, all of which have a student population of more than two-thirds women. By contrast, men are in the majority in science, mathematics and computing, and construction (EC 2007: 48).

This brings us to the issue of the number of students in science and technology, one of the benchmarks in the Lisbon Process. Among the five education benchmarks set, the increase in the number of mathematics, science, and technology (MST) graduates by 15% by 2010 is the only one that is likely to be met (EC 2005). In the EU, the proportion of enrolments in science and technology is about a quarter at ISCED Levels 5A and 5B, while it is more than a third at ISCED level 6 (EC 2007: 52). A somewhat different picture emerges for the number of graduates. Broken down into fields of study, the social sciences, business, and law account for the largest numbers, that is, about 30% to 40% of all graduates. Generally speaking, the number of graduates in science, mathematics, and computing is around 10% of all graduates, and in engineering, manufacturing, and construction between 10% and 15% (EC 2007: 165). At ISCED level 6, however, science, mathematics, and computing and, to a lesser extent, also engineering, manufacturing, and construction produce a proportionally large number of doctoral graduates (EC 2007: 166). Although the Lisbon benchmark might be met by 2010, it must be admitted that, between 1998 and 2004, only a slight increase can be observed. Moreover, the benchmark also states that the gender imbalance should decrease, but the gender gap remains with less than a third of the graduates in MST being women (EC 2007: 168).

As noted above, the age structure of the population in Europe is changing. Those above 65 years are expected to account for one-third of the population by 2050, and the age groups between 15–49 will decrease from over 50% in 1950 to 38% in 2050 (Zaidi 2008). In other words, one can expect not only a decrease in the student population but also an increase in the age of the students and the teachers. The age structure of the students in higher education in Europe currently shows a considerable amount of variation, with participation clearly the highest in the 20–24 age group (EC 2007: 54). At ISCED level 5B, the median age differs between European countries by no less than 10 years of age (EC 2007: 58). In general, part-time students and those in short vocational programmes (groups that overlap to some extent) are older. Moreover, part-time students take much more time to finish their studies, more than would be expected as a result of their studying part-time. In the EU, they are on average 6 years older (EC 2007: 11).

It can be expected, with the ageing of the population, that fewer young people will enter higher education, and, conversely, that more older people will want to study – or study again – in higher education. The expectations and needs of the students as regards their studies and the study environment can, therefore, also be expected to change. However, participation in lifelong learning, defined as participation of the 25–64 age group, is almost stable at somewhat less than 10% (EC 2005: 18). The group of lifelong learners consists primarily of people who have already had higher education. Here too, then, a participation gap can be discerned.

TECHNOLOGY AS A DRIVING FORCE

The network society could not have developed without ICT, which has become an important part of social life since the 1960s. The existence of ICT and the level of use of its instruments strongly influence the development of the network society. Inversely, too, the network society contributes to the development and dissemination of ICT. In other words, there is a dialectical relationship between the network society and ICT.

Generally speaking, Europe's position regarding ICT is still one of the most privileged although the availability and the use of ICT are expanding throughout the world. Of the 29 countries with the highest average ICT value in the world, 17 are Bologna countries (table 1). The highest scores for ICT are located in Western Europe, the lowest in the south and even more in Eastern Europe. Nevertheless, in all of the countries, the distribution and use of ICT equipment is expanding. The ICT growth of the weaker ICT inclined Bologna countries is slower than in the stronger ones. One might expect that it will take some time for them to catch up.

Table 1. Average values for several ICT indices in Bologna and other countries

Country categories	Networks index[2]	Intensity index[3]	growth rate[4]
Highest ICT value (29 countries)	432.1	451.80	54.65
- of which 17 Bologna countries *	*481.4*	*428.49*	*51.92*
Medium ICT value (28 countries)	229.6	229.66	56.17
- of which 13 Bologna countries *	*240.9*	*220.92*	*58.44*
Lowest ICT value (63 countries)	103.6	100.65	49.19
- of which 12 Bologna countries *	*123.7*	*88.15*	*55.46*

Source: ITU 2007 (* our own calculations)

The rapid development of ICT has had a tremendous impact on the development of globalization and internationalization. In universities, for instance, because of ICT, faculty mobility, recruitment of international students and researchers, the transfer of knowledge, and research collaboration have become much easier than it ever was before.

Not only have globalization and internationalization changed under the influence of ICT but so, too, have the kind and the organization of work. Observations made in Australia and Canada, two countries that are among the highest ICT developed nations, might be instructive as regards the future possible changes in the economy and the labour organization of the Bologna countries with a lower ICT level (Crow & Longford 2000; Curtain 2000). On the one hand, ICT boosted production and created new types of work but, on the other, it also made thousands of blue and white collar workers redundant (switched-off labour) The type of the preferred human capital changed. Well-educated and trained workers (self-employable labour) became necessary for the functioning of ICT, and less-skilled persons (generic labour) were threatened with dismissal. The character of work, too, underwent the influence of digitalization. On the one hand, this 'prescriptive technology' creates a type of work where the worker only can follow the prescribed procedures of the work that has to be done. On the other hand, it creates more than before the possibility for non-standard forms of employment and part-time work because a large number of complicated actions can be performed by technology. Within this context a group of flexiworkers has been created. These non-standard employed people will face 'the varying hours of work, multiple employer, open-ended contract, limited benefits, uncertain protection, and a variable place of work' (Curtain 2000: 8). It is also expected that telework, home-based work, and consulting will grow.

Turning to the EU, a recent CEDEFOP report (2008: 46) calculated that ICT certainly has influenced the employment patterns in the EU but to varying degrees in different economic sectors. Employment will decline in agriculture, fishery, manufacturing, and also for clerks Nevertheless, the number of people in other occupations will grow in numbers: technicians, professionals, and managers. Between 2006 and 2015, about 12.5 million highly qualified jobs (ISCED levels 5 and 6) will be added to the work force. The demand for skilled workers will also grow along with the demand for unskilled workers, which seems to support the development of a society divided in function of education. Nevertheless, we should be cautious about generalizing the picture for all the countries of the EHEA.

Universities play and will continue to play an important role in the training of these managers and professionals (see below). Moreover, they build and will continue to build all kinds of networks within their organizations and with other institutions, nationally and internationally. ICT as an instrument for managing universities, conducting research, and stimulating learning will increase in importance. Universities have established computer systems to support networks between lecturers, students, managers, researchers, governors, and other stakeholders not only for building networks but also for the evaluation of the work of lecturers and researchers. Similar links are being built between universities and their members, nationally and internationally, a process that is being encouraged by governments and the EU (e.g. the recently established EIT). And although GATS was not favoured by many universities, more and more of them will establish branch universities or campuses (Altbach & Knight 2007) outside Europe in order to make money. Whether this process will continue in the future is uncertain because of the changing opportunities (Healey 2008). Virtual universities (Guri-Rosenblit, 2001), already present, might grow in number.

INEQUALITY AND EMANCIPATION

In the network society, access to the networks is a minimum condition for the economic, political, and social membership of a society. Therefore, 'control over access becomes a crucial mechanism of power and domination, and the divide between the included and the excluded constitutes a line of stratification with serious political and material consequences' (Barney 2006: 31). In this way, political and material inequalities are to be expected. However, the network society at the same time holds promise for breaking down the old lines of stratification. A network has dominant actors (nodes) and values, but they do not really have a centre or a fixed hierarchy. This means that other nodes can bypass the dominant nodes by increasing their own importance in the network. Moreover, actors can build an alternative network based on other values, and compete communicatively with other networks to disseminate their alternative cultural codes. Thus, social change is possible in the network society.

ICT and Economic Inequality

In this section, we will test the hypothesis that the use of equipment for modern networking diminishes the inequality of economic remuneration. To this end, we use several indices. The networks index (NI) (see also Section 3) gives a rough indication of some of the basic instruments for building a modern network society[5]. The intensity index (II) gives a picture of the use of the Internet and the telephone for international contact. A global picture of ICT use is given by the ICT opportunity index (ICT-OI), and average annual growth refers to the growth of ICT-OI values between 2001 and 2005.

Table 2. *The means and standard deviations of NI, II, ICT-OI, and the growth rates in different Bologna areas*

	Networks index (NI) 2007		Intensity index (II) 2007		ICT-OI value		Average annual growth rate 2001–2005	
	Mean	SD	Mean	SD	Mean	SD	Mean	SD
Bologna	304.8	171.0	267.0	159.9	220.2	94.7	54.95	16.1
West[6]	463.9	125.6	411.3	112.6	306.6	58.9	48.86	11.0
East[7]	185.4	76.0	158.8	87.6	155.3	56.3	59.52	17.9
NW Europe[8]	501.1	106.5	431.8	78.9	326.1	39.2	51.83	10.6

Source: ITU, 2007 (our own calculations)

Table 3. *The Gini index and the means and standard deviations of HDI and GDP of different Bologna areas*

Area	Gini		HDI 2004[9]		GDP 2004 ($)	
	Lowest inequality	Highest inequality	Mean	SD	Mean	SD
Bologna	23	43.6	0.873[9]	0.076	20,326	13,569
West[6]	23	38.0	0.943[9]	0.014	30,201[10]	4,879
East[7]	24	43.6	0.819	0.057	10,869	6,054
NW Europe[8]	23	34.0	0.947[9]	0.009	31,769[10]	3,526

Source: The World Fact Book updated March 20, 2008
        Watkins et al., 2006 (our own calculations)

Inequality is measured, first, *within* countries by using the Gini coefficient as an indicator of the dispersion of the income in a country: the higher the coefficient, the more the inequality between the incomes in a country, the lower the coefficient the more equality. Second, inequality *between* countries is indicated by the Human Development Index (HDI) (between 0 and 1) and the GDP[11].

There is a great deal of inequality among the Bologna countries as far as the equipment for modern networking is concerned. The lowest NI score is 69.6 (Armenia) and the highest is 616.5 (Denmark). The average score is 304.8 with several lines of difference between countries. There is a large difference between the western countries (463.9) and the eastern countries (185.4). The most privileged situation can be found in NW Europe (501.1). The same pattern is found for the II and ICT-OI. Western countries have more opportunities for ICT than do the eastern ones. These countries not only score the highest on the NI, II, and ICT-OI but also show the highest average GDP ($31,769) and the highest average score on HDI (0.947). Moreover, among these countries, we find countries with small income inequality among the citizens. The Gini score (34 in comparison with 43.6 and 38) for the country with the highest income inequality is lower than in all other Bologna areas of Table 2. The lowest average score for HDI (0.819) and GDP ($10,869) is found in the eastern countries. Although the Bologna countries have many similar targets for higher education, the resources available to achieve these targets are distributed very unequally between west and east.

Table 4. Correlation between NI, II, ICT-OI, growth, the Gini index, and the HDI of different Bologna areas

	Bologna countries	West[6]	East[7]	NW Europe[8]
NI x Gini	−0.474*	−0.515*	−0.365	−0.321
NI x HDI	0.855*	0.543*	0.845*	0.008
II x Gini	−0.431*	−0.418	−0.272	−0.539
II x HDI	0.857*	0.564*	0.790*	0.291
ICT-OI x Gini	−0.476*	−0.574*	−0.311	−0.461
ICT-OI x HDI	0.902*	0.684*	0.866*	0.229
Growth ICT-OI x Gini	0.313	0.089	0.286	0.426
Growth ICT-OI x HDI	−0.328*	0.291	−0.097	0.038
Gini x HDI	−0.528*	−0.583*	−0.522*	−0.216

* $p \leq .05$

In the developed countries, it may be expected that there would be a strong relationship between HDI and the index measuring the availability of network instruments (NI). The data of the Bologna countries support this hypothesis (r=.855*), which also holds separately for the western (r=.543*) and the eastern countries (r=.845*). Table 4 also shows that it is possible to find more equipment for modern networking in countries where people enjoy more income equality (r=-.47*). If we take the groups of countries separately, the calculated relationships are only significant in the west. This brings us to the hypothesis that countries with a high level of development (HDI) and with a relatively narrow span of income inequalities (Gini) may also grow to a higher ICT-OI value than they have at this moment. Thus, it can be expected in the future that countries with an increasing level of human development and a diminishing distance between income levels may acquire more instruments for modern networking.

A similar pattern is found in the relations between II and ICT-OI, on the one hand, and the Gini and the HDI on the other. The less the income inequality, the greater the intensity of the use of ICT equipment (r=-0.431*) and the higher the ICT-OI index (r=-0.476*). After checking for the difference between west and east, we see that this relationship only holds in the west for ICT-OI (r=-0.574*). Just like above, the higher the HDI of a country, the more ICT equipment is used intensively (r=0.857*) and the higher the score for ICT-OI (0.902*). This holds not only for all the Bologna countries but also for the eastern and western Bologna countries separately. We also see that there is a weak insignificant relationship between the growth of ICT opportunities and increasing income inequality in all the Bologna countries (r=0.313). A weak relationship can also be found between increasing ICT opportunity and diminishing HDI (r=-0.328*). This seems to suggest that the growth in ICT opportunities is greater when the HDI decreases in the Bologna countries. However, this does not hold any longer when the west and the east are analysed separately.

Table 4 shows that the availability and the use of modern network equipment in the Bologna countries depends strongly on the development of the society as measured by the HDI (respectively r=0.855*, r=0.857*; r=0.902*). This still holds when we control for income inequality (Gini index) (respectively partial r=.806*, r=0.817*, r=0.869*). On the other hand, the relationship between the Gini index and NI (partial r=-0.071), II (partial r=-0.016), and ITC-OI (partial =-0.039) disappears when we control for the HDI. ICT opportunities seem to be much more influenced by the development of society (HDI) than by the inequality of income (Gini).

Migration and Mobility

The information-oriented society is looking for skilled workers, and migration is an important process in obtaining them, so well-trained people look for opportunities in societies where the information structure is richer and where their expectations may be fulfilled. Migration is very different from country to country. The lowest immigration figure is 0.6% (Romania) of the population in a country, and the highest is 37.4% (Luxembourg). We checked whether the HDI and the Gini index could be linked with these migration patterns in the Bologna countries (based on data of UN, 2006; our own calculations). We could find no significant relationship between the HDI and the Gini index, on the one hand, and the stock of migrants as a proportion of the total population in the different Bologna countries, on the other. Still, there was a growing positive correlation between the migrant figures of 1995 (r=.37*), 2000 (r=.528*), and 2005 (r=.628*) and the GDP of 2004: the higher the GDP of a country, the higher the proportion of migrants in that country. In other words, rich countries are more attractive for migrants.

Most of the migrants in 1960 in European countries were men (52%) (UN, 2006). Since the 1990s, this pattern has changed. At present, the largest proportion of migrants in Europe is composed of women (53.4% in 2005). More than before, women are trying to improve their position in other countries. However, contrary to the general pattern of migration, in 2005 there is a weak indication that the proportion of women among migrants is higher in countries with a lower GDP (r=-.242).

As countries need highly skilled workers more than previously to organize the network society, they try to influence the kind of migrants they want. Most develop a migration policy. Of 36 Bologna countries, 39% have a policy to raise the proportion of highly skilled workers among the migrants, and 53% try to maintain the level of this kind of migration. A policy to increase this number is found in a larger proportion of the NW Bologna (58%) countries than in the others (29%) (UN 2006; our own calculations).

Turning from migration to temporary mobility and particularly to the training received by youngsters in other countries than where they used to live, we see that the number of EU HE students studying in a foreign European country[12] is low: only 2.2% of all students[13] study for at least a year abroad and this percentage has not increased over the years (EC 2007: 129). And although there are more female than male students, a larger proportion of male students are studying abroad. Notwithstanding the EU's efforts to support mobility of HE students and networking between universities, professors, and students (e.g. more than 1,500,000 students have participated in the ERASMUS programme), here, too, the socioeconomic divide of the society is visible. Students hailing from better off families participate more in the programme than do the others. Moreover, the participation of students with parents having enjoyed higher education is also significantly higher than the students living in other families, and students of the richer countries also belong more to the richer socioeconomic categories than do the students coming from the poorer countries. Although this kind of networking is very much appreciated by the participants, ultimately it does not seem to guarantee salary gains or higher level jobs (Otero 2008: 141).

The Gender Gap

The network society, supported by ICT, not only reproduces the socioeconomic divide in our society but also the gender divide even when this society might change the power relations and offer local democracy and electronically stimulated participation and communication (see §1). One of the reasons is that ICT applications attract fewer women than men. Most of the Internet users in 2002 were male. The highest proportion of female Internet users (48%) could be found in Sweden (ITU 2007). In the EU, 28% of the females and 33% males (16–74 year old) use the Internet for interaction with public authorities (Eurostat 2008). Networking by ICT does not put women in a privileged position, but the network society does offer other opportunities for emancipation. One of them is gender mainstreaming, which can be defined as 'a process that seeks to advance gender equality by revising all mainstream policy arenas' (Walby 2005).

THE EHEA IN THE CONTEXT OF THE NETWORK SOCIETY

The informational economy needs 'self-programmable labour'. In other words, 'brains' are the most important 'raw material' of the informational economy. In the previous sections, we showed that the education and training of the 'brains' capable of functioning in the network society is crisscrossed by a number of demographic, technological, and social developments. Higher education in the EHEA is being confronted with these challenges. Moreover, the EHEA itself can be regarded as an expression of the network society. Castells refers to the European Union as a network state (Castells 1998). The EU is a way of cooperation between states. The EU is a transnational space in which actors on different policy levels interact in a structure that can be characterized as a network. In higher education, we have witnessed the growth of this new polity and its transnational consequences. In 30 years time, action programmes have been established, often against the policy of some of the Member States, which have had a clear impact on the mobility of students and staff, cooperation in networks of institutions, and the learning to know each others' language and culture. These are domains that are not central to the Member States' educational competence but that, nevertheless, are crucial in the light of a developing network society. Higher education is viewed in the programmes of the EU as an economic factor in the competition on the free market. The neo-liberal idea of removing barriers to the free trade of capital, goods, services, and people is thus penetrating higher education (Verhoeven 2006). The role of the EU in higher education is not replacing the policies of the Member States but is regulating a competitive market through legal initiatives and stimulatory activities.

However, the borders of what formally belongs to the EU and what, strictly speaking, does not belong to it, are permeable (De Wit 2003). Initiatives and programmes of the EU often are not restricted to EU member states, and actors and processes outside the EU are equally part of the 'networks' that constitute the European polity. Therefore, we would do better to speak of 'Europe' as the new, most relevant polity. This is true especially for higher education, and the Bologna Process is a prime example. The EU and the Bologna Process are more closely linked to each other than would appear at first sight (De Wit 2008). The EU finances the follow-up of the Bologna Process and is part of the follow-up group that is monitoring the Bologna reforms. Moreover, the EU funds transnational projects in order to create 'synergies' between the Bologna Process and the EU policy on higher education. The EU also provides the methods and instruments used to create the EHEA, that is, the method of open coordination and instruments like the mobility programmes, the diploma supplement, and the ECTS. Finally, the goals of the Bologna Process are largely the same as the goals of EU cooperation in higher education.

The aim of creating a European Higher Education Area is, in fact, situated in the market environment that is being created on a European scale for higher education (and in a similar way, for research, in the European Research Area). In this market environment, a paradox can be discerned. On the one hand, a market and, hence, competition is created. On the other, it is expected that this competition is met by cooperating on projects, in networks and consortia, etc. Moreover, the goal is increasingly to present European benchmarks alongside common standards and good practices. This is true also for the EHEA, where 'open coordination' is intended to tune policies without taking coordinating, hierarchical decisions.

This has several consequences for higher education. To begin with, higher education institutions are being confronted with market processes both in their own functioning and in their relationship with other organizations. The relationship with the government, too, can be characterized by the introduction of market operations, deregulation, liberalization, and steering at a distance.

This means that the barrier between higher education and 'external interests' is breaking down (Neave 2002). The demands of the techno-economic system and particularly of the predicted demands of the labour market become more directive. In this new normative view, higher education is expected to 'deliver' flexible, mobile, communicative, and lifelong-learning individuals, to aim at individual students as consumers and target groups, and to offer tailored education, for example, on local campuses or through distance education. In this sense, higher education institutions become enterprises that 'produce' education or human capital, and the students (and parents) become 'consumers'.

Part of the training now still provided by institutions of higher education might be taken over by the growing number of corporate universities (Mazarol & Soutar 2001: 162). Business and industry are important partners for universities in building networks, but they might also be very important competitors. In spite of the research tradition at universities, the largest amount of money for research is being spent by private industry, a development very often supported by the state. A Delphi study of European higher education experts showed that most of them fear that more than 60% of basic research would be conducted outside institutions of higher education in 2020 in Europe (Huisman et al., 2005: 33).

Furthermore, economic, and educational goals seem to be becoming ever more intertwined. Higher education institutions increasingly have to compete with each other for financing and have to enter into contractual relations with third parties. This means that they are being increasingly confronted with the diverging interests of third parties and are being asked to show their accountability and quality management.

The market-like processes might also lead to institutions of higher education functioning more like enterprises. In this sense, they might become more like network enterprises, that is, organizationally flexible, in order to be able to adapt to their environment and the variable geography of nodes in the network, using ICT to coordinate tasks, define specific goals, and manage the complexity of the network. Even in uncertain circumstances, a network enterprise is able to generate and process knowledge efficiently and to make use of it flexibly. Its success depends on linking decentralized implementation to integrated decision making. In this sense, universities have been defined as entrepreneurial (Clark 1998) or, we might say, network universities.

For institutions of higher education, the idea of functioning as a network runs counter to its predominant organizational form, that is, a professional bureaucracy. They consist of loosely coupled parts that cannot easily be moved in the same direction or adapted in the same way to a changing environment. But this is changing. New management forms are finding their way into higher education leading to the diminishing importance of collegial decision making and to the streamlining and professionalization of institutional management (Amaral et al., 2003).

Institutions of higher education have, of course, a long tradition of formal networks of disciplines and professions and informal networks of academics (Dill 1997). In a network society, however, these traditional networks are integrated to enhance the adaptive capacity of the organization, or, in other words, the diverging units of the differentiated structure can (thanks to ICT) be coordinated. These new networks follow less the traditional disciplinary dividing lines and more the path of interdisciplinary and multidisciplinary cooperation (Salmi 2001) not only as a reorganization of traditional units (e.g. departments) but also as a new set of cognitive and social practices related to 'Mode 2 of knowledge production' (Gibbons 1999).

We must keep in mind that a higher-education market is at most a quasi-market. Most consumers do not 'pay' for the product themselves; most 'producers' obtain their basic financing from the government; and the 'market' is not free but regulated. Nevertheless, on this quasi-market, commercializing research results, for example, can be used as a means to increase income, but this can also endanger the autonomy of the researcher. Tenure, too, is no longer guaranteed (Weber 1999). In other words, by becoming involved in 'academic capitalism' (Slaughter & Leslie 1999), institutions of higher education risk losing that which makes them an institution of higher education.

CONCLUSIONS AND REFLECTIONS

The network logic is penetrating the entire social structure and, hence, also higher education. Nevertheless, structure is not a one-way cause of action. That is, we must also look at how actors deal with networks, how they use them and interpret them. For example, linking computers through the Internet is one thing, having an appropriate cultural and academic setting in higher education in which the Internet is used to introduce students to the Information Age is quite another (Castells 2004).

It might be true that new social relationships are developing, but old associations like social classes have not disappeared (Halcli & Webster 2000). We have shown above that 'old' divides, based on gender, age, wealth, skills, etc. are still operative in European societies. This has important consequences for institutions of higher education and for higher-education policy.

The population of Europe and the young population in particular is shrinking. This will lead to fewer students in higher education unless older age groups participate more in higher education or unless immigration compensates for the loss in enrolment. The latter is not a certainty (Mizikaci & Baumgartl 2007).

Moreover, it is not clear whether higher education in the EHEA is ready to accommodate a growing body of international students and staff because of the language being used (the language proficiency of teachers and students, the availability of information in different languages, etc.), to the content of the curricula, to accommodation for mobile students, and so on. Regarding the older students, we have seen that the age structure of the student population is diverse but that it still consists mostly of young people and that lifelong learning is hardly growing. In other words, if the network society requires highly qualified knowledge workers and knowledge producers, there is no guarantee that the demographic challenge can be met. The consequence might be a decreasing number of students and shortages of graduates on the labour market. We could also face an excess supply of higher education (Klemencic & Fried 2007), at least in some regions. Issues of brain drain and brain gain will come more to the fore. In order to attract foreign and non-traditional students (e.g. minority students), quality as well as innovation might become an important issue. If the EHEA could show that it offers high quality education and that it takes account of new insights in learning, of the needs and expectations of non-traditional students, of new demands regarding skilled workers (communication skills, ICT skills) etc., it could become an area of interest for students from outside the EHEA. The Trends V report reaches a similar conclusion (Crosier et al., 2007).

The number of graduates in mathematics, science, and technology is increasing, for a large part as a result of growing female participation. More in general, ICT availability and use are growing although there are important differences within the EHEA. ICT availability and use are high in Western Europe but much lower in South and Eastern Europe. Moreover, there are inequalities amongst the Bologna countries with regard to equipment for modern networking. Again West and East are on opposite sides. The same goes for the standard of living. Although the Bologna countries have similar targets with regard to the EHEA, the resources available for achieving these targets are clearly unevenly distributed. The goal is to create one area for higher education, but there seem to be different areas within the EHEA. It seems important to increase the development of societies and diminish the distance between income levels because this enhances the availability and use of ICT and networking. However, societies seem to reach a saturation point with regard to the relation between wealth and ICT: at a certain level of wealth, other factors come into play, hence the importance of targeted policies, for instance to promote science and technology in education, but also in research as with the EIT.

Social and cultural factors are still important in the network society. For instance, new forms of communication strengthen existing patterns of inequality because the wealthy and educated are far more likely to use them. Along the lines of education, skilled work and unskilled work are divided and lead to divisions in the kind of work, the organization of work, etc. In the present context, the network society reproduces the socioeconomic divide.

Institutions of higher education educate the national, European, and global 'elite' that will play a central role in the network society. But the mission of higher education cannot, and should not, be limited to that. With high and increasing participation rates in higher education, they should also offer opportunities for all, so that everyone can enjoy the advantages of the network society. These institutions should, in other words, make students capable and apt for this new society and provide them with appropriate values and social skills (Salmi 2001). Mobility is one of the key means, but this means that teachers must not only provide students with information but also be 'animators and commentators in charge of giving context and in-depth understanding of an area' (Weber 1999: 10).

If the mission of higher education should be to provide opportunities for all, this does not entail that each institution of higher education should provide the same opportunities. The student body is diversified and so there could well be a diversity in institutions catering for different target groups of students, taking into account their specific characteristics and educating them through diverse pathways for the challenges of the network society.

At the same time, institutions of higher education must remain a place where a critical view on social developments is possible. 'There must be things the university will not do no matter how much money is offered, for example, permitting donors to select faculty. Conversely, there must be "useless" things it insists upon doing, for example, cross-subsidizing the teaching of classics and philosophy because it is an institution committed to cultivation and transmission of a cultural heritage as well as to economic progress' (Clark 2004: 358). One of the main challenges in furthering the EHEA, therefore, will be to make progress with the implementation of its goals while ensuring that this implementation succeeds in achieving the goals for all.

NOTES

[1] ISCED is the International Standard Classification of Education, a classification that combines levels of education with orientation (general, vocational, or pre-vocational) and destination (education or labour market). For higher education, three levels are distinguished: 5A (academic programmes), 5B (vocational programmes), and 6 (advanced research programmes, i.e., PhD programmes).

[2] "**Network index:** fixed telephone lines per 100 inhabitants, mobile cellular subscribers per 100 inhabitants, and international internet bandwidth (kbps per inhabitant)." (ITU 2007)

[3] "**Intensity index:** total broadband internet subscribers per 100 inhabitants, international outgoing telephone traffic (minutes) per capita." (ITU 2007)

[4] "The average annual growth rate (2001-2005) refers to the growth of ICT-OI values between 2001 and 2005." (ITU 2007)

[5] The following figures are based on information collected from 43 members of the Bologna Process. No information was available for Andorra, The Holy See, Liechtenstein, or Montenegro.

[6] This area is composed of all of the countries located on the West side of the line Finland, Denmark, Germany, and Austria, including Greece.

[7] This area is composed of all the countries that do not belong to the group listed in footnote 7.

[8] This area is composed of 12 countries: the first six EEC countries and those countries located northwest of them.

[9] Because of Luxembourg's very high GDP, a correction for the calculation of HDI was applied for Luxembourg.

[10] Because of Luxembourg's very high GDP, Luxembourg was excluded from the calculations.

[11] The Human Development Index is 'measured by life expectancy at birth; knowledge, as measured by the adult literacy rate and the combined gross enrolment ratio for primary, secondary and tertiary

schools; and a decent standard of living, as measured by gross domestic product GDP per capita in purchasing power parity (PPP) US dollars.' The gross domestic product per capita (GDP) is expressed in purchasing power parity US dollars, but we should not forget that GDP is also an indicator of the HDI (Watkins et al. 2006: 276).

12   In a country of the EU, a candidate country, or an EFTA/EEA member country.

13   Students from Cyprus, Iceland, and Liechtenstein are in a special position in that the provision of higher education in their country is limited, so they very often study abroad.

REFERENCES

Altbach, P. G. & J. Knight (2007) 'The internationalisation of higher education: motivations and realities,' *Journal of Studies in International Education*, 11 (3/4) pp. 290–305.

Amaral, A., O. Fulton. & I.M. Larsen (2003) 'A managerial revolution' in: Amaral, A., V. L. Meek. & I.M. Larsen (eds) *The higher education managerial revolution?* Dordrecht/Boston/London : Kluwer Academic Publishers pp. 275–296.

Barney, D. (2006) *The Network Society* Cambridge: Polity.

Castells, M. (1993) 'The University System: Engine of Development in the New World Economy,' in: Ransom, A., S-M. Khoo & V. Selveratnam (eds.) *Improving Higher Education in Developing Countries.* Washington D.C. World Bank pp. 65-80.

Castells, M. (1996) *The Rise of the Network Society. The Information Age: Economy, Society and Culture. Volume 1.* Oxford: Blackwell Publishers.

Castells, M. (1997) *The Power of Identity. The Information Age: Economy, Society and Culture. Volume 2.* Oxford: Blackwell Publishers.

Castells, M. (1998) *End of Millennium. The Information Age: Economy, Society and Culture. Volume 3.* Oxford: Blackwell Publisher.

Castells, M. (2000a) 'Materials for an exploratory theory of the network society,' *British Journal of Sociology*, 51 (1) pp. 5–24.

Castells, M. (2000b) 'Information Technology and Global Capitalism,' in: Hutton, W. & A. Giddens (eds) *On the Edge: Living with Global Capitalism.* London : Cape pp. 52–74.

Castells, M. (2004) 'Informationalism, Networks, and the Network Society: A Theoretical Blueprint,' in: Castells, M. ed *The Network Society. A Cross-cultural Perspective.* Cheltenham, UK / Northampton, MA, USA : Edward Elgar pp. 3–45.

CEDEFOP (2008) *Future skills in Europe. medium term for costs. synthesis report.* Luxembourg: Office for official publications of the European Communities.

CIA (2008) *The World Factbook,* retrieved on 31 March 2008 on https://www.cia.gov/library/publications/the-world-factbook/index.htm

Clark, B. R. (1998) *Creating Entrepreneurial Universities. Organizational Pathways of Transformation.* Oxford: Pergamon/IAU Press.

Clark, B. R. (2004) 'The Consequences of European Integration for Higher Education,' *Higher Education Policy*, 17 pp. 355–370.

Crosier, D., L. Purser & H. Smidt (2007) *Trends V: Universities shaping the European Higher Education Area.* Brussels: EUA.

Crow, B. & G. Longford (2000) 'Digital restructuring: gender, class and citizenship in the information society in Canada,' *Citizenship Studies*, 4 (2) pp. 207–230.

Curtain, R. (2000) *Changes to the nature of work. Implications for the vocational education and training system. Report to NCVER.* Kensington Park: National centre for vocational education research Ltd.

De Wit, K. (2003) 'The Consequences of European Integration for Higher Education,' *Higher Education Policy*, 16 (2) pp. 161–178.

De Wit K. (2008) *Universiteiten in Europa in de 21e eeuw. Netwerken in een veranderende samenleving.* Gent: Academia Press.

Dill, D. D. (1997) 'Effects of Competition on Diverse Institutional Contexts,' in: Peterson, M. W., D.D. Dill & L.A. Mets (eds.) *Planning and Management for a Changing Environment: A Handbook on Redesigning Postsecondary Institutions.* San Francisco : Jossey-Bass pp.88–105.

European Commission (2005) *Commission Staff Working Paper. Progress Towards the Lisbon Objectives in Education and Training.* Brussels: European Commission.

European Commission (2007) *Key Data on Higher Education in Europe.* Luxembourg: European Commission.

European Commission (2008) *EUROSTAT,* retrieved on 2 April 2008 on http://epp.eurostat.ec .europa.eu/portal/page?_pageid=1996,45323734&_dad=portal&_schema=PORTAL&screen=welco meref&open=/C/C7&language=en&product=Yearlies_new_population&root=Yearlies_new_popula tion&scrollto=0:

Gibbons, M (1999) 'Changing Research Practices,' in: Brennan, J., J. Fedrowitz, M.T. Huber & T. Shah (eds.) *What Kind of University? International Perspectives on Knowledge, Participation and Governance.* Buckingham / Philadelphia : SHRE / Open University Press. pp. 23-35.

Guri-Rosenblit, S. (2001) 'Virtual universities: current models and future trends,' *Higher Education in Europe,* XXVI (4) pp. 487-499.

Halcli, H. & F. Webster (2000) 'Inequality and Mobilization in The Information Age, ' 3 (1) pp. 67-81.

Healey, N. M. (2008) 'Is higher education in *really* ' internationalising'?' *Higher Education,* 55 (3) pp. 333–355.

Huisman, J, , P. Boezerooy, A. Dima, M. Hoppe-Jeliazkova, A, Luyten-Lub, E. de Weert & M. van der Wende (2005) ' A brief report on the Delphi study ' European higher education and research in 2020',' in: Enders, J., J. File, J. Huisman & D. Westerheijden (eds) *The European higher education and research landscaped 2020. Scenarios and strategic debates.* Enschede : CHEPS pp. 25-60

ITU (2007) *Measuring the Information Society 2007. ICT Opportunity Index and World Telecommunication/ICT Indicators,* retrieved on 17 March 2008 on http://www.itu.int/ITU-D/ict/publications/ict-oi/2007/index.html:

Klemenic, M. & J. Fried (2007) 'Demographic Challenges and Future of the Higher Education,' *International Higher Education* 47 pp. 12-14.

Lash, S. & J. Urry (1994) *Economies of Signs and Space.* London: Sage.

Mazzarol, T. & G.N. Soutar (2001) *The global market for higher education. Sustainable competitive strategies for the new Millennium.* Cheltenham (UK)/ Northampton (USA): Edward Elgar. VII + 200 pp.

Mizikaci, F. & B. Baumgartl (2007) 'Demographic Trends and Risks for European Higher Education,' *International Higher Education* 47 pp. 15-16.

Neave, G. (2002) 'On Stakeholders, Cheshire Cats and Seers: Changing visions of the University,' in: Goedegebuure, L & J. File (eds.) *The Cheps Inaugurals 2002.* Enschede : Universiteit Twente pp. 8-27.

Otero, M. S. (2008) 'The Socio-economic Background Of ERASMUS Students: A Trend Towards Wider Inclusion?' *International Review of Education,* 54 pp. 135-154.

Salmi, J. (2001) 'Tertiary Education in the 21st Century: Challenges and Opportunities,' *Higher Education Management,* 13 (2) pp. 105-130.

Slaughter, S. & L. Leslie (1997) *Academic Capitalism: Politics, Policies and the Entrepreneurial University.* Baltimore: Johns Hopkins University Press.

UN Population Division (2006) *World Migrant Stock: The 2005 Revision. Population Database,* retrieved on 31 March 2008 at http://esa.un.org/migration/index.asp?panel=2:

Verhoeven, J. C. (2006) 'Internationalization and commercialization of higher education in an era of globalization,' in: Zhang Hui (ed) *Teacher Education, Education Policy, Innovation of Higher Education, Motivation and Evaluations of Students: A Comparative Approach.* Shenyang : Liaoning University Press pp. 133-146.

Walby, S. (2005) 'Introduction: Comparative Gender Mainstreaming in a Global Era,' *International Feminist Journal of Politics,* 7 (4) pp. 453-470.

Watkins K. et al. (2006) *Human Development Report 2006. Beyond scarcity: Power, poverty and the global water crisis.* New York: Palgrave Macmillan 422 pp.

Weber, L. E. (1999) 'Survey of the Main Challenges Facing Higher Education at the Millennium,' in: Hirsch, W. Z. & L.E. Weber (eds.) *Challenges Facing Higher Education at the Millennium.* Oxford: Pergamon/IAU Press pp. 3-17.

Zaida, A. (2008) *Features and Challenges of Population Ageing: The European Perspective. Vienna: European Centre for social Welfare policy and research (Policy Brief March (I),* retrieved on 3 April 2008 on http://www.euro.centre.org

PETER MAASSEN

15. EUROPEAN HIGHER EDUCATION IN SEARCH OF INSTITUTIONAL ORDER[1]

INTRODUCTION

European integration seems to be in full swing when it comes to higher education. This is not only visible in the ongoing national reform processes in higher education, but also in European level policy documents and reform proposals, aimed at stimulating the integration of European higher education. Consequently, a stocktaking and forward-looking project like the one in the framework of which this chapter is produced can be expected to look into the state of our theoretical and empirical understanding with respect to the European integration of higher education. Where are we regarding our understanding of the dynamics of the university as the core 'Knowledge Institution' in Europe? What do recent studies into European integration efforts of higher education tell us about the possible future developments of the 'European Higher Education Area'? What are the major concepts used in these studies and how do they contribute to our understanding of the possible new directions the Bologna process might take after 2010?

Especially since the signing of the Bologna Declaration in 1999 and the Lisbon 2000 summit higher education has become more important as a policy issue at the European as well as at the national level within the (larger) EU area. The growing importance of higher education in the various policy arenas in Europe has been accompanied by a slow but steady increase in research in higher education, with a special focus on the Bologna process seen as the core European integration process with respect to higher education. However, despite the growing number of studies focused on European integration of higher education, overall there are major knowledge gaps in the European policy debates on higher education (Olsen and Maassen 2007) and inconclusive, weak and ambiguous data are often used to legitimize strong conclusions concerning the need for urgent and radical reforms.

There are a number of excellent studies on the Europeanization of higher education (e.g. Corbett 2005; Witte 2006). However, studies on European integration and higher education have often suffered from what might be called 'double-isolatedness'. Many studies have treated higher education as a sector isolated from the overall European integration processes. In addition, rarely analytical frameworks from general social sciences, and especially European studies have been used for studying European integration processes in higher education.

The starting point is that in order to improve our understanding of European integration in higher education first we have to strengthen our analytical frameworks, and second we have to carefully examine the empirical evidence used for

B.M. Kehm, J. Huisman and B. Stensaker (eds.), The European Higher Education Area: Perspectives on a Moving Target, 281–293.

legitimizing specific normative positions taken with respect to higher education dynamics in Europe.

An important argument here is that for getting a better understanding of the effects of European integration on higher education dynamics it is of relevance to discuss the notion of 'order' and relate it to some of the enduring and recurrent themes in the study of higher education and in social sciences in general, as well as to the study of the role and adaptive power of institutions. This concerns in the first place the way in which integration and change in higher education systems have been conceptualized in the academic literature on higher education (Clark 1983). In the second place the issue of unity and diversity (Olsen 2007a), i.e. balancing system-level coordination with institutional level autonomy in higher education systems.

ORDER

The concept of order is of relevance when describing and analyzing the dynamics of a higher education system. In European countries as elsewhere the need for system-level coordination is accompanied by the acceptance of the necessity of institutional autonomy. The drive for strengthening institutional autonomy leads naturally to more diversity (or disorder) within the system, while system coordination is aimed at creating unity in a system, or a minimum level of integration and order. In his seminal book from 1983 "The Higher Education System" Burton Clark has described these counter forces as follows:

> *In an infinitely complex world, the higher education system has difficulties in pulling itself together that belie simple descriptions and answers. Tasks proliferate, beliefs multiply, and the many forms of authority pull in different directions. Yet in each case, some order emerges in various parts: disciplines link members from far and wide, universities symbolically tie together their many specialists, bureaucratic structures, local and national, provide uniform codes and regulations. And the bureaucratic, political and oligarchic forms of national authority contribute to the integration of the whole.*
> (Clark 1983: 136)

The efforts to integrate European higher education are part of a more general process of integrating sovereign states in new political and institutional order (Olsen 2007a). An important element in the creation of new order with respect to higher education is the need to balance integration and change, unity and diversity, i.e. system-level coordination and university autonomy (Clark 1983; Olsen 2007a: 22-23). Maintaining such a balance has traditionally been a responsibility of the nation-state. However, the emerging "competence"[2] of the European Commission with respect to higher education (Pollack 2000; Maassen and Olsen 2007; Maassen and Musselin 2008), and the intergovernmental (Bologna) agreement to create an open European Higher Education Area, imply that the efforts to create order with respect to higher education in Europe no longer take place only at the national level, but increasingly also at the European level.

According to Clark (1983: 205) there are tensions in any higher education system between the forces that create stability and order, and those that cause adaptations, change and disorder. These forces very much contribute to the complexity of higher education institutions and systems, also because they operate in different ways at different levels in a higher education system. "Hence, it is always necessary, when speaking of a type of academic change, to specify the levels at which it operates, since an opposite disposition is likely to characterize the levels not directly in view" (Clark 1983: 209).

In principle any higher education system consists of three organizational levels, i.e. the basic academic units, the central institutional administration and leadership, and the system level governance arrangements and actors, or in the words of Clark (1983: 205) the understructure, middle structure and superstructure. In the case of European higher education an additional layer has been emerging that can be referred to as the suprastructure composed of all agencies and actors, including those representing national authorities, aimed at creating order that links together the higher education systems of the member states of the European Union.

The effectiveness of the new multi-level governance system is a clear challenge for European higher education. While institutional autonomy is continuously promoted as an aim in itself, there is now not only the need to maintain system level order in the form of an effectively coordinated national higher education system, there is the additional expectation of the creation of an integrated European Higher Education Area (EHEA). How are the fragmented basic academic units of the higher education institutions linked to the European level structures aimed at creating order in the EHEA?

The complexity of the emerging links between the various levels can be illustrated by the efforts to coordinate the creation of the EHEA through the Bologna process. An issue in this has been the representation of the academic staff in the Bologna Follow Up Group (BFUG), a structure set up to oversee the Bologna process between biennial Ministers' meetings, amongst other things, to guarantee the democratic nature of the process. The BFUG is composed of representatives of all participating countries (currently 46), the European Commission and relevant consultative members representing specific interest groups. The institutional leadership (through the EUA and EURASHE) and the student unions (through ESIB) were included as consultative members in the BFUG since its establishment. The interests of the academic staff were supposed to be represented by the EUA and EURASHE, but the lack of a direct representation of academic staff in BFUG has been seen as a democratic deficit (Neave and Maassen 2007). Therefore in 2005 an organization representing academic staff of universities and colleges called Educational International Pan-European Structure was accepted as a consultative member of the BFUG. Through the inclusion of this organization academic staff is now supposed to have a direct input into the Bologna process (Flemish Ministry of Education 2008). In the meantime representative agencies of the business world and European quality assessment agencies have also been accepted as consultative members, implying that the BFUG currently has eight consultative members.

One of the factors that cause the complexity is that adding an extra governance level at the suprastructure level does not imply that this new layer comes in a hierarchical way on top of the superstructure. Instead, the suprastructure operates next to and is partly overlapping with the superstructure. Instead of the middle structure mediating between understructure and superstructure as well as suprastructure, the three traditional structures that can be identified in any higher education system each have their own direct input into the efforts at the suprastructure to create the EHEA.

How does the integration of higher education fit the general process of European integration? Here we follow Olsen's definition by seeing integration as "a process which turns previously separated units into components of a relatively coherent and consistent system" (Olsen 2007a: 21). What are the conditions for creating a coherent and consistent European Higher Education System (or Area) with autonomous higher education institutions and autonomous national higher education systems as components?

Traditionally the efforts of the European Commission to influence the national institutional arrangements with respect to higher education have been met with suspicion and rejection of the member states. Higher education – like the rest of the education sector – has always been a nationally sensitive policy area closely related to national identity (Gornitzka 2007; Neave and Maassen 2007; Olsen 2007a: 78). The Treaty of Maastricht confirmed through the subsidiarity principle that the prime responsibility for (higher) education lies at the national level, implying that the Commission cannot undertake any initiatives itself aimed at converging European higher education (Maassen and Musselin 2008). This starting point has not been changed legally, but in practice political space with respect to (higher) education has been created at the suprastructure level in Europe (Gornitzka 2007). This is especially true since the turn of the last century with the signing of the Bologna Declaration and announcement of the Lisbon Agenda as important moments in the apparent change in attitude towards the acceptance of the need for integrating European higher education.

With respect to the implementation of the Bologna process the Ministers of (Higher) Education of the countries involved in the Bologna process decided not to set up a separate joint executive capacity to support the implementation other than a small (3 staff member) rotating secretariat. As a consequence the implementation of the Bologna process increasingly had to rely on the relevant administrative executive capacity of the European Commission, especially through organizing and funding 'evaluation studies and progress conferences and seminars'. A complicating factor is that the Bologna process encompasses not 27 but – through the Bologna process – 46 countries. This implies, amongst other things, that the change dynamics of higher education is less driven by the 6 large member states of the EU as in the case of integration processes taking place in the framework of the EU (Olsen 2007a: 43). It also means that there is a fairly unclear division of policy responsibility with respect to higher education between the supra- and superstructure, both formally and in the day-to-day policy practice. The gradual development by the Commission of competence with respect to a large number of policy issue areas (including education and research) has been referred to as 'creeping competence' (Pollack 2000). This can be argued to represent one of the main challenges with respect to the system level governance of European higher education after 2010: formalizing an effective division of authority with respect to higher education over the relevant system level governance layers: European, national, and in some cases, sub-national. Such a formalized, transparent division of policy authority can be observed in other 'federal' higher education systems, such as the USA and Canada.

Concerning the consequences of these developments two questions can be mentioned here. What kind of integration of higher education is being aimed at the suprastructure level? And: How do the traditional national (= superstructure) level efforts to create system level coordination compare to the European (= suprastructure) level attempts to realize an integrated European Higher Education Area?

These questions should be taken into account when looking at the urgent and radical reform demands European higher education institutions are currently facing (Maassen and Olsen 2007). A standard claim is that environments are changing rapidly and that the universities and colleges are not able or willing to respond in ways that are expected of them. Especially at the European level there is a perception that it is time to rethink and reform the internal organization and governance of higher education institutions, as well as their role in society simply because these institutions, and especially the research universities, do not learn, nor adapt and reorganise themselves fast enough. This can be illustrated by the following quote from the European Commission:

> *"After remaining a comparatively isolated universe for a very long period, both in relation to society and to the rest of the world, with funding guaranteed and a status protected by respect for their autonomy, European universities have gone through the second half of the 20th century without really calling into question the role or nature of what they should be contributing to society. The changes they are undergoing today and which have intensified over the past ten years prompt the fundamental question: can the European universities, as they are and are organized now, hope in the future to retain their place in society and in the world" (European Commission 2003: 22)?*

This instrumental view on the role of higher education in society forms the basis for a set of specific reform proposals, as presented, for example, in the Commission's Communication on the modernization agenda for universities (European Commission 2006), Schleicher's policy brief (Schleicher 2006), and the report by the Bruegel group presenting an agenda for reforming European universities (Aghion et al., 2008).

The nature of this set of reform proposals is based on the starting point that "European higher education systems have fallen behind over the last few decades, in terms of participation, quality, and in research and innovation" (Figel 2006: 3). The Bologna process is seen as a successful example of the reforms needed, but it only covers one aspect of the reforms needed. In addition what is needed is "root-and-branch reform of the way our universities are managed, structured, funded, and regulated" (Figel 2006: 5). The "analysis" underlying this position, using international rankings, as well as general funding and participation statistics, claims that European higher education is over-regulated, underfunded, fragmented, and insolated, and is suffering from a lack of institutional diversity, problems of cross-border recognition of academic credits and degrees, as well as poor academic career structures. The necessary reforms consist of the following elements: less government, more institutional autonomy and accountability, increased private investments in higher education (including tuition fees), partnerships with industry (also in education), and increased mobility of students and academic staff. The proposed changes are argued to advance knowledge, produce functional improvement, and benefit society in general, while the dominant language is emphasizing the economic functions of higher education.

A striking characteristic of the reform proposals is that they are based on 'strong convictions and weak evidence' (Olsen and Maassen 2007: 13-16). This implies that there are "large gaps between the claims and the solutions advocated by reformers, and the quality of the evidence they have forwarded" (Olsen and Maassen 2007: 12). An example can be found in the claimed gap between the educational revenues per student for European compared to US public higher education institutions. The before mentioned Bruegel report (Aghion et al.: 5) claims that "the EU25 spends on average €8,700 per student versus €36,500 in the US", while the European Commission (2006) suggested that there is a revenue gap of some €10,000 per student. On the other hand, a national US information center indicates that in 2006 the revenues per full-time equivalent student (public appropriations and tuition revenues) were on average less than $10,000 for all public universities and colleges in the USA (NCHEMS 2007). This example illustrates that the claims on the European side concerning the 'reform needs' are based more on perceptions of the dominance of US elite universities than on firm data and convincing evidence.

While no single group of reformers has the authority or power necessary to control reform processes and outcomes, the power-relations relevant for successful reform, are rarely analyzed. The myth of an existing, or previously existing, government command and control system is taken for granted without a careful documentation of what the historical and existing order was like and how different it is from an emerging new settlement. However, the unsuccessful attempt to found a European University (Corbett 2005) illustrates the complexity of power distributions in this policy field and so do the Bologna process and the Lisbon strategy. The use of the Open Method of Coordination (OMC) indicates the current limits of supranationalism and suggests that vagueness about what OMC means and what the method is assumed to, and can in fact, accomplish in different contexts, may be a necessary condition for agreement (Gornitzka 2007). Likewise, the uneven implementation of the Bologna process (Tomusk 2006; Amaral et al. 2008) and the uncertainties of the Lisbon strategy illustrate that actors without authority can rarely rely on (coercive) power. The causal chain from political intention and declarations to implementation can easily be broken or weakened and building support and mobilizing partners is a key process in higher education reform.

INSTITUTIONAL APPROACH

An institutional approach emphasizes the various repertoires well-established institutions use to defend themselves against changing environments and deliberate reform efforts (March and Olsen 1989, 2006 a, b). "Institutionalism supplements and competes not only with micro approaches featuring political agency and identifiable rational policy-makers and their preferences and power, but also with macro approaches giving primacy to societal forces such as economic competition, technological innovation, cross-cultural migration and demographic change" (Olsen 2007a: 3).

Institutions provide elements of order. Therefore making sense of higher education dynamics requires that we take into account the density and types of institutionalized rules and practices in which higher education is embedded, as well as the origins and histories of universities, colleges and other relevant institutions. Properties of such institutional configurations and traditions are, for example, likely to influence the degree to which universities and colleges will be able to counteract deliberate attempts at the supra- and superstructure level to alter their identity in an effort to create a specific kind of institutional order that fits a joint agenda but is alien to the basic values and norms of European universities and colleges.

Instrumental Vision

Traditionally European governments have been focused on making sure that the university as a public institution that was part of the state structure would operate on the basis of the same strict rules as other state organizations, implying, amongst other things, earmarked funding and a budgeting system on an annual basis, civil service status for all university staff and nationally determined labour agreements for university staff, strict reporting requirements, a centrally determined structure of degree systems, etc. As such the state was determining and controlling the organizational input conditions under which universities could operate, i.e. the *how* of higher education. What happened inside the university, i.e. the *what* of the university, was to a large extent left to the academics themselves to determine. Academic self-governance was part of a large democratic-constitutional social order, with partly autonomous institutions (Olsen 2000). Constitutive regulations defined these institutions and their roles, competence, social and political relationships, and responsibilities. From that perspective the academic autonomy of the university was a condition for legitimate governmental steering of the sector and peaceful co-existence of the university with other institutions.

Innovations and Change in an Institutional Order

An argument can be made for the stickiness of institutions and their less than readiness to respond to impetus for innovation. However, institutional theory suggests both inter- and intra-institutional dynamics through which change and innovation occur (March and Olsen 2006b). Institutions exist within a larger institutional setting and order – as is indeed the case with EU institutions. The point here is that innovations and change can occur in the interface between different orders of institutions and when the balance between partly autonomous

287

institutional spheres is disturbed. This can refer to balance between levels of governance (such as between EU institutions) and institutional spheres that run along sectoral lines. Friction may occur when different institutional spheres collide with each other thereby triggering institutional change (Olsen 2001). Such inter-relationships are highly relevant for the study of diffusion of organizational templates. Coercive spread implies imposition of organizational templates where institutional resilience to change or institutional inertia is trumped by hierarchy or by specific financial conditionality (DiMaggio and Powell 1991; Bulmer and Padgett 2004: 107-109). Such diffusion can also rely on the hegemonic status of one societal sphere over others.

Inherent tensions *within* a political arena can be conductive to innovation. As argued by March and Olsen (1989) there is no intrinsic need to assume that institutions represent perfect equilibriums and unambiguous and consistent frames for action in complex institutional settings. Also, political actors can reach the limits of existing procedures (Stone Sweet *et al.* 2001: 10-11), and can consequently be ripe for change and engage in search for other ways of organizing political space. *"Critical moments"* and system failure can provide opportunities for significant change (March and Olsen 1989). Such change may be induced by *skilled actions* of entrepreneurs that "create or manipulate frames that make sense of institutional or policy problems and offer persuasive solutions" (Stone Sweet *et al,* 2001:12).

OPEN METHOD OF COORDINATION (OMC) AND EDUCATION

For the role of (higher) education in the Lisbon process, the Bologna process as a political *arena* has been a site of inspiration, competition and support. The development of the EHEA related directly to fundamental and sensitive issues, such as the structure of higher education systems, national degree programme structures, and quality assurance, including the recognition of qualifications and degrees. The Lisbon process in education both feeds into and feeds on the Bologna process. The rationale of the Education and Training 2010 programme lies in its link to a greater order of the EU's Lisbon strategy and anchorage in the larger political order of the EU. This gives this process a different frame compared to the Bologna process. Competition between the two processes is also evidenced in the controversies surrounding the issue of the European Qualifications Framework (EQF) – the Bologna process has promoted a qualifications framework specifically tailored to fit higher education whereas the EU has promoted the EQF for a much broader conception of educational qualifications.

Dynamics of initiation and institutionalization of the OMC as political space should also be understood in terms of "interaction and collisions among competing institutional structure, norms, rules, identities and practices" (March and Olsen 2006b: 14). In the case of OMC education this took the shape of an inter-sectoral collision of ideas. This has came to the fore especially when education policy was defined and understood as an appendix to labour market policy and European coordination efforts in this area. The "collision" that contributed to creating new political space in the case of OMC education was between the cognitive and normative understanding of "education and learning" as part of the institutional sphere of labour market policy, rather than as education policy. Education ministers and the DG EAC headed the defense of the sectoral logics by the opportunity provided by the concept of the OMC. Such a collision meant a disagreement over appropriate "rules of engagement" for employment policy versus the education sector, since under the employment article European recommendations with respect to this policy area can be issued to member states, whereas for education this would be stepping over the remits of the Treaty. On the other hand the interaction with the larger political order of the European Union must be seen as a very important factor for the education sector making the most of the OMC template. In education the OMC became the arena that actively linked this policy domain to the larger European agenda. The way the OMC was put into practice also reflected the institutional defense, not so much of its distinctiveness, but of the sector's rightful place in European integration. The expansion and dispersion of the education agenda in Europe is sought to be coordinated within this organizational setup and as part of a translation of the Lisbon agenda. The OMC became an acceptable and recognised procedure and a signal of appropriate behaviour.

SEARCH FOR A NEW PACT

Under certain conditions change takes place incrementally within a fairly stable institutional framework. Under other circumstances institutional frameworks are themselves changing as the shared understandings underlying the political and social order are questioned and possibly modified or replaced. However, it is often difficult to say exactly under what conditions radical or revolutionary change is taking place or is likely to take place. Apparent revolutionary events, such as the democratization of higher education during the 1960s and 1970s (de Boer and Stensaker 2007), may in a longer perspective turn out to have less transformative impact than those taking part in the events believed. Neither is it unimaginable that the same observation will be made in the future with respect to the impact of the market vision (Teixeira et al. 2004; Olsen 2007b; Salerno 2007). On the other hand, consistent incremental change may over time transform the higher education system in fundamental ways.

Nevertheless, it can be argued that higher education is in a "critical period" with a potential for a far-reaching rebalancing of internal and external relations of authority, power and responsibility in institutional governance. Re-orienting European integration around the "Europe of knowledge" can be interpreted as an indication of the search for a new pact between higher education, political authorities and society at large. "A pact is a fairly long-term cultural commitment to and from higher education, as an institution with its own foundational rules of appropriate practices, causal and normative beliefs, and resources, yet validated by the political and social system in which higher education is embedded. A pact, then, is different from a contract based on continuous strategic calculation of expected value by public authorities, organized external groups, university and college employees, and students – all regularly monitoring and assessing higher education on the basis of its usefulness for their self-interest, and acting accordingly" (Gornitzka et al., 2007: 184).

Nature and Effects of European Integration Efforts with Respect to Higher Education and Research

The question can be raised of how far European integration efforts have penetrated into higher education's core activities. Such a question cannot be addressed unless we understand the institutional makeup of the European dimension in higher education and research, and the dynamics of European institution-building in these policy areas. Studying European integration and the transformation of higher education implies studying the development of political institutions and administrative capacity relevant to the "Europe of Knowledge". For more than 50 years higher education has featured on the European agenda and there are established institutional arrangements for European cooperation relevant to the way in which higher education and research operate. Yet these arrangements are in many respects still in the making, and actors and institutions involved are, if not negotiating, then at least looking to position themselves in a changing institutional order.

In addition to the market order of the EU, there is already an established European administrative order. Administrative capacity has been built up also in research and higher education to host the European dimension, linking the European executive, national, and sub-national levels of administration in these sectors. With the gradual build-up of the services of the European Commission and its functional differentiation into a DG for Research and a DG for Education, a permanent, and partly autonomous, administrative capacity has been established, organized according to sectoral lines. The two distinct, basic higher education functions of teaching-learning and research are retrieved in the political-administrative organization of the "knowledge sectors" at the European level and to some extent at the national level. At the European level this separation should be seen in light of the history of European integration and the international dimension of the two policy areas. Research policy issues have for several decades been the object of international and European coordination. Education as a policy area has traditionally been more contained by national borders and presented as nationally sensitive. The institutional horizontal split in research versus education has had important implications for the dynamics of integration even though they address in essence the same object of integration (Gornitzka 2007).

Setting the Standards

Ideas can develop into explicit standards elaborated in European processes and agreed on by EU institutions. Standards can be seen as a form of regulation that produces order as an alternative or supplement to hierarchies and market co-ordination (Brunsson and Jacobsson 2000). Standards are particularly amenable in areas of social interaction where states or other sub-national actors have regulatory autonomy (Kerwer 2005), as is the case with respect to European higher education. How are European standards formulated, how do they function across levels of governance, and across diverse national and institutional settings? Standards are definitely not a new invention in the higher education sector, with its auditing and accreditation structures and procedures. Peer review and collegial control according to academic standards and the assessment of quality have been an integral part of the research and teaching and learning process. Setting of standards at the national level, for example, concerning common national curricula, is not alien to higher education.

There are many different types of processes of European cooperation, coordination and integration that pertain to changes in the parameters of the primary activities of higher education institutions, i.e. teaching and research. Currently these processes are referred to as belonging to a "Europe of Knowledge" and to the efforts to create European areas of higher education and research. These processes are traceable and can be studied empirically down to the level of local practice, in order to see whether European integration initiatives have penetrated the universities and colleges all the way into their basic activities, that is, the day-to-day teaching and learning as well as research activities. It is a rich area for theory-based empirical studies of the multi-level character of the political order of Europe that accommodates the need to go beyond the study of European integration as merely involving the two levels of governance – i.e. the relationship between the European level and state level – and to adequately include also the middle structure and understructure.

FINALLY

The European challenge with respect to higher education and the further development of the EHEA after 2010 consist of developing a new institutional order, i.e. an appropriate balance between system level unity and institutional level autonomy, throughout all the relevant levels, i.e. not only the basic units (understructure), the institution as a whole (middle structure) and the system level (superstructure), but also the European level (suprastructure). This chapter has pointed to the difficulties arising from the differences between the current European level and national level interpretations of the appropriate unity/diversity order in higher education, and the accompanying complexities of developing an effective set of governance arrangements with respect to higher education in the emerging multi-level European governance context.

For the post-2010 European higher education system the notion of order suggests that the next steps in realizing an integrated EHEA should include an agreement on the division of policy authority between the European and national/subnational levels, implying, amongst other things, identifying policy issues that clearly represent joint interests and should therefore be handled at the European level. Such a division of authority would be comparable to a rather clear division of policy responsibilities in other federal higher education systems, such as the USA, Canada, and Australia.

NOTES

[1] Specific parts of this chapter are based on Maassen and Olsen (2007).
[2] Competence refers here in the first place to the formal agenda setting power of the Commission, and not to its formal legal authority.

REFERENCES

Aghion, Ph., M. Dewatripont, C. Hoxby, A. Mas-Colell, and A. Sapir (2008) *Higher aspirations: An agenda for reforming European universities*. Bruegel Blueprint Series Vol. V. Brussels: Bruegel. (www.bruegel.org)

Amaral, A., G. Neave, P. Maassen and C. Musselin (eds. forthcoming) *European integration and the governance of higher education and research*. Dordrecht: Springer.

Boer, H. de and B. Stensaker (2007) An Internal Representative System: The Democratic Vision. In: P. Maassen and J.P. Olsen (eds.) *University Dynamics and European Integration*. Dordrecht: Springer, pp. 99-118.

Brunsson, N. and B. Jacobsson (2000) The Contemporary Expansion of Standardization. In N. Brunsson, B. Jacobsson and associates *A World of Standards*: 1-17. Oxford: Oxford University Press.

Bulmer, S. and S. Padgett (2004) Policy Transfer in the European Union: An Institutionalist Perspective. *British Journal of Political Science*. Vol. 35: 103-126.

Clark, B.R. (1983) *The Higher Education System. Academic Organization in Cross-National Perspective*. Berkeley: University of Berkeley Press.

Corbett, A. (2005) *Universities and the Europe of Knowledge: Ideas, Institutions and Policy Entrepreneurship in European Union Higher Education 1955-2005*. Houndmills: Palgrave Macmillan.

DiMaggio, P.J. and Powell, W.W. (1991) The Iron Cage Revisited: Institutional Isomorphism and Collective Rationality in Organizational Fields. In W.W. Powell and P.J. Dimaggio (eds.) *The New Institutionalism in Organizational Analysis*. Chicago: Chicago University Press.

European Commission (2003) *The role of the universities in the Europe of knowledge*. Brussels: COM(2003) 58 final.

European Commission (2006) *Delivering on the modernization agenda for universities: Education, research and innovation*. Brussels: COM(2006) 208 final.

Figel, J. (2006) *The modernization agenda for European universities*. Ceremony of the 22nd anniversary of the Open University of the Netherlands, Heerlen, 22 september 2006.

Flemish Ministry of Education (2008) *Education International*. Official Bologna Process website 2007-2009. http://www.ond.vlaanderen.be/hogeronderwijs/bologna/pcao/Education International.htm

Gornitzka, Å. (2007) The Lisbon Process: A Supranational Policy Perspective. In: P. Maassen and J.P. Olsen (eds.) *University Dynamics and European Integration*. Dordrecht: Springer, pp. 155-78.

Gornitzka, Å., P. Maassen, J.P. Olsen, and B. Stensaker (2007) "Europe of knowledge": search for a new pact. In: P. Maassen and J.P. Olsen (eds.) *University Dynamics and European Integration*. Dordrecht: Springer, pp. 181-214.

Kerwer, D. (2005) Rules that Many Use: Standards and Global Regulation. *Governance* 18(4), pp. 611-632.

Maassen, P. and C. Musselin (2008) European integration and the Europeanization of higher education. In: A. Amaral, G. Neave, P. Maassen and C. Musselin (eds.) *European integration and the governance of higher education and research*. Dordrecht: Springer (forthcoming).

Maassen, P. and J.P. Olsen (eds.) (2007) *University Dynamics and European Integration*. Dordrecht: Springer.

March, J.G. and J.P. Olsen (1989) *Rediscovering Institutions. The Organizational Basis of Politics*. New York: The Free Press.

March, J.G. and J.P. Olsen (2006a) The logic of appropriateness. In: M. Rein, M. Moran and R.E. Goodin (eds.) *Handbook of Public Policy*. Oxford: Oxford University Press, pp. 689-708.

March, J. G. and J.P. Olsen (2006b) Elaborating the "New Institutionalism". In: R.A.W. Rhodes, S. Binder and B. Rockman (eds.) *The Oxford Handbook of Political Institutions*. Oxford: Oxford University Press, pp. 3-20.

NCHEMS (2007) *NCHEMS Information Center for State Higher Education Policymaking and Analysis*. (www.higheredinfo.org)

Neave, G. and P. Maassen (2007) The Bologna process: an intergovernmental policy perspective. In: P. Maassen and J.P. Olsen (eds.) *University Dynamics and European Integration.* Dordrecht: Springer, pp. 135-154.

Olsen, J.P. (2000) *Organisering og styring av universiteter. En kommentar til Mjosutvalgets reformforslag.* Oslo: ARENA Working Paper WP 00/20.

Olsen, J.P. (2001) Organizing European Institutions of Governance - A Prelude to an Institutional Account of Political Integration. In: H. Wallace (ed.) *Interlocking Dimensions of European Integration.* Houndmills: Palgrave: 323-353.

Olsen, J.P. (2006) Maybe it is time to rediscover bureaucracy. *Journal of Public Administration Research and Theory* 16: 1-24.

Olsen, J.P. (2007a) *Europe in Search of Political Order. An Institutional Perspective on Unity/ Diversity. Citizen/their Helpers, Democratic Design/Historical Drift, and the Co-Existence of orders.* Oxford: Oxford University Press.

Olsen, J.P. (2007b) The Institutional Dynamics of the European University. In: P. Maassen and J.P. Olsen (eds.) *University Dynamics and European Integration.* Dordrecht: Springer, pp. 25-54.

Olsen, J.P. and P. Maassen (2007) European Debates on the Knowledge Institution: The Modernization of the University at the European Level. In: P. Maassen and J.P. Olsen (eds.) *University Dynamics and European Integration.* Dordrecht: Springer, pp. 3-22.

Pollack, M.A. (2000) The End of Creeping Competence? EU Policy-Making Since Maastricht. *Journal of Common Market Studies.* Vol. 38, No. 3, pp. 519-38.

Salerno, C. (2007) A Service Enterprise: The Market Vision. In: P. Maassen and J.P. Olsen (eds.) *University Dynamics and European Integration.* Dordrecht: Springer, pp.119-132.

Schleicher, A. (2006) The economics of knowledge: Why education is key for Europe's success. *Lisbon Council Policy Brief.* Brussels: The Lisbon Council asbl.

Stone Sweet, A., N. Fligstein and W. Sandholtz (2001) The institutionalization of European Space. In A. Stone Sweet, W. Sandholtz, and N. Fligstein (eds.) *The Institutionalization of Europe.* Oxford: Oxford University Press, pp. 1-28.

Teixeira, P., B. Jongbloed, D. Dill and A. Amaral (eds.) 2004, *Markets in Higher Education. Rhetoric or Reality?* Dordrecht: Kluwer Academic Publishers.

Tomusk, V. (ed.) (2006) *Creating the European Area of Higher Education. Voices from the Periphery.* Dordrecht: Springer.

Witte, J.K. (2006) *Change of degrees and degrees of change: comparing adaptations of European higher education systems in the context of the Bologna process.* Enschede: University of Twente, Center for Higher Education Policy Studies.

Part V: The External Dimension

SIMON MARGINSON

16. THE EXTERNAL DIMENSION: POSITIONING THE EUROPEAN HIGHER EDUCATION AREA IN THE GLOBAL HIGHER EDUCATION WORLD

KEY FEATURES OF THE TOPIC

Introduction

In this era of accelerated globalization the external dimension of higher education has moved to the heart of the enterprise. Much of the activity that is shaping higher education in Europe is generated from outside Europe, and many effects of European higher education are playing out beyond Europe. The issue facing the EHEA and its systems and institutions is not whether to engage with the rest of the higher education world, but how, and to what strategic ends. How can the EHEA optimize its position on the global scale? How should it develop European global capacity? What is the gift of European higher education to the world?

Globalization is associated with the growing mobility of people, ideas, messages, money and technologies in higher education and research; new forms of delivery of higher education, and new strategies to secure global and local advantage; an 'arms race' in investments in innovation, and changes in the map of student enrolments and research. China has a new global role and is fast becoming number two national knowledge economy in the world. All of these changes call for coherent strategic responses by the EHEA in the period to 2020.

Part 1 discusses the method and assumptions of the paper, including the understanding of global relations. Part 2 overviews the global higher education terrain and its implications for Europe, and reviews prospects to 2020. It considers the mobility of academic staff and students; the new global spatiality and the strategic options in higher education and research organization that have emerged in response to it; trends in participation and research capacity; the rise of new Asian science powers, and the continuing role of the USA. Part 3 considers risks and opportunities, including the implications for diversity, and evaluates the feasibility of the Lisbon objective which imagines Europe as the world's leading global knowledge economy. Section 4 summarizes proposals regarding priorities and targets for the EHEA.

Method. The paper does not engage in statistical extrapolation across the issues. Given the complexity of the variables, the range of possible futures, the potential for reduction, and the limits of probabilistic reasoning and statistical inference (Keynes, 1921), this would be a dubious exercise. Rather, the method is *synthetic*

B.M. Kehm, J. Huisman and B. Stensaker (eds.), The European Higher Education Area:
Perspectives on a Moving Target, 297–321.

judgement. Any synthesis is partial: one chooses a particular angle, or a selected and managed plurality of angles, from which to illuminate the whole. Nevertheless the paper sets out to bring as broad as possible a set of phenomena into the frame consistent with coherence. Inevitably the findings will appear schematic and under-evidenced. But many are grounded elsewhere. The paper rests on the author's theorizations (Marginson, 1997; 2007a; 2008a), participation in policy fora and knowledge of the policy, empirical and theoretical literatures, though these are not reviewed here.

The paper aims for clear-minded realism and eschews the normative approaches common in the literature. When considering problems of strategy there is no substitute for the cold hard view: for understanding things as they are, not things as we might want them to be.

Globalization

The paper assumes that present trends in the policy settings will continue. The modernizing, quasi-corporate and performance-centred reforms associated with the New Public Management (NPM) will continue to work their way through institutions and national systems, albeit with some modifications. It is assumed also that the trend to more outwardly focused and responsive institutions, that are internationalized and engaged with communities and industry, will be sustained. It is also assumed that globalization will continue to work its way through higher education and research. The approach to globalization and the global higher education environment is set out elsewhere (e.g. Marginson, 2006; 2007a; 2007b; 2008a; Marginson & van der Wende, 2007). It is summarized briefly here.

The *global* dimension of human actions refers to a worldwide or planetary spatiality; to spaces, systems, relations, elements, agents and identities that are constituting of, and constituted by, the world as a whole or large parts of the world. For example it includes the worldwide system of English-language research publication. 'Global' as used here rests on a particular configuration of general/particular. The global dimension does not mean total or universal. It does not necessarily include every national and local element, only those elements part of the constitution of the world as an integrated world.

Thus *globalization* refers to processes of convergence and integration on a world or large regional scale; whether in economic life, culture, politics, communications or knowledge. It means 'the widening, deepening and speeding up of world wide interconnectedness' (Held et al., 1999, p. 2). Whereas international relations may involve just two nations ('inter-national'), globalization is a dynamic process that may involve many nations and draws the local, national and global dimensions together (Marginson & Rhoades, 2002). The effects of globalization are not constant but variable over time and between different parts of the world. Europeanization can be understood as one form of globalization. Here it is useful to distinguish between global convergence and global integration. Convergence means coming into proximity without blending into one system. With integration a single system is formed.

Globalization is more than a global-to-local chain of effects. Expectations by some local/global theorists that globalization would sweep away the nation-state were misplaced; especially in higher education where national funding and regulation remain crucial. Nevertheless globalization has altered the potential of national governments and generated new kinds of local-global-national configurations. For example, it is associated with the partial 'disembedding' from the nation-state of institutions that raise incomes offshore, establish campuses outsides their nation of origin, or seek accreditation from governments other than their own (Beerkens, 2004; Marginson & van der Wende, 2007). Globalization is also associated with the growing potential of global public goods produced outside the terms of the nation-state, such as the unfunded contribution of research in one nation to other nations and to the collective global system (Marginson, 2007b).

In sum, the effects of globalization are mediated by local and national factors. To understand globalization requires a 'glonacal' framework (Marginson & Rhoades, 2002): *glonacal = glo*bal + *na*tional +lo*cal*

While Europeanization can be understood as one form of global imagining, organization, convergence and integration, it cannot stand for the whole potential of globalization. A European-wide strategy is insufficient for a global strategy. Nor can Europe effectively isolate itself from the larger global dimension.

EXPECTED DEVELOPMENTS 2010-2020

Global People Mobility in Higher Education

Academic mobility. People mobility is driver and effect of global connectivity and convergence. Many national policies exhibit a prima facie bias in favour of mobility. Though mobility carries with it the real and present danger of brain drain, system closure is not an option. People cannot be stopped from leaving without decoupling the nation from the global innovation system and thus from modernization. The more the national system is open to incoming talent, the more it can compensate for outward movement. Despite this in some nations there are barriers to inward passage by non-citizens. Mobility is uneven by nation and academic category.

Data collected by the American National Science Board in the USA reveal an almost universal trend to growing cross-border collaboration in research (NSB, 2008). This is confirmed by individual country studies in Europe and elsewhere (e.g. Enders & de Weert, 2004). In the last two decades there has been significant growth in short term cross-border movement for academic purposes; research, conferences and short exchange visits; and recruitment and teaching in the cross-border degree market (OECD, 2004a). At the doctoral level many governments subsidize foreign PhD experience, while some universities that once recruited all doctoral candidates locally are now active on the national and the international planes (Enders & de Weert, 2004, p. 146). To what extent does temporary academic mobility become permanent? The Anglophone countries and some others have 'relaxed their immigration laws to attract qualified and highly qualified foreigners, including students, to sectors where there were labour shortages' (Tremblay, 2005, p. 197). However, according to Enders and de Weert (2004, pp. 146-147) intra-European cross-border mobility at the post-doctoral stage is probably stable. This would suggest that while doctoral populations are becoming more cosmopolitan this is not (yet?) associated with greater cross-border mobility at the later stages of faculty employment. One clear exception is the United States where the last two decades have seen growing inward movement at all levels. US higher education is the only unambiguous beneficiary of global mobility in the sector (Marginson, 2007b).

Is academic mobility confined to cross-border passage between national labour markets or has globalization promoted a distinctive global system of R&D labour as the OECD has argued (2004b), partly subsuming national labour markets? National academic career traditions are robust and often distinctive, particularly in larger self-sufficient systems such as France and Germany (Musselin, 2004; 2005); and in some European systems it is almost impossible for non-nationals to establish a permanent position. The last applies also in Korea, Malaysia and Thailand. National academic career structures are more conservative than those of many other professions, as indicated by the slow feminization of the professoriate. Despite these limitations the global element of academic labour is growing and is pushing beyond the logic of national systems. Some academic staff have expertise and reputation that confers superior opportunities in many countries, including researchers at the peak of their fields and globally transferable teachers in finance, accounting and, until recently, computing. Global researchers are strategic for national governments and research universities, with the potential to augment both the national innovation system and the position in university rankings. It is important not to exaggerate the size of the global pool. 'One can expect international careers to primarily include a few top academics. Most others, and especially young candidates, still develop national careers' (Musselin, 2004, p. 72), with or without international experience.

A global mobile pool of high-quality researchers does not in itself constitute a single global labour market with standardized conditions, remuneration and career structures. Rather, we have an American labour market that is global in reach and sets upper benchmarks for salaries and research infrastructure. Other national research systems are pulled towards the American benchmarks by market pressures, stratifying the academic professions between a small globally mobile upper segment and the much larger group of nation-bound researchers. Singapore has set out to create a globally competitive higher education system with expatriate faculty paid at US levels. In China some academic salaries are now globally competitive.

Global student mobility. The worldwide number of cross-border foreign students is growing at 8 per cent per year. From 1995 to 2005 it rose from 1.3 to 2.7 million (OECD, 2007a; 2008). The trend is driven by the globalization of job opportunities and educational provision, by desires for migration, and by various policies in sending and receiving nations to encourage mobility. Mobility has been facilitated by structural changes in degree programs and qualification systems. Two main templates for first degrees have emerged; the four year first degree in North America and China, and the three year first degree in Europe/UK and Australia. The three-year model is premised on a longer time spent in secondary school, an older cohort and arguably a higher level of school preparation, than applies in the USA. In contrast to the first degree level, little worldwide standardization of the Masters degree is evident. There is increasing worldwide interest in the American style of doctoral education, with its program of coursework and extended preparation prior to the research thesis, though the more extended form of thesis research traditional to the UK and much of Europe remains a significant model worldwide.

At present almost half of all European mobility is internal to the EHEA. Europe is not as attractive to cross-border students, particularly from Asia, as is the USA, UK and Australia (de Wit, 2008, p. 44) even when programs are offered in English, as at postgraduate level. There is no evidence yet to suggest that the Bologna reforms will make Europe more attractive to students from Asia or South America (Teichler, 2007, pp. 179-180 and p. 207ff.); though this is more likely than not. Neither the EHEA as a whole nor any European nation has set in place policies that would *decisively* improve the attractiveness of European higher education to non-Europeans. This problem is more fundamental than one of marketing. Though higher education in the Anglophone countries is often more expensive than in Western Europe, the Anglophone countries are more culturally open and provide incentives that encourage foreign graduates to stay. It is ironic: given the demographics, continental European higher education and society have a greater need for cross-border students and migrants than does the Anglophone zone.

Prospects to 2020. Academic mobility will increase especially at the top end of the research labour force. National innovation systems will come under increasing pressure to offer high salaries and special packages of conditions and infrastructure support to leading researchers, enhancing the bifurcation of national career structures. Nations unable to compete for high value academic labour will become, or remain, partly decoupled from the global research system. The EHEA will come under increasing pressure to develop Europe-wide solutions, such as centres of excellence, European doctoral scholarships, and special fellowship programs with augmented salaries. Nations will focus on drawing doctoral graduate nationals back from the USA and elsewhere, whether permanently or via oscillating employment. 'Bring them back' policies are already active (e.g. OECD, 2008). It is unclear that the EHEA will orient effectively to global academic mobility. Traditional career structures, recruitment conventions and salary levels are all barriers. Many national innovation systems are unable to deploy inward movement to adequately compensate for outward movement of the best and brightest to the USA. There is no evidence that the EHEA is improving its relative global position as an attractor of talent. It is likely the position is deteriorating. This is a crucial issue.

The world-wide number of mobile students is forecast to reach at least 5.8 million by 2020 (OECD, 2008; Bohm et al., 2004). The factors that have sustained recent growth in mobility will continue to affect it. The middle classes in China and India will keep expanding, and regardless of the capacity of domestic higher education, some students will seek to secure career or migration advantages by crossing borders for their education. As the domestic systems expand and improve, particularly in China, part of the cross-border student demand will shift to the postgraduate stage. In Thailand and Indonesia, which together have the population of the USA, it is likely that in 2010-2020 significant unmet demand for research university places will drive offshore enrolment. It is more difficult to anticipate the national shares of global exports. (By 'export nation' is meant nation that provides education to foreign students, i.e. exports educational services to them.) Exports from Asia are growing (Verbik & Lasanowski, 2007) and this will continue to 2020. In other words, student flows out of Asia will become more evenly balanced by flows into Asia; and the dominant role of the Anglophone nations in global exports will be modified. China is already the world's fifth largest exporter with 7 per cent of the global market, mostly students from Japan, Korea and Southeast Asia (OECD, 2007a), as well as being also the world's largest importer of cross-border education. Malaysia and Singapore between them have 4 per cent of global exports. Malaysian cross-border provision is largely confined to vocationally oriented colleges but the programs are significantly cheaper than the parallel institutions in the UK and Australia. The cross-border market is diversifying between high prestige exclusive research universities; medium prestige research institutions as in the UK, Australia and New Zealand; and vocational trainers like the University of Phoenix, franchised UK universities and the Malaysian colleges (Bashir, 2007).

Responses to Global Spatiality: Global-Local

Two kinds of practices have evolved in response to the new global spatiality. The first group of practices involve direct global-local effects: cross-border networks and consortia; Internet-based delivery; the cross-border mobility of institutions; and global referencing and ranking, in which higher education is imagined as a single global system. The second group of practices involve global-national-local effects driven primarily by governments: global competition by nations in investment in innovation; research concentrations; global hub and global knowledge city developments; and regional organization, as in Europe.

Networks and Consortia. The formalization of international cooperation with higher education institutions across the world is an early and obvious response to globalization. Many institutions invest significant executive time in establishing bilateral agreements and a smaller number have joined cross-border consortia in which the members engage with multiple partners. International agreements are designed to secure quasi-concentration benefits in research, privileged routes of student passage, perhaps jointly badged degrees, ongoing staff exchange, transferred prestige or simply the appearance of being internationally engaged.

All nations have institutions that stand out for the level of international cooperation, such as Tsinghua in China and Leiden in the Netherlands. Some partnerships and consortia lead to tangible, ongoing activity of importance to all partners, for example, in student exchange. Institutional partnerships have been instrumental in the commercial degree market, such as 'twinning' programs whereby students complete one part of the degree at home and the other part in the export nation. However, most academic visiting and research cooperation takes place outside the framework of executive-led institution-to-institution partnerships; partnerships are often less significant than they appear. Often more energy goes into the negotiation of institutional partnerships than their implementation, and there is a lack of clarity about objectives and about how the partnership will add value to the separated activities of the partners. On the other hand a small number of institutions have made very effective use of the network mode. The island nation of Singapore depends on knowledge-intensive services and a capacity to read global flows as broker and point of passage; and the National University of Singapore (NUS) is a byword for global competence. It has built a range of active partnerships with major institutions in Asia, Western Europe and the English-speaking countries, in both education and research; plays a leading role in consortia such as the Asia-Pacific Rim Universities; and hosts regional and global meetings.

Most European universities are yet to explore the fuller strategic potential of networks and consortia. This suggests potential opportunities for the EHEA, especially in relation to the emerging institutions and systems in East, Southeast and South Asia.

Internet-based delivery. Likewise, global spatiality immediately suggests research activity and educational programs via the Internet. However, while electronic research cooperation and scholarly publishing have grown so rapidly that virtual activity has become the principal mode of working beyond the local site, Internet-delivered degree programs have been marginal and problematic.

No area has been attended by higher hopes or poorer returns on capital investment than Internet-based commercial programs that deploy their courseware as intellectual property (IP). There are several reasons. High-quality interactive models of online pedagogy that explore the fuller potentials of the medium are yet to emerge (OECD, 2005, p. 14). Early prototypes rested on unit cost savings, with uniform courseware and low intensity communication in place of face-to-face teaching, and producers from English-speaking nations failed to design learning materials and methods sensitive to cultural and linguistic variations (OECD, 2005, p. 66). Online programmes were handicapped by perceptions that the degree had less status than a face-to-face programme, even when offered by leading brands such as New York University. The more important development has been non-proprietary open source models and systems (OECD, 2005, pp. 134–135). Arguably, these methods release the interactive potentials of online education more effectively than commercial learning systems. MIT has placed its courseware on the Internet without charge, enhancing MIT's global influence without diminishing the value of the onsite degree. This parallels the action of the Faculty of Arts and Science at Harvard in posting academic publishing on an open source basis, augmenting the national and global public goods that higher education provides.

Given their tradition of treating knowledge as a public good many EHEA universities are well placed to develop open source approaches, provided they invest in the necessary infrastructure and commit to communicability and openness/ transparency.

Cross-border mobility of institutions. The cross-border mobility of institutions brings the foreign education into the student's home nation. This mode of cross-border education is spreading quickly with practice often moving ahead of tracking (but see OBHE, 2008). Early cross-border institutions were in Hong Kong, Malaysia, Singapore and mainland China. Singapore has made the inward mobility of foreign providers a core element of local educational provision and global strategy. India has now become a key zone for foreign providers of both university and vocational qualifications, though private and foreign institutions are formally prohibited in much of the country. The University of Phoenix has set up campuses in India and several other nations. There are foreign campuses in South Africa. Cross-border institutions are not confined to the middle level and emerging economies. There are foreign providers in Western Europe, mostly in business education. Carnegie Mellon has a business school in Australia with local subsidies. The Australian Charles Sturt University has a teacher training campus in Ontario, Canada.

There are two main modes of cross-border institution. One is the stand-alone campus owned and built by the foreign provider. This involves often complex negotiations with local authorities, and is expensive and must be financed from home base, but enables fuller quality control over the education and engagement in the local system. The more common model is franchising with a local partner as provider. This is cheaper, and often has the potential to return a surplus. But franchised campuses are prone to lack of control from home base and weak equivalence with the home country degree, resulting in quality and reputation problems.

Unlike education provided to foreign students within the export nation, the cross-border mobility of institutions encourages hybrid approaches that combine the educational traditions of the exporting and importing nations. Unlike Internet-based degrees, which can be accessed almost anywhere regardless of the policy in particular nations (a case of the global dimension supplanting the national dimension), offshore campuses depend on the cooperation of the country concerned and are normally subject to local registration, accreditation and quality assurance requirements. Sometimes there are stipulations as to the educational program. For example foreign institutions in Malaysia must provide core subjects in Islamic Studies and Malay. Potentially, cross-border mobility of institutions is transformative at one or both ends of the relationship. It will be a site of future innovations. The nations most active in cross-border institutional mobility are the UK and Australia; and the USA whose universities have been active recently in China. Some French and Dutch institutions also have an offshore presence but for the most part European higher education is yet to explore this mode of global engagement, forgoing the important opportunity to forge deeper links in Asia. However, more EHEA institutions are creating study centres and other nodes of activity abroad.

Global referencing and ranking: The global networking of higher education institutions and systems, the enhanced cross-border engagement made possible by cheaper air travel, global academic mobility, the global character of the sciences, and the growing converges in national policy sets: all of these developments feed into imaginings of worldwide higher education as a single system – notwithstanding the heterogeneity of traditions and practices in education and research; the continuing national, cultural and linguistic differences and the partial barriers to mobility; and the gross unevenness in capacity and the level of global engagement on the world scale. This imagining of a single global system in turn has created favourable conditions for the rise and rise of global rankings. The first global rankings of institutions, by the Shanghai Jiao Tong University in China (SJTIHE, 2008) in 2003 and the Times Higher Education Supplement in 2004, quickly secured a wide impact, except in the United States where the sector stayed with national rankings by the US News and World Report. Since then further rankings systems have appeared, mostly in relation to research performance. All of these developments have powerfully strengthened the potency of the global dimension in higher education.

Rankings focus largely on research-heavy universities because research performance is more readily measured than other aspects; and league tables of leading institutions, set out in the manner of a football championship, readily secure public attention. Most of the rankings devised so far are unimportant or irrelevant for the majority of institutions which have lesser prestige or research capacity and a primarily local or national mission. The rankings tend to disadvantage or eliminate from view specialist vocational institutions; large institutions with multiple social tasks that are disadvantaged by measures focused on average research outputs or student selectivity; and non-English speaking institutions. Most ranking systems thus militate against system diversity within national systems, across Europe and on the global scale, while reinforcing the position of the strong institutions and nations. They bifurcate higher education between those placed-based but globally engaged, and those who are merely place-bound, paralleling the hierarchy created in the academic labour markets.

Nevertheless rankings will continue, gain policy importance and become more sophisticated. Metrics based on poor social science, such as those of the Times Higher Education Supplement that rest on a peer survey with a 1 per cent response rate, are likely to lose ground (Marginson, 2007c). One way out of rankings-created constraints on diversity is to establish classifications that enable separate rankings for different kinds of institution, like the Carnegie classification in the USA. This suggests a European typology (van Vught, et al., 2005), which would better position the EHEA on the global scale.

Prospects to 2020. All these global-local responses will gain more traction. For better or worse, global university rankings will play a key role in shaping the horizon of thought and triggering policies and behaviours. Rankings will strengthen external comparison and encourage convergent and imitative practices in organization and research (and if the OECD comparison of learning outcomes goes ahead, teaching). They will also generate powerful tendencies to the conflation of diversity unless corrective action is taken. The EHEA and its institutions will probably be active in designing systems of comparison. For example, comparative indicators may emerge that link graduate output to national, European and global labour markets; global patterns in doctoral education are also open to calculation and cross-border comparison; and so on.

The more diverse and specialized the rankings, the less the domination by singular models. Internet-based delivery and cross-border institutional mobility involve significant capital outlays, and institutional mobility also depends on the maintenance of a relatively open trading and cultural environment. The future of those modes is harder to predict.

Responses to Global Spatiality: Global-National-Local

National innovation policies. Global economic competition is increasingly focused on knowledge-intensive production and vectored by first mover advantages in innovation, responsiveness and adaptability. Higher education and research are now situated in the framework of innovation policy and national innovation systems. When economic competition takes place on the basis of ideas, expertise and behaviours, comparative advantage is not dependent on resource holdings or inherited traditions. It can be created by investments in education and research capacity, migration policies, and policies at the junction between the creation of ideas, the creation of applications, and business organization. The innovation policy agenda implies the extension of educational participation across the population and up the age structure, to create a more widely and deeply skilled workforce; the augmentation of knowledge creation and dissemination; national research capacity capable of attracting globally mobile corporate R&D; and global competition for mobile talent, a driver of policy in many nations (European Commission, 2006). The approach is also characterized by rising public and private investments in higher education and especially research (OECD, 2007a).

One major implication is an 'arms race' in spending on innovation. There are signs that this has begun. The Lisbon goal of Europe as the world's leading knowledge economy is one expression. China, Singapore, Korea, Malaysia, India and others are openly positioning themselves on the basis of claims to be a global knowledge economy. The first three nations have invested heavily and are test cases for the new policy. Li et al. (2008) suggest in the NBER paper 'The higher educational transformation of China and its global implications' that China's accelerated investment (see below) may be the harbinger of a new era:

> Previous efforts in other countries to use educational transformation as a mechanism either to maintain high growth or to initiate episodes of high growth have generally been regarded as unsuccessful, but the focus has been primary and secondary education, not tertiary. In china's case, these latest efforts seem to be motivated by a desire to maintain high growth by using educational transformation as the primary mechanism for skill upgrading and raising total factor productivity. If China succeeds, other countries may

follow with higher educational competition between countries as a possible outcome (Li et al., 2008, p. 4).

In research, the dominant policies of the late 1980s and 1990s sought to weaken the distinction between university research and commercial research, using the 'European paradox' narrative in which national innovation systems were marred by the inability to turn good basic research ideas into commercial product. It was argued that the essential move was to push the universities into a supply-side focus on linkages with industry. This enhanced external networking and engagement, but without necessarily fostering industry demand for higher education R&D, and often at the expense of longer term university research programs and curiosity-driven work (OECD, 2008). In policy circles, innovation systems are now seen in terms that are less zero-sum, and more complex and flexible. Key discoveries can proceed from outside as well as inside higher education, curiosity-driven basic research in higher education is an indispensable part of the mix, and higher education's contribution within national innovation systems is likely to grow. There are a number of reasons for the change of perspective. In empirical terms the so-called 'European paradox' is common to all innovation systems including the American. Commodity forms of research output constitute the particular and exceptional case, rather than the default case. Free open access knowledge dissemination is vital, as are the roles of universities in knowledge storage/processing and research training. Leading research universities have stellar power on the global scale as magnets for talent, ideas and R&D capital; critical mass in a number of disciplinary fields is a condition for interdisciplinary projects; and public good research has social and environmental as well as economic benefits. Between 2000 and 2005 the rate of growth of R&D in higher education exceeded the growth of R&D as a whole; though in half the OECD countries higher education's share of basic research fell (OECD, 2008).

This more mixed, engaged, public/private approach to innovation is conducive to those European systems that did not go as far as the Anglophone systems in refashioning research according to commodity production and market models: for example the Netherlands, Sweden and Finland. However, some European systems still lag in the level of engagement between higher education and industry that was the benefit of the 1980s/1990s policy set.

Research concentrations. Research rankings and the innovation agenda together highlight the potential of research concentrations. Via the German *Exzellenzinitiative* investment of 1.9 billion euros the designated universities may lead the regeneration of German global capacity in higher education and research. China is building a cohort of strong research universities with special funding (Li et al., 2008, p. 11). The policy question is whether concentration in itself is instrumental, as distinct from its role as a stalking horse for investment, or as a device for improving rankings. Does size matter in research? The likely answer is 'yes'. Research capacity and talent tend to attract more research capacity and talent, especially cross-border talent. Research-strong universities tend to be resource-strong and can buy more talent.

In the United States the winner-take-all higher education market, in conjunction with federal research funding, constitutes a de facto concentration of resources, research power and status power. The outcome is an exceptional group of research universities that dominate the world top 20 (Marginson, 2006) and are the primary global magnets for intellectual talent. Nevertheless the United States has a lesser proportion of the world's top 500 research universities than its economic capacity would suggest. In national systems such as Canada, the UK, Germany and the Netherlands research capacity is more broadly distributed.

Global knowledge 'hubs' and global knowledge cities. The global knowledge 'hub' model was pioneered in Singapore. The national government invites selected foreign providers of business education or research into the hub city or precinct, providing them with financial incentives. The strategic objective is to establish a central role in the global knowledge economy, able to attract foreign students and talented academics. Singapore's partners include Wharton, the Chicago Business School and MIT with whom the island state established the Singapore-MIT Alliance for Research and Technology (SMART) Centre. More recently the hub approach has been replicated in the Gulf States. The model has yet to prove viable. Outside partners exhibit a lower level of commitment than home governments, expatriate talent does not always stay, and no hub has triggered large scale foreign student flows suggesting that dependence on government money will continue into the foreseeable future. The hub strategy is more likely to work in a major global city such as San Francisco, Paris or Shanghai, places where people already want to study, work and live. Singapore is halfway to that status and the only hub so far with half a chance.

The more fruitful strategy is that of the global knowledge city, in which investment is conceived in terms of cultural economy and includes education and research. 'In principle, any place with an Internet connection can participate in a knowledge-based global economy. However, innovation continues to cluster in specific regions and the tendency for innovation to coalesce is becoming more pronounced' (OECD, 2007c, p. 41; see also Florida, 2005). Whereas industrial economies needed expansive production sites and thus located industries on the edge of cities, 'post-industrial' knowledge activities benefit more from proximity to key services, transport and communications. This favours agglomerations at city centres in which cross-field and creativity/capital synergies develop. In high technology and scientific manufacturing, media, finance, cultural and fashion activities, 'there are advantages in both clustering and in global access to knowledge' (OECD, 2007c, p. 60). Diverse knowledge workers concentrate, coming 'constantly into communication with each other in ways that help to unleash diverse innovative energies. Studies show that this process of communication is a critical factor in the generation of new ideas, sensitivities, and insights' (OECD, 2007d, p. 295). Effective higher education institutions flourish best in open regions/cities which welcome outsiders. City liveability is important. Low taxes encourage inward flows of financial capital, and entrepreneurship, but human capital is often attracted to a good and stimulating environment with better services (OECD, 2007c, p. 20).

However, few cities are first or second rank global players. This is where the EHEA is well placed – it has a relatively large number of actual or potential global cities that constitute attractive places to live and work. This suggests that if governments and/or the EHEA are to pursue strategic investments in concentration in higher education and research, the key question might be not so much 'which universities?' (or which nation) but 'which cities?'

Regional dynamics. The other move in response to global spatiality is meta-national regionalization, as in the EHEA itself. Given the scale of the USA, the EHEA and China, small to medium-sized nations have a limited set of global strategic options. Where feasible, regionalization of higher education capacities and structures seems logical. But so far regionalization in higher education is little developed outside Europe. Southeast Asian nations in ASEAN are working on recognition, student mobility and cross-border staff exchange but these activities are marginal. Argentina, Brazil, Paraguay, and Uruguay have extended educational cooperation within MERCUSOR to other South American nations. This is the most active region outside the EHEA, strengthened by the shared Spanish/Portuguese heritage.

Scale is not the only benefit or condition of regionalization. Identity and coherence are at least equally important. Here the United States and China enjoy a strong starting position as established polities and national cultures. The strategic question for regions is how to replicate these advantages, particularly coherence, without losing autonomy and diversity.

Prospects to 2020. The momentum for research concentration will be maintained, elevating selected research universities and re-differentiating some national systems. There will be a growing emphasis on knowledge city/industry/university synergies. The future of hub strategies is less clear: the jury is still out. Hubs positioned in major zones of development, such as eastern China, are more likely to succeed. Concentration should be pursued as a positive sum policy rather than a zero-sum policy. This also makes it easier to manage the difficult distributional politics. Regionalization of higher education is yet to emerge as an important factor outside Europe and in 2008 there is no indication that this is about to change.

Worldwide Growth and Distribution of Capacity

Growth of participation in higher education. There is a near universal tendency to growth of domestic participation in higher education at all ages. Between 1995 and 2005 the participation of 15-19 year olds in education increased by more than 5 per cent in almost all OECD nations. The demand for places is shaped by the growth of professional and other knowledge-intensive labour; and by social mobility and credentialism, driving the inexorable upward movement of educational qualifications over time. On the supply-side participation is fed by the funded expansion of places to meet knowledge economy objectives. Nations and regions where participation is growing rapidly can secure strategic advantage. Those that develop effective systems of adult and lifelong learning will install a more universal reflexive capacity for productivity improvement than systems in which the role of higher education is confined largely to initial preparation. In parts of the EHEA, student support and tuition discriminate in favour of young people. However, adult participation is strong in the UK and Scandinavia (OECD, 2007a).

Participation in China is expanding at all levels though policy focuses on young people. Between 1990 and 2005 tertiary student participation rose from 3 to 20 per cent of that age group (World Bank, 2008). Between 1998 and 2005, enrolled tertiary students multiplied by 4.5 times and the number of tertiary graduates multiplied by 3.7 times (Li, et al., 2008, p. 5). Not only are such rates of growth unprecedented, China's educational growth is taking place in the country with the world's largest population. It is a seismic shift on a planetary scale. China also lifted institutional quality and expanded research at similar rates (below).

In contrast, whereas between 1995 and 2005 the USA increased the participation of 15-19 year olds, along with the UK it is now in the bottom third for this age group and there continues to be high drop out. The participation of US people aged 20 and above is comparatively weak and there has been little change since 1995 (OECD, 2007a). There seems to be no policy or social impetus to address adult participation. The USA is no longer the world leader in participation. In this area European national systems, with their more focused approach to policy, might be able to secure a social and economic advantage.

Growth and pluralization of research capacity. A notable development of the last decade was the pluralization of research capacity in the sciences. Between 1995 and 2005 the annual number of scientific papers, produced in China rose from 9061 to 41,596. China was poised to overtake UK and Germany at the top of the EU table though its output remained less than one-fifth that of the EU as a whole. Between 1995 and 2005 China's annual output of papers rose by 16.5 per cent per annum. The annual rate of growth in South Korea was 15.7 per cent, in Singapore 12.2 per cent and Taiwan China 8.6 per cent (NSB, 2008). In 2003 Singapore invested 2.24 per cent of GDP on R&D, a higher figure than Canada (World Bank, 2008). In contrast, between 1995 and 2005 the number of papers produced by nations in the EU rose by 1.8 per cent per annum, with rapid growth only in outliers such as Portugal and Turkey. Papers produced in the USA increased by just 0.6 per cent per annum; in the UK the number did not increase (Figure 1).

China. Though China's researchers are unable to conduct global research conversations in their own language and China's transformation in education and research 'may still be only in its relatively early stages' (Li et al., 2008, p. 45), it is remaking the knowledge economy landscape. For example, between 2000-2005 R&D investment

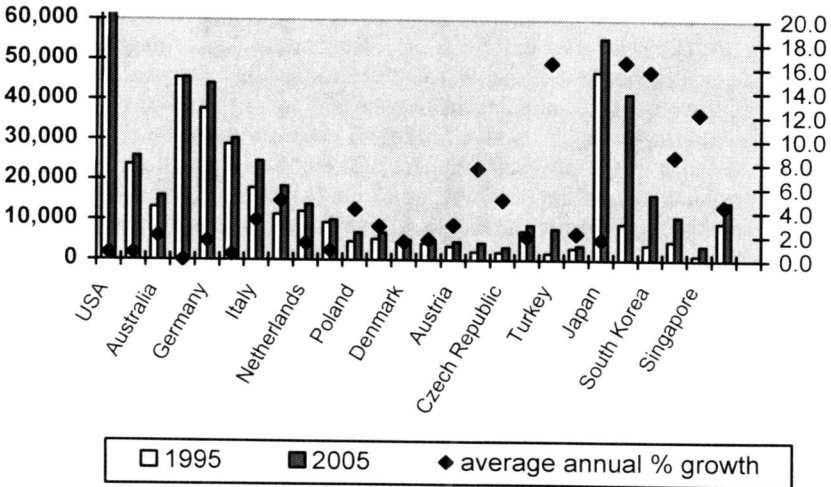

□ 1995   ■ 2005   ◆ average annual % growth

Note: European Union total papers 234,868 in 2005, USA total papers 205,320 in 2005.
Source: NSB, 2008.

Figure 1. Growth in annual number of scientific papers, EU nations producing over 2000 papers per year in 2005, and selected other nations, 1995-2005

in China rose by 18.5 per cent per year. In comparison, between 1995 and 2005 Finland led R&D investment in the European Union with an increase of 7.8 per cent per year. Investment in Germany rose by 2.5 per cent and France 1.3 per cent per year (OECD, 2007b). Between 1996 and 2005 China's investment in R&D as a proportion of GDP rose from 0.57 to 1.35 per cent (World Bank, 2008; Figure 2). In 2006 China became the world's number two R&D spender. Between 2004 and 2005 international patents filed in China grew by 47 per cent (Li, et al., 2008, p. 43).

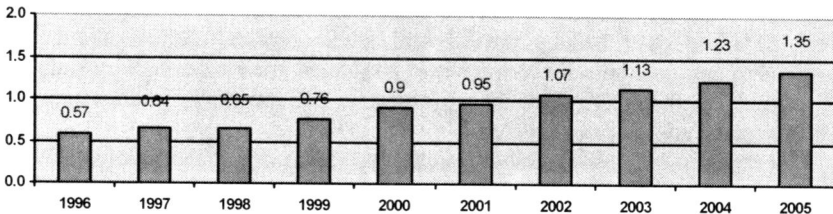

Source: World Bank, 2008

Figure 2. Investment in R&D in China as a proportion of GDP, 1996-2005

Less than one quarter of basic research in China takes place in universities, compared to over half in many OECD nations and almost two-thirds in the USA (OECD, 2008). The state enterprises receive more R&D investment than the universities. Nevertheless China is the third largest investor on R&D in higher education, after the USA and Japan, at over $10 billion in 2005 (OECD, 2007b). China's demography suggests vast long-term research potential. By 2010, *90 per cent* of all PhDs in the physical sciences and engineering will be held by Asians living in Asia, most of them produced by China (Li, et al., 2008, p. 6).

Nevertheless, and despite the fact that three Asian nations other than China have also invested in accelerated growth in research outputs, it is misleading to talk about an 'Asian region' or 'Asian leadership' in the global knowledge economy, as if the Asian nations as a whole were parallel to Europe. The geographical category ('Asia') does not translate into a unified system with coherent impact: there are no prospects of a pan-Asian education area, or an 'Asian' strategy to lift education and research. Deep animosities between China, Japan and South Korea prevent East Asian unity. The only possible combination is Taiwan and the mainland, which seems a matter of time. Singapore is a small country of less than five million people that like Switzerland moves nimbly between larger partners to sustain autonomy.

Nor is India in the same category as China as an emerging knowledge economy. For example between 1995 and 2005 its rate of growth of scientific papers was 4.5 per cent per annum, and total papers at 14,608 in 2005 was one-third the number produced in China (NSB, 2008). India has yet to indicate a coherent national policy that would lift participation and research at scale. The principal policy story of the last decade in education and research is not 'the rise of China and India' or 'the rise of Asia'. It is the rise of China; and perhaps also the rise of Taiwan, Singapore and Korea.

The United States. The rise of China has yet to challenge the dominant role of United States' higher education. The USA has no explicit policy in relation to the global knowledge economy. The cross-border dealings of American institutions in education and research are conducted by themselves, albeit with official endorsement and tacit support. Nevertheless, all agencies of education, research and government are conscious of the hegemonic position of the USA, especially in scientific research and doctoral education. The dominance of US institutions has been amassed over a long period and feeds into self-beliefs about intrinsic superiority and exceptional character. It is applied with coherence of purpose and supported by the USA's leading position in the military, political, economic, technological and cultural spheres.

The drivers are scale, resources, the established concentrations of research capacity, the ability of US institutions to attract talent, and the advantages of an English-language nation. The United States has the world's third largest population, the largest GDP, and a GDP per head above $40,000. The next higher education nation Japan has less than half the population, one-third the GDP and per capita income of just over $30,000. The USA also spends a higher proportion of GDP on tertiary education than any other nation, 2.9 per cent in 2003. This amounted to about $360 billion in 2005 in Purchasing Power Parity (PPP) terms. Japan spent

$51 billion, Germany, Korea and India each $27 billion, France $26 billion, Canada $25 billion, the UK $21 billion and Australia $10 billion (Marginson, 2008b). US investment in higher education is *seven times* that of Japan and 17 times that of the UK.

English-speaking nations constitute 71 per cent of the Shanghai Jiao Tong University top 100 universities. The UK has 11 of these. But the United States is dominant within the Anglophone group, with 54 of the top 100 and 17 of the top 20. Just 22 of the top 100 research universities are located in Western Europe aside from the UK, six in Japan, and one in each of Israel and Russia. The main Western European nations are Germany (six) France and Sweden (four each), Switzerland (three) and the Netherlands (two). None of the top 100 is in southern Europe or the Spanish-speaking countries, or China or India. India has three universities in the SJTUIHE top 500, China excluding Taiwan has 14. The USA has 166 universities (SJTUIHE, 2008). The research rankings compiled by the Higher Education Evaluation and Accreditation Council of Taiwan, which incorporate more recent citation data than the Jiao Tong, confirm these patterns. In the Taiwan ranking there are 63 United States' universities in the top 100, indicating that the US position may have strengthened (HEEACT, 2008).

On this base the USA operates as a global graduate school, subsidizing two-thirds of its foreign doctoral intake with American university scholarships (IIE, 2007) and providing work opportunities as graduate teaching and research assistants. Many foreign doctoral graduates enter post-doctoral programs and become academic migrants. American universities are more flexible and open than those of most other nations. Stay rates are high for PhDs from China, India, Israel, Argentina, Peru, Eastern Europe and Iran; and also the UK and Germany.

Prospects to 2020. The growth of domestic student participation will continue and spread to more emerging nations such as Thailand. The more spectacular changes will be in research outputs and rankings with the further elevation of the new Asian science powers. The rise of China will continue and push China's universities up the global rankings. Prospects in Latin America, Russia and Eastern Europe are harder to predict. These are the wild cards in the world setting.

Maddison (2007) has prepared a long run study of the share of world GDP by region, for OECD. In 1700 China and India produced 46.7 per cent of world product, reflecting their rural demography, with 21.9 per cent in Western Europe including the UK and 0.1 per cent in the USA. In 2003 the USA was on top with 20.6 per cent of world GDP. By 2030 China is expected to return to its historic position with 23.4 per cent of world GDP (Maddison, 2007, p. 103). This does not inevitably translate into leadership in research. But economic size helps, and it is clear that China wants to translate its size into research presence.

In 2005 China's investment in R&D in higher education was still only one quarter of the level in the United States but if present rates of growth continue, inside a generation China will exceed the investment in each of US and European higher education. Questions about quality remain. In 2008 European nations aside from the UK housed 88 of the top Jiao Tong discipline groups. The UK had 50, the

USA had 308. There were just ten in China, nine of them in engineering. One difficulty facing China is that on the whole it is more difficult for most foreign personnel to engage in a Chinese-speaking setting than to engage in an English-language Anglophone setting or the bilingual and multilingual settings of West European systems. The future of Chinese knowledge power is not simply a function of GDP shares and investment. It is also tied to the evolving global role of China in culture and language.

Table 1. World GDP shares by region, 1700-2030

	1700	1820	1952	1978	2003	2030*
China	22.3	32.9	5.2	4.9	15.1	23.1
India	24.4	16.0	4.0	3.3	5.5	10.4
Japan	4.1	3.0	3.4	7.6	6.6	3.6
Russia/USSR	4.4	5.4	9.2	9.0	3.8	3.4
Western Europe	21.9	23.0	25.9	24.2	19.2	13.0
United States	0.1	1.8	27.5	21.6	20.6	17.3

* Predicted. Source: Maddison, 2007, p. 103.

Whether there will be a closure of the gap between Europe and the USA is difficult to assess. If enough nations meet the Lisbon targets, the investment gap will narrow as it is unlikely the USA will step up its own investments in proportion in the next period, unless there is a major Sputnik style policy response to the perceived threat from China. Whether Europe narrows the gap between itself and the USA as an attractor and retainer of research talent partly depends on factors relating to mobility such as pay rates and openness to foreign employment. Moves towards aggregation of European research budgets will help. Research aggregation augments strategic capacity and builds EHEA coherence and identity.

RISKS AND OPPORTUNITIES

Globalization and Diversity

Globalization tends to weaken the variety of higher education unless, as with the European project, that variety is deliberately sustained. Although a culture-heavy domain such as research ought to lend itself to multiple expressions, here there are significant problems of homogenisation due to the normalizing effects of performance counts and rankings and the monolingual system of publication in which scholarship in languages other than English is downgraded. There is a more secure potential for continuing diversity in teaching, especially where this is based cn the national language. The challenge is to devise common global systems in higher education where a broad range of independent thought is sustained. The EHEA is experienced in this problem and can make a crucial contribution to the global architecture of the sector.

It is important not to overstate the threat to diversity. In higher education and research the global setting is more open and less closely regulated that a national polity or even the EHEA. Further, there are risks in certain forms of diversity. To what extent will global cultural relations inside and outside higher education become played out on the basis of cultural dialogue, as the traditions of higher education would suggest, or on the basis of the 'clash of cultures' called up from time to time in the larger political economy? Much of the worldwide sector has failed to sustain intellectual links with key institutions in the Middle East. On the other hand universities in China have built strong relations with foreign institutions, including American universities, helping to modify the global potential of US/China rivalry and contributing to the partial liberalization of civil society in China. Again, the EHEA has a potential contribution through the design of inclusive and cosmopolitan approaches.

Yet a lack of interest in East and Southeast Asian nations is sometimes evident in higher education circles in Europe. The problem is not confined to higher education which in this respect mirrors the larger setting. To take one example among many, between 1998 and 2003 French publishing houses purchased the rights to 3941 foreign novels. Only 90 (2.2 per cent) of those novels were from Asian nations. Such a pattern of translation bears witness to 'a distinct lack of openness towards this continent' (Benhamou & Peltier, 2007, pp. 101–102).

The European Global Project

The risk here is strategic insularity: that the EHEA will be so preoccupied with intra-regional reform, with itself, that it will lose sight of the global setting and the need to build long-term active relationships beyond Europe. The danger will be reinforced if the global dimension is read simply as a domain of threat that the EHEA needs to protect itself 'against'. It is true that there is potential for the US's domination in higher education and research to crowd out or weaken the global functions of European institutions, and weaken their standing at home. China is a formidable emerging global player in higher education, research and innovation. But there is nothing the EHEA can do to modify the endogenous dynamics of Asian and American higher education. What it *can* affect is its own responsiveness, initiative and capacity; and here the risk is that European global engagement will be inadequate.

There is no lack of opportunity for weak or fractured cross-border engagement. Efforts to attract talented foreign students and researchers may be retarded by immigration delays, quasi-discriminatory selection or cultural hostility; or weaknesses in services and lack of supporting policies (for example for families); or lack of scholarships and living support or work for students. Likewise migrant researchers could face steep walls at the point of entry into national career structures, decisively handicapping higher education in Europe vis-à-vis the USA. It is possible that salaries in Europe will become increasingly uncompetitive and career structures too inflexible and/or seniority-based, prompting bright researchers to go where rewards for merit are more immediate and better.

A more subtle risk is that the EHEA will focus on the global setting in solely competitive terms, becoming preoccupied with Europe's relative standing as a knowledge region as an end in itself without sufficient regard for the contribution of the EHEA to the global public good beyond Europe. Again the risk is that European identity building will become short-circuited by closure towards the external world. Europe then becomes defined not by what it is, but by what it is not (and by who it keeps out). If so the larger potential of the European project, which is one of the hopes of the world, will be squandered.

The 'leading knowledge economy' objective. The foregoing also raises the question of the global viability of the Lisbon agenda. The Lisbon strategy sets out to establish Europe as the leading knowledge economy region in the world by building on, developing and where appropriate, integrating the strengths of European higher education and research. States are expected to increase the funding of research and development (R&D) to 3 per cent of GDP and the funding of higher education to 2 per cent of GDP. The Lisbon objectives have been joined to the Bologna process of standardization of programs, nomenclature, equivalences, credentialing, credit transfer and quality assurance to facilitate the process of European system building while sustaining national diversity. They also dovetail into the formation of the European Research Area, the partial integration of research budgets, growing research collaboration across European borders; measures to encourage student and researcher mobility in Europe; and continued reform of national systems and institutions (de Wit, 2008).

How feasible is the goal of leading knowledge economy? Before answering the question it is necessary to review the strategic thinking it entails. The Lisbon agenda imagines the global knowledge environment as a contest of first among equals between Europe, the United States of America (USA) and emerging Asian powers. It is true that in terms of institutions and students, the size of the EHEA looks similar to that of the USA. In Europe there are about 4000 institutions of higher education, 3300 in the European Union; and in 2000 there were about 17 million students, 12.5 million in the EU; and 1.5 million staff with 435,000 researchers. In the USA figures published in 2006 showed 4216 two and four year institutions of higher education, 17.3 million students and 1.2 million academic staff (de Wit, 2008, p. 167 & pp. 199–200). The EHEA is also comparable to higher education in China, which enrolled 21.3 million tertiary students in 2005 (World Bank, 2007), though eventually the size of higher education in China and India will dramatically exceed those of the USA and Europe.

Nevertheless to imagine the USA, Europe and China/Asia as having equivalent global roles in higher education is to be misled. In a contest of first among equals, the goal is global primacy rather than global domination. But this is not a competition of first among equals. Higher education in the United States is dominant on the world scale. It now exercises a larger role than the EHEA wants for itself in future, and this role blocks the EHEA's ambition.

When the UK and the rest of Europe are combined they constitute 33 of the Jiao Tong top 100 universities compared to the 54 in the USA. This might seem closer to comparability. But the assumption that UK universities are strategically integrated into the common EHEA is difficult to justify. Though the United Kingdom (UK) is second nation in research it can no longer exercise world leadership in its own right. UK higher education, despite its strengths, finds itself in an ambiguous position: poised between on the one hand more fully embracing and integrating into the larger European project in higher education, on the other hand the idea of a partnership of equals with the USA. Despite a shared Anglo-American culture the USA shows no sign of wanting such a partnership but the UK is unable to fully commit itself to Europeanization. Further, even if the UK was thoroughly integrated into the EHEA the comparison would be misleading .United States' higher education is more closely coherent and much more powerful. As noted, the USA has 17 of the top 20 universities and US higher education houses 308 of the discipline groups listed in the world's top 100 for research in their fields: over 60 per cent of the world's academic centres of excellence. In social science the USA has 77 of the top 100 disciplinary groups. In engineering research, where capacity is more pluralized, it has 49 out of 100 (SJTUIHE, 2008). Notwithstanding reservations about the measures, including the biases in favour of the hard sciences, medicine and English-language research; this signifies a very strong position indeed. It is comparable to the US global dominance in film and television and in the holdings of advanced military weapons.

Any measure of performance can only be a symptom of global leadership. The main features of the American sector find their way into reform templates all over the world. Researchers from all over the world migrate to the USA, not because of the indicators, but because American society provides an open system of opportunity, its possibilities augmented by size, diversity and internal mobility. In 2003 three quarters of EU citizens who obtained a US doctorate said they had no plans to return to Europe (Tremblay, 2005, p. 208).

The question is not simply whether the EHEA could overtake the USA in measured performance. The question is whether policy strategies designed to achieve a position of first among equals, based on benchmarks of comparative performance expressed in statistical terms, are likely to modify the existing role of a hegemonic power. The USA's sway in higher education and research rests on more than material capacity and cultural authority in those sectors alone. There are no sign of endogenous decline in that hegemony or in the larger complex of elements that sustain it. By the same token, Europe's success as a global knowledge economy is grounded in more than higher education and research. Much can be done to spark innovation and creativity in higher education but the ultimate economic take-up (and often the genesis) of new ideas depends also on industry, government and civil society.

Regardless of whether total European spending on innovation exceeds total US spending or not, the EHEA is highly unlikely to become the world's leading knowledge economy region. This is not to say that the Lisbon goals and targets have been without merit. By using them to drive investment and reform, the EC installed a reflexive dynamic of continuous modernization, innovation and creativity with positive economic, social and cultural spin-offs. Moreover a modified version of the Lisbon goal could be achievable. Europe will not become the leading knowledge economy but it could become the most creative, most innovative and most globally engaged higher education region, create many public and private benefits.

Nothing is forever and the best interests of higher education everywhere, including American institutions, lie in fostering the plurality and diversity of the global sector. Here the EHEA can fulfil part of its strategic objective. If, as this paper argues, the framework of competition is shaped by American hegemony, then the EHEA and China and other emerging Asian nations have a common interest in reducing this. For this reason alone the rise of China is more opportunity than threat to the EHEA and fostering engagement in China should become a principal strategic priority. China does not and will not exercise the kind of hegemonic role in worldwide higher education able to retard European ambitions or achievements talent. It is more likely to be source of talent than competitor for it.

STRATEGIC OBJECTIVES AND TARGETS

Strategic Objectives

The stated objective of the Lisbon strategy was global effectiveness. The unstated assumption was that Europe had to be built first: fuller global engagement was postponed to later. This contrasts with the immediacy of response to globalization in the Anglophone and East Asian nations. There are opportunity costs in failing to engage. Arguably, the stronger the EHEA's global performance, the more that European achievement and coherence are enhanced.

This paper suggests five areas for evolving the external activities of the EHEA. First, more attention could be given forming and communicating European higher education identity outside Europe. What are the distinctive values, purposes and practices of teaching and research that are common to higher education in Europe, and constitute European higher education's gift to the world? Second, and most important, priority could be given to engagement with higher education in Asia, and especially in China. Third, much could be achieved through a targeted program of external initiatives in research, teaching, and partnership building in Asia and elsewhere, including student recruitment and exchange, and using mobility of institutions. Fourth, it is vital to dismantle the barriers to inward mobility of people and ideas. Finally, there are strategic gains to be made in developing subsidized centres where research and global links have priority, perhaps within the framework of global knowledge city development. The paper will briefly expand on three of these areas.

Europe-Asia Engagement

Augmented engagement with Asian higher education would build on existing activities but will be conducted on a larger scale. It would encompass active consortia, research partnerships, joint degrees, student and staff exchange, and scholarships for Asian doctoral students. Much of Europe provides attractive places to live with pleasant urban precincts and supportive social policies. The academic cultures of many EHEA institutions embody a profound commitment to scholarship and the life of the mind. These features could be deployed effectively to draw foreign talent. If efforts to reach out to China are underpinned by a growing capacity in Chinese language they will be more successful.

Inward Mobility

Measures to ease the inward passage of non-European students and researchers would incorporate immigration regulations; civil order, toleration and anti-discrimination legislation; services and supporting policies; scholarships and living support or student work; and for migrant researchers, salaries and access to national career structures. The EHEA might benefit from a Europe-wide scheme of salary supplements for high flying researchers.

Concentration of Global Capacity

This strategy would consist of investment in research capacity in selected institutions located in cities strongly placed in the global setting, either as established global cities (Paris, Berlin, etc.) or as cities such as, say, Barcelona, Amsterdam, Copenhagen or Prague with the potential to become front rank global cities. Building global critical mass and connectivity on the base of city/university synergies would be more effective than concentrating resources on selected universities regardless of location, or creating one mega-university in Europe, or funding of network which would become preoccupied by its own internal relations.

Targets for 2020

If the Lisbon-style targets are revisited it would be better for the EHEA to aim at becoming the most creative and globally engaged higher education environment in the world, and for Europe to become the most *innovative* knowledge economy.

Further, the EHEA might formally seek to achieve by 2020:
- Growth in the number of EHEA universities in the top 100 and top 40 research universities;
- Growth in the number of foreign doctoral students;
- Growth in the proportion of non-citizen academic staff in each national system;
- Growth in the foreign student share at first degree and Masters levels;
- Allocation of a fixed minimum of the European research budget to partnership activities involving China;
- An increase in the proportion of first degree European students learning Chinese.

More important than particular targets is to achieve the values and behaviours consistent with effective global engagement. The key is to combine a strong sense of identity and proactive strategy; with openness, engagement with the other and a willingness to change.

REFERENCES

Bashir, S. (2007). *Trends in International Trade in Higher Education: Implications and options for developing countries*. Education Working Paper Series, Number 6. Washington: The World Bank.

Beerkens, H. J. J. G. (2004). *Global Opportunities and Institutional Embeddedness: Higher education consortia in Europe and Southeast Asia*. Center for Higher Education Policy Studies, University of Twente. Accessed on 10 February 2006 at http://www.utwente.nl/cheps/documenten/thesisbeerkens.pdf

Benhamou, Francois and Peltier, Stephanie (2007). How should cultural diversity be measured? An application using the French publishing industry, *Journal of Cultural Economy*, published online 3 April.

Bohm, Anthony (2004). *Vision 2020: Forecasting international student mobility. A joint study by the British Council and IDP Australia*. London: British Council.

Enders, J. and de Weert, E. (eds.) (2004) *The International Attractiveness of the Academic Workplace in Europe*. Herausgeber und Bestelladresse, Frankfurt.

European Commission (2006). *1976-2006: Thirty Years of European Cooperation in Education*. Brussels: Office for Official Publications of the European Communities.

Florida, Richard (2002). *The Rise of the Creative Class*. New York: Basic Books.

Held, David, Anthony McLew, David Goldblatt & Jonathon Perraton (1999). *Global Transformations: Politics, Economics and Culture*. Stanford: Stanford University Press.

Higher Education Evaluation and Accreditation Council of Taiwan, HEEACT (2008). *2007 Performance Ranking of Scientific Papers for World Universities*. Accessed on 6 February 2008 at: http://www.heeact.edu.tw/ranking/E02Australia.htm

Institute for International Education, IIE (2007) Data on international education in the United States. Accessed 12 January 2007 at: http://www.iie.org/

Keynes, John Maynard (1921). A Treatise on Probability. London: Macmillan and Co.

King, Lily, Gibson, Chris, Khoo, Louisa-May and Semple, Anne-Louise (2006). Knowledges of the creative economy. Towards a relational geography of diffusion and adaptation in Asia, *Asia Pacific Viewpoint* 47 (2), pp. 173-194.

Li, Yao, Whalley, John, Zhang, Shunming and Zhao, Xiliang (2008). *The Higher Educational Transformation of China and its Global Implications*. NBER Working Paper No. 13849. Cambridge: National Bureau of Economic Research.

Maddison, Angus (2007). *Chinese Economic Performance in the Long Run. Second Edition*. Paris: OECD.

Marginson, Simon (1997). *Markets in Education*. Sydney: Allen and Unwin.

Marginson, Simon (2006) Dynamics of national and global competition in higher education, *Higher Education* 52, pp. 1-39.

Marginson, Simon (2007a). The new higher education landscape: Public and private goods, in global/national/local settings. In S. Marginson (Ed.) *Prospects of Higher Education: Globalisation, market competition, public goods and the future of the university*, pp. 29-77. Rotterdam: Sense Publishers.

Marginson, Simon (2007b). The public/private division in higher education: A global revision, *Higher Education* 53, pp. 307-333.

Marginson, Simon (2007c). Global university rankings, in S. Marginson (Ed.) *Prospects of Higher Education: Globalization, market competition, public goods and the future of the university*, pp. 79-100. Rotterdam: Sense Publishers.

Marginson, Simon (2008a). Global field and global imagining: Bourdieu and relations of power in worldwide higher education, *British Journal of Educational Sociology*, 29 (3), pp. 303-316.

Marginson, Simon (2000b). Vers une hégémonie de l'université globale (transl. Rachel Bouyssou), *Critique Internationale*, 39, April-June, pp. 87-107.

Marginson, Simon and Rhoades, Gary (2002). Beyond national states, markets, and systems of higher education: A glonacal agency heuristic, *Higher Education* 43, pp. 281-309.

Marginson, Simon and van der Wende, Marijk (2007). *Globalization and Higher Education*, Education Working Paper Number 8, Organization for Economic Cooperation and Development. Paris: OECD. Accessed 31 October 2007 at: http://www.oecd.org/dataoecd/33/12/38918635.pdf

Musselin, C. (2004) Towards a European academic labour market? Some lessons drawn from empirical studies on academic mobility, *Higher Education*, 48, pp. 55-78.

Musselin, C. (2005) European academic labour markets in transition, *Higher Education*, 49, pp. 135-154.

National Science Board, NSB (2008). *Science and Engineering Indicators*. Accessed on 8 March April 2008 at: http://www.nsf.gov/statistics/seind04/

Observatory on Borderless Higher Education, OBHE (2008). Website and publications. Accessed on 30 April 2008 at: www.obhe.ac.uk [password protected]

Organisation for Economic Cooperation and Development, OECD (2004a). *Internationalisation and trade in higher education*. Paris, OECD.

Organisation for Economic Cooperation and Development, OECD (2004b) *OECD Science, Technology and Industry Outlook*. Paris: OECD

OECD (2005), *E-learning in Tertiary Education: Where do we stand?* Paris: OECD

OECD (2007a). *Education at a Glance: OECD Indicators*. Paris: OECD.

OECD (2007b). *Science and Technology Indicators*. Paris: OECD.

OECD (2007c). *Higher Education and Regions: Globally competitive, locally engaged*. Paris: OECD.

OECD (2007d). *Competitive Cities in the Global Economy*. Paris: OECD.

Organisation for Economic Cooperation and Development, OECD (2008a). *Tertiary Education for the Knowledge Society: OECD Thematic Review of Tertiary Education*. Paris: OECD.

Shanghai Jiao Tong University Institute of Higher Education, SJTUIHE (2008). *Academic Ranking of World Universities*. Accessed 23 March 2008 at: http://ed.sjtu.edu.cn/ranking.htm

Teichler, Ulrich (2007*). Higher Education Systems: Conceptual frameworks, comparative perspectives, empirical findings*. Rotterdam: Sense Publishers.

Tremblay, K. (2005) Academic mobility and immigration, *Journal of Studies in International Education*, 9 (3), pp. 196-228.

de Wit, Hans (2008). International student circulation in the context of the Bologna Process and the Lisbon Strategy, in Hans de Wit, Pawan Agarwal, Mohsen Elmahdy Said, Molatlhegi T. Sehoole & Muhammad Sirozi (Eds.), *The Dynamics of International Student Circulation in a Global Market*, pp. 167-198. Rotterdam: Sense Publishers.

World Bank (2008). Data and statistics. Accessed 22 March 2008 at: http://go.worldbank.org/47P3PLE940

Verbik, Line & Lasanowski, Veronica (2007). *International Student Mobility: Patterns and trends*. Report, The Observatory on Borderless Education. Accessed 21 March 2008 at: www.obhe.ac.uk [password protected]

van Vught, Frans, Bartelse, J., Bohmert, D., Burquel, N., Divis, J., Huisman, J. and van der Wende, Marijk (2005). *Institutional Profiles. Towards a typology of higher education institutions in Europe*. Report to the European Commission. Accessed 1 January 2007 at: http://www.utwente.nl/cheps/documenten/engreport05institutionalprofiles.pdf

LIST OF AUTHORS

Barbara M. Kehm is Professor of Higher Education Research and Director of the International Centre for Higher Education Research (INCHER-Kassel), University of Kassel, Germany. E-mail: kehm@incher.uni-kassel.de

Jeroen Huisman is Professor of Higher Education Management and Director of the International Centre for Higher Education Management (ICHEM), University of Bath, United Kingdom. E-mail: j.huisman@bath.ac.uk

Bjørn Stensaker is Head of Research at the Norwegian Institute for Studies in Innovation, Research and Education (NIFU STEP) in Oslo and Professor (II) at the Institute of Educational Research, University of Oslo, Norway. E-mail: bjorn.stensaker@nifustep.no

Dr. Harry F. de Boer is senior researcher at the Center for Higher Education Policy Studies (CHEPS), University of Twente, Netherlands. E-mail: h.f.deboer@utwente.nl

Dr. Ben W.A. Jongbloed is senior researcher at the Center for Higher Education Policy Studies (CHEPS), University of Twente, Netherlands. E-mail: b.w.a.jongbloed@utwente.nl

Jürgen Enders is Professor of Higher Education Policy Studies and Director of the Center for Higher Education Policy Studies (CHEPS), University of Twente, Netherlands. E-mail: j.enders@utwente.nl

Julien Barrier is a PhD candidate at the Centre for the Sociology of Organisations, University of Sciences Po in Paris, France. E-mail: j.barrier@cso.cnrs.fr

Christine Musselin is a Research Professor of CNRS and Director of the Centre for the Sociology of Organisations, a research unit at the University of Sciences Po in Paris, France. E-mail: c.musselin@cso.cnrs.fr

John Brennan is Professor of Higher Education Research and Director of the Centre for Higher Education Research and Information at the Open University, United Kingdom. E-mail: j.l.brennan@open.ac.uk

Dr. Rajani Naidoo is Director of the programme Doctor of Business Administration in Higher Education at the University of Bath, United Kingdom. E-mail: edsrn@management.bath.ac.uk

Kavita Patel is a research assistant at the Centre for Higher Education Research and Information at the Open University, United Kingdom. E-mail: k.patel@open.ac.uk

Dr. Kurt De Wit is an officer at the Office for Education Policy at the Catholic University of Leuven in Belgium. E-mail: Kurt.DeWit@dowb.kuleuven.de

Jef C. Verhoeven is Professor of Sociology and former Head of the Centre for Sociology of Education at the Catholic University of Leuven in Belgium. E-mail: jef.verhoeven@soc.kuleuven.be

Jan De Groof is President of the European Association for Education Law and Policy, Professor at the College of Europe (Brussels, Belgium) and at the University of Tilburg (Netherlands), he is also Government Commissioner for Universities (Belgium, Flemish Community) and UNESCO Chargé de Mission for the Right to Education. E-mail: Jan.DeGroof@ua.ac.be

Marek Kwiek is Professor in the Department of Philosophy and Director of the Center for Public Policy at Poznan University, Polen. E-mail: kwiekm@amu.edu.pl

Peter Maassen is Professor of Higher Education at the University of Oslo, Director of HEDDA, and Research Professor at NIFU STEP, the Norwegian Institute for Studies in Innovation, Research and Education. E-mail: peter.maassen@ped.uio.no

Simon Marginson is Professor of Higher Education in the Center for the Study of Higher Education at the University of Melbourne, Australia. E-mail: s.marginson@unimelb.edu.au

Guy Neave is Honorary Professor at the Centre for Higher Education Policy Studies (CHEPS), University of Twente in the Netherlands and Senior Principal Researchers at the Centre for Research in Higher Education Policies (CIPES), Matosinhos, Portugal. E-mail: guy.r.neave@gmail.com

Dr. Åse Gornitzka is senior researcher at Arena-Centre for European Studies, University of Oslo, Norway. E-mail: ase.gornitzka@arena.uio.no

Ulrich Teichler is Professor of Higher Education in the International Centre for Higher Education Research (INCHER-Kassel) at the University of Kassel, Germany. E-mail: teichler@incher.uni-kassel.de

Pedro Teixeira is Associate Professor at the Faculty of Economics, University of Porto, Portugal and senior researcher at the Centre for Research in Higher Education Policies (CIPES), Matosinhos, Portugal. E-mail: Pedrotx@fep.up.pt

Jussi Välimaa is Professor of Higher Education Studies and leader of the higher education studies team at the Institute for Educational Research, University of Jyväskylä, Finland. E-mail: jussi.valimaa@ktl.jyu.fi

Sir David Watson is Professor of Higher Education Management at the Institute of Education, University of London, United Kingdom. E-mail: d.Watson@ioe.ac.uk

Dr. Paul Temple is senior lecturer in Higher Education Management at the Institute of Education, University of London, United Kingdom. E-mail: p.temple@ioe.ac.uk

Frank Vandenbroucke is Deputy Minister President of the Flemish Government in Belgium and Minister of Work, Education, and Training.

Lightning Source UK Ltd.
Milton Keyres UK
177312UK00005B/39/P